The Longest Boundary

How the US-Canadian Border's Line came to be where it is, 1763–1910

Volume 2 – Consolidation, Confirmation and Completion

J. P. D. Dunbabin

Grosvenor House
Publishing Limited

This book is published by
Grosvenor House Publishing Ltd
Link House
140 The Broadway, Tolworth, Surrey, KT6 7HT.
www.grosvenorhousepublishing.co.uk

A CIP record for this book
is available from the British Library

ISBN 978-1-80381-638-8
eBook ISBN 978-1-80381-639-5

Preface

During a splendid Alaskan holiday, we were given what seemed to be two contradictory accounts of how the local boundary with Canada had been determined (though I now believe one informant was talking of the Chilkoot, the other of the Chilkat, Pass). Shortly afterwards, while gazing up Glacier Bay (rightly awarded to the United States in 1903) towards the Canadian mountains beyond, I decided to explore the surprisingly neglected process through which what is now the US-Canadian border, the world's longest, came by stages between 1763 and 1910 to its present line – the precise location of its disputed starting point, the 'true St. Croix', being ascertained in 1797-8 largely through archaeological excavation ...

'Of the making of books there is no end'; and this one has taken far longer than I anticipated, so long indeed that doubts were widely voiced as to whether it would ever emerge. Delay did, though, have the unlooked-for effect of extending my research into the internet age, and so opening sources I would not otherwise have encountered. The outcome has been a long book, too long, many people rightly warned, for today's academic publishers. So I am very grateful to Grosvenor House Publishing for producing it, rapidly, helpfully, and efficiently, on a self-publishing basis.

More could usefully have been done. But while writing I have consulted and been helped by archives extending from the Algemeen Rijksarchief at The Hague to the Levens Hall MSS., Cumbria – and more especially by Libraries and Archives Canada in Ottawa, by Maine State Archives in Augusta, by the Library of Congress and the National Archives in Washington, by the National Archives and the British Library in London, and by All Souls College and the Bodleian Library in Oxford. I have enjoyed the hospitality of the William L. Clements Library at Ann Arbor, Michigan, and (as a British Academy Exchange Fellow) of the

Newberry Library in Chicago. I must also thank Georgetown's Professor John Hirsh, both for entertainment and encouragement in Washington and for copying a document from the Library of Congress, and my Combe neighbour, Sue Goodman, Architect, for drawing the 'North-East Boundary disputes' map.

This book might best have been written in Ottawa, using the resources of Libraries and Archives Canada. But almost as well placed has been the University of Oxford, relatively close to the UK's National Archives, with the impressive and helpful Bodleian Library (and more especially its Vere Harmsworth Library/Rothermere American Institute component), and with the stimulus and encouragement (extending long after my formal retirement) of my colleagues and college, St. Edmund Hall.

In my last book I wrote that my grandchildren were too young 'to have yet made any academic contribution'; this time, when Bodley's hard copy was locked up through Covid, Callie extracted for me material held electronically by her university, Exeter. Over a longer period, I have received love, care, interest, and encouragement, from my daughters Bridget and Penny, and above all from my wife Jean (despite my strewing our rooms with disorganised book papers).

John Dunbabin   St. Edmund Hall, Oxford

About the Author

J.P.D. Dunbabin was for many decades Fellow & Tutor in Politics and Modern History at St. Edmund Hall, Oxford (acting as its Principal in 1998–9), and latterly also University Reder in International Relations. He retired in 2004 but has continued to be academically involved. His previous books are *Rural Discontent in Nineteenth Century Britain* (1974) and *International Relations since 1945*, Volume 1 *The Cold War* (2nd. edn. 2008), Volume 2 *The Post-Imperial Age* (1994). He has also published articles and chapters on a wide range of nineteenth and twentieth century British, and twentieth century world, history, plus four articles on Canadian history.

Table of Contents

Notes

i) The usual exchange rate was just under $5 to the £
ii) The military ranks in use were often brevet ones, thus Captain (not Lieutenant) Pickett
iii) The book contains some maps, but others are readily available from the internet, as are portraits or photographs of most people mentioned

VOLUME 2
Consolidation, Confirmation and Completion

Previous chapters have dealt with the agreeing of successive sections of a border that eventually stretched from coast to coast. The treaties involved have lasted better than have most others, but only because locals chose to build their polities within the prescribed boundaries, not to seek for radical change. Accordingly the focus of chapters 10-13 is more domestic: the evolution of 'Canada', and the confederation of the provinces of British North America into a single Dominion (in part to preserve their independence from the United States); the way in which that Dominion expanded to the Pacific to keep the West out of American hands; and the much slower subsequent consolidation of actual Canadian control over the newly incorporated areas.

CHAPTER 10

The road to Canadian Confederation

The 1783 treaty closing the Revolutionary War had accepted the presence on the continent of both the United States and British North America and had described the general line of the border between them. Over time treaties and Commissions pinned down this border's precise course, and matched the United States' western growth by extending it first to the Rockies in 1818 and finally in 1846 to the Pacific. But this boundary might have been set aside or radically changed had either of the countries involved disintegrated. It was initially unclear whether the United States could control all the land the 1783 peace treaty had assigned it. Vermont had briefly established its *de facto* independence. In 1780-1 its leaders negotiated, cautiously but not necessarily insincerely, over becoming a British province; and before it finally acceded to the United States in 1791, there were ideas, encouraged by its prominent Allen family and shared by Upper Canada's prospective Lieutenant-Governor, John Graves Simcoe, that a Canada-Vermont partnership might lead other areas to follow suit. In 1787-8, indeed, the Revolutionary War General and Kentucky politician, James Wilkinson, had secretly sworn allegiance to Spain, and he sought to induce the Spanish Governor of Louisiana to 'admit' Kentuckians 'under protection as vassals'. Then in 1804-6, by which time he was himself Louisiana's American Governor, both he and the former Vice-President Aaron Burr appear to have been involved in a conspiracy either to detach Louisiana from the United States or to carve themselves an independent state out of the neighbouring Spanish territory. These designs related to land south – in the case of Louisiana well south – of the Canadian border; but the War of 1812 led to talk of New England leaving the Union, though it ended before things had proceeded any further. Between 1820 and 1861 the United States encountered periodic internal crises, but the compromises these engendered left its internal polity essentially intact; and though the South's secession did then trigger a major Civil War, the greater part of the country, that abutting on British North America, remained whole, while the War ended with the restoration and strengthening of the Union.

* * * * *

South of the border, the belief was widespread that British North America, or at least Canada, was anxious to join the US. This was put to the test during the War of 1812. The Maritimes and most of Lower Canada were shielded from land operations by New England's reluctance to get involved, and were in any case strongly loyal. Upper Canada was another matter: Simcoe, its first Lt. Governor, had encouraged American settlers; and 'as the means of obtaining land have been extremely easy', the flow continued, perhaps amounting in all to between fifteen and twenty thousand. An 1814 *Geographical View* represented the population as equally divided between, on the one side, British immigrants, Loyalists, and their children, and on the other, 'natives of the United States with their children'.[1] Antecedents did not necessarily determine allegiance – the heroine Laura Secord's parents had come from Massachusetts in 1795, but she herself had married the son of a Loyalist. Still there was a good deal of pro-American sentiment, like that overheard in a Niagara tavern in 1807: 'if Congress will only send us a flag and a proclamation declaring that whoever is found in arms against the United States shall

---

[1] Elizabeth Jane Errington, 'British Migration and British America, 1783-1867' *in* Phillip Buckner ed., *Canada and the British Empire* (Oxford, paperback edn. 2010) p. 144; M. Smith, *A Geographical View of the British Possessions in North America…* (Baltimore, 1814) p. 288 – quoted in E.A. Cruikshank, 'A Study of Disaffection in Upper Canada 1812-15', Royal Society of Canada, *Transactions*, series 3 vol. 6 (1912), Section 2 p. 18. Statistics Canada, *Censuses of Canada 1665 to 1871, The 1800s* (online, accessed 15/5/19) gives estimates of 77,000 for Upper Canada's population in 1811, 95,000 in 1814

forfeit his lands, we will fight ourselves free without any expense to them'. Encouraged by such reports, the geographer John Melish wrote in 1810 that 'if 5,000 were sent into Upper Canada with a proclamation of independence the great mass of the population would join the American Government'.[2] And General Hull began his invasion by proclaiming that

'Many of your forefathers fought for the freedom and Independence we now enjoy; being ... therefore of the same family with us ... the arrival of an army of friends must be hailed by you with a cordial welcome. You will be emancipated from tyranny and oppression and restored to the dignified position of freemen...'

This, Lt. Governor Brock reported in July 1812, had 'considerable effect': numbers of people joined Hull's army, and the belief 'that the Province must inevitably succomb' made magistrates and militia officers 'sluggish and indifferent'. However Brock's dash and Hull's incompetence turned things around, and in September 1812 an American spy reported that

'Most of the inhabitants would willingly have submitted, but when it was found that private property was seized without [compensation], the public sentiment entirely changed. The success of General Brock established the change of sentiment. He has since made the most of it, and ... A determination now prevails among the people to defend their country.'[3]

---

[2] British officials believed such sentiments were fostered by 'secret agents'; and in 1812 Nathaniel Cogswell did represent himself to the Governor-General as having been funded by Jefferson (and, less well, by Madison) to promote a move for an 'independent Govt.' of Canada (as a prelude to its later annexation) – Cruikshank, 'Disaffection' pp. 11-16
[3] Cruikshank, 'Disaffection' pp. 20-2, 25-6

Thereafter things see-sawed. A few people either joined US forces or quietly left for America.[4] Many more served in the British militia, some enthusiastically, others sluggishly. Most, perhaps, kept their heads down, welcoming whichever troops were in position locally. After the Americans had occupied Niagara, over 500 came in early June 1813 to give their paroles. But at the end of the month a British magistrate observed that the passage of troops *en route* for Niagara had 'occasioned an obvious change in the manners and language of the people' in his district. He told Governor-General Prevost that stationing regulars at York (Toronto) would 'have an excellent effect in confirming the loyal and overawing the disaffected'; but should there be a serious reverse, 'little reliance is to be had in the power of the well disposed to... keep down the turbulence of the disaffected who are very numerous'.[5]

In the long run this implied a loyalist ascendancy since (Amherstburg apart) United States forces never managed to maintain themselves in Canada for any length of time. But their attacks naturally reinforced official suspicions of the American element of the population. Initially this had been treated rather gently: while in occupied York/Toronto in 1813, the American Commodore Chauncey observed 'that he never heard of any place that contained half the number of persons publicly known ... to be enemys to the government & country to be allowed to remain at rest'.[6] But after US forces had left, pressure for a tougher line mounted. An inquiry led in September to 34 treason charges,

---

[4] Forty-eight people 'joined the enemy' between June 1812 and June 1814 'from the limits of the 2nd Regiment of Norfolk', while there is a list of 43 'Disaffected Persons in the London and Western Districts' (most of whom provided the Americans with active assistance). An official list of landholders 'who did voluntarily withdraw from the Province without license during the late war' held 336 names, and Cruikshank thinks many more landless men probably left — Cruikshank, 'Disaffection' pp. 54-8, 60-4

[5] General Dearborn to the War Secretary, 3 June 1813; William Dummer Powell to Prevost, 28 June 1813 (Cruikshank, 'Disaffection' pp. 31-3)

[6] Major William Allen, 3 Aug. 1813, reporting a conversation between Chauncey and Dr. Strachan (Cruikshank, 'Disaffection' p. 34)

though with few immediate consequences. November saw the capture of 18 Norfolk settlers who had used American arms to terrorise their neighbours, and a commission for the trial of all accused of treason was issued with a view to making examples. Deputy Attorney-General Robinson insisted on civil rather than military process, and a Court opened in Ancaster with three King's Bench Justices. Of the prisoners charged, 4 were acquitted, 17 condemned to death. But the administrator General Sir Gordon Drummond thought 'many examples' unnecessary 'to convince the Province that Treason will meet with its due reward', and so, after a careful review by Robinson, only 8 were hung: their heads, though, were then paraded around local villages.[7]

Meanwhile legislation had been passed in February 1814 to declare landholders who had voluntarily withdrawn to the US to be aliens incapable of holding land; and as the war came to an end, it was decided to try to reduce the American proportion of the population. Drummond was therefore told, on taking over the Governorship from Prevost, not to grant land 'to Subjects of the United States' and to use his 'best endeavours to prevent their Settling in either of the Canadas'.[8] This was easier said than done. Already by September 1815 there were complaints that Americans were again 'pouring into' Upper Canada. Commissions were appointed to confiscate 'Forfeited Estates', and to administer the 1814 Alien Act. It was also decided not to proffer the Oath of Allegiance to any non-office holders except descendants of the original Loyalists, and to these only if they or their parents/ husbands had done their 'duty in defence of the Province'. One could not secure a land title without taking the oath, so this discouraged American land purchases. But when it started to take

---

[7] Fifty people who had fled to America were also charged *in absentia – Dictionary of Canadian Biography*, Jacob Overholser, Sir John Beverley Robinson, Elijah Bentley, Abraham Markle; Mark McNeill, 'Bloody Assize Revisited', Hamilton *Spectator* (updated 29 Feb. 2020)

[8] Bathurst to Drummond, 10 Jan. 1815 (ed. W. Wood, *Select British Documents of the Canadian War of 1812*, iii Part 2 (Toronto, Champlain Society, 1926) p. 509

effect, large landholders anxious to sell jibbed. In 1817 a committee of the Legislative Assembly condemned the policy, leading Lt. Governor Gore to complain that its real aim was to transfer 'this devoted Province to the United States of America'.[9] Controversy became acute in 1821 when an American settler was elected to the Assembly but then expelled as ineligible; and the alien question 'remained as a first-class' issue until legislation in 1827 confirmed Americans who took the Oath of Allegiance 'in all the privileges of British birth'. They later showed their gratitude to those who had taken their part against the establishment, 'and their votes became the largest prop of the growing reform movement'.[10]

Keeping Americans out of Canada was one side of post-war British policy; the other was 'diverting to the British Colonies that part of the Population which would otherwise emigrate to the United States'. To this end the government in 1815 provided some 2000 Scots with free passages, and settled a number of demobilised troops. And though direct official interventions were mostly rather ineffectual, British North America received more UK immigrants than the United States until the later 1830s, while even thereafter their absolute numbers continued to rise. In 1867 'about 60 per cent. of Canadians were of British origin',[11] and the resultant 'British' sentiment would influence the country well into the twentieth century.

This did not mean that the 'home' government and its representatives in British North America encountered no political problems. Indeed after 1820 'critics emerged in every colony to challenge the official factions ... that had long dominated its government', factions pejoratively termed in Upper Canada

---

[9] Cruikshank, 'Disaffection' pp. 54, 59-60, 64-5; Gerald M. Craig, *Upper Canada. The Formative Years 1784-1841* (London, 1963) pp. 87-91

[10] Craig, *Upper Canada* pp. 114-22. Though often evaded, New Brunswick's similar ban on American ownership of land lasted into the 1830s

[11] Bathurst to Drummond, 20 March 1815 (*British Documents of the War of 1812*, iii Part 2 pp. 788-9); Errington, 'British Migration and British America' pp. 141, 146

'"the Family Compact", in Lower Canada the "Chateau Clique", in Nova Scotia "the system" ... The new generation of critics (they liked to call themselves reformers) were more energetic than their predecessors, and ... often more willing to employ public opinion in their opposition.' Lower Canada apart, they 'saw themselves as provincial Britons, claiming ... the right to self-governing institutions similar to those possessed by the metropolitan British, a cry which came to be summed up in the phrase "responsible government"'. And though the issues differed from one province to another, all came to 'responsible government' at much the same time: Nova Scotia and Canada in 1848, Prince Edward Island in 1851, New Brunswick in 1854, and Newfoundland in 1855.[12]

That said, the process occasioned no more than minor troubles in the Maritimes, but in 1837-8 rebellions in both Canadas. This is not the place to discuss them. But their sequels did much to frame the political structure of the future Canada. In the 1830s Lower Canada had set the pace in agitation, and over the decade this became increasingly a French-Canadian cause, the reformers styling themselves 'Patriotes'. They were reacting to immigration and Anglicisation: business was largely in Anglo-phone hands; in 1833 the 'waste lands' of the Eastern Townships were assigned to what the Assembly would term 'speculators residing in England'; and almost half the city of Quebec, more than half that of Montreal, was English-speaking.[13] Overall, though, such immigrants were in a minority, and the Assembly was correspondingly dominated by Canadiens. They sought, in a way reminiscent of the 17th century English House of Commons, to bend the government to their will by denying it supply, but with the more modern aim of securing power and patronage by making the Executive and Legislative

---

[12] J.M. Bumsted, 'The Consolidation of British North America, 1783-1860', and Phillip Buckner, 'Canada and the British Empire', *Canada and the British Empire* pp. 5, 52, 58

[13] Fernand Ouellet, *Lower Canada 1791-1840. Social Change and Nationalism* (Toronto, 1980) p. 331; James Sturgis, 'Anglicisation as a theme in Lower Canadian History 1807-1843', *British Journal of Canadian Studies* 3 (1988) pp. 210-33

Councils elective. Hopefully this would correct a situation where, in 1832, only a third of the local magistrates and 47 of the Provincial Administration's 204 salaried officers were of French origin.[14] In 1834 the Assembly sent its demands to London in the form of Ninety-two Resolutions. In April-May 1837 Parliament rejected them: some changes were desirable, but neither the Legislative nor the Executive Council should become elective. Also, as the Assembly had made no provision for the administration of justice and the 'support of the civil government' since October 1832, the Governor was authorised to draw on provincial revenues to cover the outstanding costs of £142,000. With their hopes thus dashed, or bluffs called, the Patriotes moved beyond the Assembly to mass meetings that tapped into a rising peasant discontent, and to further preparations (though their extent is disputed) for military action and the establishment of an independent state.[15] Fighting broke out in November, and by December the insurgency had been crushed, with most of the leading figures fleeing to the United States. A year later some of these mounted an invasion and touched off a second and more radical rising, but this too was put down in short order.

Throughout the 1830s Upper Canada reformers had been in contact with their Lower Canada counterparts. But they were much less strongly placed. Composition of the Upper Canadian Assembly swung from one election to the next; and when in 1836 it voted to suspend supply, Sir Francis Bond Head dissolved it and secured the defeat of most leading Reformers, which he followed up by dismissing officials and judges with Reform sympathies. Most Reformers then withdrew to private life, which left the way clear for the impetuous William Lyon Mackenzie to copy the Patriotes. As 'a challenge to the rebels to change agitation into attack', Bond Head sent off all his regular troops In November 1837

---

[14] 'The Ninety-Two Resolutions of the Legislative Assembly of Lower Canada' (Wikisource, accessed 21/5/19) esp. no. 75
[15] Ten 'Resolutions intended to be proposed by Lord John Russell ... relative to the affairs of Lower Canada' (Wikisource); Fernand Ouellet and André Lefort, 'Viger, Denis-Benjamin', *Dictionary of Canadian Biography*

to help the authorities in Lower Canada;[16] and Mackenzie fell into the trap, seeking to seize Toronto and establish a Reform government. He might have garnered more support had he been less incompetent, but his force was quickly dispersed, and he fled to the United States. Once there, Mackenzie recruited American sympathisers by promising land in Canada; with their help he briefly occupied Navy Island, Niagara, and proclaimed a Canadian Republic. The chief effect of such filibustering was to intensify loyalist backlash in Upper Canada, leaving some former Reform leaders so uncomfortable that they contemplated decamping to America.

Salvation from this despond came from Britain's attempt to recast the Canadas in the wake of the rebellions. Lower Canada could not be left indefinitely with no popular participation in government and an appointed Council in lieu of its Assembly, but restoring the Assembly might lead straight back to the troubles of the 1830s. Hence the policy of merging the two Canadas. This proved easier said than done. There would be a single parliament, in which it was hoped that loyal Upper Canada would control Lower; but as the latter was the more populous (some 650,000 as against 456,000), the two had to be accorded equal representation. They remained for many purposes distinct, since differences in their laws made it necessary to continue separate legal establishments and officials in each; and this had the effect of preserving separate patronage (and hence political) systems in 'Canada East' and 'West'. The merger, first recommended by Governor-General the Earl of Durham but pushed through by his successor Poulett Thomson, was unpopular in both Canadas, though more especially in Lower whose anglicisation was clearly aspired to (the French language ceased to be official). However perceptive politicians saw the possibility of controlling the new Assembly through a Patriote-Reformer combination, and using this majority to extort the

---

[16] Head to General Sir John Colborne, 20 Nov. 1837. Head later explained that to demonstrate the province's underlying loyalty he had wanted 'to await the outbreak, which I was confident would be impotent' (S.F. Wise, 'Head, Sir Francis Bond', *Dictionary of Canadian Biography*)

changes they required. Until November 1837 Louis-Hippolyte LaFontaine had been deeply involved in the Patriote agitation, but he had drawn back from rebellion. Many previous leaders had then fled abroad, and LaFontaine managed (with his wife's assistance) to position himself as an intermediary between those who had been imprisoned and the government, and as many exiles' advocate to the latter. In 1839-40 he was contacted by Francis Hincks with the message that the Canadiens 'would never obtain their rights in a Lower Canadian legislature. You want our help as much as we do yours.'

Hincks was a protégé of the leading Upper Canadian Reformer Robert Baldwin. Baldwin had long been telling anybody who would listen (including Lord Durham) that it was 'the genius of the English race in both hemispheres to be concerned in the Government of themselves'; without it they would break away, but with it there would be 'a permanent connection between the colonies and the Mother Country'. By 'the Government of themselves', Baldwin, like his father before him, meant a government whose ministers depended, as in Britain, on retaining the confidence of the Assembly, and Durham recommended this, coining the phrase 'responsible government'. It was not the policy either of London or of Governor Thomson. But Hincks assured LaFontaine that in the Assembly of the united Canada there would be an 'overwhelming Reform majority' and that 'we will make' the Ministry give Responsible Government 'whether they like it or not'. In an address to his constituents, LaFontaine accepted the desirability of thus cooperating to achieve responsible government by exploiting the union of the two Canadas; and he later claimed to have used this union, 'the rod by which it was intended to destroy my countrymen' to place them 'in a better position than they had occupied before'.[17]

---

[17] Robert Baldwin to Lord Durham, 23 Aug. 1838; Francis Hincks to LaFontaine, 17 June 1840; Craig, *Upper Canada* esp. pp. 257, 274; LaFontaine to 'the Electors of Terrebonne', 25 Aug. 1840; Jacques Monet, 'La Fontaine, Sir Louis-Hippolyte', William G. Ormsby, 'Hincks, Sir Francis', and Michael S. Cross and Robert Lochiel Fraser, 'Baldwin, Robert' in the *Dictionary of Canadian Biography*

In other words, cooperation with friendly Anglo-phone politicians was the key to the *survivance* the Patriotes had in the 1830s pursued by more confrontational means.

The 1841 elections did not go entirely smoothly: LaFontaine had to withdraw from the contest in his own constituency. But this cemented his alliance with Baldwin, who provided him with a Toronto seat (a favour LaFontaine repaid in kind in 1843), and the two became personal friends. The Reform majority was not 'overwhelming', but the new Governor-General Sir Charles Bagot concluded in 1842 that the Assembly would not function unless he came to terms with LaFontaine. LaFontaine accepted office as Canada East's Attorney-General, on condition that Baldwin was also brought in. Bagot was pleasantly surprised by their performance as ministers, and, while his health collapsed, left them increasingly free to function as if heads of a party government. This, however, did not commend itself to Bagot's successor, Charles Metcalfe, who, though in many ways liberal, was determined to be neither a 'nullity' nor 'a tool in the hands of party'. He insisted on himself controlling patronage. The government resigned, and in 1844 Metcalfe dissolved the Assembly. In the resultant election he secured the votes of many moderate Reformers, but also played on the theme of loyalty with striking success among recent British immigrants to Upper Canada, where the government won all but a dozen seats. Though less successful in Canada East, it enjoyed a small overall majority. Metcalfe, however, was mortally ill; and though he had sought to maintain the Governor's independent authority, power slid into the hands of what became a moderate Conservative administration.[18] LaFontaine thus had to struggle to maintain his leadership in Lower Canada without the resource of patronage, and against the background of government attempts to co-opt other eminent Canadiens.

He succeeded. Hincks moved to Montreal to provide journalistic support, with financial assistance from both Baldwin and LaFontaine. LaFontaine further developed his political

---

[18] 'Metcalfe, Charles Theophilus', *Dictionary of Canadian Biography*

machine, helped in Montreal by George-Étienne Cartier, who had fought for the rebels at the start of the 1837 rising but next year wrote (from exile) that he had not 'forfeited his allegiance'. (In 1853 he named his daughter 'Reine-Victoria'.) Though strongly anti-clerical in 1837, LaFontaine now mended relations with the Church, earning the gratitude of Bishop Bourget of Montreal for his help in 1845-6 over bills on education and Jesuit estates. Over time this clerical support became increasingly important for a party that became known as the *bleus*, in opposition to its more secular and anti-clerical critics, the *rouges*.

In the 1847-8 elections, the LaFontaine Baldwin alliance triumphed, securing majorities in both halves of Canada. Lord John Russell had once held that Governors, who were appointed by the London government, could not have two masters, as would be the case with 'responsible government'. Peel and his Colonial Secretary Lord Stanley agreed, applauding Metcalfe's stand, and rewarding him for his 1844 election victory with a peerage. But Lord Grey, the Colonial Secretary in Russell's 1846-52 Liberal government, laid down, in the context of Nova Scotia,[19] that a Governor should not identify himself 'with any one party' but keep an administration while it could manage the legislature, and accept its adversaries if they in turn gained this control; he should, too, exercise great caution in refusing assent to a government measure. Grey showed this instruction to his new Governor-General, Lord Elgin, before he left for Canada.[20]

In 1848 there was general agreement that a LaFontaine Baldwin government would have to be tried. For 'If we over-rule the Local Legislature we must be prepared to support our authority

---

[19] A split there over denominational education led to a situation where Lt. Governor Lord Falkland was in effect acting as a political partisan. He had to go, and Lord Grey instructed his successor Sir John Harvey to assume a position of political neutrality, adding (in March 1847) that Harvey should be prepared to accept party government. After an election victory later that year, a reform ministry duly took office in 1848
[20] Earl Grey, *The Colonial Policy of Lord John Russell's Administration* (quoting his 3 Nov. 1846 despatch to Harvey) i (London, 1853) pp. 209-13

by force, & in the present state of the world & of Canada, he must ... be an insane politician who would think of doing so.'[21] Still this was seen as a gamble, as the 1848 Nova Scotian change was not: Elgin was told the experiment would 'probably determine not only whether ... [Canada's] connection with this Country is to last, but also whether it is to have the advantage of a mixed and well regulated Govnt or is to be given up to Extreme democracy.' Russell had talked of reinforcing the garrison as a precaution, and he continued to monitor Canadian developments very closely. But he recognised that 'a liberal ministry' would be 'the best safeguard – if Baldwin is true', and he hoped that a 'friendly and determined' attitude would 'rapidly reduce annexationists to miniscule numbers'.[22]

In the long run, accepting 'responsible government' both had that effect and proved the necessary condition for major colonies remaining within the British connection. But in 1849 Elgin's support for LaFontaine and Baldwin combined with economic troubles to create a surprising crisis. British North American produce, notably grain, flour, and lumber, had enjoyed preferential access to the UK. But the 1840s move there towards free trade ended this just as UK demand subsided with the end of the railway-building boom. And it was natural, though apparently mistaken, for the colonies to view the tariff change as the chief cause of the severe depression that then struck them. It seemed a poor reward for their past loyalty.

Their other potential market was the United States. This was heavily protectionist. But access would be gained were the colonies to join it, leaving their unappreciative mother country. Such reasoning gave rise to small movements for annexation in other

---

[21] Grey to Elgin, 22 Feb. 1848 (ed. Sir Arthur Doughty, *The Elgin-Grey Papers 1846-1852* (Ottawa, 1937) pp. 120-1) – Grey's Conservative predecessors Stanley and Gladstone were said to agree
[22] Russell to Grey, 12 and 16 March 1848 – Russell guessed that Canada was currently split two-to-one in favour of the imperial connection (Ged Martin, 'The Elgin-Grey Papers 1846-1852: A Triangular Correspondence', on-line version); Grey to Elgin, 22 March (Doughty, *The Elgin-Grey Papers* pp. 125-9)

provinces.[23] And in Montreal, which had been particularly hard hit,[24] economic resentment fused with political backlash against the LaFontaine-Baldwin ministry. In February-March 1849 this carried through the legislature a bill to pay compensation for all losses incurred in the 1837-8 Lower Canada risings, including those of insurgents. The idea was neither new nor exclusively 'Reform', but the bill encountered violent Tory opposition, partly tactical but also fuelled by revulsion against an 'insult to every man who bore arms in 1837 and a positive robbery of every man who was not a rebel against the Queen ... one of a chain [of measures] long cherished in the Lower Canada Parliament and now revived ... to put the Anglo-Saxons of Canada East ... under the feet of the French'.[25] LaFontaine was burnt in effigy, and Elgin was petitioned either to withhold assent or to dissolve the Assembly. Instead, he drove in to give assent, sparking two days of rioting that burned the parliament building and included attacks

---

[23] In New Brunswick there was relatively little overt press support for annexation. But it was said to be often privately discussed as a possibility if trade failed to revive; and July 4 was marked by demonstrations of pro-American feeling – including the cruise of people from St. John to Eastport, Maine, singing a parody of 'a great New Brunswick hymn':

> '...Clear the way for Annexation/To the nearest greatest Nation.

> To British policy a prey,/Kick'd and plundered by Earl Grey,/Clear the way for Annexation,/...

> On loyalty we cannot live,/One ounce of bread it will not give,/Clear the way for Annexation...'

However M. Ruth Nicholson concludes that the movement 'sprang from commercial distress only', and that, with a revival of trade and prospects, it had died out 'by the summer of 1850' – *Relations of New Brunswick with the State of Maine and the United States, 1837-1849* (M.A. thesis, University of New Brunswick, Aug. 1952) pp. 127-134). See also Michael S. Cross, *Free Trade, Annexation, and Reciprocity, 1846-1854* (Toronto, 1971: Canadian History Through the Press Series) p. 12
[24] Exports from Montreal fell from $3.3m. in 1847 to $1.5m. in 1848; and Lord Elgin would report that three-quarters of the commercial men there were bankrupt – Donald Warner, *The idea of continental union: agitation for the annexation of Canada to the United States, 1849-1893* (Lexington, Kentucky, 1960) pp. 10-11
[25] *Montreal Gazette*, 16 Feb. 1849 (J.M.S. Careless, *The Union of the Canadas. The Growth of Canadian Institutions, 1841-1857* (London, 1968) pp. 235-6n.)

on the houses of LaFontaine and Hincks.[26] Conservatives then mounted a mission to persuade the London government to intervene, but to no avail.

Quite how important all this was in inclining people to 'annexation' in order to protect themselves against this British backing of 'the French', it is hard to say. It will not have influenced Liberal annexationists. But it was in these terms that, many years later, the repentant Sir John Abbot (soon to become Conservative Prime Minister of Canada) explained his and other signatures of the annexation manifesto: 'They were exasperated by the fact that when 10,000' former sufferers by the rising petitioned the Governor-General to reserve for royal decision 'a Bill which they believed to be ... for paying the men whom they blamed for the trouble', he went out of his way to sanction it, 'in contempt for their ... loyalty'.[27]

The *Montreal Herald* first advocated annexation in late June 1849; and 'One by one' over the course of the summer, commented the *Montreal Transcript*, 'the Conservative journals have come over' to it, while 'many influential Conservatives, who not long ago would have rejected the address with scorn, are now its shameless and unflinching advocates'. By the autumn, most of Montreal's anglophone press was, Elgin reported, 'more or less avowedly annexationist. And all are bitterly opposed to the French and to constitutional Govt. which gives the French a share in the Govt. of the Country.'[28] A manifesto arguing in studiously moderate terms for annexation was produced in October, and quickly acquired over a thousand signatures. Though Elgin described it as an 'emanation from a knot of violent protectionists

---

[26] By way of precaution and punishment, Montreal lost its position as Canada's capital, with the legislature now alternating between Toronto and Quebec
[27] Senate speech, 15 March 1889 – Cephas D. Allin and George M. Jones, *Annexation, Preferential Trade and Reciprocity ... the Canadian Annexation Movement of 1849-50* (Toronto, 1912) p. 115
[28] *Montreal Transcript*, Oct. 1849 (Allin and Jones, *Annexation* p. 115); Elgin to Grey, 1 Nov. 1849 (Doughty, *The Elgin-Grey Papers* pp. 528-30); Cross, *Free Trade, Annexation, and Reciprocity* pp. 11, 16

and disappointed party men', it seems that Montreal's 'larger commercial interests' favoured annexation, while those signing the rapidly assembled counter-document were 'socially and commercially less impressive'. Fewer than a quarter of the manifesto's signatories were francophones, though they included Louis-Joseph Papineau (the leader of the Patriotes until 1837, who had returned from exile but retained his American republican proclivities) and his younger 'Rouge' followers.[29]

Annexationists looked to the Rouges to deliver the French vote. But an early 1850 Quebec by-election showed that LaFontaine's rapprochement with the Church had marginalized Papineau: for the mainstream French vote now crushed the annexationist candidate Joseph Legaré.[30] Disappointment also came in the anglophone Eastern Townships. Their exposed situation had led to an initial surge of support for annexation, with 1,200 people pressing it on their MLA, the rising businessman Alexander Galt; and he duly declared it to be 'the only sure cure for our manifold ills'. But this went down badly with his London superiors in the British American Land Company. Partly for this reason, he resigned his legislature seat; and in the ensuing by-election the annexationist candidate only just scraped home.[31] By then the Governor-General and the Reform party had, with the backing of the imperial government, come out strongly against annexation; and to counter the common belief that this would enjoy the mother country's blessing, they dismissed those officeholders who

---

[29] Elgin to Grey, 14 Oct. 1849 (*Elgin-Grey Papers* p. 522); these *Papers* print the manifesto and its signatures (pp. 1487-94); Allin and Jones assess the signatures (*Annexation* pp. 114-17, 149-51), while Cross notes the interests of leading members of the Montreal Annexation Association (*Free Trade, Annexation and Reciprocity* p. 11)

[30] When Legaré had stood as Papineau's ally in 1848, he had (though not elected) received a majority of the francophone vote. As an annexationist in 1850 he now secured an Anglophone majority, but, on a much higher poll, he was heavily defeated by the francophones – see the triumphalist analysis of the two votes in *Canada de Québec*, 2 Feb. 1850 (*Elgin-Grey Papers* pp. 596-600)

[31] 'Galt, Sir Alexander Tilloch', *Dictionary of Canadian Biography;* Cross, *Free Trade, Annexation and Reciprocity* pp. 11, 64, 67-70; Warner, *The Idea of Continental Union* p. 19

persisted in endorsing it. Annexation had never cut much ice in Canada West (which Elgin had been carefully cultivating); and Hincks was able to make full use of Barings' warning that the money needed to service past canal projects and public works could not be raised 'until perfect reliance' could be placed on the 'future political condition of the colony'.[32] So when the legislature convened in Toronto in 1850, it held only seven clear annexationists, and the two efforts to raise the question were heavily defeated.[33]

The annexation movement was little more than a bubble, subsiding quickly with the return of economic prosperity. But Elgin had concluded that Canada would only remain quiet if 'you put our trade on as good a footing as that of our American neighbours'. For much of its 'exportable produce' had 'to seek a market in the States', paying a 20% duty that 'would remain in the pocket of the producer if we were republicanised'. To compensate for the loss of preferential access to the UK, Canadian businessmen had for some time been looking to a US tariff deal, 'Reciprocity'; and in 1849 Elgin wrote that it was 'either this or annexation'. Similarly, New Brunswick's Executive Council warned that without such a deal the public would soon seek relief 'by incorporation with the neighbouring republic'.[34] A doctrinaire free trader, Elgin continued to press for Reciprocity even after the annexation bubble had deflated. So, until 1852, did

---

[32] Hincks had been told this in September 1849, when in Britain trying to place £500,000 worth of bonds. On returning to Canada, he pressed for the dismissal of annexationist officeholders; news that this had been done enabled Barings to sell the bonds – Ronald Stewart Longley, *Sir Francis Hincks. A Study of Canadian Politics, Railways, and Finance in the Nineteenth Century* (Toronto, 1943) pp. 168-72, 175

[33] Warner, *The Idea of Continental Union* pp. 27-8; Allin and Jones, *Annexation* pp. 334-50

[34] Elgin to Grey, 23 April, 11 June, and 8 Nov. 1849 (*Elgin-Grey Papers* pp. 349, 370, 534); W.S. MacNutt, *The Atlantic Provinces. The Emergence of Colonial Society 1712-1857* (Toronto, 1965) pp. 238-9. Grey even ascribed the failure to obtain reciprocity in 1850 to the counter-productive over-enthusiasm of 'the Colonists & especially the N. Brunswickers' (25 Oct. 1850 – *Elgin-Grey Papers* p. 722)

the Lieutenant-Governors of the Maritime Provinces, with New Brunswick's Sir Edmund Head echoing the view that only thus could annexation be avoided. British ministers in Washington agreed, Crampton in 1854 describing reciprocity as 'of the greatest political importance, as removing the only disadvantage under which the Colonies labour in consequence of not being members of the American Union, and thus taking away every motive for annexation.'[35] And governments in London were happy to back the idea.

But securing Reciprocity was not easy. In 1848 and 1849 legislation had passed the House but stalled in the Senate, partly through fear that tariff concessions to Canada would become generalized, partly through the belief (encouraged by the American consul in St. John, Israel Andrews) that better terms could be obtained. From 1850, neither House showed much interest; and in late 1851 Stephen A. Douglas, who had previously sponsored the measure in the Senate, spelt out the difficulties to Crampton: since no National or Party feelings were involved, both support and opposition came

'not on any general Principle, but from various local or peculiar considerations ... the only means of getting it [through] is therefore one which involves great knowledge of men's characters, of their local interests and prejudices ... and above all great labor in keeping account of the 'ayes and noes' etc.'

Douglas himself was now too busy 'to undertake much of that kind of work', but 'there is a man, who – if we could get him

---

[35] Donald C. Masters, *The Reciprocity Treaty of 1854* (London, 1936) pp. 12-18; John Crampton to Lord Clarendon, 12 June 1854 (James J. and Patience P. Barnes, *Private and Confidential. Letters from British Ministers in Washington to the Foreign Secretaries in London* (Selinsgrove, Pennsylvania, 1993) p. 102

to act – with the assistance of some others whom he could command – ... I think, would secure our carrying the Bill.'[36]

This dimension of mid-nineteenth century business tends not to feature in general accounts. We have seen [above pp. 323-5] that F.O.J. Smith (who also promoted and backed telegraphy) proposed, first to Van Buren and then to Webster, that he be employed 'for a few thousand dollars' as an agent to plant newspaper articles and persuade Maine's politicians to authorise compromise negotiations. In the years that followed, British interests encountered similar figures, some of whom canvassed for employment by explaining (more fully than would have been necessary to Americans) just how the system worked. Thus in late 1850 Israel Andrews told both the British minister in Washington, Sir Henry Bulwer, and Lord Elgin in Canada that they had gone the wrong way about promoting Reciprocity: they had relied on personal approaches to individual Congressmen and had not built a supportive public opinion at the local level. 'Motives of pecuniary interest must be made to operate upon leading' local newspapers and politicians 'in different parts of the Country' and generate resolutions and petitions 'favorable to the measure'. It was, too, 'customary and indispensable to have every important measure before Congress in charge of intelligent special Agents who are relied upon to furnish facts [to Congressmen] and solicit votes'. And, given the diversity both of local interests and of Congressional business, 'There must be a reciprocity of votes, and means must be used to obtain the ... cooperation of the Agents and friends of the [other] great measures which will be before Congress'. All this would be expensive – $50,000 had been spent to secure passage of a bill to establish 'a line of Steamboats'.[37]

---

[36] Crampton to Elgin, 3 Nov. 1851 – quoted at length in James J. Barnes, *Authors, Publishers and Politicians. The Quest for an Anglo-American Copyright Agreement 1815-1854* (London, 1974) pp. 180-3. Chapters 9-12 of this book must constitute one of the fullest portraits of the then network of Congressional promoters and lobbyists

[37] Andrews gave Elgin this memorandum when visiting Toronto in November 1850, having previously left a copy with Sir Henry Bulwer in Washington – *Elgin-Grey Papers* pp. 747, 753-4

Though they sometimes were, or affected to be, shocked, the British knew that 'a great deal was done in Congress in this way'.[38] In 1847 Sir George Simpson visited Washington to try to sell the Hudson's Bay Company's [HBC's] property south of the new Oregon border. He was soon talking with the well-connected George N. Sanders, who told him that to get even $300,000 out of Congress would require promising 10% of any amount over $250,000 to 'A, B, C, D, and E', 5% to '1, 2, 3, and 4', 1 or 2% to a few others, and the remaining 12-15% to Sanders himself. Further negotiations led in 1848 to an agreement: Sanders would seek to sell the property for $410,000, receiving 2½% as commission plus anything he secured beyond $410,000. Sanders spent heavily on legal opinions ($5000 to Webster, an unspecified sum to Richard Coxe, and, he said, $10,000 on further legal fees); he offered Senator Clayton $1,500 for his 'legal opinion and support', and probably extended similar inducements to other Senators. In February 1849 Sanders was confident of success – too much so, Simpson reported, since he brought his Resolution forward without 'having all his friends in the house to support the measure'.[39]

It was not a happy precedent – Sanders had received some HBC money, but undoubtedly made a loss. However the Reciprocity project soon attracted other would-be agents. In 1849 Andrews had been given a secret mission as a US special agent in the Maritimes. He lost no time in establishing contact with the leading Canadian proponent of Reciprocity, W.H. Merritt, not,

---

[38] Crampton to Elgin, 3 Nov. 1851 (Barnes, *Authors, Publishers and Politicians* pp. 180-1)
[39] John S. Galbraith, 'George N. Sanders, "Influence Man" for the Hudson's Bay Company', *Oregon Historical Quarterly* 53:3 (1952) esp. pp. 162-4. The real difficulty, though, was that Palmerston had refused to accompany the sale with a treaty relinquishing British rights to navigate the Columbia south of 49°, which the otherwise supportive Secretary of State Buchanan required. Sanders argued that an HBC sale would terminate them, but the Senate would have been happier with a treaty. In any case, President Polk disliked the idea as 'a project of speculators who hung about the lobbies of Congress ... and whose only object was to make a handsome sum for themselves'

one imagines, solely for statistical purposes.[40] Bulwer had already advised entrusting Reciprocity to 'a skilful lawyer accustomed to managing bills in Congress', paying him 'a good fee' and promising more 'in case of success', and had suggested promising Andrews 'a handsome consideration' should the bill pass. Andrews maintained that 'without gaining the influence of the local Press' Reciprocity could never pass 'Congress, where it would be opposed by local interests', and had committed his thoughts to writing. He struck Bulwer as probably anxious to carry the question, but also as seeking 'to get employed in the matter and to better himself by doing so' – something 'by no means' uncommon for inadequately paid US agents. At this stage Andrews had not mentioned money, and Bulwer expected 'to find no difficulty in giving him' 'a small sum' if this seemed likely 'to influence' his report to Congress.[41] But Andrews seems to have wanted more: the British government, Bulwer told Elgin, 'will let me give him 100£ or so but he requires 300£ or 400£ & 2,000 or 3,000£' if the Reciprocity bill passed.[42] For good measure Andrews appears to have threatened to block the measure 'unless it is made my interest to write for it'.[43] A more formidable approach was made

---

[40] Ostensibly, Andrews was to make statistical reports on trade. But he could have done so from his previous position as Consul in St. John; nor does this provide any motive for secrecy – Donald C. Masters, 'A Further Word on I.D. Andrews and the Reciprocity Treaty of 1854', Canadian Historical Review [hereafter Can.H.R.] 17:2 (1936) pp. 159-60, citing Clayton to President Fillmore, 20 July 1850; William D. Overman, 'I.D. Andrews and Reciprocity in 1854: An Episode in Dollar Diplomacy', ibid. 15:3 (1934) p. 248

[41] Bulwer to Palmerston, 1 July and 7 Oct. 1850 – Barnes, Authors, Publishers and Politicians p. 185; FO 5/515 fos. 158-9. Palmerston authorised Bulwer 'to incur any reasonable expense which he may find useful' (FO 5/515 fo. 171)

[42] Andrews conveyed these terms to Bulwer after getting 'nothing definite' during his Canadian visit (extract of letter from Bulwer, forwarded by Elgin to Grey on 17 Dec. 1850 – Elgin-Grey Papers p. 777)

[43] 10 Nov. 1850 letter to Elgin, enclosed in Elgin to Grey, 17 Dec. 1850. The signature has been obliterated, but both the context and the writer's description as 'an employé of the U.S. Govt.' fits Andrews. However Masters, 'A Further Word' p. 164, attributes it to George W. Brega (who did indeed work as one of Andrews' agents for reciprocity from at least 1851) – Overman, 'Andrews and Reciprocity' p. 260n.)

to Crampton next year by President Polk's former private secretary, Joseph Knox Walker, on behalf of a group that really did style itself the 'Organization'. This represented itself as able to carry Reciprocity through Congress but indicated that it would kill it were its terms not met. Crampton, admittedly a man with a 'natural love of intrigue', believed both claims, especially after he had consulted Douglas and been advised to put himself in Walker's hands. He told Elgin, whose summary of the letter was that 'the whole question of our getting or not getting Reciprocity appears to hinge on our booking up £20,000'.[44]

The 'Organization' contained former members of Polk's administration, who were now seeking to repair their own fortunes: Polk's private secretary, Knox Walker; Treasury Secretary R.J. Walker; Secretary of War William Marcy; Navy Secretary John Mason; and (though he joined rather later) Vice-President George Dallas. A later addition was a lawyer with Whig connections, Lewis C. Levin.[45] The HBC turned to the Organization, R.J. Walker agreeing to secure $1m. for its American property on a commission basis; after this had come to nothing despite payments of $21,500, it worked with Levin and Dallas, who were to receive 10% in the event of a satisfactory sale.[46] Meanwhile Bulwer's son, Robert Lytton, Bulwer himself, and Crampton helped conclude a deal whereby British authors and publishers would pay the Organization for legislation to protect British copyrights from American pirating. When a copyright treaty was signed, Levin received £1000 on

---

[44] Crampton to Elgin, 3 Nov. 1851 (Barnes, *Authors, Publishers and Politicians* pp. 180-3), and Elgin to Grey, 15 Nov. (*Elgin-Grey Papers* p. 939); J. L. Morison, *The Eighth Earl of Elgin* (London, 1928) p. 166

[45] Barnes, *Authors, Publishers and Politicians* pp. 194-215.

[46] Galbraith, 'George N. Sanders' p. 174, and his *The Hudson's Bay Company as an Imperial Factor* (1977 edn., New York) pp. 269-71. This had to be abandoned when Marcy, now Secretary of State, reproved Simpson for Sanders' attempts to bribe Congressmen. Thereafter, the HBC and the British minister of the day negotiated more conventionally with successive US administrations; arbitration was eventually agreed on in 1863, and the company was awarded $650,000

account; but as the treaty was never submitted to the Senate for ratification, we cannot tell how well he had prepared the way.[47]

Dealings over Reciprocity were less advanced. But they are mentioned in letters of November 1852 in which Levin undertook to continue working despite a recent rift with Knox Walker. When Congress met, he would 'go on, in good faith,' with Copyright and HBC compensation. He would also, 'if you approve it, lay the foundation for the certain passage of the reciprocity Bill', provided the British colonies did nothing 'to exasperate our people'. He would concentrate exclusively on these three projects, and 'undertake no other business'.[48] By then, however, the Organization was breaking up, and it is not clear whether there were further dealings with it – though in June 1853 Crampton would, at the suggestion of Marcy (now Secretary of State), have a long conversation with R.J. Walker.[49] But Walker soon annoyed first Marcy and then the Pierce administration generally, and this may have again left the field open to Andrews, with whom the Canadian government had never lost contact.

The more conventional way of seeking Reciprocity was of course diplomatic. Initially the British negotiating position was weak. For, as Crampton pointed out, the UK's move to free trade had already given away the tariff concessions that might otherwise

---

[47] The initial deal was for payment of $60,000, but Levin cut his terms when it transpired that Bulwer had mis-stated the price when approaching the British authors – Barnes, *Authors, Publishers and Politicians* chaps. 11, 12

[48] 'Mr. Tucker of Philadelphia [another member of the Organization] has promised me his active co-operation in carrying the reciprocity bill ... and I am willing to undertake it on a contingency basis without asking any retainer. The fee however ought to be a considerable one' – Levin to Crampton, 2 Nov. 1852, and to T.W.C. Moore (an intermediary between Claims Agents and the British Legation), 15 Nov. (ibid. pp. 230-1)

[49] Crampton extolled Walker's familiarity with attitudes towards commercial questions 'in each State ... in Congress generally, and even in the minds of each important Member ... His opinion therefore as to ... what can or cannot be done upon any commercial question, is extremely valuable'. Crampton also noted Walker's sincere support for free trade and his favourable attitude towards Britain – to Lord Clarendon, 19 June 1853 (Barnes, *Private and Confidential* pp. 74-5)

have been used for bargaining.[50] But in 1852 the British side acquired a powerful lever. By then the Maritimes were no longer so keen on Reciprocity, especially if it meant losing the Fisheries; and the new Conservative government in the UK responded to their concerns by extending naval support for fishery protection. Most of the fishing was in fact done by American vessels, some 2,500 in 1852,[51] which rejected the British view as to how the three-mile limit should be measured, and which were anyway inclined to follow the fish across that limit. Naval enforcement remained light. But there was inevitably a danger of clashes with US warships sent to protect the fishers, and both countries feared an incident that might set them by the ears.

Secretary of State Webster had been in no hurry to move over Reciprocity, but the prospect of a fisheries clash galvanized him into action. The situation was, he told Crampton, 'full of danger'. He had recommended to President Fillmore immediate negotiations on 'the whole subject of the fisheries and Canada trade'. And he summoned both Crampton and Andrews to his country home. Talks there went well, leading to the agreement of draft treaties on HBC compensation and on copyright – though Webster doubted whether it would be worth submitting them to the Senate in the coming session. Over Reciprocity and the Fisheries, he had greater concerns. For, he told Fillmore, if 'no arrangement be made', he looked either 'for a half-belligerant [sic] state of things between us and the Provinces, and great difficulty respecting the Fisheries; or for a united rush by the Colonists themselves and [Stephen Douglas'] Young America, for their annexation to us', both of which he would 'most deeply deplore'.[52] Where all this would have gone had Webster lived, we cannot say.

---

[50] Crampton to Clarendon, 19 June 1853 (ibid. p. 76)

[51] Masters, *Reciprocity Treaty* p. 41; ed. Kenneth E. Shewmaker and Kenneth R. Stevens, *The Papers of Daniel Webster. Diplomatic Papers, Volume 2. 1850-1852* (Hanover, N.H., 1984) p. 871

[52] Webster to Crampton, and to Andrews, 17 July 1852 (Manning, *Diplomatic Correspondence* iv (Washington, 1945) p. 43); Webster to Millard Fillmore, *Diplomatic Papers 1850-1852* esp. pp. 703, 705-6)

But he became increasingly confident that the 'Fishery affair will come out right and bright'; and 'during his last illness' he was discussing with Andrews 'that great matter' – the prospect of negotiating a 'comprehensive Treaty with Great Britain'.[53]

After Webster's death things hung fire until the advent of a new administration. Then in August 1853 Crampton and Marcy settled down to detailed tariff discussions. Marcy made much of Congressional difficulties: 'almost every State, however strong in favour of Free Trade generally, makes its exception as to some particular article ... as for example Pennsylvania – coal and iron; ...Maine and New Hampshire ... – ship-building; Maine and Massachusetts – the bounty on fishing'. Crampton warned that the British Provinces would be reluctant to give anything up on a mere 'promise' (which no US administration could guarantee to implement) 'of receiving an equivalent by American Legislation'.[54] So Marcy submitted a definite draft treaty. But as this did not provide for any of the main points Crampton had been instructed to obtain, it did not strike the Foreign Secretary Lord Clarendon as *Reciprocity;* and in February 1854 he suspended negotiations.[55]

However both sides worried about the fisheries, and both turned to new ways of getting things moving. Marcy called Andrews in for consultations. Andrews went back north, and soon reported that though opportunities had been missed and the Provinces' terms for relinquishing the fisheries had risen, he had done much to remedy the situation. But to 'complete the work', he

---

[53] Webster to James Watson Webb, 15 Aug. 1852, and to Richard Milford Blatchford, 24 Aug. (*Diplomatic Papers* p. 712); Andrews to Cass, 15 April 1857 (Manning, *Diplomatic Correspondence* iv p. 690). After Webster's death his private secretary told the new Secretary of State that Crampton had hoped Webster would be able to resolve 'by another great treaty all the questions with England respecting the fisheries, the navigation of the St. John and St. Lawrence, reciprocity, Hudson's Bay Company, and copyright' – G.J. Abbot to Edward Everett, 28 Oct. 1852 (Barnes, *Authors, Publishers and Politicians* pp. 229-30)

[54] The discussions are described in Marcy's diary (Charles C. Tansill, *The Canadian Reciprocity Treaty of 1854* (Baltimore, 1922) pp. 56-8, and Crampton to Clarendon, 2 Aug. 1853 (Barnes, *Private and Confidential* pp. 78-83)

[55] Buchanan to Marcy, 1 Nov. 1853 (Manning, *Diplomatic Correspondence* iv pp. 532-3); Masters, *Reciprocity Treaty* p. 47

'must be speedily furnished' with 'the sinews of war', $8 or 10,000. With this, a fraction of the costs on the money market alone of a 'single angry collision on the fishery grounds', Andrews could secure a satisfactory and permanent settlement; otherwise, there was no hope of further progress. Marcy was sceptical; but he put the issue to President Pierce, who deemed 'it to be his duty to use all proper means at his disposal'. Andrews was told Pierce expected him 'to produce results'. Difficulties came not from the UK but from 'the Colonies – It is with them that we are to labor to remove these obstacles.' And Marcy concluded that 'Whatever is done must be done promptly – for the fishing season will come soon'.[56]

Andrews' preparations had probably already started: he had been told in previous years to lobby 'the most influential men' in New Brunswick and Nova Scotia, and he would appear to have spent freely from at least the autumn of 1853.[57] He was to some extent also working with the Canadian government. Indeed, he had in February 1854 met the Canadian premier, Hincks, and (he later said) arranged to 'undertake the management of matters in the Lower Colonies, which Mr. Hincks confessed were beyond the power of either himself or Mr. Crampton'.[58] But the pace increased

---

[56] Andrews to Marcy, 31 March and 3 April 1854; Marcy to Andrews, 10 and 15 April 1854; Caleb Cushing to Andrews, 12 April 1854 (authorising expenditure of $5000) – Manning, *Diplomatic Correspondence* pp. 84, 544-55, 588-90

[57] Webster to Andrews, 13 Oct. 1851; Marcy to Andrews, 12 Sept. 1853 – ibid. pp. 38-9, 81-3. Overman believes that 'during this period' he incurred expenses of over $18,000 ('Andrews and Reciprocity in 1854' p. 250n.), while in 1854 Andrews told the US administration that most of his $50,911 bill for services from May 1850 to 5 Aug. 1854 related to moneys spent between December 1853 and the following August (Lester B. Shippee, *Canadian-American Relations 1849-1874* (New Haven, Conn., 1939) p. 77n.)

[58] Andrews' explanation of his expenditure, made in 1854 after the passage of the treaty (Tansill, *Canadian Reciprocity Treaty* p. 72). Overall, Andrews received $40,000 from the Canadian government; this included $15,000 spent on the election expenses and personal debts of 'members returned to the Nova Scotia and New Brunswick Parliaments who might be favorable to said treaty' (Irene W. Hecht, 'Israel D. Andrews and the Reciprocity Treaty of 1854',

after President Pierce's instructions. Much of the action was overt – Andrews persuaded the Maritime provinces to send delegates to New York for discussions with Marcy. But there was a covert component – $8,051 'Paid privately and by myself to officials, leading persons and the press and others whom it was not proper to ask for ... vouchers'. And some even of the expenditure for which vouchers were forthcoming was revealing: £210 to the New Brunswick politician W.H. Needham, who had moved assembly resolutions against surrendering the fisheries, but who now switched to supporting the treaty; $1,150 to P.F. Little, an assembly member who had done 'the Treaty good service in Newfoundland', where 'the Government and its party were opposed to any arrangement'; and $3,900 spending by Andrews' Halifax associate E.H. Fuller that extended from postage and dinner parties through payments for newspaper articles to money for 'influential persons in the Fishery Districts' and 'Contribution to Election Expenses'. Andrews also contacted the Lt. Governors of Nova Scotia and New Brunswick. Both wanted a treaty. But Head followed 'red-tape' and was 'unwilling to assume any responsibility in order to effect it'; this contrasted with the 'manly straight-forwardness' of Nova Scotia's Sir Gaspard Le Marchant, who was 'quite willing to assume any responsibility ... that the exigencies of the case might seem to demand'.[59]

Though there were limits to what Lord Clarendon would concede, he certainly wanted a treaty – the Crimean War had just broken out, and it was, he told Elgin, 'of the utmost importance in the present state of the World that we should settle the fishery question'.[60] Marcy had for some time been lamenting that, unlike Lord Elgin, Crampton did not enjoy a high social position.

Can.H.R. 54:4 (1963) p. 321) and $5000 each to two Canadian politicians and to 'Morrison an editor' (Shippee, *Canadian-American Relations* pp. 73, 76)

[59] Andrews to Marcy, 13 May 1854, and the further explanation of his expenses after the treaty had been secured – Tansill, *Canadian Reciprocity Treaty* pp. 69-73; Manning, *Diplomatic Correspondence* iv esp. pp. 568-72

[60] Elgin's briefing of Le Marchant, 14 April 1854 (Masters,_*Reciprocity Treaty* p. 48)

And Hincks had in February promised Andrews that he would, during his spring visit to Britain, suggest sending Elgin to Washington as a plenipotentiary.[61] Clarendon did so, though to prevent Elgin's appearing there as a supplicant, it was given out that he was merely making a courtesy call on his way back to Canada from home leave.

When Elgin reached Washington, the social season was at its height, and both he and his entourage plunged in – so much so that its detractors said the ensuing treaty had been 'floated in champagne'. Particular attention was paid to Democratic senators. Many of these were Southerners, worried that Reciprocity would draw British North America on into joining the US. This was, indeed, its attraction to supporters like Andrews. But Elgin saw Reciprocity as the way to scotch any revival of annexationist sentiment there, and presumably made good use of this argument. Anyway, he appears to have been able to reassure the administration that a treaty could pass the Senate.[62] Negotiations resumed, and quickly led to a treaty that combined a measure of Reciprocity for primary products with concession to the US of access to the fisheries and to Canada's canals and the St. Lawrence. The United States still drove a hard bargain, refusing the import of Maritime-built ships, but it did now permit the access of Nova Scotian coal (even though this lost the treaty Pennsylvanian votes).

The treaty signed, Elgin departed, leaving the administration to secure ratification and the legislation needed for its implementation. The timetable was tight, but success was obtained on the last day of the session. Crampton wrote that it was done by pacifying the South, mobilising party loyalty, and applying 'the "screw" very vigorously'. Crampton himself played a part, 'counting noses' with Marcy, inducing 'some of the better disposed Southern men' to drop the idea of an amendment extending the Fugitive Slave law to Canada, and appealing 'to my old friend Mr. Clayton' to pull his

---

[61] Tansill, *Reciprocity Treaty* p. 72; Shippee, *Canadian-American Relations* p. 77
[62] For a colourful account of Elgin's social diplomacy, see Laurence Oliphant, *Episodes in a Life of Adventure* (1896 edn., Edinburgh) esp. pp. 47-53

punches and allow the Senate to go into secret session.[63] But it was widely felt that Andrews had played the chief role.[64] Much of his action, like arranging for letters to be sent to Congressmen and soothing a Committee Chairman who felt slighted by the administration, was entirely proper. But, as an 1854 Canadian report put it, 'to carry the bill through speedily and successfully, it was found necessary to subsidize many parties both within and without ... Congress'.[65] In September 1854, Andrews' US bill included $3,000 'Paid in Washington' that he would only account for personally to the President or the Secretary of State since the 'circumstances under which it was applied are of so delicate a nature'.[66] How much Andrews had spent overall it is impossible to say, since his claims expanded steadily as the authorities tried to scale them back.[67] In any case, Reciprocity was carried, and over the

[63] Crampton to Clarendon, 26 June, 24 July, and 7 Aug. 1854 (Barnes, *Private and Confidential* pp. 103, 104, 106)

[64] Senator Mason, the Foreign Relations Committee Chairman, declared in 1858 that Andrews had rendered the treaty 'very valuable services', while Head (now Canada's Governor-General) wrote in 1856 that 'but for his services there would have been great difficulty in obtaining' the treaty's ratification (Masters, *Reciprocity Treaty* p. 84)

[65] The report said $118,000 had been spent on 'subsidizing some ninety individuals', but this will have included Andrews' actions in British North America – Overman, 'Andrews and Reciprocity' p. 257. During the treaty's passage through Congress, Andrews sent Elgin 'a running fire of telegrams and letters' about his activities. Elgin would not answer directly, but had one of his ministers send 'notes of encouragement' in case Andrews was tempted to change sides and block the measure; these notes were later held to commit the Canadian government to reimbursing him for expenditure in Washington as well as north of the border (Masters, 'A Further Word' pp. 160, 164, 166)

[66] Tansill, *Canadian Reciprocity Treaty* pp. 71-2

[67] Masters thinks Andrews' claims totalled nearly $200,000, for which he was repaid some $132,000 ('A Further Word' pp. 164-7); Irene W.D. Hecht, 'Andrews, Israel de Wolfe', *Dictionary of Canadian Biography* puts his expenditures at $50-60,000 on behalf of the US, and $40,000 on that of the Canadian, government. In expectation of repayment, Andrews had raised much of the money by loans, sometimes guaranteed by sympathisers (amongst whom the eminent figures A.T. Galt and L.T. Drummond proved effective in pressing Canada to repay); in 1854 he was expecting reimbursement of $20,000 by merchants of Boston (who did contribute $14,000), $20,000 by New York and Oswego (which did not). In after years Andrews was 'sued, and sometimes

next decade trade between the United States and British North America expanded greatly. Economists now explain this in terms of the wider economy, notably the stimulus of the American Civil War. But at the time the credit was widely given to Reciprocity, especially in the Maritimes which enjoyed an apparent 'golden age'.

* * * *

The early 1850s also saw major upheavals in Canadian politics. Baldwin's Reform and LaFontaine's Canadien parties had come together to get 'responsible government' and correct French and other grievances. But by 1850 young men in Upper Canada had become impatient with the limitations of Baldwin's policies, and had started to push, in the 'Clear Grit' movement, for more advanced American-style reforms. This worried those, particularly in Lower Canada, who were increasingly happy with what they had already achieved and the political position they now occupied: Elgin forecast that if 'clear Gritism absorbs all the hues of Upper Canadian liberalism the French ... will fall off from them and form an alliance with the Upper Canada Tories'.[68]

Religious developments gave this another impulse. The parochial clergy had in 1843 secured control of ordinary schools in Lower Canada.[69] But 'while pro-clerical Catholic influence was spreading' there, 'the spirit of voluntarism was advancing in Canada West'. Its most powerful voice was that of George Brown, owner/editor of the Toronto *Globe*. Brown's family background lay in religious journalism; and while he had developed beyond this, he was a firm adherent of the Free Kirk that had emerged from the 1843 Scottish 'Disruption'. In 1850-1 his *Globe* also

---

imprisoned for portions of ... [his] indebtedness'. But the US did appoint him Consul-General for British North America, while (in response to a plea from Head) the UK government contributed £1000 towards his relief

[68] Elgin to Lord Grey, 2 Aug. 1850 – Careless, *The Growth of Canadian Institutions* p. 169

[69] Marcel Lajeunesse, 'L'Evêque et l'instruction publique au Bas Canada, 1840-1846', *Revue d'Histoire de l'Amérique Français* 23:1 (1969) pp. 44-6

took up the cry of 'Papal Aggression' with which Lord John Russell had greeted the Vatican's re-establishment of Roman Catholic bishoprics in Protestant Britain. In July 1851 the *Globe* proclaimed independent reform the 'one course for the opponents of priestcraft and state churchism': proceeds of the sale of the Clergy Reserves should go to the state, not to the Anglican and official Presbyterian churches as specified by the British parliament in 1840; and it demanded exclusively non-sectarian schools, whereas the *bleus* promoted religious corporations for educational and welfare purposes at home, and in Upper Canada pressed for separate schools for the Catholic minority. To voluntarists, the passage of legislation to permit these represented 'French domination' – 'Are we slaves to Popish prelates?' asked the Toronto *Examiner*.[70]

Their remedy was a fairer distribution of parliamentary seats. In 1840 it had been Lower Canada that had resented the according of equal representation to both units. But in 1852 the census confirmed that Canada West was now the more populous, by 952,000 to 890,000; and in 1853 Brown first sought 'rep[resentation] by pop[ulation]'. In 1854 he also called for the annexation of the empty Hudson's Bay Company territory beyond the Great Lakes, where settlers would then swell Canada West's population and enable it, once 'rep. by pop.' was obtained, to dominate parliament for the benefit of Brown's causes.

Baldwin and LaFontaine both left politics in 1851. Baldwin's successor was not Brown but Hincks, who had for some time been at odds with him. Brown accordingly left Hincks' Reform party and went independent. In 1854 Hincks was tainted with scandal, and after the elections that year he was defeated over the choice of Speaker. Lord Elgin asked Sir Allan MacNab, who after 1849 had led the Conservatives back towards the political centre, to form a government; and, with Hincks' support, he managed to do so in coalition with the *bleu* leader Augustin Morin. Morin and Hincks both left parliament in 1855, followed next year by the elderly and gouty MacNab. Control of the coalition thus passed to the

---

[70] 15 July 1855 – Careless, *The Growth of Canadian Institutions* pp. 173, 197

combination of the liberal Conservative John A. Macdonald, who represented Kingston in the *east* of Upper Canada, and Morin's successor as *Bleu* leader, George-Étienne Cartier; they proved a formidable combination. The 'Clear Grits' had moderated their original posture, shedding the American proclivities Brown had deplored, but welcoming his general voluntarist line. And in 1857 a convention adopted the policies Brown had campaigned for, 'rep. by pop.', annexation of the HBC's North-West, non-sectarian education, and free trade, thus establishing the Liberal party. Significantly, though, this was generally known as the 'Grits'. In *bleu* eyes it retained some of their alarming characteristics. Nor were the *bleus* reassured by the links the Liberals fashioned with the anti-clerical *rouges*.

In subsequent years the Macdonald-Cartier combination generally had the upper hand as the *bleus* commanded more of Canada East's vote than did the Liberals of Canada West's. But the balance was very even, with Liberals holding office from 1862-4. John Sandfield Macdonald's ministry then resigned following a parliamentary defeat, but its successor (Sir Étienne Taché, John A. Macdonald and Cartier, the sixth government in six years) was clearly very shaky. As George Brown would tell Parliament, 'repeated endeavours year after year to get a strong government formed have resulted in constant failure, and we now stand ranged, Upper and Lower Canada, in such an attitude that no dissolution ... is likely to bring about a satisfactory change'.[71] Brown remained determined to secure 'rep. by pop.' and emancipate Upper Canada from what he saw as control by the Conservative Quebec *bleus*. But he had come round to seeking this through a constitutional agreement to be worked out in a cross-party parliamentary committee. He gained this committee in May 1864 by securing most of the Upper Canada votes, Conservative as well as Reform, and steered it towards a federal solution. Most *bleus* had opposed the committee, but they probably felt that 'rep. by pop.' could not

---

[71] 17 June 1864 (while negotiations to form a Grand Coalition were in progress) – J.M.S. Careless, *Brown of the Globe* ii (Toronto, 1963) p. 134

be indefinitely delayed, and saw that a federal system might shield them from Upper Canadian dictation and enable them to remain *'maîtres chez nous'* in Quebec. In June 'a federative system, applied either to Canada alone or to the whole British North American Provinces', was backed by seventeen committee members including Cartier, who thus split from John A. Macdonald, one of the only three to dissent.[72] This left Macdonald 'with but a small following from his own province, and with by no means complete control over that'.[73] His position at the head of Canadian politics required *bleu* support; and, as a calculating man, he must have wondered how long it would be, in a federation of only Upper and Lower Canada, before the *bleus* concluded that they must switch to dealing with the Liberals running the other province. To escape, Macdonald turned, in something of a 'flight forward', to promoting a union of all the provinces of British North America, which might, and in fact did, enable him both to keep the *Bleus* and to attract 'loose fish' from the other provinces into a consolidated Conservative party.

At this point the Taché, Macdonald, Cartier government was defeated in Parliament. As a Liberal one had so recently fallen, another election would normally have followed. But this was unlikely to produce any clear-cut result, and, encouraged by the Governor-General Lord Monck, Brown broke the deadlock by indicating readiness to join a Coalition Government to bring in constitutional change. Negotiations (chiefly between Brown, Macdonald and Cartier) quickly produced agreement on removing

---

[72] Careless, *Brown* pp. 117-129. Macdonald attributed the American Civil War to federalism, and held that any future British North American union must be a 'legislative' one like the United Kingdom; but Cartier declared bluntly, 'That is not my policy.'

[73] Sir Richard Cartwright, *Reminiscences* (Toronto, 1912) p. 62. Cartwright also says (p. 65) that Macdonald only consented to Confederation when he 'was bluntly told by his French allies that they were utterly tired of his failure to secure any adequate support from Ontario, and that if he refused to join they would make what terms they could with Mr. Brown'. But Cartwright had become Macdonald's political opponent, and these *Reminiscences* may have exaggerated Cartier's readiness to drop him and cultivate Brown

'existing difficulties by introducing the federative principle into Canada' with provisions that would permit the incorporation of the Maritimes and the HBC's North-West Territories 'into the same system' – thus creating either a purely Canadian confederation (Brown's preference[74]) or, should this prove feasible, a broader British North American one. Macdonald later wrote, in 1866, that he had had 'the option of either forming a Coalition Government [on this basis] or handing over the administration ... to the Grit Party for the next ten years'.[75]

Ideas of a broad British North American federation were not new – there had been some eighteen proposals before 1858. Lord Durham would have liked to effect one, but in his *Report* had talked of it only as a matter for the future. By the 1850s the idea of some merger, whether of the Maritime Provinces or between these and Canada, had started to stir again. It was more widely endorsed within distant Britain than within North America, where people were better aware of the problems. But the common pursuit of Reciprocity in the early 1850s led to meetings between Provincial delegates, though no formal institutional collaboration. The decade also ushered in an era of railway building – in 1851 Sir Allan MacNab had declared, post-prandially, that 'all my politics are railroads',[76] and most other major politicians were likewise

---

[74] To overcome the disfunctions of a unitary Canada, Brown would accept either a broader federation or one between the two Canadas alone. But he had initially preferred the latter, to give time for the organisation of his province 'so that, when federation of all the British North American provinces does come, it may be formed with Upper Canada as the central figure'. And when the 1865 New Brunswick elections seemed likely to block broader Confederation, his first thought was, 'it is a very serious matter for the Maritime provinces, but magnificent for us'. He did, though, soon modify this into a determination to proceed with Confederation as before; but if 'it fails after all legitimate means have been used, we will go on with our scheme for Canada alone' – Careless, *Brown* pp. 111 [1863], 189-90 [March 1865]

[75] Careless, *Brown* pp. 131-5; Ged Martin, *Britain and the Origins of Canadian Confederation* (Basingstoke, 1995) pp. 47-53; Christopher Moore, *1867. How the Fathers made a Deal* (Toronto, 1997) esp. pp. 26-9; Macdonald, Sir John A., *Dictionary of Canadian Biography*

[76] MacNab, Sir Allan Napier – *Dictionary of Canadian Biography*

deeply involved. Railway promotion could generate grandiose geo-political visions. As early as 1847, Nova Scotia's Speech from the Throne had talked of the projected 'Intercolonial Railway' from Halifax to Quebec as constituting 'the most important link in that great line of communication which may be destined at no remote period to connect the Atlantic with the Pacific Ocean'.[77] Even Joseph Howe, a railway enthusiast but someone who, when push came to shove, wanted no change in Nova Scotia's provincial status, had foretold in 1851 that many of his audience would live to hear steam engines whistle in the Rockies and to journey from Halifax to the Pacific in five or six days, while later in the decade he had dreamed of 'British American Colonial Union, and of a British Pacific Railway'.[78] And in the early 1860s the British Colonial Secretary, the Duke of Newcastle, shared the belief of the railway promoter, Edward Watkin, both that union between Canada and the Maritimes would be 'the necessary, the logical result' of building the Intercolonial, and that a Pacific railway and transcontinental union would come together sooner than most people expected.[79]

Talk, though, was one thing, reaching agreement another. In 1858 the Canadian government sought to promote discussion of a possible federation, but an unprepared and insecure British government kicked this into the long grass.[80] Meanwhile little progress had been made with the Intercolonial Railway, largely because of disputes over its best route and difficulties in securing an Imperial loan guarantee to cut the cost of borrowing to build it. In 1861-2 Nova Scotia sought to revive the railway by linking its

---

[77] Jay Underwood, *Built for War: Canada's Intercontinental Railway* (Montreal, 2005) p. 25

[78] Howe's 1851 prophecy is cited by Lyle Dick, '"A New History for the New Millenium": Canada: A People's History', *Can.H.R.* 85:1 (2004) p. 98, his later dream by Alexander Morris, *Nova Britannia; or, Our New Canadian Dominion Foreshadowed* (Toronto, 1884) p. 335. Morris had himself looked in 1858 to a 'railway and telegraph linking the Atlantic with the Pacific', probably within the next twenty years (ibid. pp. 78, 88-9)

[79] Ged Martin, *Britain and Canadian Confederation* pp. 109, 111-13, 136-7

[80] Ibid. pp. 102-8

approach to Britain for a loan guarantee with suggestion of a move towards Provincial Union. This led to a Quebec conference between Canada, New Brunswick, and Nova Scotia that soft-pedalled the constitutional question but agreed a formula for funding the Intercolonial. However when this was taken to London, Gladstone made the loan conditional on the establishment of a sinking fund. Such funds were not normal Canadian practice, and the Canadian delegates brought proceedings to an acrimonious close by rejecting the idea. So although both British North American union and the Intercolonial Railway were familiar projects by the 1860s, no tangible progress had been made with the former, and little with the latter.[81] In 1864 the Lt. Governor of New Brunswick, Arthur Gordon, managed to arrange a meeting of New Brunswick, Nova Scotian, and Prince Edward Island delegates in Charlottetown in September to consider a legislative union of the three provinces. The idea commanded little enthusiasm, and Nova Scotian and New Brunswick politicians may have been looking rather to make progress informally on the Intercolonial. But instead, the Charlottetown delegates were persuaded to let a large Canadian party join them and explain its ideas for a broad grouping. These ideas went down well in a convivial atmosphere, and it was agreed to send delegates to another conference in Quebec to see whether satisfactory terms could be worked out. This was duly done in October. The outcome chiefly reflected the wishes of the Canadian government, partly because it had done most preparatory work, partly because of Macdonald's drafting and man-management skills, and partly because Canada would be so much the largest unit.[82] But the Maritimes, with Québécois assistance, insisted that the new state should be not a 'legislative union' on the model of the United Kingdom, but a 'Confederation' based on those existing

---

[81] Martin, *Britain and Canadian Confederation* pp. 102-8, 198, 229-32; Peter B. Waite, 'A Chapter in the History of the Intercolonial Railway, 1864', *Can.H.R.* 32:4 (1951) pp. 356-7
[82] By contrast, Nova Scotia, whose delegation had no financial or business background, allowed itself to be trapped into an unfavourable financial deal that had, eventually, to be revised after Confederation had taken effect

provinces that joined it, plus Canada East and West (renamed Quebec and Ontario).[83] It should also undertake to build the Intercolonial Railway.

The causes of Confederation, and even of its timing, seem thus to have been internal to British North America: vague aspirations towards unity that antedated the American Civil War; the felt need to remodel the governance of Canada; anxiety in Nova Scotia and New Brunswick to secure the Intercolonial Railway (which has been described as 'probably the most important single influence affecting the course of the Confederation Movement' there in 1864, 'indeed the *sine qua non* of their entrance into Confederation');[84] and though the British government carefully left the initiative to the provinces, knowledge that Confederation was what the 'Mother Country' wanted (together with more direct British pressure on the Lt. Governors of New Brunswick and Nova Scotia to promote it). But all this time the American Civil War was raging. And if Confederation's origins were largely independent of developments south of the border, perceived threats from the United States loomed large in the justifications that would be advanced for it: heavy-handed American policies in 1864-5, US attempts to exploit anti-Confederation sentiment to derail the project, and, above all, cross-border raids mounted from US territory by Fenian filibusters.

Some of the United States' 1864-5 policies were responses to actual and rumoured Southern raids from Canadian territory, rescinded once that danger had ebbed. But the Canadian Parliament's debates on Confederation, in February-March 1865, took place in their shadow. As the head of the Coalition government, Sir Étienne Taché, put it at the start of debate, Canada, lacking the open seaboard that would come from Confederation with the Maritimes, 'was shut up in a prison ... for five months in fields of ice'. There had indeed been access to the sea through the

---

[83] The term 'Confederation' was attractive as differing from the US 'federal' system. But it did not then have its modern connotation of a union whose constituent parts are more legitimate and powerful than the central government; many people, including Macdonald, hoped for the reverse
[84] Waite, 'A Chapter in the History of the Intercolonial' p. 356

United States, but with the Civil War 'difficulties' had arisen. First 'we had been threatened with the abolition of the transit system' whereby goods could be railed through the US 'in bond' without payment of duties; 'then the Reciprocity Treaty was to be discontinued' (as indeed it was, subject to a year's notice, in March 1865);[85] 'then a passport system was inaugurated, which was almost equivalent to a prohibition of intercourse, and the only thing that really remained to be done was to shut down the gate altogether'. John A. Macdonald also made these points; Cartier feared withdrawal of the bonding system; and after referring to the 'insane threat' to end this, Brown presented 'colonial union' and the Intercolonial Railway as the remedy.[86] An opponent observed that when the Government had been formed, it had not talked of the danger of invasion or suggested that 'if we did not form a Federal union we would be annexed to the United States'.[87] But events had gifted it with these arguments; and whatever their merits – it was, after all, open to Canada to build the Intercolonial without Confederation – they were presumably believed to be persuasive. Several other speakers also made them, the Confederation scheme worked out at Quebec was comfortably endorsed, and Queen Victoria was petitioned accordingly.

But Confederation was also urged on a basis that transcended immediate Civil War pressures. Taché had declared the British provinces to be on an 'inclined plane'; 'if we do not cultivate' with the Maritimes

'a close commercial, political and social intercourse – being all of us British subjects, all of us monarchists, owing

---

[85] The assault on Reciprocity in the House may have owed more to protectionism; but Charles Sumner ascribed abrogation's easy passage through the Senate to anger over the St. Alban's raid (P.B. Waite, *The Life and Times of Confederation, 1864-1867* (Toronto, 1962) p. 32)
[86] *Parliamentary Debates on the subject of the Confederation of the British North American Provinces* (Quebec, 1865) pp. 6-7 (Taché), 32 (Macdonald), 55 (Cartier), 106-7 (Brown); Public Archives of Canada, *Index to the Confederation Debates of 1865. Compiled by M.A. Lapin* (Ottawa, 1951)
[87] *Confederation Debates* p. 1016 (Lucius Huntington)

allegiance to the same Crown..., we run a great danger. We are, in our present position, small, isolated bodies, and it may probably be with us, as in the physical world, where a large body attracts to itself the smaller bodies within the sphere of its influence ... we shall lose little by little our attachment to the Mother Country...; and we shall become more democratised, before we are aware of it.'

By the time Taché said this, two other speakers had given as reasons for supporting the Quebec scheme that 'we were fast sliding [down an "inclined plane"] into the republic of the United States', that the choice lay between Confederation and 'going by driblets into the American Union'. And the government pushed the argument strongly – Cartier had led off by declaring that 'rep. by pop.' could only be safely achieved in a federation, adding that 'The matter resolved itself into this, either we must obtain British North American Confederation or be absorbed' into an American one; those who thought Confederation was not needed 'to prevent absorbtion into the vortex of American Confederation ... were mistaken.'[88]

Not everybody agreed. But few differed as to the undesirability of a move into the American embrace. Instead, opponents depicted Confederation as likely to bring on, not avert, this misfortune: the frictions inherent in a federal system would lead Upper Canada 'to look to the other side of the line for union'; the cost of the military spending that accompanied Confederation would destroy today's loyalty and readiness to resist any American invasion; and Confederation would lead to 'the early cutting' of 'the tie between these provinces and the parent state' and to 'absorbtion into the republic to the south'.[89] Only one speaker, the prominent *rouge* Antoine Dorion, condemned the attempt 'to establish a political system founded on a political principle contrary to that of the United States – on the monarchical

---

[88] Ibid. pp. 343 (Taché), 326 (Oliver Blake) and 329 (David Edward Price), 54-5 (Cartier)
[89] Ibid. pp. 456 (M.C. Cameron), 355 (Henri Joly), 539 (Christopher Dunkin)

principle'. 'You may decry as much as you choose the democratic system, and laud the monarchical ... – the people will ... ever know which will suit them best'. Even so, he stressed that he did not call for annexation, 'nor do the people desire it' – though the proposed changes were 'the surest means of bringing it about'.[90] Much more typical was the view that it was a choice 'as between annexation to the United States and connection to Great Britain – as between republicanism and monarchy – between Canada, our country, and Canada, our [US] state';[91] and though annexationism could briefly be encountered in Upper Canada when Confederation later faltered,[92] Cartier had been on firm ground in brushing aside 'the old Papineau Tail – whose idea was annexation to the United States'.

This was all very well for Canada, to whose political problems Confederation represented an answer. The real question was whether it would be accepted in the Maritimes, which were under no immediate pressure to change. Canada was, as Sandfield Macdonald put it, 'imploring them, against their will to step in and save us, forsooth, from destruction'; but were coercion attempted, 'they will be like the damsel who is forced to marry against her will, and who will, in the end, be most likely to elope with someone else'.[93] Prince Edward Island did refuse to join Confederation in the 1860s, while Newfoundland held aloof until the 1940s. But the project did not need them. It would, however, have been dead without New Brunswick and Nova Scotia, and they were evenly divided. Precision is impossible – after all, the 1865 and 1866 New Brunswick elections produced diametrically opposed results. But one electoral analysis computes the popular

---

[90] Ibid. pp. 869-71
[91] Ibid. p. 903 (Walter Shanly). Among the advantages claimed for 'monarchism' (besides its general British connotations) was that it precluded the election of an executive President, which was blamed for recent American troubles.
[92] Waite, *Life and Times* pp. 157-9
[93] *Confederation Debates* pp. 741-2

vote as split 58% anti-, 41% pro-, Confederation in Nova Scotia, 51% – 47% in New Brunswick.[94]

As the Civil War wound down, the United States had in fact ended some of the measures complained of in the February-March 1865 Canadian debates.[95] But it went ahead with the abrogation of Reciprocity. Populist papers like the New York *Herald* boasted that economic pressure would soon reduce British North America to suing for annexation, and such extreme views were well publicised north of the border. Encouragement was also drawn from the routing of Confederation in the 1865 New Brunswick election; and in 1866 the Chairman of the House Committee on Foreign Affairs, N.P. Banks, played to this by tabling a bill for the admission of the British provinces as US states, on terms in some ways rather better than those of the Quebec Confederation scheme.

More immediate pressure came from 'Fenian' recruitment of significant numbers of former Civil War soldiers in the hope of freeing Ireland from British rule:

'We are the Fenian Brotherhood, skilled in the arts of war,
And we're going to fight for Ireland, the land that we adore.
Many battles we have won, along with the boys in blue,
And we'll go and capture Canada, for we've nothing else to do.'

The *Herald* thought it needed only 'a word of encouragement to the thousands of Fenians who are eagerly awaiting an invitation to invade Canada, for our government ['forever'] to settle the

---

[94] Figures cited by P.B. Waite in the 'CHR Dialogue: "The Maritimes and Confederation: a Reassessment"', *Can.H.R.* 71 (1990) p. 31
[95] Indeed Allen P. Stouffer points to both American and Anglo-Canadian efforts to still alarm and reduce tension in the spring of 1865. They were helped by the outpouring of sympathy following Lincoln's murder; and in August General Grant was enthusiastically received during his unofficial tour of Canada. But in 1866 further issues 'appeared on the scene to open a new era of tension' – 'Canadian-American Relations in the Shadow of the Civil War', *Dalhousie Review* 57:2 (1977) pp. 332-46

question of a Canadian monarchy with an English Guelph upon the throne'.[96] In 1866 a thousand-odd Fenians gathered around Eastport, Maine, staging such incidents as landing on a New Brunswick islet and stealing the customs officers' Union Jack, and for some months generating tension. Outgunned and outnumbered by British warships and regulars, they would, militarily, have had no chance even had the local US commander not intercepted their weapons and ammunition. But they sought to latch onto, and stimulate, the hostility to Confederation then widely prevalent in New Brunswick and Nova Scotia. Thus the commander of the Eastport 'Convention', Bernard Killian, declared that they were out to defeat Confederation, while a Fenian proclamation in St. John, New Brunswick, announced that, through Confederation, 'English policy' was seeking 'to bind you in an effete form of monarchism'. Full play was made of this – had Killian been 'in the pay of the Canadians' and his speech written by D'Arcy McGee, ruefully commented the St. John *Morning Freeman* on 21 April, 'he could not have said anything better suited' to their purposes. During the May New Brunswick election, the *St. Croix Courier* declared the strongest argument for Confederation to be the need 'for a good and efficient system of mutual defense'. It had not always thought so; but 'when we see ... how our enemies may [suddenly] concentrate within a gunshot of our doors, the man must be blind ... who can fail to recognize its force.' 'At the very moment when we have but just been delivered from the Fenian invasion by the prompt action of the British forces', the Roman Catholic Bishop Richards asked, 'are we ... to prefer, not the wish of [the 'Mother Country'] our protector, parent, and friend, but that of her and our enemies?' New Brunswick's anti-Confederate majority was reversed,[97] while in Nova Scotia the Lt. Governor,

---

[96] Supposed Fenian marching song, quoted e.g. by Robert L. Dallison, *Turning back the Fenians. New Brunswick's last Colonial Campaign* (Fredericton, N.B., 2006) p. 73; New York *Herald*, 15 March 1866, duly quoted on 21 March by the Ottawa *Citizen* – Waite, *Life and Times* p. 264

[97] Waite, *Life and Times* esp. pp. 272-3; Dallison, *Turning Back the Fenians* p. 110; William M. Baker, 'The 1866 Election in New Brunswick: the Anglin-Rogers

Sir Fenwick Williams, had reported a 'great change' in local attitudes towards Confederation following the emergence of the Fenian threat.[98] Of course, neither Fenian pressure nor British advice could have influenced behaviour had there not anyway been substantial support for the idea of Confederation (and probably a growing doubt as to the possibility of improving the scheme's details). But at a crucial moment, when Confederation had seemed dead in the water in both New Brunswick and Nova Scotia, and therefore also in Canada, the Fenians had done much to unblock the project.

By 1867 the local temperature had cooled. New Brunswick and Nova Scotia had made largely pro forma attempts to get details of the Confederation scheme modified at a conference in London, and Nova Scotia opponents an unavailing effort to persuade the British government to shelve it. The necessary legislation was going through the imperial Parliament; and Nova Scotia's assembly held a final debate. Some of the arguments differed from those deployed in Canada: was there any reason to merge with a province with whom one had so few dealings;[99] would not the proposed terms, more especially the financial terms, of Confederation prove disastrous; and should the Nova Scotian electorate not be consulted, as New Brunswick's had been, before the province was finally committed to Confederation? Also, in a province where the franchise was wider than in Canada, supporters were less likely to praise Confederation's non-democratic tendency. But, as in Canada, the province's British and monarchical heritage loomed large, and the danger of falling into the United States was

---

Controversy', *Acadiensis* 17:1 (1987) pp. 97-98. Waite gives reason to believe Killian's proclamation genuine, though its distribution may have been assisted by Confederation supporters

[98] Williams to Governor-General Lord Monck, 12 March 1866 (*Life and Times* pp. 224-5)

[99] Nova Scotia probably had 'more ships in the Port of Calcutta, in any day of the year,' a shipbuilder would soon declare, 'than ... in all the ports of Canada' – (McLelan, Archibald Woodbury – *Dictionary of Canadian Biography*)

much stressed, though here it could be pressed into service on both sides of the debate.

J.G. Bourinot led off by explaining his 1866 change of opinion. He had been impressed by the breadth of British advocacy of Confederation and by

'the wish of the Imperial Government ... to see Union consummated; then came the Fenian excitement, and the abrogation of the Reciprocity Treaty; and, at length, when our own territory was threatened, I felt that the moment had arrived when a ... lover of his country should decide'.

So he resolved to back Confederation. Later speakers descanted on similar themes, the Premier Dr. Tupper declaring Confederation 'the only means by which British America can remain British America', the Liberal but pro-Confederation A.G. Archibald that it was the only way 'we can prevent our Provinces from being absorbed in the American Union'.[100] The leading opponent, William Annand, thought the opposite: 'You cannot graft this mongrel system upon monarchical institutions – when you change you must become a Republic,[101] and the game played by the American Government in Mexico will be played over again here.' He looked on Confederation 'as a first step towards a separation from the Mother Country' and foretold that 'ten years will not pass before this new nationality will drift into the United States'. That, Annand obviously felt, would be a bad thing. But he unwisely continued that their geography and interests required

'these Maritime Provinces to belong to a great maritime power – the first in the world if they are allowed – and if not

---

[100] *Debate on the Union of the Provinces in the House of Assembly of Nova Scotia, March 16th, 18th, and 19th, 1867* (Foreign and Commonwealth Office Pamphlet Collection, 1867 – JSTOR) pp. 3 (Bourinot), 16 (Tupper), 37 (Archibald)
[101] 'You may', Annand later explained, 'call the Confederation ... monarchical, with a Governor-General at its head, but it must become a Republic' (ibid. p. 46)

to the second, they cannot and will not be governed ... by a people living in the Canadian backwoods. We must, therefore, belong either to the mother country or to the United States, and if we are once separated from England, there is no question about our final destination.'[102]

This enabled critics to pile in: one said Annand should put on his newspaper the motto, '"The United States rather than Canada," ... and let the people know what the true issue is'.[103] This was a travesty. Annand repeated at length that what he would really like was some measure of integration with the United Kingdom. Failing that, he just wanted Nova Scotia to stay as it was, a position echoed by his supporters. 'The people of Nova Scotia have no idea of joining the United States,' Mr. Blackwood continued, 'unless they are driven to it'. But, he warned, 'if you stir up hostility by such legislation as will embitter their minds ... the British feeling will be driven out of their British hearts.'[104]

There was point to this warning. Britain did pass the legislation incorporating Canada, New Brunswick, and Nova Scotia into the new Dominion of Canada. At the first elections, Nova Scotia sent eighteen opponents and only one supporter of Confederation to Ottawa, with a similar outcome in its own Assembly elections; and the new provincial government was headed by Annand. Matters were made worse by economic depression following the ending of Reciprocity and of the failure of the fisheries in 1866 and 1867, and by the extension to Nova Scotia of the higher Canadian rate of customs duties. The new provincial assembly tried in vain to interest New Brunswick and Prince Edward Island in a Maritimes union as an alternative to

---

[102] *Debate on the Union* pp. 20-1
[103] Ibid. p. 39 (Samuel Shannon); cf. also pp. 22-3 (James Macdonald), 54-5 (Tupper), 56 (Fraser)
[104] Ibid. pp. 25, 43-5 (Annand), 57 (Blackwood), 61 (Stewart Campbell). Personally, Blackwood declared, he could 'never feel otherwise than degraded by being subjected to the Stars and Stripes'

Confederation; and in February 1868 it petitioned the Queen, saying that Confederation would rob its people

> 'of their revenues, take from them the regulation of their trade and taxation, expose them to arbitrary taxation by a Legislature over which they would have no control..., deprive them of their invaluable fisheries, their railroads and other property, and reduce this free, happy, and hitherto self-governed province to the degraded position of a servile dependency of Canada.'

Joseph Howe, Tupper's great rival and the best-known local politician, went to beg London to release Nova Scotia, and was joined by Annand and other delegates from the provincial government. The Canadian Governor-General Lord Monck took this very seriously, arguing that were Confederation broken up, 'the maintenance of British power or the existence of British institutions will soon become impossible'. He believed that many 'who lend themselves to the anti-Union agitation would withdraw ... if they realized ... that the Union cause is really identified with the maintenance of British institutions'; and he urged the Colonial Secretary to gamble on Nova Scotia's basic loyalty by telling its deputation

> 'that the plan of Union, though adopted at the request of the Colonies, is considered essential, as much on imperial as on provincial grounds. That a refusal to allow any influence to ... the suggestions of the Imperial Government and Parliament is virtually to sever the connection between the mother-country and the Colony, and that if Nova Scotia desires the continuance of that connection, it must be by the maintenance of the Union.'[105]

---

[105] The Nova Scotian Assembly's unanimous Resolutions and its Address to the Queen, 21 Feb. 1868; Lord Monck to the Duke of Buckingham, 13 Feb. 1868 (CO 880/4/12, Confidential Print, *Nova Scotia. Despatches from the Governor-General of Canada ... pp.* 3-4, 11-13)

The Colonial Office feared that if Nova Scotia left Confederation, New Brunswick would do so too, and then 'Upper and Lower Canada might call for separation, as appeared probable a few years ago'. The Colonial Secretary accordingly rejected the delegation's contention that Confederation had been illegitimate since it had not been referred to Nova Scotia's electorate, and declared that his government would not reverse 'a great measure of State, attended by so many extensive consequences already in operation, and adopted with the ... previous consent of every one of the Legislatures involved.' [106]

The news sparked an outcry: 'Nova Scotians', declared the *Yarmouth Herald* on 4 August, 'have been proud of their connection with England. What have they to be proud of now? ... the people of Nova Scotia will never be loyal to the Dominion of Canada ... never ... consent to such an alliance'.[107] But it was not clear what they could do about it, especially as the Provincial government showed no interest in Howe's idea that it might try creating constitutional deadlock by resigning and voting down any replacement. Instead, there was talk of annexation to the United States, but much of this was bluster. Thus when Attorney-General Wilkins was carpeted by the Lt. Governor, he backtracked and protested his loyalty to the Empire. Annand had told Howe that if the petition to London failed, he would go for annexation; but in August he sought a 'back-stairs' interview with Sir John Macdonald, now the Dominion Prime Minister, to investigate a possible deal. Howe too had concluded that there was no alternative to a deal. He had made his first overture as early as July; and talk of resistance to Confederation or of annexation will have confirmed him in this course – he warned Macdonald in the autumn that 'a clear and unfettered vote of the people might take

[106] CO 880/4/10, Confidential Print, *Confederation of British America*. Precis by T.F. Elliott, 8 April 1868; CO 880/4/11, *Draft of a proposed despatch on the Nova Scotia address against Confederation, May 1868* esp. p. 4
[107] Donald Warner, 'The Post-Confederation Annexation Movement in Nova Scotia', *Can.H.R.* 28:2 (1947) p. 160

it into the American union'.[108] Howe met Macdonald in August, and the rest of 1868 saw a leisurely exchange of letters through which Macdonald sought to recruit the big name, Howe, while excluding Annand. The last obstacle was removed with the dashing of Nova Scotian hopes that Britain's new Liberal government would prove more sympathetic than its Conservative predecessor. In January 1869, following a meeting held in Maine so as to exclude the Provincial government, Howe secured marginally 'Better [financial] Terms'. He then joined Macdonald's government on 30 January – as Macdonald put it, Nova Scotia took 'the shilling' and enlisted 'in the Union, though I'm afraid it will consider itself for a time as a conscript rather than a volunteer'.[109]

This required Howe to seek parliamentary re-election; the contest was unexpectedly bruising, and even his personal prestige plus (in Macdonald's phrase) 'Holy War' support from Ottawa (in the form of money and patronage appointments) only just brought Howe to victory. Meanwhile, a young Liberal, backed by the local financial establishment, had comfortably carried the family seat of Yarmouth on an annexationist platform. To some, annexation now seemed the only available alternative: in June the 'Anti-Confederation League of the Maritime Provinces' changed its name to the 'Annexation League', declaring that 'Our only hope of commercial prosperity, material development and permanent peace lies in closer relations with the United States', and resolving to use all legitimate means 'to sever our connections with Canada and to bring about a union on fair and equitable terms with the American Republic'.[110] Such sentiment was

---

[108] Howe to Macdonald, 29 Oct. and 16 Nov. 1868 (Warner, 'Post-Confederation Annexation Movement' p. 162)

[109] Warner, 'Post-Confederation Annexation Movement' pp. 156-62; Richard Gwyn, *Nation Maker. Sir John A. Macdonald: His Life, Our Times* ii *1867-1891* (Toronto, 2011) pp. 49-52, 60-3; Bruce Fergusson, *Joseph Howe of Nova Scotia* (Windsor, N.S., 1973) pp. 128-31; *Dictionary of Canadian Biography* entries for the people most involved

[110] This was very much the line taken by R.J. Walker when consulted (in December 1868) by the 'Nova Scotia League' as to the possibility of the province joining America as a state and the likely effect on its welfare; Walker noted that,

strongest in the fishing and the coal districts, and in cities hoping for access to the US coastal trade. But it did not last. Defections were evident by December in the coal district; the last annexation meeting in the south seems to have been in February 1870; and the following December even the *Yarmouth Herald* recognized that the time was not ripe for political union with the United States. Like the 1849 Montreal movement, that of Nova Scotia was a boom-and-bust protest, vulnerable to the realization that Britain would never permit (nor the United States take drastic action to secure) 'annexation'. Nova Scotian anger would fade with returning prosperity. It had not prevented the establishment of the Dominion of Canada. But it did make Macdonald more cautious and conciliatory in his handling of the Dominion's later expansion.[111]

---

even with the present tariffs, Nova Scotia's exports to the US were more than eight times as large as those to 'the Canadas', and proclaimed 'the absurdity of sacrificing' the former to the latter – *Letter of the Hon. Robt. J. Walker on the Annexation of Nova Scotia and British North America* (Washington, April 1869) p. 4

[111] Warner, 'Post-Confederation Annexation Movement' pp. 162-5; Gwyn, *Nation Maker* p. 63

CHAPTER 11

From Rupert's Land to Manitoba: Canada's purchase arranged, 1869; Métis 'Resistance', Louis Riel's Provisional Government, and Red River's 1870 entry into Confederation as 'Manitoba'

In 1869 the American publicist R.J. Walker would contrast the 'proposed' continent-wide Canadian Dominion, 'composed of detached parts, incapable of intercommunication, or of being consolidated into one empire', with the United States, and ask how long the 'constantly augmenting force of mutual attraction of kindred race, of language, of institutions, of interest and geographical position' could be resisted.[1] But things did not develop as he (and many others) expected; and our next three chapters recount the Dominion's 1870 expansion to incorporate the North-West as far as the Rockies, followed next year by British Columbia on the Pacific coast, and then describe the far slower process of consolidating Canadian governance in, and building rail communication to and between, these new accessions.

Initially Canada only stretched to just past Lake Superior. Beyond lay Rupert's Land. Charles II had granted this to the

---

[1] Walker instead highlighted the 'system that has carried the sisterhood of States from the Atlantic to the Pacific, and now binds them together by our first great Continental railroad ... [which] will be followed by the great Northern and Southern routes' – *Letter of the Hon. Robt. J. Walker on the Annexation of Nova Scotia and British North America* (Washington, April 1869) pp. 11, 16-17

Hudson's Bay Company [HBC] (for 'two elks and two black beavers' payable to the King whenever he should 'happen to enter' the territory[2]), and his Charter had been periodically renewed. The region was still mostly the domain of the First Nations (some 40,000 in all), with in addition largely seasonal prospectors, 'adventurers', and 'plains hunters'. There was also a scattering of missionaries, and of 'forts' where, in splendid isolation, the HBC conducted its core fur-trading business. But to feed and service these, there had grown up around Fort Garry (Winnipeg) a more or less settled population of 11,963 in 1871 - larger than the 10,586 Europeans in British Columbia, though well below the 94,000 of the smallest eastern Province, Prince Edward Island.[3] For most of its history this settlement, Red River, had been isolated. Major supplies came by sea through Hudson's Bay, which was only briefly unfrozen; people and mail could reach Canada by canoe, but there was no quicker or higher capacity way of crossing the inhospitable Canadian Shield. South of the Lakes, though, the terrain was easier, and during the 1850s Minnesota was settled, its population growing from 6,000 to 172,000. The US postal service reached the border at Pembina in 1857, and 1859 saw an international steam-ship service down the Red River. In the next decade passage through Minnesota became Red River's normal link with the outside world, generating

---

[2] E.H. Oliver ed., *The Canadian North-West. Its Early Development and Legislative Records* (2 vols. continuously paginated, Ottawa, 1914-15) p. 144. Within the area between Canada and the Rockies, the HBC made some administrative divisions (chiefly as between the partly settled Red River border zone and the purely Indian fur bearing interior), and Canada sometimes distinguished between the 'North-West Territory' and the more southern part of the area (also referred to as the 'Fertile Belt'). But in what follows both 'Rupert's Land' and the 'North-West Territory' (or 'Territories') should be taken as referring to the whole area
[3] George F. Stanley, *Louis Riel* (Toronto, 1963) pp. 164-5; Statistics Canada (www.statcan.gc.ca), 'Censuses of Canada 1665 to 1871, The 1800s'. The 'Census of Canada, 1870-71' estimate of Indian numbers between Ontario and the Rockies was 40,200 (in 15 main groups) – ed. George F.G. Stanley, *The Collected Writings of Louis Riel. Les Ecrits Complets de Louis Riel*, ii *1875-1884* (Edmonton, 1985) pp. 19, 20n.

forecasts that the settlement would look to, or even wish to join, the United States. South of the border, business, political, and newspaper circles hoped that St. Paul, Minnesota, would become the development hub for the British prairies, and the departure point for a railway tapping their business on its way to the Pacific coast. And there was always a fair amount of annexationist sentiment, articulated and promoted by men like Senator Ramsey and the activist James Wickes Taylor.[4]

Red River was not particularly hard to control, as was shown when small detachments of British troops were stationed there from 1846-8 and 1857-61. In their absence, the HBC struggled. This was partly because it never raised an effective coercive force of its own like, say, Cecil Rhodes' later British South Africa Company Police. But it also reflected the HBC's vulnerability, at a time of hostility to statutory monopolies, to allegations of tyrannous maladministration that fed into campaigns against its Charter. In 1821 decades of competition between the HBC and the Montreal-based North-West Company had ended in a merger, sealed by the concession to the new body of a trading monopoly. In 1838 Parliament renewed the concession for 21 years. But by the 1850s the political climate was adverse. As one factor told Sir George Simpson, 'free trade notions' were making such progress that the day would soon come

> 'when ours, the last important British monopoly, will necessarily be swept away like all others, by the force of public opinion, or by the still more undesirable but inevitable course of violence and misrule within the country itself – it would therefore be better to make a virtue of necessity than to await the coming storm, for come it will.'[5]

---

[4] Alvin C. Gluek, *Minnesota and the manifest destiny of the Canadian north-west: a Study in Canadian-American Relations* (Toronto, 1965)

[5] Donald Ross (from Norway House) to Simpson, 21 Aug. 1848 – John S. Galbraith, *The Hudson's Bay Company as an Imperial Factor 1821-1869* (New York, 1977 reprint) p. 331

The idea of making a virtue out of necessity and surrendering the Company's property, *against compensation*, had some appeal to the HBC's leaders. But in 1856 the then Governor, John Shepherd, thought it would be better to ask the government to renew the trade monopoly and to send troops to keep order in Red River.[6]

The Colonial Office did not wish itself to assume control of Red River, officials remarking that this was 'simply impossible under present circumstances'.[7] But a new option was emerging, a Canadian takeover of some or all of Rupert's Land. George Brown's *Globe* and William McDougall's *North American* had long been attacking the HBC, and during the 1856 election the agriculture minister Philip VanKoughnet declared

> 'The Charter of the Hudson's Bay Company – no charter – no power could give to a few men exclusive control over half a continent. That vast extent of territory stretching from Lake Superior and Hudson's Bay belonged to Canada – or must belong to it.'

This rising interest led to Canadian government sponsorship of Henry Youle Hind's 'Exploring Expeditions' of 1857 and 1858, and British of John Palliser's more extensive surveys of 1857-9. Both reported the presence of much good land.[8]

1857 also saw wide-ranging examination of the HBC by a Select Committee of the British Parliament. Taking evidence from both the Company's friends and enemies, this addressed the Red River settlement's 'present condition' and noted 'the growing' Canadian wish to acquire 'the means of extension

---

[6] Simpson to Shepherd, 2 Aug. 1856, and Shepherd's 1 Sept. reply (Galbraith, *Hudson's Bay Company* pp. 74, 331-2, 338-9)

[7] Colonial Office Minute on a petition seeking direct British rule, 4 July 1856 (ibid. p. 339)

[8] Galbraith, *Hudson's Bay Company* p. 336; Irene Spry, 'Captain John Palliser and the Exploration of Western Canada', *Geographical Journal* 125:2 (1959) pp. 149-84

and ... settlement ... over a portion' of the HBC territory.[9] Perhaps the most important witnesses were Simpson and Canada's Chief Justice William Draper. Simpson declared Rupert's Land unsuited to agricultural settlement: the land was mostly bad, frost often took the crops, and there was little wood for fuel or building. Simpson's views had their supporters (though he had to explain away his earlier travel-writing likening of the river between Rainy Lake and the Lake of the Woods to the Thames at Richmond, with, in future, 'crowded steamboats' and 'populous towns').[10] Other witnesses suggested that settlement south of the northern Saskatchewan and west of Lake Winnipeg was not only possible but also needed to stop Americans flooding in across the invisible border. If 'something is not done', said Draper, 'that territory will in some way or other cease to be British'; Canada would then be cut off 'from all possible communication with the Pacific', a prospect that he said many Canadians viewed 'with extreme anxiety'.[11]

Draper also argued that the HBC's claim to the entire Hudson's Bay watershed was relatively recent, and that most of its fertile southern part was in fact owned by Canada as the heir to New France. Much would later be made of this claim, and Canada's despatch of Draper to London to present it. But what his mission really portrayed was Canadian ambivalence. With no instructions, Draper could only give his personal views and speak of his own reading of Canadian opinion. He thought Canada in no position to undertake Red River's immediate government. So any new arrangements there would have to be of an 'interim'

---

[9] Parliamentary Papers [hereafter P.P.] 1857 Session 2, xv p. 3; the Committee also considered the proper administration of Vancouver Island
[10] P.P. 1857 Session 2, xv questions 716-24, 773, 874-8, 1425-6
[11] Ibid., questions 4059-63. The Index heading 'Colonisation and Settlement' lists evidence given on 'Unfitness generally of the Territory for Settlement and Cultivation', 'Evidence to a contrary Purport', 'Course recommended as regards the Land fit for Settlement', and 'Expediency of Settlement North of the American Frontier'. Edward Ellice was alone in maintaining that the country should be left 'as it is', since settlement, whether from the US or Canada, was unlikely for years to come (questions 5841, 5845-81)

nature, in other words, some form of direct Imperial rule.[12] This view was confirmed next year by Governor-General Sir Edmund Head. He favoured establishing 'a colony or colonies' to cover the Red River settlement and the Saskatchewan, but warned that while Canada would 'assert her claims and rights in the abstract', she would not 'not readily undertake the Government of the Red River ... as a charge on her own revenues'. So he suggested only the vesting in Canada of the reversionary interest in the colony, and the placing of two Canadians on its governing Council.[13]

Canada's ambivalence would long continue. To some extent this reflected the state of its economy – depression in late 1857 damped down the Western aspirations felt earlier in the year. In part, too, it was a matter of individual outlook. Men like McDougall and Alexander Morris were Western visionaries; but others feared the cost of expansion and/or the American-style Indian wars this might provoke, while yet others became involved as railway promoters. There was, too, an institutional interest. Good land in Canada West was becoming scarce;[14] and it was natural to look west and hope to replicate, north of the border, the flood of settlement in Minnesota. Should this happen within Canada's then constitutional framework, Reform politicians might harvest support from the new areas, use these votes to help force 'Rep. by Pop.', and with it Canada West's political preponderance. Such prospects did not appeal to the Macdonald-Cartier coalition that more usually held the government; and while this would not court trouble by openly defending the HBC or opposing western colonisation, it moved only slowly, and felt that any immediate change in Red River or Rupert's Land should take the form of a new British colony like British Columbia.

---

[12] P.P. 1857 Session 2, xv questions 4056, 4059-66 and Appendix 5

[13] Head to the Colonial Secretary Sir Edward Bulwer Lytton, 9 Sept. 1858 (G. de T. Glazebrook, 'A Letter on the West by Sir Edmund Head', *Canadian Historical Review* [hereafter *Can.H.R.*] 21:1 (1940) pp. 58-9)

[14] P.P. 1857 Session 2, xv question 4067 (Draper); A.R.M. Lower, 'The assault on the Laurentian Barrier, 1850-1870', *Can.H.R.* 10:4 (1920) pp. 295, 300, 302, 303

The 1857 Select Committee had nearly recommended that the 'country capable of colonisation' should simply be taken from the HBC. But instead it looked to arrangements between the 'Government and the Hudson's Bay Company by which these districts may be ceded to Canada on equitable principles'. It hoped all parties would 'approach the subject in a spirit of conciliation and justice', and looked to early legislation to 'lay the foundation of an equitable and satisfactory arrangement'.[15] However no settlement was reached till 1869. The HBC always declared its readiness to sell. But Canada, though never the English law officers, doubted the validity of the HBC's title to the lands in question. That aside, there was the question of price, and of whether Britain or Canada should pay. Lastly there was, for many years, uncertainty as to whether territory the HBC relinquished should pass directly to Canada, or be organised as a separate colony (or colonies).

The Liberal Colonial Secretary Henry Labouchere would have liked to ask the Judicial Committee of the Privy Council how much land really had been conveyed to the HBC by its Charter. But when the Company proved reluctant, he instead proposed that it surrender to Canada the lands wanted for settlement, with compensation set by a commission representing the province, the Company, and the imperial government. The HBC accepted, but Canada did not. By then Labouchere had been succeeded by the Conservative Bulwer-Lytton. More hostile to the HBC than his predecessor, Lytton tried to force it to agree a reference to the Privy Council not just of its boundaries but, as Canada wished, of the validity of the Charter itself. The HBC dug in its heels, and Canada too drew back. Lytton considered legislation; but the Conservatives lost office before this could come to anything.

In 1860 Lytton's successor, the Duke of Newcastle, reverted to a scheme whereby the HBC would surrender lands wanted for

---

[15] P.P. 1857 Session 2, xv, Report pp. iii-iv, and p. 14 (Gladstone's take-over resolutions, which were silent on compensation for the HBC and were defeated by Labouchere's casting vote)

settlement, with arbiters awarding compensation – but only for the HBC's immoveable property, not for the territorial and other rights it claimed under its Charter. The Company again proved recalcitrant, and to put pressure on it, Newcastle withdrew the troops sent to Red River in 1857. Talks continued, but at a glacial pace, with Governor Berens suggesting, as a solution, that Britain simply buy the whole Company for £1.5m. That, though, was not what Newcastle wanted, and he was reluctant to include, in arrangements for taking over fertile areas from the HBC, anything that would sanction its claims 'to the fee simple of the vast Continent of British North America'. An impasse seemed to have been reached.[16]

However a new element emerged in the form of British bankers, capitalists, and railway promoters. Edward Watkin (of the Manchester, Sheffield and Lincolnshire Railway) had been asked by Barings to turn around the Canadian Grand Trunk. He thought its running could be improved. But securing 'a *great success* in a few years can only be done in one way ... through the extension of railway communication to the Pacific'; and this could only be achieved through cooperation with the British and Canadian governments, and by associating the railway with some large 'land' and 'emigration' scheme.[17] In June 1861 Watkin set up an interview between financiers interested in Canadian railways and the Duke of Newcastle, whom he already knew through English railway dealings;[18] and he remained in frequent informal contact with the Duke. Both men had visions of a string of British colonies, linked by rail and extending right across the continent.

---

[16] Galbraith, *Hudson's Bay Company* pp. 347-53, 365-8; P.P. 1857-8 xli, 'Hudson's Bay Company ... Correspondence ... in consequence of the Report of the Select Committee', 1859 Session 1 xvii, 'Papers relating to the Hudson's Bay Company's charter and license of trade'; Newcastle's 12 July 1861 note on T.W.C. Murdoch's observations on his 19 Feb. meeting with Governor Berens (CO 6/33 fos. 257-73)

[17] Watkin to Thomas Baring, 13 Nov. 1860 (Sir Edward Watkin, *Canada and the States. Recollections 1851 to 1886* (London, 1887) pp. 12-15)

[18] Elaine Allan Mitchell, 'Edward Watkin and the Buying-out of the Hudson's Bay Company', *Can.H.R.* 34:3 (1953) pp. 223, 226-7

And though Watkin's memoirs may exaggerate, they discussed tactics, sharing grouses about Gladstone's Treasury tight-fistedness, and daydreams of revising the border with the United States to acquire Superior City (at the head of Lake Superior), presumably as a departure point for a railway to Fort Garry and the West.[19]

At this stage lobbying chiefly concerned finance for the projected Intercolonial Railway: arrangements were made for Maritimes politicians to see the Prime Minister and the Chancellor of the Exchequer. In 1862 talks between Canada's Cartier and the HBC's 'Overseas Governor' added the building through Rupert's Land of a road and telegraph line to British Columbia (linking there to the projected line to Europe through Alaska and Russia). Thomas Baring and other capitalists wrote to Newcastle declaring their readiness to participate, but first asked what the government would do to help – would it make a grant of land? The correspondence was passed to the HBC, which stalled. However, Newcastle mentioned to Watkin that the Company was ready to sell 'their *whole* rights' for £1.5m. Newcastle feared that such a purchase might be 'just now impracticable', but in December he promoted a meeting between the HBC and Watkin's associates.[20]

---

[19] Watkin, *Canada and the States* pp. 65-65+, chaps. 7, 8. In 1862 Watkin envisaged, as a possible way of raising money to buy out the HBC, selling part of its territory to the US for £1m. – E.E. Rich, *The History of the Hudson's Bay Company, 1670-1870*, vol. 2 *1763-1870* (London, 1959) pp. 832-3). Newcastle had told Watkin he would not *sell* the United States land, but would 'exchange' with it; 'and, studying the map, we put our fingers upon the Aroostook wedge, in … Maine – upon a piece of territory at the head of Lake Superior, and upon islands between' Vancouver Island and B.C. – 'which might be the equivalent of rectification of boundary on many portions to the Westward along the 49th parallel' (Watkin, *Canada and the States* pp. 122-3, 129). In 1861 Newcastle told Watkin he had heard that 'Maine wants to be annexed to our territory' (p. 65+); and in 1863 Watkin, when in Canada, hoped to arrange 'an exchange of territory between the Hudson's Bay and the United States with … Superior City [Wisconsin] being brought into British territory' – the 'negotiation looked very hopeful at one time, but it was not followed up in London' (p. 205)

[20] Mitchell, 'Watkin and the Buying-out' pp. 228-30, 233-8; Newcastle to Watkin, 14 Aug. 1862 (Watkin, *Canada and the States* pp. 128-30)

While negotiations over the construction of a (subsidised) road and telegraph route continued, Watkin struck an independent deal for the purchase of the HBC. He had hoped that the government would either buy the Company itself or lend the £1.5m. required, but Newcastle declined – 'Were I a minister of Russia I should buy the land. It is the right thing to do...; but [British] ministers must subordinate their views to the cabinet'. Some of Watkin's original associates also backed away. So when faced with the need to raise money in a hurry, he turned to a venture capital fund, the International Financial Society.[21] The purchase went through, and the Society then promptly floated a new Hudson's Bay Company on the stock exchange for £2m. Its first Governor, selected by the Duke of Newcastle, was Sir Edmund Head, until recently Canadian Governor-General; and his two successors were front-bench politicians, the Liberal Earl of Kimberley and the Conservative Sir Stafford Northcote.[22]

For profit the new Company looked to rapid settlement and land sales. Its Stock Exchange prospectus declared much of its southern territory to be 'well adapted for European civilization', with soil producing wheat 'in abundance' and 'capable of sustaining a numerous population'. This district would therefore 'be opened to European colonization, under a liberal and systematic scheme of land settlement', with Watkin visiting it to report on how this should be done.[23] But Watkin did not actually go beyond Canada, and his reports were unhelpfully general. He ascribed much of Red River's unfortunate condition to the 'false economy' of withdrawing the Canadian Rifles, and declared firm government a prerequisite for land settlement. This might in principle be provided by the HBC.

---

[21] This also floated a loan for one Austrian railway, financed another, plus an Anglo-Italian bank, and a land company for Mauritius, and took a major part in the conversion of Mexico's public debt – Rich, *History of the Hudson's Bay Company* vol. 2 p. 836

[22] Mitchell, 'Watkin and the Buying-out' pp. 233-41; Galbraith, *Hudson's Bay Company* pp. 386-90; Watkin, *Canada and the States* pp. 115-19,121-6; P.P. 1863 xxxviii, 'Correspondence between the Colonial Office and the Hudson's Bay Company...'; Rich, *The Hudson's Bay Company* vol. 2 chap. 29

[23] P.P. 1863 xxxviii fos. 98-9

But that would require 'arming the Governor with a military force', something no British government showed any disposition to do. So Watkin felt the 'great object' should be 'to induce the Imperial Government to found a Crown Colony under arrangement with the Hudson's Bay Company'. The other possibility was annexation by Canada 'under some reasonable arrangement with the Hudson's Bay Company'.[24] Both would require an arrangement with the HBC; but in the subsequent negotiations, Britain, Canada, and the HBC all took a fairly narrow view of their own interests.

The 1857 Select Committee report had reflected Canada's apparent wish to take over at least the fertile southern belt of Rupert's Land. But the wish cooled. In March 1863, when reports of gold finds on the Saskatchewan led to fears of an influx of American miners (like that into British Columbia in 1858), the Canadian government was sufficiently worried to call London's attention to the problem and regret that nothing had been done '*to organize the Saskatchewan Territory*' into a Colony. The Colonial Office was not enthusiastic, minutes asking 'what adequate reason there could be' for taxpayer support 'for an isolated little Govt., buried in the middle of the American Continent, and surrounded by nothing but dwindling hordes of wandering savages'. The general assumption was that the British government would not assume responsibility for the area. But Newcastle would not tell the HBC this. For he was himself rather drawn to the idea: that summer he gave Watkin 'many interviews' to discuss schemes for state purchase of the HBC, whose lands would then be organised into 'a Crown Colony ['Hysperia'], like British Columbia'.[25]

During Watkin's 1863 visit to Canada, he discussed the HBC territories with leading politicians. Brown and the Grits, he reported, had favoured of annexing them and 'thereby securing that preponderance which would settle ... the future government' of all Canada. And when Watkin sent Brown a project for a

---

[24] Watkin, *Canada and the States* pp. 163, 165-9, 184. The printed text has 'Colonial' not 'Imperial' Government; but colonial governments could not establish Crown colonies, so this must be an error

[25] CO 42/633 fos. 49-53; Watkin, *Canada and the States* pp. 120-3

separate Crown Colony there, it was returned with the message that 'It would not do at all'. However the then Premier, the moderate Liberal Sandfield Macdonald, expressed 'a strong opinion in favour of ... a separate Crown Colony', as did John A. Macdonald, Cartier, and the leader of 'the Catholic party in Lower Canada', Vicar General Charles Cazeau.[26] Next month the directors of the new HBC resolved that it was 'expedient' that authority 'over the Red River Settlement and the South Western portion of Rupert's Land should be vested in officers deriving ... [it] directly from the Crown'. Negotiations followed. But when ill health forced Newcastle's retirement in April 1864, he and the Company were still at odds over what compensation it should receive in return. His successor, Edward Cardwell, summarised the state of play on the 'Proposed Colony in Rupert's Land', and took the question to the Cabinet.[27]

Late that year the well-connected 'British North American Association' still believed 'arrangements' were 'contemplated between the Imperial and Canadian Governments, and the Hudson's Bay Company' to make the Red River Settlement into a Crown Colony and throw the 'Fertile Belt' open to colonisation.[28] But matters had moved on. In view of a possible rush of American miners to the Saskatchewan, there had been suggestions that the Imperial Government, British Columbia, and the HBC should concert arrangements to issue licenses and preserve order.

---

[26] 'It would not do at all', ibid. p. 173; the remainder, Watkin to Head, 24 July 1863 (pp. 180-1). Later, though, Watkin wrote that Brown had favoured 'a Colony' within the Canadian customs union, but with 'a separate Government' (to Macdonald, 18 Feb. 1865 – Sir Joseph Pope ed., *Correspondence of Sir John Macdonald* (Garden City, N.Y., 1921) p. 22

[27] Galbraith, *Hudson's Bay Company* pp. 395-400; CO 880/4/2, Confidential Print, '"Proposed Colony in Rupert's Land". Memorandum by Edward Cardwell, Secretary of State...', 2 May 1864

[28] British North American Association, *Confederation of the British North-American Provinces, being extracts from Speeches recently delivered on this subject...* (London, 1865 – JSTOR Foreign and Commonwealth Office [Pamphlet] Collection) p. 18. The Association comprised bankers and businessmen interested in Canadian railways and in the projected overland telegraph to British Columbia; it was close to Watkin

'Mr Gladstone & Mr Cardwell', a later Colonial Office minute stated, 'knocked that on the head' Instead they determined that developments there should be 'dealt with by the HBC and the Canadian [not the Imperial] Government – with the object' of annexing the territory to Canada.[29] And Canada too had muted its backing for the idea of a Crown Colony. When it pulled out of the overland telegraph project in February 1864, it revived its claim to that part of 'Central British America which can be shown to have been in [French] possession' in 1763. Cardwell responded by asking whether Canada would undertake the government of part of the HBC territory; if so, it should send somebody to London for discussions.[30] By then Brown had joined the Canadian government, which will have reinforced Canada's interest in the prairies. That November Canada's Executive Council declared itself 'more than ever impressed with the importance of opening up the lands between Lake Superior and the Rocky Mountains ... The first step ... must be the extinction of the proprietary rights and privileges of the Hudson's Bay Company.' It added that Brown would be coming to London 'to communicate freely on the whole subject'.[31]

His visit did not prove useful. He represented the HBC as 'seeking to sell ... territory to which they had no title under their charter', and suggested ascertaining 'what validity there was' in the Company's claims, 'what land the Company really had to sell'. In any case, it was for the Imperial Government to 'secure the extinction of the [Hudson's Bay] Company's claim to proprietary rights'. That done, Canada would be prepared to open up 'communication with the country' and establish local government

---

[29] Minute by the Colonial Office's senior civil servant, Sir Frederic Rogers, on R.G. Smith to T.F. Elliot of 12 July 1867 – CO 6/42 fo. 147

[30] 18 Feb. 1864 report of a committee of the Executive Council, forwarded next day by the Governor-General Viscount Monck; Cardwell to Monck, 1 July 1864 (P.P. 1864 xli pp. 129-30, 645-6)

[31] Executive Council Minute, 11 Nov. 1864 (forwarded by Monck to London next day); the quotation is from the Colonial Office's 'Abstract' of the very verbose Minute – CO 42/643 fos. 275-84, 287

'in the settled parts'.[32] This was unwelcome. For the British government accepted its law officers' view that the HBC's charter and claims were almost certainly valid; nor did it want itself to buy land for Canada. So the negotiations 'rested' until the visit to London of a broader Canadian delegation - Brown, Macdonald, Cartier, and Galt. Before he left Canada, Macdonald would, ideally, still have preferred 'to leave that whole Country a wilderness for the next half century' rather than see its colonisation 'drain away our youth and strength'. But 'if Englishmen do not go there Yankees will'; and if Canada was 'to remain a Country separate from the United States', it was essential that the US 'should not get behind us by right or force and intercept the route to the Pacific'. To prevent this, Macdonald would gladly have seen 'a Crown Colony established there'.[33] But Cardwell did not want to ask Parliament to create one, and, despite civil service warnings that this would only delay things, seemed instead 'very anxious' to get Canada 'to take all the responsibility'. British ministers accordingly reached agreement with the Canadian delegation that the North-Western Territory 'should be made over to Canada'. But the Canadian government would first have to negotiate 'the termination of their rights' with the HBC, the purchase price, 'if any', being met by a loan that Canada would raise under Imperial guarantee.[34]

---

[32] Confidential Print, CO 880/4/13, 'Summary of negotiations for the surrender by the Hudson's Bay Company of their territory; and for the completion of Passenger and Telegraphic Communication between the Atlantic and the Pacific...' p. 7. Brown was, though, only restating the Executive Council's position that it was for the Imperial Government, not for that of Canada, to bring 'to an end a monopoly originating in an English Charter' (CO 42/643 fo. 287)

[33] Macdonald to Watkin, 27 March 1865 (Library and Archives Canada, on-line doc. MIKAN no. 566855), in answer to Watkin's letter of 18 Feb. asking whether Confederation had changed the views Canadian leaders had held during his 1863 visit. Macdonald did say that Canada would be prepared to 'open up the communication from its western boundary' and enter into mutually beneficial customs and other arrangements with a new Crown Colony

[34] Galbraith, *The Hudson's Bay Company* pp. 401-2; Watkin to Macdonald, 18 Feb. 1865 (Pope, *Correspondence of Macdonald* p. 22); Cardwell to Monck, 17 June 1865 ('Papers relating to the Conferences ... between Her Majesty's

'Negotiations, however, did not follow.' This upset both the HBC, whose shareholders were pressing for some return on their investments, and the Colonial Office, which feared that the situation on the ground might become so bad that Britain would after all have to step in and establish a Colony.[35] But Canada would not address the North-West question until Confederation had come into effect. The question was then put before the first Dominion Parliament in the Speech from the Throne, which anticipated 'a new nationality' whose bounds would 'ere long' extend 'from the Atlantic to the Pacific Ocean'.[36] In December 1867 the Commons debated resolutions on the takeover of Rupert's Land. In moving them, McDougall urged prompt action: at a time when the Americans were pushing up to the border, its inhabitants were 'without Government'; were no attention paid to their calls 'for protection and assistance ... they must look elsewhere, and there were already movements on foot in that direction'. Another speaker cited the recent American purchase of Alaska, and a number referred to the way in which Texas had passed to the USA. Timothy Anglin, however, scouted the idea of the US absorbing the territory 'if we delayed action'; for Britain would not permit it.[37] The rising Liberal Edward Blake noted

---

Government and a Deputation from the Executive Council of Canada...', P.P. 1865 xxxvii pp. 437-9). The agreement was sanctioned by the British cabinet

[35] After yet another HBC warning that if the Territory was to be retained 'as British soil', something would have to be done to assert 'its British character' and maintain 'law and order within it', the Colonial Secretary Lord Carnarvon commented, 'I wish either Canada or the U.S. had it'!

[36] *Canada. House of Commons Debates – First Session – First Parliament*, ed. P.B. Waite (Ottawa, 1967) pp. 5-6 – subsequently cited as *Commons Debates – First Session*. Until 1875 there were no official transcripts of debates, only newspaper reports that reduced the speeches to, at most, one-third of their length. Waite reproduces the fullest reports available, but other newspapers sometimes chose to record different aspects of a speech. Some of my quotations are therefore from the 'scrapbook' record reproduced as Canada Parliament, Canadian Library Association, Microfilm Committee, *Parliamentary Debates, 1866-1870* (hereafter *Parliamentary Debates)*

[37] *Commons Debates – First Session*, pp. 182 (4 Dec. 1867, McDougall), 187 (4 Dec., Anglin, and 5 Dec., Johnson), 190 (5 Dec., McGill), 225 (8 Dec., Sir John Macdonald)

Colonial Office fears, should gold be discovered, of 'a large influx of [American] adventurers … who might be disposed to the assertion of their political independence'. A 'strong Government' would indeed then be needed. But it would be for Britain to provide it, the task being beyond Canada's resources; and Canada would be none the worse were the territory to become a Crown Colony. Joseph Howe, too, repeatedly attacked the proposed expansion as ruinously expensive, observing that the 'frog made himself ridiculous when he attempted to blow himself out to the dimensions of the ox'. Instead, he suggested asking Britain to form Rupert's Land into a Crown Colony.[38] Cartier, however, held that the expenditure involved would give a four- or five-fold return, and asked whether they should grudge 'the paltry sum of five or six million dollars to extend the Dominion to British Columbia'. Sir John Macdonald also descanted on the territory's value as an outlet for both 'the future teeming of Western Canada' and for European immigrants. Settling it was something Canada would have to do for itself – Britain could not be expected to pay for it, any more than for the settlement of central Australia. He added that when the Quebec Confederation scheme had been submitted to Parliament, it was 'perfectly well understood' that the 'full design … was that it should include the whole of British America, from the Atlantic to the Pacific', a sentiment also voiced by the Liberal leader Alexander Mackenzie.[39] Some opponents of Confederation agreed: the Halifax MP Alfred Jones declared that 'any one who had gone in for Union, pure et simple, was bound to follow it to its logical conclusion'. As an opponent of Confederation, 'he could not do so.' Debate accordingly sometimes relapsed into a re-run of the Confederation issue; one Nova Scotian asked whether the Territory's inhabitants were 'willing' to come into Confederation, 'or were they to be dragged in against

---

[38] Ibid., pp. 202, 204 (6 Dec., Blake), pp. 184, 224 (4 and 9 Dec., Howe)
[39] Ibid., pp. 187 (4 Dec., Cartier), 195 (5 Dec., Mackenzie), 224-5 (9 Dec., Macdonald)

their will' like his own province?[40] In the final ballot Nova Scotia voted almost unanimously against moves to acquire the North-West Territory, joined chiefly by Quebec *Rouges*.[41]

The resolutions so carried were forwarded to London, accompanied by a declaration that transfer to Canada 'should not be delayed by negotiations ... with private or third parties' - that is with the HBC. Instead the Company's 'legal rights' would be placed under the 'protection' of Canadian courts.[42] In which case, Macdonald had told Parliament in a passage promptly seized on by the HBC, 'the moment it was known that the country belonged to Canada, and that the ... Canadian courts had jurisdiction there', the Company's 'chief protection' would be 'gone forever'; 'We would [then] get the country at the cost of a comparatively small sum'.[43] For good measure, the Canadian government declared that, given Washington's 'avowed policy ... to acquire territory from other Powers, by purchase or otherwise', 'not a day' should be lost. So could London please cable back, saying whether the 'Imperial Cabinet' would approve the transfer of Rupert's Land on these terms? This, however, was a try-on. For the Canadian Parliament had anticipated that there might be negotiation with the HBC and had sought a veto over any agreement reached.

The Colonial Office's receipt of the Canadian request coincided with the arrival of the HBC's protest against it, and with advice from the English Law Officers that it would not be 'advisable' to seek to legislate on Rupert's Land against the

---

[40] Ibid., p. 245 (11 Dec., Luther Holton), 187 (4 Dec., Chipman, King's, Nova Scotia); *Parliamentary Debates* p. 75 (6 Dec., Jones, Halifax)

[41] *Commons Debates – First Session*, p. 255 (11 Dec.). The Quebec votes, however, represented only 23% of that Province's MPs

[42] 'Report of a Committee of the Privy Council' (approving recommendations submitted by McDougall), and Parliament's 'Resolutions for the Incorporation of Rupert's Land and the North-Western Territory with Canada', enclosed in Monck to Buckingham, 1 Jan. 1868 (P.P. 1868-9 xliii pp. 378-9)

[43] *Commons Debates – First Session* p. 225 (9 Dec. 1867); Head to Buckingham, 25 Jan. 1868 (P.P. 1868-9 xliii pp. 396, 398)

Company's wish 'while the Charter continues to exist'.[44] So the Colonial Secretary, the Duke of Buckingham, put the question to the Cabinet, advocating a position intermediate between those of the Dominion and of the Company. He would seek 'an amicable arrangement with the Company' for its surrender to the Crown of 'rights claimed under the Charter'. This would involve leading the HBC to recognise that its own interests required it to make a proposal neither 'immoderate nor calculated to compel any long discussion'.

Negotiations started fairly well, with a discussion between Buckingham and the HBC's Deputy Governor, Sir Curtis Lampson. Buckingham had ruled out the simple cash payment the Company would have preferred: 'Great Britain ought not to be expected to find an indemnity. Canada cannot.' Instead, he had suggested, like Newcastle in 1864, that the Company should receive a shilling for each acre sold, plus a quarter of any 'gold revenue'.[45] He and Lampson agreed on royalties on land sales and gold revenue, to a total value of £1m.; but trouble arose over the HBC's wish also for a free grant of a tenth of all land sales. They did agree to negotiate further. But when the HBC formally stated its terms, these included the right to select 5000 acres for every 50,000 sold. Buckingham waited till he had secured legislation empowering the Crown to transfer the Territory to Canada on its surrender by the HBC, and then invited the Company's Governor, the Earl of Kimberley, to come and discuss their differences.[46]

Buckingham's attitude towards Canada was initially rather cavalier – 'It would be necessary' he had told the cabinet when first proposing negotiating with the HBC, 'afterwards to inform Canada of the terms'. His colleagues pointed out that these would

---

[44] Confidential Print, CO 880/4/16, 'Hudson's Bay Company. Law Officers' opinions; latest Address of the Canadian Parliament; letter from the Company', passim
[45] CO 880/4/14, Confidential Print, '"Pending questions about the Hudson's Bay Territory." Memorandum by the Duke of Buckingham…', 25 Jan. 1868, esp. pp. 2-3
[46] CO 880/4/17, Confidential Print, 'Summary of proposals discussed confidentially between Sir. Curtis Lampson and the Duke of Buckingham…', 12 March 1868, p. 1; the Earl of Kimberley to C.B. Adderley, 13 May 1868, and Sir Frederick Rogers to Kimberley, 7 Aug. (P.P. 1868-9 xliii pp. 398-401)

have to be acceptable to Canada, since otherwise the British Government might be landed with the Territory. Buckingham received an unofficial warning from Governor-General Monck. But he went ahead, merely telling Monck in August that he would be starting formal negotiations with the HBC, 'and shall not fail to keep your Lordship informed of … [their] course'.[47] Unsurprisingly, the Canadian government asked to join in, and in October 1868 Cartier and McDougall arrived in London. Buckingham invited them to his country seat for talks; and both he and his deputy C.B. Adderley appear to have been shaken by their resistance to previous proposals. Two further conferences with Buckingham – one of three-and-a-half hours – now left Kimberley pessimistic: he submitted a modified offer, but in the expectation that negotiations would be broken off since 'Canada evidently wishes to get the territory for nothing'. Things were then delayed by the British general election. And when Cartier saw that this had gone badly for the Conservatives, he pressed Buckingham to reply to Kimberley's offer, hoping thereby to commit the incoming Liberal Colonial Secretary 'in our favour against the Company's demands'. Buckingham agreed, and Cartier and McDougall were consulted over the drafting of his final offer, dated 1 December. They gave it a tepid acceptance, subject to the approval of the Canadian Parliament.[48]

The major sticking points were the royalties to be paid to the HBC from future Canadian government land sales, the reserves it

[47] Buckingham's 'Pending Questions…' memorandum; Galbraith, *Hudson's Bay Company* pp. 416, 418-9; Buckingham to Monck, 8 Aug. 1868 (P.P. 1868-9 xliii p. 389)
[48] R.S. Longley, 'Cartier and MacDougall, Canadian Emissaries to London, 1868-9', *Can.H.R.* 26:1 (1945) pp. 29-31, 38, which draws on Cartier's letters reporting developments to Prime Minister Macdonald; ed. Angus Hawkins and John Powell, *The Journal of John Wodehouse First Earl of Kimberley for 1862-1902* (Royal Historical Society, Camden Fifth Series vol. 9, 1997) pp. 225-6 [18 Sept., 17, 24, 27 Oct. 1868]; Kimberley to Adderley, 27 Oct. 1868 (P.P. 1868-9 xliii p. 401)

would retain around its trading posts,[49] and the way in which the further lands allotted to the Company should be chosen. Buckingham now felt that given the likely low land prices and the costs of opening the Territory up for settlement, the shilling an acre royalty on all land sold would for years leave Canadian governments no prospect of profit. Instead, he offered 3d. an acre on land grants and a quarter of the price of land sales. The HBC rejected this, feeling that were settlement to prove slow, it might incur 'very heavy contributions ... without receiving the smallest benefit in return'. Moreover, whereas the HBC's plan would have given it land near newly established townships that would have 'an actual value in the market', under Buckingham's proposal it would get only a predetermined scatter of 'tracts of wild land', many valueless, or, if taxed, 'a heavy burden'.[50] Since Kimberley had now joined the government, it fell to his successor as Governor, Sir Stafford Northcote, to deliver the Company's rejection of Buckingham's proposal. Northcote stated that the HBC would stand by Kimberley's offers but added that it would be much better if Canada simply bought the Territory, paying in cash or bonds.

Cartier, a Conservative, had always been concerned about Britain's new Liberal government. His apprehensions were reinforced when Chancellor of the Exchequer Lowe told him informally that he thought Canada ought not to want the icy regions of the North-West, and that the HBC would never accept Buckingham's terms. John Bright also felt Canada should 'let the Company alone'; and Cartier suspected Kimberley of continued advocacy for the Company he had once governed. The Colonial Secretary, Lord Granville, was slow to decide. But eventually he pressed Cartier and McDougall to answer Northcote's letter. Their reply was long and confrontational. And they supplemented it by

---

[49] The Colonial Office calculated that the Company's latest demand would give it 500,000 acres, while the HBC put the figure at 50,000

[50] Adderley to Kimberley, 1 Dec. 1868; Kimberley to Adderley, 27 Oct. 1868, and Sir Stafford Northcote to Rogers, 13 Jan. 1869 (P.P. 1868-9 xliii pp. 401, 409-10)

inspiring newspaper comment, by lobbying the Conservatives, and finally by threatening to go home.[51]

Granville had asked the Canadians to comment on a simple buying out of the Company. They could see no basis for paying the HBC more than £106,431. If it held out for more, sovereignty over the whole Territory should at once be passed to Canada 'subject to the rights of the Company'. Alternatively, Canada should receive 'all the territory not ... validly granted to ... the Company under its Charter' (the Fertile Belt), leaving the HBC the far north.[52] The HBC's response was that a transfer to Canada 'subject to the rights of the Company' would be fine *if* these were defined in advance; otherwise there would be endless litigation. As for a transfer of the territory not validly held under the HBC's Charter, would its boundaries be defined? If not, there would be 'constant conflicts of authority'. Having thus shot down the Canadian proposals, Northcote reverted to the HBC's real desideratum, a Crown Colony. Should Britain establish one, the Company would gladly surrender enough of its 'proprietary rights to cover the cost to the Imperial Exchequer'. Or it might keep these rights and get its shareholders to raise money to meet that cost, recouping themselves from the profits accruing from land settlement after the Colony's establishment. Lastly, Northcote replied to some rather pointed Colonial Office questions as to how the Company would protect life and property in its territory as long as it remained responsible for this – which might be quite some time. It would, he said, itself establish a firm government, provided Britain passed 'any needful' legislation and protected the settlement from Canadian trespass or interference.[53]

With the ball thus back in Granville's court, he decided that the Canadians would have to be brought to accept some serious cash payment to the HBC and suggested £375,000 plus a twenty-fifth of all surveyed land. Cartier might have accepted, but

---

[51] Longley, 'Cartier and MacDougall' pp. 32-4, 35-7, 38-9
[52] Cartier and McDougall to Rogers, 9 Feb. 1869, summarised in Rogers to Northcote, 22 Feb. (P.P. 1868-9 xliii pp. 413-14, 428-39)
[53] Rogers to Northcote, 22 Feb. 1869, and Northcote's 26 Feb. reply (P.P. 1868-9 xliii pp. 413-16)

McDougall proved tougher – 'very huffy and imperious', as Granville later described him. £350,000 was similarly rejected. But eventually Granville got Cartier to join him in 'forcing' McDougall to accept a revised package of £300,000 (to be raised through bonds backed by an Imperial guarantee) plus a twentieth of the surveyed land.[54]

Granville then turned to the HBC, not mentioning his prior understanding with the Canadians, but presenting his proposals as an award that could only be modified by agreement between the parties. Rejection would bring reference of the whole question to the Judicial Committee of the Privy Council.[55] The chief obstacle now was the resentment of HBC shareholders: when Granville's proposals were read to the Company's directors, all agreed that they were unjust, while three advocated defiance.[56] But the HBC had proved unable to effect land settlement on its own. Moreover, defiance would both alienate the British government and ensure yet further delay while the Judicial Committee of the Privy Council reviewed the legal position. So most directors recommended accepting the proposals, albeit with major modifications. This led to discussions with Cartier and McDougall, who rejected most HBC demands but made one substantial concession: on the laying-out of a township, instead of simply being assigned lands by lot, the Company should have up to ten years to select those it wanted.[57]

---

[54] Longley, 'Cartier and MacDougall' p. 39; Granville to Gladstone, 11 March 1869 – ed. Agatha Ramm, *The Political Correspondence of Mr. Gladstone and Lord Granville 1868-1876* (Camden Third Series no. 81, 1952) nos. 39, 40. All Granville's packages also included HBC retention of agreed reserves around its trading posts

[55] Longley, 'Cartier and MacDougall' p. 47; Rogers to Northcote, 9 March 1869, and his *pro forma* letter of that date to the Canadian Delegates (P.P. 1868-9 xliii pp. 416-18, 439-40). Cartier and McDougall had both told Macdonald on 6 March of their agreement with Granville

[56] Galbraith, *Hudson's Bay Company* pp. 405-8

[57] Northcote to Cartier and McDougall, 11, 12, 16 March 1869; Cartier and McDougall to Northcote, 15 and 18 March; Northcote to Rogers, 22 March; 'Memorandum of Agreement[s] between the Delegates of the Dominion and the Directors of the Hudson's Bay Company', 22 and 29 March (P.P. 1868-9 xliii pp. 384, 418-22)

When the final Agreements were taken to a special meeting of the HBC's General Court, they met with cries of 'Treachery'. However on 9 April a stormy three-hour meeting agreed that there was no alternative and endorsed the settlement by two to one – but reluctantly, the Secretary adding to his minute the words, 'The argument of the minority was the more cogent, but the reasoning of the Chairman, as the event proved, was found to be the more convincing.'[58]

In Ottawa, things went more smoothly, with both government and parliament readily accepting Cartier and McDougall's report and recommendations. Two apparently minor developments, however, would prove to have important consequences: the date for the transfer of Rupert's Land to Canada slipped from 1 October to 1 December; but so as not to waste a season, the Canadian government obtained permission to begin land surveys while governance was still in HBC hands.

* * * *

The chief components of the settlements by now thinly spread around the Red River and the Assiniboine in the general neighbourhood of the then village of Winnipeg were the Francophone and Catholic métis, 5757 in 1871, and the 4083 Anglophone and Protestant 'half-breeds'. There were also 1575 Europeans (half born in the settlement), and 558 Indians (mostly

---

[58] Galbraith, *Hudson's Bay Company* pp. 424-6, and chap. 9 generally; Rich, *The Hudson's Bay Company* vol. 2 chap. 30. The critics' fears were well-founded. For by 1873 the HBC had received a mere $6,000 from land sales. Mackenzie's government then felt that the unallotted HBC landholdings would cause 'difficulties with settlers', and it wanted complete freedom to grant land so as 'to fill up the country rather than to attempt to make money' by sales. So in 1875 Mackenzie almost purchased the entire land stock (apart from 30,000 acres around trading posts) for £500,000 to £550,000. But the economic depression scuppered the deal, and land sales brought the Company 'little revenue until the twentieth century' – when it rode the great prairies land boom, with a net profit of £2.7m. from sales between 1908 and 1913 – John S. Galbraith, 'A Note on the Mackenzie Negotiations with the Hudson's Bay Company, 1875-1878', *Can.H.R.* 34:1 (1953) pp. 39-45

the settled and Christian 'Swampy' Indians).[59] The Métis and 'half-breeds' both descended from marriages 'after the custom of the country' between fur trade personnel and Indians, but they had developed their own group cultures. The 'half-breeds' were the more agriculturally settled; and in this pursuit they overlapped with the retired HBC employees from the Orkneys and with Lord Selkirk's settlers from northern Scotland. There were prosperous Métis farmers and traders. But more of that community were 'hivernants', employed in the summer as peripatetic boatmen and carters, or were periodically away from Red River on their far-flung buffalo hunts. These last were massive collective efforts, conducted in semi-military fashion under an elected 'President'; and their practitioners were correspondingly armed and formidable. The HBC, of course, had both half-breed and Métis servants, but also more senior traders and other officials (many of Scots descent), headed by the Governor – for most of the 1860s, William Mactavish, who combined the roles of Governor of 'Assiniboia' (basically the Red River settlement) and of the Company's more northern and exclusively fur-trading posts. Lastly, besides these by now traditional groupings, there had as the decade progressed come to be a small but increasing number of external immigrants, some few American, but chiefly 'Canadian'.

Relations between the Métis and the 'half-breeds' were broadly friendly. But there was an underlying fear of communal conflict, and a reluctance to do anything that might provoke it. In 1863 the Reverend Griffith Corbett was imprisoned for attempts to procure an abortion but sprung from jail by half-breed supporters. He had earlier denounced the increasing number of Roman Catholics on the governing Council of Assiniboia; and the Métis offered to raise a force to restore order and return Corbett to jail. But the then Governor declined, since he did not want to start a civil war, setting the French against the English. Similarly in 1868, when the leader of the 'Canadian' party Dr. John Schultz

---

[59] Stanley, *Louis Riel* pp. 164-5, and p. x (map of the 'Red River Settlement 1870')

was forcibly released from jail, Governor Mactavish declined to enlist Special Constables from among the (all too willing) Métis to re-arrest him.[60]

Segmented communities often coexist tranquilly until change in their area's governance is threatened, and this seems to have been the case in Red River. In time past the HBC had sometimes used its legal powers to repress trade competitors, encountering direct action Métis resistance. But by the mid-1860s it essentially operated as a weak and non-interventionist local authority, and membership of the Council of Assiniboia had been broadened to include most local community leaders. The HBC's regime accordingly came to enjoy at the least widespread acceptance, and many officers, notably Governor Mactavish, were personally popular. But it was equally clear that Company rule was on the way out. The Queen, British troops, and the 'imperial' parliament were held in some respect, so the most popular alternative would probably have been a Crown Colony. But after 1865 a Canadian takeover seemed increasingly likely. Within Red River this prospect was vociferously promoted by a small group of 'Canadians', headed by Schultz and by the settlement's only newspaper, the increasingly extreme Nor'Wester. This paper, the trader and postmaster Andrew Bannatyne later deposed, so 'misrepresented ... the feelings of the people' as to generate a counter-petition with over 800 signatures, both French and English. This the Nor'Wester initially refused to publish. So a crowd of Métis assembled to seize its printing press and had to be personally dissuaded by the Governor.[61] In themselves, Schultz and

---

[60] Fred Elmer Bartlett, *William Mactavish: the last governor of Assiniboia* (University of Manitoba, M.A. thesis, 1964) pp. 144-6 (Corbett), 155-7 (Schultz); Joseph J. Hargrave, *Red River* (Montreal, 1871) chaps 19-20 (Corbett), 29 (Schultz). Similarly in 1866 Mactavish had commuted a death sentence passed on a Métis murderer as it 'would have excited feelings that would not so soon have been allayed'; it was replaced by banishment to British Columbia (Bartlett, *Mactavish* pp. 158-9; Stanley, *Riel* p. 47)
[61] *Report of the [Parliamentary] Select Committee on the Causes of the Difficulties in the North-West Territory in 1869-70* [hereafter *Select Committee Report*] (Ottawa, 1874) p. 123; Hargrave, *Red River* pp. 433-4; Bartlett, *Mactavish* p. 132

the *Nor'Wester* were only irritants. But they gained consequence from their apparent links with the Canadian government. It was, Alexander Begg wrote in 1869, known that the Schultz 'clique' were in communication 'with the chief men' in Ottawa, while Mactavish reported that the 'chief cause of [Métis] hostility' was that they thought the Canadian officials who came to Red River were 'too intimate with Dr. Schultz and his party' and that they acted 'under the doctor's influence'.[62]

The first such 'officials' came in 1868 to start building a road to Lake Superior – both to provide relief in a year of crop failure, and to establish a direct link that would facilitate the intended Canadian takeover. They also, until Mactavish intervened, bought land from the Indians some of it already claimed by Red River settlers. And they sent letters back to Canadian newspapers: Bannatyne recalls these as maligning the Assiniboia Council and 'stating that they would soon have another Government there, and then they would teach ... the people in the territory about law'. He did not add that the letters' comments on half-breed women had led his wife to take a riding whip to one of the correspondents.[63]

By mid-1869, Mactavish was reporting 'considerable excitement' at the prospect of being transferred to Canada.[64] Yet both London and Ottawa concentrated entirely on arrangements with the HBC's directors and shareholders. Nothing was done to take precautions on the ground, and little to address local concerns. In 1868 the Anglican Bishop of Rupert's Land, Robert Machray, had written to the Colonial Secretary to ask for a small detachment of troops, as there was 'imminent risk any day of some outbreak leading to the utter prostration of law and order'. He added that before sanctioning the transfer to Canada,

---

[62] ed. W.L. Morton, *Alexander Begg's Red River Journal and other papers relative to the Red River resistance of 1869-70* (Toronto, Champlain Society, 1956) pp. 157-8; Mactavish to the HBC's W.G. Smith, 7 Sept. 1869 (ibid. p. 14n.)
[63] *Select Committee Report* p. 123; *Dictionary of Canadian Biography*, 'Bannatyne, Andrew Graham Ballenden'
[64] Mactavish to W.G. Smith, 24 July 1869 (Bartlett, *Mactavish* p. 203)

the Colonial Secretary should see whether there were any questions that needed 'to be set at rest by imperial authority'; and he stressed that any transfer should include 'proper provision for the tenures and titles of the present occupiers of land'.[65] The advice was sound. But London was trying to shed, not assume, colonial burdens, and in 1868-9 it thought only of brokering a deal between Canada and the HBC. Yet after the deal's conclusion in the spring of 1869, there would still just have been time to send out troops by the traditional Hudson's Bay route; and once stationed at Red River, their presence would almost certainly have averted the subsequent troubles.

Machray also blamed the Canadian government, both for not sending out troops (100, he thought, would have been enough), and for its almost complete misunderstanding of Red River opinion. It 'seemed to believe that the people ... were oppressed by the Company ... and ... looking so impatiently for the Advent of Canada that there had to be little care as to the arrangements for that Advent'. But only people like Schultz and the *Nor'Wester's* editor W.R. Bown thought like this, as Ottawa would have realised had it sent out 'a Statesman of judgement and experience' to check on their reports. This 'Series of Government blunders' was completed by the HBC's London management, which 'thought only of their shareholders' and forgot the responsibilities of the authority they were surrendering. So neither they nor the Dominion gave any reassurances as to 'the character or policy of the new Government', and nothing was done 'to set at rest the doubts of the malcontents'.

It has, indeed, been suggested that the Canadian government disregarded explicit warnings of a coming Red River insurrection. But this developed quickly in October-November 1869, and even then came as a surprise. When Governor Mactavish and the Roman Catholic Bishop Taché were in Ottawa that summer, they cannot have had foreknowledge of rebellion, but merely concerns

---

[65] Machray's later account to Governor General Young, 18 March 1870 – Morton, *Begg's Red River Journal* pp. 502-10 (esp. p. 504)

as to the type of behaviour that was likely to be resented, or even blocked, by the kind of direct action that was by no means unprecedented in the Settlement. That said, Canadian ministers declined to listen to HBC officers or those close to them. Mactavish told Taché that he had, in mid-summer, been unable to get Ottawa to accept any of his recommendations, for 'These gentlemen are of opinion, that they know a great deal more about this country than we do.' Taché, too, voiced his private apprehensions to Cartier in mid-July, but he was an opponent of Confederation: Cartier brushed him off, supposedly saying 'he knew it all a great deal better than I did, and did not want any information'. And when Taché made a further effort in October, he was refused an interview. He did write advising against sending McDougall out as Governor-designate, but by then it was too late.[66]

Bishop Taché wanted Ottawa to send Commissioners to ascertain popular feelings and report on steps that would be 'satisfactory to the people' – including popular election of some of the new governing council. He would also have liked to see Mactavish reappointed as Governor. When London took British Columbia from the HBC in 1859, it continued Douglas as Governor, and this had proved a success. But Mactavish was ill (in fact dying) and eager to quit, as was his *de facto* deputy, Judge Black. Rather than go down this road, Ottawa selected William McDougall as the prospective Lieutenant-Governor. The choice was a natural one, given McDougall's long-standing involvement with the acquisition of Rupert's Land; but he was an Ontario Protestant who had once described French Canadians as 'a foreign race' and their creed as 'not the religion of the Empire'. A Roman Catholic Quebecker would have been better.

That said, Canada's approach was more cautious than is sometimes suggested. Howe, now the responsible minister, did pay Red River a flying visit in October 1869. He earned brownie

<hr>

[66] Taché's testimony (*Select Committee Report* pp. 10-14) in 1874, by which time, admittedly, Cartier was dead and unable to give his version; Bartlett, *Mactavish* p. 404; Beccles Willson, *The Life of Lord Strathcona and Mount Royal* i (Boston, 1915 edn.) p. 300n.

points by not accepting hospitality from Schultz; and he reported that 'by frank and courteous explanations to leading men who largely represent the resident population', he had done much to 'clear the air' of 'absurd rumours'. Unfortunately, the source of trouble was to prove not so much the 'resident population' as the mobile Métis, the carters, boatmen, and buffalo hunters who that month returned to the Settlement for the winter; and they were not really to be reached through private conversations with 'leading men'. To get reassurances across, Howe would have had to go public. But though he was in the Settlement at the time when Métis activists started to block land surveys, Howe refused to 'speak at a public meeting'.[67] Such meetings were later successfully held in far more fraught circumstances, so this may have been a missed opportunity.

Canadian reassurances would have been partly, but only partly, in order. McDougall had been told to go to Red River to set things up in advance of its takeover. He should offer Council seats to Mactavish and Black, and put forward, as prospective Councillors, 'several of the residents of character and standing in the Territory, unconnected with the Company'. There was meant to be a fair degree of continuity with the current Council of Assiniboia. And if McDougall's instructions left open the possibility that people like Schultz would figure among the 'residents of ... standing', after his visit to Red River Howe strongly advised McDougall to turn, not to Schultz's 'clique', but to Mactavish and 'the more influential elements of society'. Reprehensibly, neither this letter nor McDougall's instructions addressed the vital question of the current settlers' land rights.[68]

---

[67] Howe to Macdonald, 10 Oct. 1869 (Willson, *Lord Strathcona* i p. 256); A.C. Roberts, 'The Surveys in the Red River Settlement in 1869', *The Canadian Surveyor* 24 (1970) p. 247

[68] 28 Sept. 1869, Preliminary instructions to McDougall, *Correspondence and Papers connected with the Recent Occurrences in the North-West Territories* (Ottawa, 1870 – Canada, Sessional Papers, 1870 vol. v no.12 – hereafter *Sessional Paper*) pp. 153-4; Howe to McDougall, 31 Oct. 1869 (Willson, *Lord Strathcona* pp. 262-4). See more generally, Ged Martin, 'Manitoba

But there was no intention to trench on these. Where there were 'ranges of farm lots laid out by the [Hudson's Bay] Company', Ottawa meant to leave these 'intact as independent grants'. And Colonel Dennis, the survey director, published in the *Nor'Wester* the assurance that 'his instructions are to respect the grants made by the Company' and to survey other existing holdings with a view to 'giving to the owners proper deeds confirming the titles'. His new 'township surveys' would only apply to lands 'not yet granted or ... still unsettled'.[69] There were, then, grounds for Ottawa's denial of any intention of 'ignoring the municipal and political rights of the people of the North-West'.[70] But that said, the whole point of taking over Rupert's Land was to make possible settlement on a scale that was both bound to transform society and meant to do so. McDougall was accordingly to report on the lands 'it may be desirable to open up at once to settlement', and to submit a plan showing 'the number of Townships' that were to be laid 'out at once'.[71] Privately, Macdonald wrote that while 'it will require considerable management to keep those wild people quiet', in 'another year the present residents will be altogether swamped by the influx of strangers'.[72] Any judgement of McDougall's intentions, though, can only be academic, since he was barred from entry into the Territory.

At Red River the news that Canada had paid £300,000 for Rupert's Land did not go down well. Almost everybody felt payment should have been made to them, not to shareholders in London; senior HBC personnel also believed they had legal rights

---

Report – Parts 1, 2. Report for the Department of Justice ... Re: Manitoba Metis Federation et al. vs. A.G. of Manitoba and A.G. of Canada' (accessed 4/2/20)
[69] Memorandum from the Minister of Public Works, 22 Sept. 1869 (*Sessional Paper* p. 152); J.S. Dennis' testimony, 21 May 1874 (*Select Committee Report* p. 186); Roberts, 'Surveys in the Red River Settlement' pp. 241-2
[70] Howe to the Very Rev. Thibault, 4 Dec. 1869 (*Sessional Paper* pp. 45-6)
[71] Dennis' 12 Feb. 1870 'Rough Diagram ... intended to illustrate Report on Township Surveys' (facing p. 1 in Morton, *Begg's Red River Journal)* indicated sites for five Townships north of the settlements along the Assiniboine
[72] Macdonald to J.Y. Bown, 14 Oct. 1869 (Library and Archives Canada, MIKAN 542766)

to compensation deriving from their position as 'winterers' under the merger between the North-West Company and the HBC.[73] But discontent first came to a head when 'Canadians' were seen staking out land claims close to the parish of St. Norbert. A local meeting, called after mass on 4 July, organised patrols to protect Métis lands. The prosperous Métis William Dease, an Assiniboia Council member, then summoned another meeting through an insert in the Nor'Wester that was read out after services in a number of parishes. At this meeting Dease declared that the £300,000 was not owed to the HBC, and advocated overthrowing the local HBC government, seizing its funds, and setting up an independent government 'to treat with Canada or any other country'. Though Dease had his supporters, something, perhaps the insert in the Nor'Wester, led the St. Norbert curé Father Noel Ritchot to suspect that he had links with Schultz; and the clergy coached John Bruce to speak successfully against him. Métis Community leaders called various follow-up meetings. But, according to Ritchot, they gave up over the summer, whether through lack of energy or through pessimism as to the outcome of the enterprise. However some Métis, 'galvanised by one of their young men' [Louis Riel], met to see whether means could be found 'at least to make a clear protest against the injustice and injury done to the nation by Canada'.[74]

That autumn the combination of Dennis' surveys, McDougall's imminent arrival as Governor-elect,[75] and the seasonal return to

---

[73] Duane C. Tway, 'The Wintering Partners and the Hudson's Bay Company, 1867-1879', Can.H.R. 41:3 (1960) pp. 215-223

[74] Philippe R. Mailhot, Ritchot's Resistance: Abbé Noel Joseph Ritchot and the Creation and Transformation of Manitoba (University of Manitoba, D. Phil. Thesis, 1986) pp. 16-21, 29-30 - Mailhot draws extensively on a notebook in the Parochial Archives of St. Norbert, Manitoba, the Cahier Historique I containing 'a narrative of the early stages of the Resistance in Ritchot's handwriting', and cites, inter alia, Father Georges Dugas's 24 July 1869 letter to Taché; Bartlett, Mactavish pp. 209-11

[75] Already by 29 August Father Dugas reported talk of telling McDougall, on his arrival, 'to take the road back to Toronto'; and on 11 Sept. the US Consul, Oscar Malmros, reported that the 'mass of the settlers' were strongly inclined 'to get up a riot to expel the new Governor on his arrival here' – Dugas to Taché (Morton,

Red River of Métis transport workers and buffalo hunters generated a perfect storm. In some places, it was later reported, recent Canadian arrivals had marked off for themselves 'extensive, and exceptionally valuable tracts of land, thereby impressing ... the people with the belief that the time had come when, in their own country, they were to be entirely supplanted by the stranger.'[76] Dennis declared these land claims invalid, and thought he had reassured the people he talked to. He stressed the Canadian government's intention to 'deal honourably and fairly' and inserted in the *Nor'Wester* his assurance that it meant to issue deeds confirming existing land titles. Also, on 31 August, he called not only on Governor Mactavish but on the Catholic priests at the Palace of St. Boniface. The latter professed themselves satisfied, and promised to explain things to their people. But they did not deliver.[77] And the issue was too good for activists to neglect.

Louis Riel had earlier warned surveyors off land near Oak Point. He now saw Dennis, was apparently convinced that the Métis need have no fear for their lands, but still told the crowd after mass next Sunday 'to organize and prevent the Canadian Government coming in until their just claims were recognized and settled'.[78] Then on 11 October he led seventeen armed Métis in halting a survey party near St. Vital. Dennis complained to Dr. Cowan, who summoned Riel to an interview. Riel declared

---

Begg's Red River Journal p. 410); Malmros to J.C.B. Davis (ed. Hartwell Bowfield, *The James Wickes Taylor Correspondence 1859-1870* (Vol. III, Manitoba Record Society Publications, 1968) p. 82)

[76] D.A. Smith to Howe, 12 April 1870 (hereafter Smith's Report) – CO 880/4/26, Confidential Print, 'Correspondence relative to the recent disturbances in the Red River Settlement' [20 Aug. 1869-9 June 1870], p. 175

[77] Roberts, 'Surveys in the Red River Settlement' pp. 238-40; W.L. Morton's Introduction to *Begg's Red River Journal* p. 39. Father Lestanc, in charge of the diocese during Bishop Taché's absence, is said initially to have declined to try to influence his people as it might suggest that the Church 'was in sympathy with the Government' and so weaken its religious influence' (CO 880/4/24, Confidential Print, 'Memorandum regarding the disturbances in the Red River Settlement' p. 2)

[78] Mailhot, *Ritchot's Resistance* pp. 29-30; Dennis' testimony, *Select Committee Report* pp. 186-7; Roberts, 'Surveys in the Red River Settlement' p. 239

that the party had had no right to survey, or indeed to be in the Settlement at all. Cowan countered that the operation had been sanctioned by the HBC and would do the people no harm. Next day Riel was taken to see Mactavish, who repeated that he was acting illegally, and that the survey would not affect people's land rights. Riel, however, would not back down; he was ready to go to prison if jailed. This, Mactavish believed, would only invite further trouble. So Dennis' complaint was dropped.[79] Riel's defiance had proved successful, but Mactavish saw it as a purely political move:

'The men who have thus interfered say they know the survey could proceed without injury to anyone, but stopping it was always a beginning; and they are desirous to let the Canadian Government know that it is not wanted by them; that ... if the Canadians wanted to come here, the terms on which they were to enter should have been arranged with the local government here, as it is acknowledged by the people.'[80]

Thereafter, Métis resistance developed rapidly. Riel had been training for the priesthood in Montreal but had dropped out and drifted gradually back to his mother in Red River, arriving in 1868. He had discussed 'the changes which were preparing for our country' with his friend Louis Schmidt, and the two had agreed to take a hand when the time came. The disengagement of more established community leaders opened the way for Riel; and there were first 'small secret meetings', then 'more numerous assemblies'.[81] If the surveys furnished the first opportunity, rumours attending

---

[79] Roberts, 'Surveys' pp. 243-7
[80] Mactavish to W.G. Smith, 12 Oct. 1869; Mactavish had already written on 16 August that it would have been better if surveys had not started 'till the Canadian Government was in authority here', and that he expected the Métis and Indians to stop them 'until their claim [to the land] is satisfied' (Bartlett, *Mactavish* pp. 212, 214-15)
[81] 'Les Memoires de Louis Schmidt, 8 Juin 1911' (typescript copy, Morton MSS Collection, University of Saskatchewan, http://scaa.sk.ca/ourlegacy/permalink/ 25702) pp. 68, 71

McDougall soon provided a better. On the Sunday after the 11 October confrontation, Riel supposedly claimed that Ottawa meant 'to take their farms from the French half-breeds and give them to Canadians' and urged people to prevent McDougall's entry.[82] McDougall was known to be bringing rifles and was wrongly believed to be escorted by a small army. To counter this, Métis organisation grew apace. The various parishes had in 1868 chosen representatives to apportion famine relief, and meetings were now again held to select Councillors. These met on the 20th at Bruce's house and resolved to institute the 'laws of the prairie, according to the custom of the country'.[83] Captains were sent out to meet McDougall's supposed army, 'which advances into the country ... in the name of a foreign power, whose authority is absolutely unrecognised by the nation'. But next day, when it became apparent that McDougall's party was no army, a note from the 'National Committee of the Métis' was substituted, ordering him 'not to enter the North-West Territory without a special permission from this Committee'.[84]

A fence was erected in St. Norbert across the trail from Pembina, and people came in to man it – the more readily since many were now back from the Prairies with no occupation for the winter. Had the original timetable for a Canadian takeover on 1 October been adhered to, with McDougall arriving in advance during the summer, it would have been less easy to find people to bar him. As it was, there were by 28 October some 150 men at the barricade, fed by Ritchot on condition that they left his chickens alone. Not everybody approved. Dease made two efforts to get the barricade removed, the second at the request of the Council of

---

[82] Dennis' 12 Jan. 1870 letter to the *Globe* – Morton, *Begg's Red River Journal* p. 487

[83] For these 'laws' governing the conduct of the buffalo hunt, see George F.G. Stanley, 'The Half-Breed "Rising" of 1875', *Can.H.R.* 17:4 (1936) p. 401

[84] Mailhot, *Ritchot's Resistance* pp. 33-6; Mailhot draws on Ritchot's *Cahier II*, 'the Minute Book of the Métis Council, which sat for the most part in Ritchot's Presbytery. Although Riel was the Secretary of these meetings, the notes are in Ritchot's hand'

Assiniboia. On the 27th he came to a meeting with eighty 'of the more respectable [members] of the French community'. Though present, Father Lestanc took little part in the proceedings; but Ritchot 'was very violent in favour of the insurgents, calling upon them to maintain their ground.' The upshot was that twenty of Dease's men changed sides to support the resistance.[85]

The resistance leaders Bruce and Riel had been summoned before the Assiniboia Council, which Riel treated to an impressive exposition. His 'party were perfectly satisfied with the present [HBC] Government', but objected to one 'coming from Canada without their being consulted' and would never admit any non-HBC Governor

> 'unless Delegates were previously appointed with whom they might negotiate as to the ... conditions under which they would acknowledge him; ... [the Métis] were uneducated and only half civilized and felt that if a large immigration were to take place they would probably be crowded out of a country which they claimed as their own; ... it was just because they were aware [that they were 'poor and insignificant'] ... that they had felt so much at being treated as if they were even more insignificant than they really were; ... their existence, or, at least their wishes had been entirely ignored; ...if Mr. McDougall were once here most probably the English speaking population would allow him to be installed as Governor and then he would be our "Master" ... therefore they intended to send him back...'

In so doing, they were acting 'for the good of the whole Settlement', and they wanted the aid of 'their English speaking fellow countrymen ... in securing their common rights'. There might be some opposition from the local 'Canadians', 'but for that they

---

[85] Mailhot, *Ritchot's Resistance* pp. 33-40; Dennis to McDougall, 27 Oct. 1869 (Oliver, *The Canadian North-West* p. 882); 'Memorandum regarding the disturbances in the Red River Settlement' pp. 4-5

were quite prepared'. Though Riel was unmoved by the Council's criticism, he agreed to put it to his party and later report back to the Governor – which he did in no uncertain terms: the 'English' might be willing to let 'the Canadian Government establish itself here' and question

'the conditions later if they were going badly, but this is not the way we choose to do it. It is, it seems to us, only simple prudence to prevent the wolf's entry into the sheep-fold ... [rather] than have to throw it out later. To us, the Canadian Government, that is the wolf ... We remain loyal subjects of Her Majesty, but we refuse point-blank to recognize the authority of Canada.'[86]

Later, Mactavish had a three-hour session with Ritchot. What he made of it is unclear, but his expectations will not have included the actual outcome – Ritchot's return to his party declaring that the Governor was 'favorable to their designs'.[87]

Meanwhile the Governor and Council had to decide on a response to the Resistance. Had he been well, Mactavish would, his secretary believed, have gone 'up to bring in Mr. McDougall', and 'in spite of everything, [have] been able so to exert his influence as to break up the affair'.[88] Not all Métis thought it wise to bar McDougall's entry, and the Governor's intervention just might have tipped the scales. But though he still conducted business, Mactavish was too ill even to attend Council meetings. In Council, Bishop Machray urged putting down the rising by force; and he still felt next year that an 'Active Man of Spirit at the

---

[86] Assiniboia Council Minutes, 25 Oct. 1869 (Oliver, *The Canadian North-West* pp. 616-18); Bartlett, *Mactavish* pp. 234-5, 454; 'Memorandum regarding the disturbances...' pp. 3-4

[87] Judge Black said after the interview that Mactavish had failed to bring Ritchot to reason, Dr. Cowan some years later that Mactavish had communicated his impression that Ritchot would help in restoring order. Both sources agree as to Ritchot's subsequent behaviour (Dennis' narrative of events, 28 Oct. 1869 – *Sessional Paper* p. 25; Cowan's 1874 testimony, *Select Committee Report* p. 128)

[88] J.J. Hargrave, *Select Committee Report* p. 185

head of Affairs might perhaps have ... trampled it out', though he admitted that 'in the then temper of the English Section' a call for Special Constables might not have had much of a response. In any case, Machray had stood 'alone'. The Council considered escorting McDougall in by a roundabout route or else sending 300 unarmed men to bring him along the direct road. But it feared that even these courses would precipitate 'a collision between different sections of the people, which might plunge not only the settlement but the whole [North-West] Territory, into all the disasters of a war of races and religions'. And on 30 October they advised McDougall to stay in Pembina pending 'a peaceful dispersion of the malcontents'.[89] So Riel had gained his point by being ready to risk communal conflict when most of his potential opponents were not. This pattern would be repeated.

While the formal authorities were thus inactive, Riel's Resistance was not. He had told Council on the 25th that he was happy with the 'present [HBC] Government'. But his group had already styled itself, in its message telling McDougall to keep out, 'The National Committee of the Métis of the Red River'; and following Dease's challenges to its authority, it moved quickly to formalise its position with resolutions providing for the choice of a President, Vice President, and Secretary. On 30 October the laws of the prairie were endorsed by a mass meeting as a legal code for the Métis, and a Council (including Ritchot) was sworn in. So when McDougall's Secretary reached St. Norbert on 1 November, he was told his exposition of Canada's good intentions came too late – the Métis had already formed a government, framed a constitution, and held elections.[90]

The decisive step, however, came on 2 November, when Riel's men occupied Fort Garry, the HBC post at the heart of the

---

[89] Machray to Young, 18 March 1870 (Morton, *Begg's Red River Journal* p. 507); minutes of the 25 Oct. 1869 Assiniboia Council meeting, and Mactavish to McDougall, 30 Oct. (Oliver, *The Canadian North-West* pp. 618, 585-7); 'Memorandum regarding the disturbances...' pp. 4-6
[90] Mailhot, *Ritchot's Resistance* pp. 52-4, 56-7; J.A.N. Provencher to McDougall, 3 Nov. 1869 (*Sessional Paper* p. 28)

settlement. In an exculpatory letter Mactavish later asserted that neither he nor Cowan had had any reason to anticipate this seizure. Schultz, though, claimed that there had been twelve hours' warning;[91] and in 1874 Cowan testified that he and Mactavish *had* considered putting Fort Garry into a state of defence, but had decided not to since they 'could not get a sufficient force to do so, those who were best affected to the Company [the Métis] being then in insurrection'.[92] It is easy for historians to second-guess such decisions, and it is true that on the afternoon of the 2nd Cowan had only fourteen men (plus the invalid Governor). But the gates were not even closed; and this inaction contrasts with Douglas' demonstrative manning of Fort Vancouver in 1848 against the possibility of seizure by Oregon's anti-Indian expedition. Fort Vancouver was, of course, stronger than Fort Garry. But the latter also had both guns and defences; and while one can understand a reluctance to turn to the 'Canadians', there were 'loyalists' from both other communities who had offered their services to resist McDougall's entry. Protecting the Governor would have been less controversial. And an open attack on Fort Garry would have been an act of rebellion against a government that still retained some legitimacy, hence something people might have been reluctant to undertake.

As it was, Riel's men moved quietly through Fort Garry's open gates and refused to leave, saying they had come to protect it

---

[91] Letter 'supposed to be from Dr. Schultz, and others' to McDougall, 5 Nov. 1869 (*Sessional Paper* p. 31); W.R. Bown also talked of prior warnings in his somewhat imprecise 1874 testimony (*Select Committee Report* p. 114)

[92] Mactavish to Howe, 14 May 1870 (Bartlett, *Mactavish* pp. 244-5); Cowan's 1874 testimony, *Select Committee Report* p. 128. Bishop Taché, a leading member of the Council, also described the Métis as 'the party on whom the Government had for several years relied for assistance in difficulties'. He thought the past behaviour of the 'Canadian' party such that it was 'almost impossible' for the Government to call on them for assistance, and he doubted whether the Anglophone half-breeds would have responded. So he felt that the only resource available would have been the few (elderly) remaining Chelsea pensioners. Taché also claimed that the seizure of the Fort took the Government by surprise; but he was himself abroad at the time (ibid. p. 13)

from the 'danger' of McDougall's appearance before the Fort.[93] Though they promised not to stay long or touch anything, they stayed put; and there could be no question of dislodging them that winter: it would have needed field guns to blow down the walls; the Fort held almost all such guns in the Settlement, and none could come from Canada or Britain until after the spring thaw. Meanwhile, Riel could use Fort Garry as a centre of power to conduct business, hold prisoners, and keep the Governor under house arrest. Its possession also enabled him to retain the men he soon came to call his 'soldiers' throughout the winter, something St. Norbert's resources would not have stretched to. Riel was soon drawing first on the HBC's food stores, then on its money. And this financial self-sufficiency also meant that he did not need the money that some of his Minnesota well-wishers would gladly have supplied in hopes of edging him towards declaring the full international independence that they saw as leading inevitably to joining the United States.

Riel always sought the Anglophones' support – on his own terms – not merely because this would strengthen his negotiating hand, but because they and the Métis were really one people. To this end, on 6 November, the 'President and Representatives of the French-speaking population' invited their 'friendly fellow inhabitants' to send twelve representatives from their parishes 'to form one body' with the existing French Council of Twelve 'to consider the present political state of this Country'. The invitation was accepted, and a first meeting of the resultant 'Convention' was held in Fort Garry on the 16th. In some ways the two groups were not that far apart. For when the French presented their 'List of Rights' – 'the conditions upon which the people of Rupert's Land would enter into Confederation' with Canada – there was little dispute.[94] There was, though, no agreement as to the proper way to obtain them. The 'English' protested against 'the taking up

---

[93] Mactavish to McDougall, 9 Nov. 1869 (*Sessional Paper* pp. 53-4)
[94] Morton, *Begg's Red River Journal*, 1 and 5 Dec. 1869, pp. 193, 209-10; 'Louis Riel's Notes of the Sessions of the November Convention of English and French, November 16 to December 1, 1869' (ibid. pp. 420-28)

of arms by the French, against their seizure of the Fort, and against their illegal opposition' to McDougall's entry. Such acts of rebellion were, they thought, both morally wrong and potentially disastrous: 'we shall draw down on the colony misfortunes such as it has never known', with perhaps 'a military expedition against us, if we do not act with moderation'. Riel, by contrast, denied that they had in any way acted against 'the English Government' or the Queen in rebelling 'against the Company which sold us and … Canada which wants to buy us'. Nor did he fear military coercion: 'winter will protect us with its snows and storms … Hudson's Bay, Thunder Bay, and the American territory are not easy barriers to break in order to reach us here in the spring … we have six months before us and … during that time we shall have a settlement with Canada'.

Matters were further complicated when Riel persuaded the Métis to declare their organisation a 'Provisional Government'. Even though it was often colloquially styled 'government', Riel had to overcome his colleagues' 'incredible misgivings', chiefly their fear of 'the appearance of a rebellion against the Queen'. He countered by protesting, probably sincerely, 'that we remain faithful to the Queen'. Indeed, if she 'knew what we wanted, she would listen to us.' By contrast, the current 'Government of Assiniboia' was 'only a name', too weak to protect them, and, if it made contact with McDougall, likely to deliver them into his hands. With such arguments he induced his colleagues to go forward, and to invite the 'English' to join in forming 'a provisional government for our protection and to treat with Canada'. Perhaps surprisingly, the invitation was not turned down. Some intense politicking outside the Convention came up with a compromise that would have retained the existing Council of Assiniboia as a legislature but provided for an elected 'Executive Council' to conduct negotiations with McDougall. Riel, however, backed out of this. And though the Convention, when it resumed on 1 December, could agree a 'List of Rights', it broke up over how this should be negotiated. An angry Riel then told the 'English' to return to their farms, but 'watch us act. We are going to work and obtain the guarantee of our rights and yours. You will come to share them in the end.'[95] One doubts whether Riel had encountered Rousseau during his training for the priesthood. But he behaved as if he, and that majority of the Métis which followed him, incorporated the general will of the whole Red River settlement.

McDougall had not liked the Assiniboia Council's advice to stay out of the Territory. He stressed that, as Governor, Mactavish was legally required to 'resist any lawless exhibition of force', and he urged a Proclamation. In reply, Mactavish explained why he had not gone beyond informal attempts to procure McDougall's entry, adding that, since this now seemed impossible, McDougall should return home. McDougall thought this a 'somewhat extraordinary communication'. His informants told him that most HBC officers were 'either actively or tacitly encouraging the insurrection'. So he decided to 'force the [HBC] authorities into a public declaration' that would either disprove this or compel them 'to show their hand'. To that end, he encouraged 'the loyal inhabitants' to lobby the Governor.[96]

---

[95] *Begg's Red River Journal*, 27 and 30 Nov. 1869, and Riel's Notes of the November Convention (Morton, *Begg's Journal* pp. 188, 190, 428); 'Memorandum regarding the disturbances' p. 16 prints the 'List of Rights'

[96] McDougall to McTavish, 2, 4, and 7 Nov. 1869, and to Howe, 13 and 20 Nov., Mactavish to McDougall, 9 Nov. 1869 (P.P. 1870 l pp. 21-3, 31, 36-9). Whether some HBC officers encouraged Riel's Resistance was debated both at the time and later. Their Governor, Sir Stafford Northcote, made enquiries when in Ottawa in 1870. Schultz thought HBC officers had done so but would name no names. McDougall named Sheriff McKenna and the postmaster Andrew Bannatyne (members of the Assiniboia Council, though not HBC employees) and the HBC supply clerk at Fort Garry, John M'Tavish. Donald Smith felt that some HBC officers 'had connived at, or even encouraged,' Riel's proceedings, named M'Tavish, and implied that Bannatyne was strongly influenced by his wife 'who took Riel's part in the early days of the troubles'. Judge Black did not believe any HBC officers 'had abetted Riel's movement, though some had, perhaps, been lukewarm', and explained that all M'Tavish had done 'was to endeavour to keep on good terms with those who had the power'. It was widely felt that the officers were less able than in the past, were upset by receiving nothing from the North-West's sale to Canada, and were demoralised by the prevailing inflation. But Bishop Machray did not think this dissatisfaction 'had anything to do with these troubles' – Northcote's Diary, 21, 23, 24, 29 April, and 6 May, 1870 (*Diaries 1869, 1870, 1875, 1882, of the First Earl of Iddesleigh* (privately printed, 1907) [hereafter *Iddesleigh Diaries*] pp. 109, 110-11, 116, 120, 127-8, 148-9)

Mactavish did issue the Proclamation. But the way in which the *Nor'Wester* greeted this showed that it was 'in secret contact' with McDougall; had McDougall, Mactavish later wrote, deliberately 'set himself to damage his cause in the estimation of the' Métis, 'he could not more effectively have done so'.[97] In response the 'Representatives of the [French-speaking] people in Council' adopted a 'Declaration of the people of Rupert's Land and the North-West' to the effect that they had 'established a Provisional Government, and hold it to be the only and lawful authority now in existence in Rupert's Land and the North-West'. Riel also occupied the public offices in Fort Garry with their records and papers and made prisoners of the officers in charge of public funds.[98]

The Proclamation not having gained McDougall entry, he concluded that he would have to make his own arrangements. He knew the Canadian takeover of Rupert's Land had been set for 1 December; and though he had been told not to act on this without further instructions, he decided to anticipate these. So he crossed into British territory, and on 1 and 2 December issued Proclamations announcing Red River's transfer to Canada, his own assumption of office as Governor, and Mactavish's consequent displacement. McDougall also commissioned Dennis to act as his 'Lieutenant and a Conservator of the Peace', with power to 'attack, arrest, disarm or disperse the ... armed men so unlawfully assembled and disturbing the public peace', and to call on support 'in the name of ... the Queen'.[99]

Dennis reached Winnipeg early on 1 December. That evening, after showing his Commission to its keeper, he took possession of

[97] Mactavish to Howe, 14 May 1870 (Bartlett, *Mactavish* p. 263)
[98] 'Memorandum regarding the disturbances' pp. 6, 15-16. The 'Declaration of the people' (published only on 8 December) resembles the US Declaration of Independence, but also proclaims 'readiness to enter into such negotiations with the Canadian Government as may be favourable for the good government and prosperity of the people'
[99] Alexander Begg, *The Creation of Manitoba; or a History of the Red River Troubles* (Toronto, 1871) pp. 130-3

'Stone Fort', which was some way from the centre of the Settlement and smaller than Fort Garry but the only other fortified post. There he was joined by Swampy Indians, fifty of whom he retained to guard the Fort. Next day he received many promises of recruitment, and he wrote telling McDougall to get ready to come in when summoned. Thus encouraged, McDougall declared himself confident that this display of 'determination to ... maintain by force, if need be, the authority of the New Government' would 'compel the Traitors ... to cry, "God save the Queen," or beat a hasty retreat'.[100]

The confidence proved misplaced. Already by 4 December Dennis was ordering Schultz and his adherents to withdraw from their exposed position in Winnipeg, adding *'You speak of enthusiasm. I have not seen it yet with anybody* but' the Swampy Indians. Most Anglophones disapproved of Riel's actions but felt that as Canada had got them into the mess it was its job to get them out. Other inhibiting factors probably included the false rumour that 1100 formidable Sioux were moving on the Settlement,[101] and the 4 December publication 'List of Rights', whose demands many people found attractive.[102] The Anglophone tendency, therefore, was towards non-involvement. By contrast, a

---

[100] Dennis to McDougall, 2 Dec. 1869, and McDougall to Howe, 6 Dec. (P.P. 1870 l pp. 63-5)

[101] Schultz apparently sought support from the Sioux at Turtle Mountain, but the Métis 'plain hunters' persuaded them to keep quiet. Report spread that McDougall was behind this approach. He admitted to threatening 'the insurgents and their annexation leaders with an Indian as well as a civil war, if they persisted', but did nothing to actualise this, evading offers from several Indian chiefs to help deal with Riel; and he told Dennis to stop using even the Swampy Indians lest their employment excited 'the war-spirit of more distant bands, who may not be so easily restrained'. However he sent to tell Chiefs around the Lake of the Woods that the Queen might 'want them to help her soldiers to make war against the French in the early spring'; McDougall was probably thinking of logistic assistance to a Canadian expeditionary force, but the Canadian government scrambled to find the messenger and recover McDougall's letter – Begg, *Creation of Manitoba* pp. 146, 148-9; McDougall to Howe, 29 Nov. and 8 Dec. 1869, and to Dennis, 8 Dec. (P.P. 1870 l pp. 56, 86-92); Confidential Print CO 880/4/25, 'Memorandum relating to the Disturbances in the Red River Settlement. (Continued...)', p. 1

[102] Begg, *Creation of Manitoba* pp. 146, 148, 152-3, 157, 159

report that men were assembling to attack Fort Garry led Métis previously opposed to Riel's party to ask to be allowed to join it. This, Begg commented, 'shows that when it comes to fighting all the French will join together no matter what their differences may be now.'[103]

The end came swiftly. Schultz's adherents had refused to evacuate his house, where they were guarding the 'government pork' originally intended for the survey parties. On 7 December Riel brought cannon from Fort Garry and gave the defenders fifteen minutes to surrender before he opened fire. They all did, and were marched off to captivity in the Fort. Next day Dennis received from Bishop Machray an appeal not to fight: success was unlikely, and, anyway, a victory would be only slightly less fatal 'to the Settlement and the interest of the Canadian Government than a defeat'. On the 9th Dennis issued a 'Peace Proclamation' calling things off, and on the 11th he left for Pembina. By the time he got there, McDougall too had decided to go back to Canada.[104]

The capture of Schultz's party was followed next day by the formal announcement of the 'Provisional Government', and two days later by the hoisting of its flag (white, with a fleur-de-lis). Over the next month the government's structure was fleshed out. A 'Military Council' was added, with Riel as Commander-in-Chief and tribunals operating what was termed 'martial law'. A £10,000 loan was demanded of Mactavish; he refused, but the Government helped itself to the HBC safe in Fort Garry containing £1090.[105] On 27 December Bruce gave up the Presidency on grounds of health. Riel succeeded, and appointed ministers, including, as Treasurer, the controversial Irishman W.B. O'Donoghue.

By now Riel was very much in charge, and the question was what use he would make of his power. In his heart of hearts he may have wanted more,[106] but he always said his aim was to

---

[103] *Begg's Red River Journal*, 3 Dec. 1869 (ed. Morton, p. 198)
[104] Begg, *Creation of Manitoba* pp. 161-5, 173-9, 183
[105] 'Memorandum relating to the disturbances' pp. 8-9
[106] In mid-1869 he had put to Ritchot projects that the priest, though he hoped 'Providence could at least use them for the honour of the Métis nation', was

secure acceptable terms on the basis of which Red River would join Canada. There must, though, have been at least a tacit fall-back position in case Canada refused to negotiate. And this became apparent in January when the HBC postmaster, Andrew Bannatyne, agreed to join the Provisional Government: the object, it was then said,

> 'was to treat if possible with Canada for a just union with that country or England – failing these two to look elsewhere... It is to be understood that Annexation to the States is not the direct policy of the Provisional Government – Mr. Bannatyne declares himself a loyal subject of Great Britain but if utterly ignored by that country he is ready to follow the general voice of the people in whatsoever direction is found to be for the good of the settlement.'[107]

Riel's movement, though, did not always seem to adhere to these priorities. From the beginning, Minnesota expansionists had latched onto it: Riel's former Secretary Louis Schmidt wrote of 'their constant efforts to shake our British allegiance and draw us into their Republic', and said Riel was offered 'large sums of money ... and also men and munitions to repel Canadian troops' should they try to force their way into the country.[108] This was penned long after the event. But Begg observed at the time that some Americans were trying to 'mislead' Riel towards 'annexation to the States. H.S. Donaldson, Major Robinson, Oscar Malmoras [recte Malmros, the US Consul in Winnipeg] and Stutsman at Pembina are all admitted to the secret councils'; and he cited a

---

unable to bless 'because of the near impossibility of their success'. Ritchot later tore his description of these projects from the record (Mailhot, *Ritchot's Resistance* p. 33). So they must have been something other than the aim Riel both declared and achieved, the negotiation of satisfactory terms for accession to Canada

[107] *Begg's Red River Journal*, 6 Jan. 1870 (ed. Morton, p. 253). Begg and Bannatyne were on close terms

[108] 'Les Memoires de Louis Schmidt' p. 86. Admittedly, Schmidt was concerned to stress Riel's 'Loyalty to England' and resistance to such temptations

letter from Enos Stutsman giving Riel tactical advice and sending regards to 'friend Donohue'. Already by early November Malmros had reported that though some people wanted to become a British Crown Colony, the likelihood was that 'the country' would soon 'be a unit in favour of independence, ie., annexation to the United States' and that 'should this revolution be successful', within 'two years ... all the British Colonies on this Continent will apply for admission into the Union'. Malmros did his best to forward this, managing in late December to get the first issue of Riel's new semi-official paper, the *New Nation,* to lead with an article he had dictated, 'Annexation Our Manifest Destiny'. On 6 January 1871 he boasted to Minnesota's Senator Ramsey that without outsiders suspecting his 'real position', he had 'materially assisted in producing the present situation' and 'prevented many mistakes on the part of the popular leaders'; and on the 15th he urged the State Department to give Riel $25,000 'to secure the success of the independence movement'.[109] It seemed, Begg wrote on 26 December, to be Riel's intention 'to declare for [Red River's] independence – be recognized by the United States and afterwards be admitted into the Union as a Territory'. And when Macdonald's agent Donald Smith arrived at Fort Garry on the 27th, he felt that the 'drift of the whole thing is annexation'.[110] That said, the annexationist tide soon went into decline; in early February a ball for Washington's birthday had to be cancelled for want of funds; and people came to believe that Riel 'had only been making use' of the Americans 'to answer his own purposes'.[111]

---

[109] *Begg's Red River Journal,* 26 and 27 Dec. 1869 (ed. Morton, pp. 240, 242); Alvin Gluek, 'The Riel Rebellion and Canadian-American Relations', *Can.H.R.* 36:3 (1955) pp. 202-6

[110] *Begg's Red River Journal,* 26 Dec. 1869; Pope, *Correspondence of Sir John Macdonald* p. 114. Another of Macdonald's agents, Jean-Baptiste Thibault, also observed that when he reached Red River, 'everyone ... spoke of annexation to the States' (to Howe, 20 March 1870 – 'Correspondence relative to the recent disturbances' p. 182)

[111] Gluek, 'The Riel Rebellion' pp. 206-7; Begg, *Creation of Manitoba* pp. 197-8, 201

Once Sir John Macdonald realised that McDougall might well be kept out of Red River, he suspended Canada's payment to the HBC and refused to take the Territory on in its present lawless condition. He worried that if HBC authority lapsed while Canada was unable to govern in the area, the Provisional Government might '*ex necessitate*' acquire a legal status that the US might be tempted to recognise. But reassurance came when these fears were referred to London, and the Crown's Legal Officers advised on 21 December that they were 'unfounded'.[112] Macdonald's second action was to send out two French-speakers, Grand Vicar Jean-Baptiste Thibault and Colonel Charles de Salabery, who might be expected to be well received in Red River. They were to explain Canada's good intentions; and they were briefed with arguments proving that 'it would be hopeless to expect any aid' from the US government 'even should the people wish to substitute republican institutions for the authority of the Queen', while they would in any case be far better off as a Canadian province than as a US state.[113] But Macdonald did not look only to diplomacy. For it was soon arranged that the senior HBC officer in Montreal, Donald Smith, should also go out, ostensibly only as an HBC officer but carrying a Canadian Commission. He took a letter to McDougall, saying Macdonald hoped that, while Thibault and de Salabery were 'acting upon' the Métis, Smith would 'organize the English and Scotch half-breeds & the whites, who are loyal to Canada'. McDougall should 'sit down with these gentlemen & lay out a plan of operations', seeking, through Thibault and de Salabery, to bribe 'the prominent Insurgents' – given the 'enormous' 'cost of sending a Military Force' to Red River, it would be well worth spending 'a considerable sum of money buying off the Insurgents'. McDougall should also 'arrange with Mr. Smith a plan by which he might ...

---

[112] Ged Martin, *Manitoba Report ... for the Department of Justice ... Re: Manitoba Metis Federation ... vs. A.G. of Manitoba and A.G. of Canada, Part 2* (accessed 12/2/20)
[113] Morton, *Begg's Journal* pp. 81-2n.

without observation, organize a body of Scotch and English to take possession of Fort Garry...'.[114]

By the time the Commissioners reached Red River, McDougall had left the region. So there could be no question of the kind of coordinated policy Macdonald had sketched. Thibault and de Salabery eventually met Riel's Council, but this lost interest in them when it transpired that they could not treat on the terms for an accession to Canada. What followed is unclear. Malmros reported that de Salabery had, 'rather inopportunely', been allowed to talk with 'a number of people', and had managed to create 'a desire of negotiating with Canada'.[115] And Thibault later claimed that, through cautious 'conversations with single individuals', he and de Salabery had done much to secure the despatch of Red River delegates to negotiate in Ottawa.[116] Smith, as we shall see, thought very differently. Though Riel restricted his movements, he managed to work through his half-breed brother-in-law Richard Hardisty. He had, he later reported, found the Anglophones 'greatly divided' between union with Canada and 'the formation of a Crown colony', and had managed to swing opinion towards the former.[117] Smith had also set out to 'secure partisans'. One tool, noted by Malmros, was the offer of summer employment as HBC boat and trip men;[118] and, as Smith's biographer puts it, 'where promises would not serve, pecuniary

---

[114] Macdonald to McDougall, 12 Dec. 1869 (Library and Archives Canada, MIKAN 543527). Smith was also to put 'back-bone' into Governor Mactavish, with whom McDougall should be careful to 'act in Concert'

[115] Malmros also wrote that he had been 'reliably reformed' that de Salabery had tried to bribe Riel and been 'contemptuously refused' (to J.C.B. Davis, 15 Jan. 1870 – *James Wickes Taylor Correspondence* pp. 107-8). Begg, too, recorded unsuccessful offers 'from Canadien sources to Riel to make a pecuniary settlement of the difficulties' (ed. Morton, *Red River Journal*, 26 Dec. 1869, p. 241)

[116] Thibault to Howe, 17 and 20 March 1870 ('Correspondence relative to the Recent Disturbances' pp. 180-2)

[117] Smith's Report p. 175

[118] Malmros feared poverty might force the Métis to succumb to such 'tempting offers' but told Acting Secretary of State Davis that $25,000 'promptly sent' would counteract them – 15 Jan. 1870 (*James Wickes Taylor Correspondence* pp. 107-8)

bribes', generally of less than £10, 'proved effective'.[119] But Smith and Hardisty also tapped into the growing belief that Riel was going too far. Even before Smith's arrival, Charles Nolin had left Riel's Council;[120] he came to head a small but significant opposition fraction. Smith had early concluded that no good would come of negotiating with Riel's Council. Instead, he worked with people like Nolin to restore Mactavish to power, and indeed rumours reached Ottawa that this had been effected. Fairly soon, Riel demanded to see Smith's Canadian Commission. This Smith had left on American soil for safe-keeping; and there ensued a struggle between adherents of Riel and of Smith for its possession that could easily have led to shooting.[121] Smith's group, led by Pierre Leveiller, won, occasioning great 'excitement', and Leveiller's group 'insisted upon keeping a guard in the Fort [Garry] as well as Riel's men'.[122] Riel and Smith agreed that there should be a mass meeting of the whole settlement; and on 18 January Smith told Macdonald he hoped this would agree to appoint delegates with whom he would negotiate 'for the transfer of the territory to Canada'.[123] But then, Smith later complained, 'Thiebault & Salabery ... spoilt the chance of an arrangement which had been almost made when Père Lestanc [Bishop Taché's deputy] got hold of Thiebault & took him [at 3 am.] to talk to the French [in Fort Garry] who were falling off from Riel, the end of

---

[119] Willson, *Lord Strathcona* pp. 328-30. In 1874 Smith said he had given £500 'to the loyal French half-breeds, whose assistance had been absolutely necessary in my position as Canadian Commissioner' – *Select Committee Report* p. 94
[120] *Begg's Red River Journal*, 23 and 24 Dec. 1869 (ed. Morton, pp. 238-9)
[121] For this episode, and the complicated politics of the next couple of months, see Morton's Introduction to *Begg's Red River Journal*, Stanley's *Louis Riel*, and Smith's Report (the Confidential Print, 'Correspondence relative to the recent disturbances in the Red River Settlement' version of which (pp. 169-76) contains passages omitted in the published official papers)
[122] 'Memoirs of Louis Schmidt', and *Begg's Journal*, 18 Jan. 1870 – Morton, *Begg's Red River Journal* pp. 265, 469
[123] Smith to Macdonald, 18 Jan. 1870 (Pope, *Correspondence of Sir John Macdonald* p. 120)

which was that they all returned to their allegiance to him.'[124] The alternative view, voiced by the Chaplain to Riel's 'soldiers', was that but for 'Father Lestanc and G.V. Thibault blood would have run'.[125]

As it was, over a thousand people trooped in to Fort Garry on 19 and 20 January to listen to lengthy speeches in the intense outdoor cold (-20° F.) but the only outcome was agreement that the 'English' and 'French' communities would each elect twenty representatives to consider 'Mr. Smith's commission, and ... what would be best for the welfare of the country'.[126] Many of these elections were genuinely contested, with Riel gaining only seventeen of the French seats and Nolin three. The resultant Convention drew up both a structure for a new Provisional Government and a new 'List of Rights' to be demanded of Canada. Over this Riel was twice defeated when Nolin's group sided with the 'English': for the Convention voted not to insist on joining Canada as a Province (rather than a Territory), and not to seek to annul 'all bargains with the Hudson's Bay Company for the transfer of this territory'. On 8 February Smith was asked to comment on the List. He could accept some of the demands but said others would have to go to the Canadian government, and he suggested sending delegates to Ottawa to discuss them.

At this point Riel demanded that the Convention recognise his Provisional Government. Some people still regarded Mactavish and his Council as the legitimate government, so a group was sent to seek his consent. Mactavish would not delegate his powers, but

---

[124] Sir Stafford Northcote's account (to Sir Curtis Lampson, 21 April 1870 – British Library Add. MS. 50,056 fos. 14, 15) of Smith's complaints; cf. also Smith's more inhibited Report pp. 170-1, 175, which locates Lestanc's and Thibault's visit on the night before the first mass meeting, not, as is sometimes stated, on that between the two meetings. Begg notes de Salabery's presence in Fort Garry, but says nothing about his behaviour – *Journal*, 18 Jan. 1870 (ed. Morton, p. 265)

[125] Father Giroux to Taché, 12 Feb. 1870 (Morton, *Begg's Red River Journal* p. 387n.)

[126] *New Nation* report, quoted in *Begg's Journal*, 20 Jan. 1870 (ed. Morton, p. 275)

told them to go ahead, form a government, 'and restore peace and order to the Settlement'. The structure of this government was then quickly agreed. But on 10 February there was a final row over whether Riel should become President or go with the other delegates to negotiate in Ottawa. Riel again blew his top. He was then voted into office, and promptly nominated the delegates: Ritchot, Judge Black, and the 'American' Alfred Scott. Everybody spilled out in relief to celebrate, setting off the fireworks Schultz had originally procured to welcome McDougall.

All, however, was not well. For Riel had been slow to release his prisoners. Though some of those taken in December had been discharged and others, including Schultz, had escaped, several remained. There had been calls at the January meetings for their release. But Riel had demurred, indeed had (as we shall see) added to their number in February. Then, to secure acceptance of his Provisional Government, he promised their release. The most eminent were promptly freed, but there were problems over the remainder. Under the reluctant leadership of a Major Boulton, a party (chiefly of youngsters who 'thought the whole thing a splendid idea') set out to liberate them. Their progress from the most remote parish, Portage la Prairie, was slowed by a mammoth blizzard, but resumed on 14 February. An attempt to seize Riel at the house outside Fort Garry where he often slept failed, as he was not there. So did a move to contact Dease and enlist Riel's Métis opponents. But Schultz (and the Swampy Indians) did rise, and Schultz' men marched to the Scottish parish of Kildonan, singing a variant of a well-known Jacobite song:

'Hey, Riel are ye waking yet
Or are ye're drums a-beating yet,
If ye're nae waking, we'll nae wait,
For we'll take the fort this morning.'[127]

---

[127] Stanley, *Louis Riel* p. 388n.

In Kildonan their enthusiasm evaporated in the face of discouragement from the Protestant ministers. Meanwhile, though, Boulton's party had, in a sense, achieved his objective – release of the prisoners. For news of its march had led Riel to resume their discharge. The chief delaying factor was now the refusal of many to swear not to oppose his government. But on 15 February Bannatyne (who was always anxious to seek out compromise) and a young Canadian visitor, Miss MacVicar, managed to persuade the recalcitrant that they were really only being asked to keep the peace.[128] They then took the oath and were freed. This news further dampened the insurgents' ardour, as did a tragic shooting that heightened fears of civil war.[129] So an insurgent 'Council of War' asked for official confirmation of the release, demanded a general amnesty, and declared that four 'English' parishes would not recognise the Provisional Government. Riel's response was uncompromising: 'although the President desired peace, he was fully ready for war.'[130] Rapid Métis mobilisation showed that there was no chance of upsetting his Government. Schultz prudently fled the country, and most insurgents decided to go home. Unfortunately the Portage la Prairie contingent passed by Winnipeg, perhaps believing they had a safe-conduct, and were seized and taken prisoners to Fort Garry.

Riel had never been notable for self-restraint, but that February he was unusually tense and volatile – on the 24th he would be briefly struck down by 'brain fever'. On losing a vote in the Convention on 5 February he had burst out: 'The devil take it; we must win. The vote may go as it likes; but the measure ... must be carried' and rounded on 'those traitors', Nolin's group. Then on the 10th, when his election as President was in question, he threatened the representatives of the western parishes with war in a fortnight if they did not support him and declared that 'if the

---

[128] *Begg's Journal*, 15 and 16 Feb. 1870 (ed. Morton, pp. 308, 310-11, 315)
[129] In trying to escape from the insurgents, Norbert Parisien shot and killed a bystander. On his recapture, Parisien was so beaten that he later died. These were the first casualties of the Resistance conflict
[130] 'Memorandum relating to the Disturbances in the Red River Settlement. (Continued...)' p. 5

prejudices of your people are to prevail, they may do so, but it will be in my blood'.[131] Nor had Riel stopped with words. Following his outburst against Nolin, he stormed at Cowan and Mactavish, threatening to shoot them 'within three hours', sent Cowan to a prison cell, and placed a 'close guard' on Mactavish. Next day Bannatyne was also jailed when he insisted on seeing Mactavish, and an attempt was made to add Charles Nolin, though it was resisted and would have led to casualties had the guns on both sides not misfired.[132] But Riel had not, in the end, killed anybody.[133] Now he wanted blood. Four of the Portage prisoners were promptly sentenced to death, and though Riel quickly reprieved three, he insisted that Major Boulton must die next day. Figures of all persuasions in the Settlement flocked to persuade him to relent, Miss MacVicar flinging herself melodramatically on her knees crying, 'Mercy! Mercy! Mercy!'[134] For a long time Riel said he would do so only if Schultz could be captured and shot instead. He said the English, and more especially the Canadians, despised the Métis, 'believing that they would not dare to take' anyone's life; 'under these circumstances it would be impossible to have peace and establish order in the country; an example must therefore be made'. However, after long argument with Donald Smith, Riel switched course and, in effect, traded Boulton's life for an undertaking by Smith to use his influence to get the 'English' to elect Councillors and accept the Provisional Government. Riel then woke Boulton up to announce his reprieve and, on the rebound, tried to persuade him to join that Government as leader of the 'English people'. Boulton finessed that offer, but Smith redeemed his promise. With Archdeacon McLean, he toured the

---

[131] Stanley, *Riel* pp. 94, 98; *Begg's Red River Journal*, ed. Morton, Introduction p. 99, and 5 Feb. 1870 (p. 296)

[132] Mactavish to W.G. Smith, 12 Feb. 1870 (Bartlett, *Mactavish* pp. 305-6); Stanley, *Riel* p. 95; *Begg's Journal*, 6 Feb. 1870 (ed. Morton, pp. 297-8)

[133] A captured insurgent messenger, William Gaddy, was condemned to death. But this may have been only for show, since the firing party merely told him to leave the country and keep quiet – Morton, *Begg's Journal* p. 313n.

[134] *Begg's Journal*, 20 Feb. 1870 (ed. Morton, p. 318)

English parishes persuading them to hold elections to the Provisional Council, on the basis that this would secure 'the transference of the country to Canada' and in the meantime assure safety of life and property.[135]

Riel had thus obtained, with the blessing of Macdonald's Commissioners, the regime he had long sought – a 'Provisional Government' under his control, but formally accepted by both halves of the Red River community. He quickly blighted this achievement. For on 3 March news broke that Thomas Scott had been condemned to death by a kangaroo 'court martial'. Scott had been a consistent opponent: captured at Schultz's house in December, he had escaped, joined the February rising, and been captured again. He had not been among the people Riel initially proposed to shoot, but he had insulted and got across his jailers. Many of these may have wanted to punish him. But two of his judges had favoured a lesser penalty, and Riel could quite well have commuted the sentence. The general expectation was that he would, but this time Riel refused all pleas. Scott, Riel said, was a bad man who had insulted his guards and dissuaded some prisoners 'from making peace; so I must make an example to impress others and lead them to respect my government.' 'We must make Canada respect us.'[136]

Regimes have sometimes gained status by thus taking life. But Scott's execution was 'worse than a crime, a blunder'. Admittedly, its immediate effects were slight: in Red River it was met with no more than sullen acquiescence; nor did it prevent the successful negotiation of adhesion to Canada. But fanned by Schultz, by the nationalist 'Canada First' group with which he had links, and by Scott's brother, the news aroused demands for vengeance in Orange Ontario, and countervailing Quebec sympathy for the Métis.[137] Looking to both provinces for support, Macdonald's

---

[135] Smith's Report p. 173; Stanley, *Riel* pp. 109-10

[136] Smith's Report pp. 174-5; Stanley, *Riel* pp. 111-15; Morton, *Begg's Journal*, Introduction pp. 110-16

[137] Even within the government, Hector Langevin ('the representative of the purely French section') pressed Smith to drop from his report 'passages which reflect on the French party and the priests', while Morris ('who speaks for the

government did its best to dodge the issue. No real effort was made to bring Riel to justice. But equally he could not, as Macdonald had originally hoped, be brought into the Canadian establishment as a Senator,[138] or even be allowed to sit as an MP. Instead, Riel was kept dangling until 1875 when he was finally accorded an amnesty conditional on his leaving Canada for five years.

This, though, still lay in the future. In Red River the situation seemed to depend on the success of the delegates sent to Ottawa to present 'the terms upon which the people of Assiniboia will consent to enter into confederation'[139] – a former Minnesota Governor, visiting on railway business, would be told in April that if the Provisional Government's demands were met, Riel would lead the North-West into Canada, but if not, he would seek American aid.[140] Meanwhile, the next noteworthy event was Bishop Taché's return. He had been summoned back from Rome by a penitent Canadian government, and now carried both copious assurances of its goodwill and assurances that Red River's delegates would be well received. Initially they were not. For Ontario was so aroused by Scott's execution that Ritchot and Scott had to bypass it and be escorted to Ottawa by the Intelligence chief Gilbert McMicken. Once there, a private prosecution (Colonel Dennis' s idea[141]) secured their arrest as accessories to murder, and this in turn angered Quebec. It took ten days for counsel (quietly briefed by the government) to secure their discharge, and serious talks did not start until 25 April. The political background was not propitious.

---

opposite school') wished him to omit 'what reflects on the Canadian Govt & Macdougall' – Northcote to Lampson, 26 April 1870 (Add. MS. 50,056 fo. 26)
[138] 'There is no place in the ministry for him to sit next to [Nova Scotia's] Howe,' Macdonald had written before hearing of Scott's execution, 'but perhaps we may make him a senator for the [North-West] Territory!' – to Sir John Rose, 23 Feb. 1870 (Pope, *Correspondence of Sir John Macdonald* p. 128)
[139] The words of the delegates' 22 March commission from the Provisional Government (Stanley, *Riel* p. 123)
[140] Governor Marshall's conversation with O'Donoghue and Riel himself, as described in N.P. Langford's 10 July 1870 letter to James Wicke Taylor (Gluek, 'The Riel Rebellion' p. 207)
[141] Northcote's Diary, 22 April 1870 (*Iddesleigh Diaries* p. 113)

For there seemed to be a real possibility of Cartier's losing control over his Quebec MP's, which would have collapsed the government. So it is not surprising that, on the Canadian side, he and Macdonald conducted the negotiations on their own, telling their colleagues very little. For the delegates, Ritchot made the running, with Black sometimes seeking compromise, and Scott allegedly more interested in the hotel bar.[142]

The Red River Convention had elaborated a 'List of Rights' to be put to Ottawa. But with characteristic disregard for the constitution he had just helped frame, Riel discarded this, giving the delegates new instructions and then supplying Ritchot with a yet further list. This insisted that 'the territory of the North-West' should only enter Canada 'as a province, ... with all the rights and privileges common to the different Provinces of the Dominion', and that its 'Local Legislature' must have 'full control over all the lands of the North-West'.[143] Cartier and Macdonald would have preferred Red River to enter as a Territory, but they were ready to see it a Province, 'Manitoba', and to settle matters relating to its representation in Ottawa, and to its constitution and finances. But they made it clear that Manitoba could not incorporate the whole North-West, and instead proposed limited 'postage-stamp' boundaries; these the delegates accepted, provided they gave the new province access to both Manitoba Lake and Lake Winnipeg.[144]

---

[142] The reports Northcote sent back to London in April recur repeatedly to political difficulties and the threat they posed to the Cartier-Macdonald relationship. Northcote also said the Governor-General seemed 'to know very little' of how the talks were going, while Howe (the minister departmentally responsible) and Hincks were 'also in the dark'; he himself owed what knowledge he had of 'what is passing with the two chief Ministers' to Judge Black and Donald Smith – Northcote to Granville, and to Lampson, 26 April 1870 (Add. MS. 50,056), and to Disraeli, 28 April (Add. MS. 50,016 fos. 78-80)

[143] The Third and Fourth 'List of Rights', clauses 1 and 11 – W.L. Morton, *Manitoba: the Birth of a Province* (Vol. 1, Manitoba Record Society Publications, 1965) Appendix 1 (which also prints the First and Second Lists)

[144] Ritchot's 'Remarks on Twenty-Six Clauses [of the draft of what became the 'Manitoba Act'] April 28 and 29, 1870', appended to his 'Journal' of his time in Ottawa (translated in Morton, *Birth of a Province* pp. 157-60); Macdonald's 2 May 1870 speech in Parliament (*Ottawa Times*, 4 May 1870, reprinted in

Far more difficult was the issue of who should control the unoccupied ('waste') land within Manitoba. For this went to the heart of the Métis 'Resistance'. Bishop Machray thought that the fundamental cause of the troubles was that the Métis would not permit any considerable immigration 'unless they can raise some breakwater'; he believed the rights they had demanded in the Convention 'are not what they really care for ... they wish for a section of the country to be restricted to the French population'. And Riel did indeed instruct Ritchot, albeit too late to influence the negotiations, to 'demand that the country be divided in two [by the local Legislature] so that this custom of the two populations living separately may be kept for the safeguarding of our most threatened rights'.[145]

Macdonald told Northcote (who was in Ottawa, discretely observing proceedings) that 'we do not mean to give the local legislature power over the lands, because we have to provide for the extinction of the Indian title, for our engagements to the H.B.Co., and for the construction of a Railway.'[146] Judge Black thought this reasonable, but Ritchot forced him to admit that Red River would never accept federal control of the lands *tout court*. Ritchot therefore asked again for 'the control of those lands as requested in our instructions'. But when told this was 'impossible', he switched to seeking 'compensation or conditions which for the population actually there would be the control of the lands of their province'; and this opened the way to haggling.[147] Macdonald and Cartier offered, besides confirmation of existing holdings, 100,000 acres 'to be bestowed on the children of the métis'; in

---

'Correspondence relative to the Recent Disturbances' p. 200). Ministers wished to keep Portage la Prairie out of Manitoba to serve as the nucleus of a future purely English Province but were forced by Parliamentary opposition to change course in Parliament and include it. Ritchot would have liked to extend Manitoba east to the Lake of the Woods, but feared this would cause further trouble

[145] Machray to Governor-General Young 18 March 1870 (Morton, *Begg's Journal* p. 506); Riel to Ritchot, 19 April 1870 (*Collected Writings of Louis Riel,* i *1861-1875*, ed. Gilles Martel p. 86)

[146] Northcote's Diary, 2 May 1870 (*Iddesleigh Diaries* p. 134)

[147] Ritchot's Journal, 26 and 27 April 1870 (Morton, *Birth of a Province* p. 140)

reply Ritchot suggested that current settlers should each be able to select 200 acres, as should, for 50 to 75 years, all their descendants on reaching the age of 16, 'with a safeguarding law to keep the land in the family'. Such an indefinite prolongation of the process would have been unworkable, and the negotiators shifted to determining an immediate total entitlement, the ministers offering 350,000 acres and Ritchot claiming three million. They agreed on 1,200,000 (raised to 1,400,000 when Portage la Prairie was added to Manitoba).

Ritchot thought they also agreed that the provincial legislature should oversee the selection of these lands, distributing them to 'heads of families in proportion' to their current number of children, and perhaps passing 'laws to ensure the continuance of land in the métis families'. The government's understanding was rather different. Cartier told Northcote that when blocks of land were set out for development, each recognised Métis claimant 'would receive an order entitling him to claim his allotment at any time' (just as the HBC would claim its twentieth share as agreed in 1869). The process would, Macdonald explained, be controlled by the federal government, 'taking care not to put' the Métis 'all together'.[148] Unsurprisingly, the Bill introduced into Parliament followed this understanding. The Red River delegates accepted that it would be counter-productive to try to amend its wording, but they secured a promise that, before they left Ottawa, an Order-in-Council would provide for a committee 'to select these lands and divide them among the children of the half-breeds'. The committee's members were to be jointly agreed; Macdonald began by proposing Bishop Taché, with Ritchot tactfully then suggesting Bishop Machray. But nothing further happened, and though Ritchot pressed repeatedly he could get no more than an assurance from Cartier that the regulations governing the 1.4 million acres

---

[148] Ritchot's Journal, 26 April to 2 May 1870 (Morton, *Birth of a Province* pp. 97, 103, 140-3), and Northcote's Diary, 2 and 4 May (*Iddesleigh Diaries* pp. 134, 142). Though Riel's 19 April letter envisaged a distinct block of land on which the Métis would live separately, Ritchot always said claimants should be able to select land wherever they pleased

reserved for 'the families of the half-breed residents' would be of a nature to meet Métis wishes and 'guarantee in the most effectual and equitable manner, the division of that extent of land amongst the children of the heads of families of the half-breeds' resident in Manitoba at the time of its transfer to Canada.[149]

If the question of land was difficult, that of amnesty for all actions committed during the Resistance was, given the storm Scott's 'execution' had aroused in Ontario, quite impossible. Ritchot had at first declared a general amnesty to be 'a condition *sine qua non* of any settlement.' But conceding this, a memorandum by Cartier later explained, would have split the Canadian government and prevented any settlement. So Macdonald and Cartier argued that amnesty could come only from Queen Victoria, partly because she had, in December 1869, already issued a Proclamation bearing on the topic, and partly because Canada had no authority over Rupert's Land when the offences were committed. They also gave copious assurances, though never in writing, that they would join in persuading Victoria to grant a full pardon, and that it could easily be obtained. 'Without these assurances', Cartier's memorandum declared, 'it is more than probable' that the delegates 'would not have felt themselves justified in negotiating.'[150] Cartier got Ritchot to petition the Queen and wrote his own supportive memorandum. These were forwarded to London with the plea that, in view of 'the jealousies and animosities' the issue raised in Ottawa, the Imperial Government would itself 'pronounce on the question'. But this refused to act unless asked to do so not merely by individual ministers but formally by the Dominion Government. The parcel was passed to and fro across the Atlantic, but no such collective

---

[149] Ritchot to Cartier (who was now running the government following Macdonald's near-fatal collapse), 18 May 1870, and Cartier's 23 May reply (*Select Committee Report* pp. 73-4)

[150] 'Memorandum on a general Amnesty, prepared by ... Sir George Etienne Cartier for the Governor-General, July 26 1870' (Morton, *Begg's Journal* pp. 554-7)

request was ever forthcoming, and no formal amnesty was forthcoming until 1875 (below, pp. 848-9).[151]

In Red River, people were pleased by news of the Manitoba Act, but unclear as to whether a general amnesty had or had not been granted. They knew troops were being sent out, and some people thought of raising a force to oppose them. To counter such ideas, Bishop Taché took it upon himself to promise, in the name of the Canadian government, that 'a complete and entire amnesty (if not already bestowed) will surely be granted before' the troops' arrival.[152] Ritchot, too, was determinedly optimistic, and he returned to a Red River very ready to believe in his achievements: it 'now seems', noted Begg, that Ritchot's mission had been very 'successful ... and it is rumoured that a general amnesty is to be declared', or even that Ritchot was carrying one. In January Riel had insisted on seeing the Canadian Commissioners' exact powers, but now he went along with the general euphoria. So Ritchot's report to the Legislature on the doings in Ottawa was, Begg says, adjudged 'very favourable. The Assembly accepted the terms and a special messenger is to be sent' to invite the prospective Lieutenant-Governor 'to come in immediately'. 'It appears', Begg continued, 'that an amnesty has been granted by promise of Sir Clinton Murdoch and [Governor-General] Sir John Young as special commissioners from the crown'; and the troops would not leave [Canada] till they had heard that the Provisional Government (which both 'England and Canada fully recognized') had accepted the Ottawa terms. 'This 24rth day of June therefore is the turning point in the affairs of the Settlement. Some of the members of the Legislative Assembly got drunk ... in honour of the occasion.'[153]

---

[151] CO 880/6/70, Confidential Print, 'Proposed Amnesty to the Red River Insurgents', 3 July 1873. The Colonial Secretary noted that Cartier's Memorandum had 'not been submitted to his colleagues, and that he is not inclined to open a discussion upon the subject with them' (30 June 1870 – ibid. pp. 4-5)

[152] Taché to Howe, 9 June 1870 (Morton, *Begg's Journal* pp. 550-3)

[153] Begg, *Red River Journal*, 17, 20 and 24 June 1870 (ed. Morton, pp. 382-5)

Such enthusiasm was, no doubt, chiefly felt by the Provisional Government and the Métis. For Begg also noted an 'English' feeling 'that the French are getting all the concessions and they nothing', while Bishop Machray recorded 'much feeling ... on the subject of an Amnesty' for Scott's 'deliberate murder': though not wanting the death penalty, 'the body of the people here will feel deeply' if nothing was done to vindicate the law. Machray also condemned the grant of land 'to the half breed part of the community' as 'a most dangerous provision', and deprecated any 'attempt to limit a special tract of the country to a special class of the people and religion'.[154] Trouble was therefore likely in the future. But for the time being, both sides of the Red River community could look forward to the advent of Canadian rule.

Negotiating with the Red River delegates had constituted only half of Macdonald's policy. For he always retained 'the unpleasant suspicion' that Riel was 'only wasting time by sending this delegation, until the approach of summer enables him to get material support from the United States'. Terms might be agreed with the delegates, 'but that will not prevent Riel from refusing to ratify the arrangement, if he pleases'. So, while receiving the delegation 'with all kindness' and making 'an arrangement with them', 'we shall, at the same time, prepare' for a military expedition 'to leave by the end of April or the beginning of May'.[155] But though Canada was 'strong enough to enforce her authority ... unaided', Macdonald needed a contingent of regular British troops. For the view was common in the US,

'and has, *we know*, got possession of ... the President and his Cabinet, that England wants to get rid of the North-West if possible, and will not willingly raise her hand to retain it.

---

[154] Machray to Governor-General Young, 16 July 1870 (Morton, *Begg's Journal* pp. 560-1)
[155] Macdonald to Sir John Rose, 11 March 1870 (Sir Joseph Pope, *Memoirs of the Right Honourable Sir John Alexander Macdonald...* ii (London, 1894) pp. 62-3)

A mixed force will also show that England and Canada are acting in complete accord & unity in the retention of British North America under British Sovereignty.'[156]

As for the North-West, any 'one who knows the country and its people will acknowledge the influence which the Queen's name and the emblem of her power possess. No force which either Canada or the Hudson's Bay Company could exercise could take its place – the announcement that she will intervene to enforce order will go far to accomplish it' – whereas the locals might see in 'the absence of any imperial Troops ... a reason why they should attack any Force of another kind'.[157]

The use of 'Imperial' troops had been canvassed from the outset. In December 1869 both the HBC's Governor Sir Stafford Northcote and the eminent, though now 'semi-detached', Canadian politician Sir Alexander Galt urged Lord Granville 'to take the Red River into the hands of the Imperial Government and to settle the questions that had been raised before transferring it to Canada'. And as soon as he heard of McDougall's exclusion from Red River, Sir John Rose, the banker who operated as Macdonald's representative in London, asked Granville to assure the Governor-General that 'the weight of the Queen's authority' would be 'extended to enforce the orderly establishment' of government there. Since the Métis respected that authority, Rose believed that 'the co-operation of even one Company of Her Majesty's Forces' would lead to a speedy back-down by 'the designing men' who, 'for their own purposes', had 'stirred up the

---

[156] Macdonald to Rose, 5 Feb. 1870 – C.P. Stacey, *Canada and the British Army 1846-1871* (Toronto, 1963 edn.) pp. 234-5.

[157] Macdonald's paper 'Canada and the North-west', his 26 Jan. 1870 letter to Rose, and 'Memorandum respecting the Force to be sent to Red River', all enclosed for Granville's benefit in Rose to R. Meade, 17 Feb. 1870 – 'Correspondence relative to the Recent Disturbances' pp. 348-52

difficulty'. Privately he suggested that the mere promise of a company of Rifles would be 'sufficient'.[158]

Granville did indeed ask Gladstone in November whether he might promise Canada the company of troops 'in case they are wanted some months hence'. But nothing came of this. Instead, Canadian views were sought on another of Northcote's suggestions, that a 'Commission' 'composed of English public men of position and others' should be appointed for Red River. Granville tactfully added that this would, of course, require the concurrence of the Canadian government. But he reverted to the idea when Bishop Taché passed through London on his way back from Rome: would not Taché's 'hands be strengthened' by a Royal Commission 'with or without representatives of Imperial and Colonial Governments, and of [Hudson's Bay] Company or population'?[159] Neither Taché nor Macdonald thought so: 'to send out an overwashed Englishman, utterly ignorant of the country and full of crotchets, as all Englishmen are, would be a mistake. He would be certain to make propositions and consent to arrangements which Canada could not possibly accept.'[160]

Macdonald's reaction on hearing that McDougall had been barred from Red River had been that 'We have certainly no intention of giving up the country, and we shall make preparations for operations in the spring, *via* Fort William'. He did, though, for the benefit of the London government, draft a Minute to the effect that every 'other course should be tried before resort is had to force': Commissioners had been sent to remove 'misapprehensions' and 'reconcile the people to the change' from HBC to Canadian

---

[158] Northcote's Diary, 11 May 1870 (*Iddesleigh Diaries* p. 153); Northcote to Disraeli, 28 April (Add. MS. 50,016 fo. 80); 'Memorandum by Sir John Rose', accompanying his 22 Nov. 1869 letter to Granville ('Correspondence relative to the Recent Disturbances' p. 345), and Granville to Gladstone, 29 Nov. (Ramm, *The Political Correspondence of Gladstone and Granville* no. 165)
[159] Granville to Gladstone, 29 Nov. 1869 (Ramm, *Political Correspondence* no. 165), and Granville's cables to Governor-General Young of 29 Dec. 1869 and 25 Jan. 1870 ('Correspondence relative to the Recent Disturbances' pp. 221, 223)
[160] Macdonald to Rose, 21 Jan. and 23 Feb. 1870 (Pope, *Correspondence of Sir John Macdonald* pp. 121-2, 127)

rule, and it was 'confidently hoped' that they would succeed. But in case they did not, his Government was making preparations to send 'a Military Force in early spring'. Personally, Macdonald told Rose, he did not expect the Commissioners to succeed; and should they fail, 'the only thing left is the preparation of an expedition in the spring, *via* Thunder Bay.' 'In this view, we must know what Her Majesty's Government will do'.[161]

In London, the Red River question continued under discussion.[162] But Granville had come to 'doubt the expediency of sending Imperial troops', and in late January 1870 Sir Curtis Lampson found him determined to await 'further information before taking any decided stand'. Indeed, Lampson gained the impression, though he stressed only the 'impression', that 'if the Insurgents continue in force, and a majority of people at Red River wished annexation to the United States the Government' might negotiate with the United States.[163] However in February Granville proved more forthcoming. Rose had been told that Macdonald's preparations were well advanced. Volunteers would be forthcoming, but some British regulars would be needed – chiefly for their moral effect, though they should also bring mountain guns 'to shell the forts in case they are held'. Rose was to put this to Granville, aided by a powerful Memorandum demonstrating that Canada, the HBC, and the Imperial Government all had a common interest in such action, and that 'employment of the Queen's troops under such circumstances' was, though unusual, not unprecedented. A more formal request duly followed in the form of a Canadian Privy

---

[161] Macdonald to McDougall, 27 Nov. 1869, his Privy Council Minute, sent by Governor-General Young to Granville on 17 Dec. 1869, and his 31 Dec. 1869 'Private' letter to Rose – 'Correspondence relative to the Recent Disturbances' pp. 29, 61-2; Pope, *Memoirs of Macdonald* ii pp. 60-1

[162] Granville called on Gladstone 'about the Red River' (Granville to Gladstone, 25 Jan. 1870 – Ramm, *Political Correspondence* no. 195), and a 'Memorandum regarding the Disturbances in the Red River Settlement' (CO 880/4/24) was printed for the Cabinet on 31 January

[163] Granville's 25 Dec. 1869 minute (CO 42/679, cited by George F. G. Stanley, *The Birth of Western Canada* (Toronto, 1960 edn.) p. 129); Lampson to Northcote, 31 Jan. 1870 (Add. MS. 50038 fos. 58-9)

Council minute seeking 2-300 'of Her Majesty's light troops now in Canada' plus some light artillery, with the Governor-General asking for a reply by cable.[164] Rose had already discussed the question with Granville, and he now cabled Macdonald 'to the effect that Her Majesty's Government will co-operate in the expedition'.[165] So it is not surprising that on 5 March Granville told the Cabinet that, 'in concert' with the Secretary for War and the Prime Minister, 'he had found it needful ... to afford some military aid' to establish order in Red River. Then, armed with Cabinet approval, he conveyed this to Ottawa by telegram.[166]

Gladstone, however, got cold feet. He had, he told Granville, 'thought the armed force was only to subdue outliers not to overawe the community'; and he now wondered whether it had been an error to hand 'the Red River people to ... Canada without their consent'. He raised the possibility of holding a plebiscite, and trusted that things could be settled 'by negotiation before May when the force moves'. Granville replied that the 'Red Riverites' should have been, not 'consulted', but 'managed'. As to a plebiscite, it would be 'a farce to collect the votes ... of a few hundred Europeans and ten thousand half savages scattered over this vast territory. (Not to mention the Indians.)' The 'best way of getting the assent of the people' would be by dealing with the delegates now being sent to Ottawa. The Canadians were 'fully alive to the extreme danger of bloodshed'; Granville saw no alternative to standing by them; 'and if so the prompt assertion of authority is probably the safest.' This drew a convoluted reply. What Gladstone now wanted was pre-emptive recognition of 'the

---

[164] Rose to Meade, 17 Feb. 1870, enclosing the memorandum Granville had asked for and other documents ('Correspondence relative to the Recent Disturbances' pp. 347-52); Sir John Young to Granville, 12 Feb. (enclosing the Minute) and 24 Feb. 1870 (ibid. pp. 120-2, 128)

[165] Macdonald to Rose, 23 Feb. 1870 acknowledging Rose's cable of the 22nd (Pope, *Correspondence of Macdonald* p. 128); on 22 Feb. Meade noted that Granville had 'discussed this matter' with Rose (CO 42/695 fo. 281)

[166] Gladstone's report to the Queen on the 5 March Cabinet meeting (National Archives, Kew, Cab 41/2/11), and Granville to Young, 5 March 1870 ('Correspondence relative to the Recent Disturbances' p. 225)

title of the Red River people', or acknowledgment of their 'rights' as 'independent settlers', but 'on their own ground only'. This would isolate them geographically. For, outside 'the land they now hold', they would have no 'claim whatever beyond a right of way'. So American filibusters crossing the international border would be unable to claim that they had reached the land of the people for whom they were going to fight.[167] Gladstone hoped that 'something *might* be hammered out of this', and the Red River question returned to the cabinet on 16 and 19 March. It was finally decided 'to send an agent to Ottawa to watch & if need be guide' 'the negotiations between the Delegates from the Settlement and the Canadian Government'.[168]

Broadly, the London government had two requirements. If military assistance were accorded, Canada should proceed with the acceptance of Rupert's Land that it had stalled in late 1869; this occasioned no difficulty, and Canada also volunteered to meet the bulk of the expedition's costs. Secondly, 'reasonable terms' should be given to the 'Red River settlers', with the Canadian government accepting 'decision of Her Majesty's Government on disputed points of Settlers' Bill of Rights'.[169] This was potentially more difficult. Granville had, as early as February, arranged for the senior civil servant Sir Clinton Murdoch to pass through Ottawa, ostensibly on emigration business, and had assured Macdonald that 'he knows all that has passed, and could probably tell you more ... about our views, than we have probably been able to make clear in

[167] Gladstone to Granville, 5 and 7 March 1870, Granville to Gladstone 6 March – Ramm, *Political Correspondence* nos. 208-10; Granville's 6 March letter to Rogers about Gladstone's missive of the day before (PRO 30/29/57 fos. 258-60). See also the discussion in Ged Martin, *Manitoba Report Part 2*. Concern over the possibility of intervention by American filibusters was quite often voiced in London
[168] CAB 41/2/12 and CAB 41/2/13; Gladstone's note of the 19 March cabinet (ed. H. C. G. Matthew, *The Gladstone Diaries with Cabinet Minutes and Prime Ministerial Correspondence* vii *January 1869-June 1871* (Oxford, 1982) pp. 257-8)
[169] This constituted the third of the conditions laid down in Granville's 23 April cable to Young ('Correspondence relative to the Recent Disturbances' p. 230)

our correspondence'. Murdoch was to help make administrative arrangements about the expedition. But he had also been told that 'troops should not be employed in forcing the sovereignty of Canada on the [Red River] population should they refuse to admit it'.[170] This upset Macdonald: it would, he complained to the Governor-General shortly after Murdoch's arrival, render the troops 'of no use. If we accept the country we are committed to its conquest; we cannot return ... [it] to Her Majesty or to the Hudson's Bay Company. Again, why should we be called upon to pay for troops that may be ordered not to act when they get in to Fort Garry?'[171] But Macdonald need not have worried. When Murdoch saw the Red River demands brought by Judge Black, he shared the general view that several were inadmissible. He accepted assurances that the Canadian government would give the settlers 'very reasonable terms – as liberal indeed as were given to New Brunswick and Nova Scotia. More cannot in reason be demanded.' And he added that, 'whatever the result of the negotiations', the military expedition could not be delayed without risking 'a collision between the opposing parties in the settlement' and prolonging 'the reign of terror which it is admitted has now existed there' for over four months.[172]

On 5 May, with Parliament set to accept the Manitoba Bill, the Governor-General cabled Granville 'Negotiations with delegates closed satisfactorily' and outlined the settlement. Next day he added, 'I presume I am now at liberty to issue the final orders for Troops to proceed to Red River', and was duly told,

[170] Granville to Macdonald, 23 Feb. 1870 (Pope, *Correspondence of Macdonald* p. 131); instructions to Murdoch, 22 March, quoted in Sir Clinton Murdoch to Rogers, 28 April 1870 (CO 42/695 fo. 182). Granville also persuaded Sir Stafford Northcote to visit Ottawa to observe generally and to handle any questions that might arise over the HBC's interests; but Macdonald and Cartier kept him at arm's length till they had settled with the Red River delegates
[171] Macdonald to Young, 10 April 1870 (Pope, *Memoirs of Macdonald* ii p. 63)
[172] Murdoch to Rogers, 21 April 1870; more is added on the inadmissible demands in Murdoch's letter of the 28th (CO 42/695 fos. 178-9, 181-2)

'Yes, the Troops may proceed.'[173] The only remaining political obstacle was that of passage through the American Sault Ste. Marie canal. It had never occurred to Canadian ministers that this might be denied – the US had sent military supplies through Canadian canals during the Civil War. But the Grant administration's first impulse was to refuse passage in order to block the North-Western Expedition. However, it soon drew back, fearing Canadian retaliation against American use of its St. Lawrence canals,[174] and instead pressed for a Proclamation amnestying Riel – to no effect.[175] With political difficulties thus removed, there remained only physical ones – including 47 portages. These were overcome, partly through the leadership of Colonel Wolseley (later a famous British general), and partly because, for much of the way, the force did not have to move on foot, as in the past, but could travel by river in Macdonald's purpose-built boats.

Riel had sent Delegates to negotiate for adhesion to Canada, and at home had moved in an increasingly 'British' direction, flying the Union Jack, banning the Stars and Stripes, and taking the *New Nation* from its annexationist editor. But he had been worried by accounts of the Expeditionary Force, and still more by Ritchot's and Scott's arrest on their arrival in Ottawa. So, though his resources were now reduced by the return of many of his men to their summer employments, he still kept up some defence preparations. Indeed the US Vice-Consul reported that the idea of resisting the troops had been before the 'Provisional Council' on 3 June, but had been postponed till Ritchot got back to Red River.[176] Ritchot then dissipated fears: he said Cartier had told him Riel should 'continue to maintain order and govern the

---

[173] Young to Granville, 5 and 6 May 1870, Granville to Young, 8 May ('Correspondence relative to the Recent Disturbances' pp. 188, 211, 231)

[174] Steamers were therefore allowed to pass, provided the troops and military materiel were portaged over Canadian territory

[175] Young to Thornton, 21 May 1870 (CO 42/691 fo. 625)

[176] Vice-Consul Robinson to J.C.B. Davis, 7 June 1870 – *James Wickes Taylor Correspondence* p. 175. Schmidt says that news of Ritchot's and Scott's arrest prompted the Americans to renew their efforts 'to shake our British allegiance' ('Memoires' p. 86)

country' until the arrival of the new Canadian Governor, and then 'be at the head of his people to receive' him.[177]

The prospective Lt. Governor A.G. Archibald could well have gone to Minnesota by train (as McDougall had done in 1869) and come on to Winnipeg from there. There were, indeed, repeated rumours in Red River that he was on the point of arriving. But neither he nor the amnesty he was expected to bring came. This revived some uneasiness, and Bishop Taché set off again for Canada to find out. While there, he tried to hurry Archibald's journey by persuading him to go to the North-West Angle of the Lake of the Woods, where he would be met and escorted onwards by a joint party of Métis and Anglophones. Had this come off, Archibald might well have overtaken the troops (as Taché probably wanted for political reasons). But Archibald's guide could find neither the North-West Angle (though he spent a day looking for it) nor any trace of the escort, and it later transpired that Riel had not sent one. So Archibald had to go back and follow in the wake of the troops.[178] Meanwhile O'Donoghue (with his Fenian and annexationist proclivities) revived fears of the troops' intentions and encouraged resistance. Riel may briefly have contemplated this. But he decided to go through with the policy of welcoming the new Governor, and was no doubt encouraged by a Proclamation from Colonel Wolseley declaring his mission to be one of peace.[179] On 23 August Taché returned to Red River, still full of reassurances – he had a tendency to believe that what ought to be actually was. That evening Riel told him he had been deceived: the troops were at hand and looked to surprise Fort Garry early next morning. Taché denied it: 'the soldiers will

---

[177] Ritchot's testimony (*Select Committee Report* p. 77)

[178] Archibald's testimony (*Select Committee Report* p. 135), and Taché's account (ibid. pp. 44-5). Taché mentions that General Lindsay (the Expedition's overall commander) wanted Archibald to arrive before the troops since no provision had been made for the civilian government of Manitoba if the troops arrived first. Cartier did not

[179] Stanley, *Riel* pp. 152-3; Morton, *Begg's Red River Journal* p. 145n. To O'Donoghue's dismay, Riel had the Proclamation printed and publicised

not be here for a fortnight, they reassured me of it in Ottawa'. Riel was right. Next morning, he saw troops advance on Fort Garry, and a horseman dashed up telling him to fly or he would be lynched. Riel and O'Donoghue abandoned their breakfast, crossed the river to tell Taché to come and see the soldiers – 'Do you believe it now?' – and then headed for the border.[180]

---

[180] Abbé Dugas' account of events on 23 and 24 August 1870 (ed. Morton, *Begg's Red River Journal*, p. 565); Taché's recollection (*Select Committee Report* pp. 45-6). General Lindsay had in fact told Taché the troops would reach Fort Garry sooner than originally anticipated

CHAPTER 12

The Crown Colony of British Columbia, 1858-71

With Manitoba's entry into Confederation and the takeover of the North-West Territories beyond it, Canada now bordered on the young and still lightly settled Crown Colony of British Columbia [B.C.]. For all practical purposes, though, this could be accessed only from the Pacific – 'commercial intercourse', Governor Musgrave observed, 'would be easier with Australia than with Canada'.[1] Nevertheless B.C. joined Canada in 1871.

To follow this story, we must go back to 1846. North of the new border the Oregon treaty made no immediate difference. But the incoming Colonial Secretary, Earl Grey, felt that, given 'the encroaching spirit of the U.S.', it was important to strengthen Britain's 'hold upon the territory now assigned to us' by encouraging its settlement by British subjects. He also believed this 'could only be effected under the auspices' of the sole British concern in the area, the Hudson's Bay Company [HBC]. There were difficulties. For the Company was widely hated as a monopoly; and many felt that it was ill-fitted it to sponsor a colony of settlement by reason of the incompatibility between agriculture and the wild animals whose furs the HBC existed to harvest. Equally, the HBC was reluctant to assume a role that would certainly expose it to further attacks. Eventually, though, the Company decided that unless it took on Vancouver Island, this

---

[1] Governor Musgrave to Lord Granville, 30 Oct. 1869 – ed. James Hendrickson and the Colonial Despatches project, *The Colonial Despatches of Vancouver Island and British Columbia 1846-1871* (University of Victoria, online, https://bcgenesis.uvic.ca), hereafter *Despatches*

would go to some other concern that would then trench on HBC operations on the mainland.[2] So in 1849 the HBC received a Crown grant of the Island and transferred control of its western operations from Fort Vancouver in now American Oregon to Fort Victoria. But the mainland was left, as before, to its First Nations residents with no more than a scattering of HBC trading posts.

Vancouver Island's first Governor was an outsider. But in 1851 he was succeeded by the HBC's senior local officer, James Douglas, who held the two posts jointly, reporting both to the Company and to the Colonial Office. He was (as we have noted in connection with the San Juan archipelago) concerned to prevent American encroachment on what he saw as British territorial rights. Most immediately worrying were the 'Queen Charlotte Islands' (Haida Gwaii). In 1850-1 Indians had brought gold nuggets to trade at HBC posts there. The news spread; American as well as HBC ships visited the islands; and Douglas became apprehensive. Their vessels, he reported, were chartered by 'adventurers', who meant, if they succeeded in digging gold, 'to colonise the island, and establish an independent government [as had, of course, been done in Oregon], until, by force or fraud, they become annexed to the United States'. They expected British opposition, but spoke 'confidently' of being able to recruit 'to almost any ... extent, from ... California', and considered their 'ultimate success' as 'admitting scarcely of a doubt'. Douglas warned the British Naval Commander in the Pacific that there were probably 500 Americans on the Island, who 'if left unmolested' would 'attempt to wrest that valuable possession from the British Crown'.[3] His solution was two-fold: HBC expeditions to buy gold from the Indians and mine the gold-bearing vein; and the barring of foreign ships from the Islands (after which 'a flourishing

---

[2] John S. Galbraith, *The Hudson's Bay Company as an Imperial Factor, 1821-1869* (New York, 1977 edn.) pp. 283-47, 291

[3] Douglas to Grey, 16 Dec. 1851 and 29 Jan. 1852, and to Admiral Moresby, 29 Jan. 1852 – 'Correspondence relative to the Discovery of Gold at Queen Charlotte's Island', Parliamentary Papers [hereafter P.P.] 1852-3 lxv pp. 34-5, 38. It was not then realised that the archipelago comprises more than one island

trade [in supplies] would soon flow into this colony').[4] Earl Grey
turned down the idea of excluding American vessels, a decision
later reaffirmed by his Conservative successor.[5] However H.M.S.
Thetis was sent to assert sovereignty, paying Haida Gwaii a brief
(but, it was thought, effective) visit in mid-1852.[6] The legal position
was regularised by Douglas' appointment as Lieutenant-Governor
of Queen Charlotte's Island. He was, though, told there was no
'design of colonizing the country', so he should not make laws or
permanent grants of land, but only represent British authority and
issue gold mining licenses, broadly on the Australian model. Next
spring Douglas duly issued regulations requiring licences to be
taken out at Victoria.[7] By then the gold excitement had subsided,
and, with it, Douglas' dream that, with the Americans discouraged,
'the mines would be left to ... Her Majesty's subjects', in effect to
the HBC.[8] But if this gold rush proved a damp squib, it would soon
be replayed, on a far greater scale, on the Fraser River.

Gold was found on a tributary, Thompson's River, by an
Indian picking up what he had thought was a pebble. 'The whole
tribe immediately began to collect the glittering metal';[9] and a few
Europeans soon joined them. In April 1856 Douglas told the
Colonial Secretary of reports that gold was being dug 'in
considerable quantities' and that many other 'valuable deposits'
were likely to be found. He asked whether the government wished
to tax the miners but suggested that this could not be done
'without the aid of a military force' whose cost would probably
exceed the income derived. The response was that the government

[4] Douglas to Grey, 29 Jan. and 28 May 1852 – P.P. 1852-3 lxv pp. 35, 41-2
[5] Douglas to Grey, 31 Oct. 1851, and Grey's 4 Feb. 1852 reply; Sir John
Pakington to Douglas, 27 Sept. 1852 – ibid. pp. 33, 43
[6] P.P. 1852-3 lxv pp. 34-40; *Despatches*, documents enclosed in W.A.B. Hamilton
(Admiralty) to Herman Merivale (Colonial Office), 25 May 1852
[7] Pakington to Douglas, 27 Sept. 1852, and Douglas to the Duke of Newcastle,
11 April 1853 – P.P. 1852-3 lxv pp. 43-4, 51-3
[8] To Grey, 28 May 1852 (ibid. pp. 41-2)
[9] Douglas' MS. 'Diary of Gold Discovery on Fraser's River in 1858', 14 Sept.
1860, cited in Dan Marshall, *Claiming the Land: British Columbia and the
Making of a New El Dorado* (Vancouver, 2018) p. 35

did 'not at present look for a revenue from this distant quarter of the British dominions' and was not 'prepared to incur any expense on account of it'. Keeping order should people flock 'into this new gold district' was therefore left to Douglas' discretion.[10] By February 1857 enough gold had reached Victoria to induce Douglas to tell an HBC officer 'to test the gold diggings' by taking a large party of Indians to search for 'the precious metal' and buy it 'from them as fast as they can collect it'.[11] Douglas' son-in-law, Dr. John Helmcken, said he 'attached great importance' to this gold, 'and thought it meant a great change and a busy time. He spoke of Victoria rising to be a great city.' Anticipating 'a great rush of people into ... Thompson's River', Douglas wrote in September that 'nothing but the most energetic measures will serve to protect our interests': HBC officers must 'strive to secure the trade in our own hands', circulating the works to supply the miners' wants and buy the gold.[12]

American attempts to mine in Haida Gwaii had been constrained by Indian hostility, and Douglas seems to have hoped for a repetition. In July 1857 he told the Colonial Secretary that the 'tribes of Thompson's River ... had lately taken the high-handed, though probably not unwise course, of expelling all the parties of gold diggers ... [chiefly Americans] who had forced an entry into their country'; they had said they would 'resist all attempts at working gold ... both from a desire to monopolize the precious metal ... and from a well-founded impression' that otherwise their 'principal food', the migrating salmon, would be driven off.[13] But Douglas' HBC superior, Sir George Simpson, was soon warning that the Indians would not be able to stop 'whites

---

[10] Douglas to Colonial Secretary Henry Labouchere, 16 April 1856, and Labouchere's 4 August reply (*Despatches*)

[11] Douglas to Donald McLean, 10 Feb. 1857 (Marshall, *Claiming the land* pp. 37-8)

[12] Ed. Dorothy Blakey-Smith, *Reminiscences of Doctor John Sebastian Helmcken* (Vancouver, 1975) p. 154, and numerous letters of instruction sent by Douglas to HBC officers on the mainland (Marshall, *Claiming the land* pp. 37-43)

[13] Douglas to Labouchere, 15 July 1857 (*Despatches*)

working these diggings, and should we [the HBC] encourage them to resist the influx of gold diggers, we may become embroiled in serious difficulties' and 'incur public censure for checking colonization'. In November Douglas cautioned Chief Trader Donald McLean accordingly; McLean should instead both 'inculcate upon the Indians the duty of being kind to all white men' and warn incoming Europeans that they were 'dangerous and not to be trusted'.[14]

By late 1857 Douglas combined hopes that 'Fraser's River will prove a second Sacramento' with fear of 'serious affrays' between Indians and 'the motley adventurers' who would be attracted' from the United States and would 'probably attempt to overpower the opposition of the natives by force of arms'.[15] Anticipating such an influx, and acting as 'the only authority commissioned by Her Majesty within reach', Douglas issued a Proclamation in December that declared all gold in the area to be Crown property, though people might work it on taking out a licence in Victoria. He had the Proclamation published in American newspapers, perhaps with the aim of prompting a small miners' influx that would be supplied from Victoria and boost the value of property there. What he got was a 'Great Excitement' that at its peak brought up to 33,000 people to the mining area – 'We are crazy with gold fever. Everybody that can get away is off to Frazer's river after gold.'[16]

---

[14] Simpson to Douglas, 16 Sept. 1857, and Douglas to McLean, 23 Nov. (Marshall, *Claiming the land* pp. 45-6, 48)

[15] Douglas to Dugald McTavish, 18 Dec. 1857 (ibid. p. 74); Douglas to the HBC's Secretary W.G. Smith, 18 Feb. 1858, and to Labouchere, 15 July 1857 ('Correspondence relative to the Discovery of Gold in the Fraser's River District', P.P. 1857-8 xli pp. 251-2, 253)

[16] Donald J. Hauka, *McGowan's War* (Vancouver, 2003) p. 224 (citing Averill Groenveld-Meijer, 'Manning the Fraser Canyon Gold Rush', University of British Columbia MA thesis, 1994); *Daily Alta California*, 19 March, 1858 (reprinting 6 March reports on gold in the *Olympia Pioneer and Democrat*), San Francisco *Bulletin*, 19 March (reporting the arrival of newspapers from Portland), 15 and 19 April (reporting the scheduled departures of one ship for Victoria and one for Port Townend, WA.) – Marshall, *Claiming the land* pp. 63-4, 286n., and chap. 3 generally; John Nugent to Secretary of State Cass, 8 Jan. 1859 (William R.

Some trekked in directly over the border, but most came by ship to Victoria. They made an unexpectedly good impression. Victoria's merchants were delighted by the 'wealth and business' their arrival brought, and strongly in favour of making the port 'a stopping point between San Francisco and the gold mines' as 'both in going and coming the miners would spend a great deal of money'. In May 1858 Douglas set out the position for the Colonial Secretary. One option was to arrange for steamers to take the prospective miners from Victoria to the head of the Fraser navigation, from whence they could 'readily' access the diggings on foot. The 'whole trade of the gold regions would [then] pass through Fraser's River, and be retained within British Territory'. It might, though, be dangerous to allow foreigners unrestricted immigration without first requiring them to 'take the oath of allegiance' or give other security. For if most were American, 'there will always be a hankering in their minds after annexation to the United States, and with the aid of their countrymen in Oregon and California, at hand, they will never cordially submit to British rule'.[17]

Douglas added that if the diggings proved remunerative, he did not think immigration could be checked 'even by closing Fraser's River, as the miners would then force a passage [overland from the Columbia] into the gold district' in which case its 'valuable trade ... [would] be driven ... into a foreign channel, and entirely lost'. On 8 May he was still seeking the Colonial Secretary's instructions. But by the 19th he had decided that further American entry from US territory left him no option. So to escape 'the greater evil' of making people turn to 'unlawful' ways of 'entering the country', he moved 'to legalize' the miners' entrance 'into Fraser's River', on conditions 'which at once assert the rights of the Crown, protect the interests of the Hudson's Bay Company', and 'draw the whole trade of the Gold Districts through Fraser's River' to Vancouver Island and its British 'Mother Country'. He therefore offered an American

---

Manning, *Diplomatic Correspondence of the United States. Canadian Relations 1784-1860* iv (Washington, 1945) pp. 756, 774-5)
[17] Douglas to Labouchere, 8 May 1858 (*Despatches*); Douglas to W.G. Smith, 27 April (P.P. 1857-8 xli p. 261)

company a contract to run steamers to the head of the Fraser navigation, paying the HBC $2 a passenger, and carrying only HBC goods and people who had taken out a British gold mining licence; boats not so authorised by the HBC would be liable to seizure. This arrangement, Douglas said, would also 'give the Government a decided control over the mining population of the interior'.[18]

Events would soon show up the paucity of this control. Miners were initially tolerated by the Stó:lo people south of the Fraser canyons: an 'amicable understanding' was reached whereby the local village let miners access 'Washington Bar' outside 'fishing hours'; near Yale, Europeans were allowed to work on Indian land on payment of 'a tax of a blanket or a shirt' for each miner; and at Hill's Bar, Douglas' Diary noted in late May, '80 Indians and 30 white men' were at work together.[19] But when visiting the gold fields next month, Douglas found 'great alarm' at Hill's Bar 'on account of a serious affray … with the native Indians, who mustered under arms … and threatened to make a clean sweep of the whole body of miners assembled there'. Douglas attributed the trouble to 'provocations on both sides' and to a natural Indian resentment 'at the large quantity of gold taken from their country by the white miners'. He spoke 'with great plainess [sic]' to the miners, lectured the Indians 'soundly on their conduct', and took 'the leader of the affray', Chief Kowpelst, 'into the Government service', where he proved 'exceedingly useful in settling other Indian difficulties'. Douglas also cautioned the Indians 'against taking the Law into their own hands'; they should instead apply for redress to George Perrier, whom he appointed a magistrate. And he chose 'Indian Magistrates … to bring forward' any Indians 'charged with offences against the [British] Laws of the country'. Nevertheless, Douglas noted, Indian 'audacity' had been stimulated by news of the defeat of a US unit in Oregon, and

---

[18] Douglas to the new Conservative Colonial Secretary, Lord Stanley, 19 May 1858 (*Despatches*)
[19] Marshall, *Claiming the land* pp. 53, 58, 60, 286n.

he concluded that it would 'require ... the nicest tact to avoid a disastrous Indian war'.[20]

Matters worsened, not helped by mining parties who, having had to fight Indians to get through the Washington Territory, continued doing so north of the border. The 'Oregonians', an American diarist wrote, 'have got to Thompson River and they clear out Indians wherever they come across them'. Chief Nicola [Huristesmexe'qEn] confronted one party that crossed into British territory in July, wantonly destroyed stores, and killed Okanagans. He said he could have raised nearly two thousand warriors and annihilated them; but the war chiefs would then 'have usurped his power and carried on a general war against the whites, Americans and English'. So he had listened to advice from McLean and 'other good men, & priests', and merely required the American party to release some hostages they had taken. Nicola had, his great-granddaughter believed, been asked by tribes on both sides of the border 'to join them in war against the whites', but though preparing for war should no settlement be reached, he held his people back from immediate participation.[21] Not everybody was so restrained. Already by June the San Francisco *Bulletin* was reporting that though on the lower Fraser miners were doing well, the Thompson River Nlaka'pamux were 'not permitting any one to go up'. On 9 August two Frenchmen were shot (perhaps in retaliation for a rape), and widespread assaults followed, more especially above the Fraser canyons. One party of 26 miners on the Thompson was told Indians were killing all white men in the area; they fled south, losing men 'nearly every day', and only five were left by the time they were rescued. Above Yale, miners were largely 'driven from their claims', with numerous corpses thrown into the Fraser and drifting down to Yale and Hope. So 'alarming

---

[20] Douglas to Stanley, 15 June 1858 (*Despatches*); Hauka, *McGowan's War* pp. 35-7
[21] George Wesley Beam, MS. Diary, 22 Aug. 1858, and Marie Brent's rendering of family tradition (Marshall, *Claiming the land* pp. 150-2); Hauka, *McGowan's War* pp. 80-3, citing D.B. Nunis ed., *The Golden Frontier: the Recollections of Herman Francis Reinhart, 1851-1869* (Austin, Texas, 1962)

was the news ... that hundreds' of men started to leave the lower Fraser 'to return to their homes'.[22]

Others were more pugnacious. Miners formed armed 'Companies' to rescue fugitives, exact revenge, and intimidate the Indians into peace – though as most miners were located below the Fraser River's falls, the Indians they initially attacked were quite likely to have been friendly. One such Company, under the former Texas Ranger Captain Rouse, routed Indians near Spuzzum who took refuge in the mountains, and 'burnt three of their rancheries [villages], destroying all their provisions'. Rouse's men claimed not to have 'molested any but those they knew were implicated in murders and robberies', but another source says 33 Indians from a friendly tribe were killed and their huts and winter provisions destroyed. Chief Kowpelst was brought captive to Fort Hope 'to find out the authors of the several outrages'. But once there, Kowpelst was vouched for by the HBC trader Ovid Allard, and it was decided to return him 'in safety' to his house and to return the guns 'taken from his people ... on condition of their remaining peaceably at their fisheries, and not troubling the whites'.[23]

Meanwhile miners flocked to Hope and Yale. Meetings were held and demands put to HBC officers; in Wesley Beam's words, 'The miners have went to Forts Yale and Hope, and made them give all of the arms and ammunition they had. Mr Walker of Hope did not want to do it but they shoved him aside'. On 16 August a Company, the Pike Guards, was formed 'to procede at once up the

---

[22] Marshall, *Claiming the land* pp. 152-8; Hauka, *McGowan's War* pp. 79, 84-5; Edwin Stout, 'A Pioneer of '58', in W. Wymond Walkem, *Stories of Early British Columbia* (Vancouver, 1914) pp. 55-8; H.M. Snyder to Douglas, 28 Aug. 1858 (ed. Daniel P. Marshall, 'Documents ... The Fraser River War', *Native Studies Review* (Saskatoon) 11:1 (1996) pp. 139-45). Another reason for going home was that the lower Fraser workings had been largely inundated by the seasonal floods

[23] Captain Snyder's account in the *Victoria Gazette*, 24 Aug. 1858, 'An Indian War Broken Out', *San Francisco Bulletin*, 1 Sept., and Alfred Waddington, *The Fraser Mines Vindicated, or, The History of Four Months* (Victoria, 1858) p. 57 – all cited in Marshall, *Claiming the Land* pp. 159, 255

river', with H.M. Snyder, who enjoyed considerable prestige as correspondent to the San Francisco *Bulletin*, elected as its Captain. He proposed 'to take an interpreter with us and make pease' with the Indians 'by peasible (sic) means if we could, and by force if we must'.[24] Ovid Allard supplied William Yates as an interpreter, thinking 'it would be as well for him to go with them & try to stop as many murder[s] and rob[b]ery ... as possible'; and the party took a supply of white flags 'to give ... [to] the Indian Chiefs along the river as a guarantee not to bother the whites in any shape or form'. Snyder would ascribe much of the credit for his success to Yates and 'our other interpreter' Mr. Battiece, without whom 'I do not believe we would of seen one dozen of Indians'. None were visible on the party's arrival just short of Sailor's Bar, but the interpreter explained their peaceable 'object' to a chance encounter, who accompanied them for two miles and then shouted. Indians emerged from every direction and appeared 'delighted with what we had proposed'. A 'Treaty' of peace was made with them, and the Chief sent his son to escort them up to a rancherie near Spuzzum, whose sixty inhabitants concluded another peace and were given white flags to indicate it. But matters were then complicated by the presence of another Company, the Whatcom Guards, whose Captain Graham supposedly responded 'To h--ll with these flags, we are here to find out and kill those who are responsible for the dead bodies ... floating down the river'.[25] This course, Snyder found, 'had driven the Indians into the mountains', and progress was unlikely unless Graham could be restrained.

Eventually, though, Graham agreed to let Snyder's party go on alone, sending back a white flag if they managed to make peace

---

[24] Snyder to Douglas, Fort Yale, 28 Aug. 1858 (Daniel P. Marshall, 'Documents ... The Fraser River War' pp. 140-5. The 'war' is covered in pp. 85-92 of *McGowan's War*, and Chapter 5 of Marshall, *Claiming the land*. Both draw largely on Snyder's letter to Douglas, supplemented by the 'Reminiscences of William Yates' (the HBC interpreter who accompanied him), no date (B.C. Archives), the 'Account of Capt. Snyder's Expedition', *Victoria Gazette*, 1 Sept. 1858, and Snyder's 'Letter from Fort Yale', *Bulletin*, 25 Sept. 1858

[25] Walkem, *Stories of Early British Columbia* p. 59

with the Indians above the canyon. At the Chinese miners' camp Snyder's party (now reinforced by a like-minded French Company) again met Chiefs who not only themselves made peace but accompanied the miners to others further up; and, according to the sanitised[26] account Snyder later sent Governor Douglas, they were then passed from one Chief to another until they met David Spintlum [Cexpe'ntlEm], the 'war chief of all the tribes for some distance up & down the Frazer River and for one hundred miles up Thompson River'. Spintlum had been summoned from some 75 miles away, and, according to tradition collected forty years later, had joined hundreds of warriors assembled from all parts of the Upper Thompson country. There had been 'fiery speeches', the war chief CuxcuxesquEt urging 'the people to drive out the whites' and ending all his speeches with a war dance. In opposition, Spintlum 'talked continually for peace, and showed strongly its advantages', eventually securing majority support.[27] After a preliminary meeting with Spintlum on 21 August, Snyder proceeded next day to a 'grand council' with 'Eleven Chiefs and a very large number of other Indians ... from above and below' the canyons. Snyder's message was that 'this time we came for pease [sic], but if we had to come againe, that we would come not by hundreds but by thousands and drive them from the river forever', and he believed the Indians were 'supprised and frightened to see

---

[26] Years later Edwin Stout said Snyder was occasionally 'unable to control his men', who were 'fairly maddened by the sight of numerous corpses floating down' the river, 'and in disobedience to orders ... killed numbers of natives at Chapman's' and Boston Bars (ibid. p. 60). Travelling two days behind Snyder's party, a *Bulletin* correspondent noted two burnt Indian villages, four or five corpses, and several smashed-up fishing lodges (*Claiming the Land* p. 177), though this may not have been the work of Snyder's men

[27] Marshall, *Claiming the land* esp. pp. 176, 178-9 – drawing on James Teit, 'Mythology of the Thompson Indians: The Jessup North Pacific Expedition VIII:2', *American Museum of Natural History Memoir* 12 (Leiden, 1912) p. 412, '"The Coming of the White Man" as told by Mary Williams' in Mamie Edwards (ed.), *Our Tellings: Interior Salish Stories of the Nha7Kápmx People* (Vancouver, 1996) pp. 130-1, Marshall's own transcription of a 1927 memorial to the (by then long dead) Chief David Spintlum, and evidence given by Chief Andrew Paul to a Canadian Parliamentary Committee in 1946

so many men with guns'.[28] Snyder's position was actually very weak, since his men were almost out of food. But peace was made, and that done, the party rushed back, very hungry, to Yale, escorted by Indian chiefs to spread news of the peace and to prevent ambushes. (On the way they learnt of the Whatcom Guards' collapse: when sent a white flag to indicate the making of peace at the head of the canyon, Graham simply threw it away; that night his party seems to have been attacked, presumably by Indians worried by his behaviour, and in the ensuing confusion both he and his Lieutenant were killed, probably by 'friendly fire'.)

What Snyder and Spintlum had agreed, Indian traditions suggest, may have been a deal giving Indians one side of the river, miners the other; also miners should not seize Indians suspected of crime for delivery to the law without their Chief's consent. The precise terms are not important since they could not bind Douglas and what became the government of British Columbia. But we should note the almost complete absence of British authority on the ground: the miners had taken control of the HBC's arms and its positions at Forts Yale and Hope; and their campaign was conducted by improvised but disciplined bodies of hundreds of armed men, some, at least, with 'the stars and stripes at their head'.[29] It came close to sparking an Indian war, in which both sides would have gathered support from across the American border. The credit for avoiding this must rest chiefly with Snyder and Spintlum (and their respective supporters), not with the distant Douglas.[30]

---

[28] Marshall suggests that Snyder's numbers may have approached 250 (*Claiming the Land* p. 171), but Snyder believed that as they marched in single file, they seemed three times as many (to Douglas, 28 Aug. 1858)

[29] Jason Allard (Ovid's son), '...Some Stories of Yale in the Gold Rush', MS., University of British Columbia – cited by Marshall, *Claiming the land* p. 159

[30] Indian attitudes will, though, have been influenced not only by calculations as to the likely outcome of hostilities but also by their decades-long relationship of mutual benefit with the HBC

The 'War' does not figure in Douglas' despatches to London. But both Snyder and the Secretary of the miners' meeting at Hope wrote to him, and he set off up the Fraser to enforce 'such laws as may be found necessary for the maintenance of peace and good order among the motley population of foreigners', 'and to assert the rights of my Country'. Douglas was accompanied by 35 sailors from the warships at its mouth, an 'absurdly small [military force] for such an occasion', 'in hopes', he told London in a broad hint, 'that early measures will be taken by Her Majesty's Government, to relieve the country from its perilous state'. At Hope his 'first attention was devoted to the state of the Indian population', which was 'much incensed against the miners'; he received 'visits from the Chiefs of Thompsons River', 'distributed presents of clothing ... as a token of regard', and 'gave them much useful advise for their guidance in the altered state of the country'. Douglas then turned 'to the state of the white population', hearing minor cases and arranging for a murder trial, laying out a town site for traders who wished to settle, and promising legal land titles. After a week, he went slowly upstream, calling at every bar, hearing complaints and explaining his regulations. At Yale, as at Hope, Douglas found the Indians assembled. They 'made no secret of their dislike to the white miners ... and in all cases where redress was possible, it was granted'. What this amounted to is unclear: the only example given in the despatch is the marking out of, and removal of miners from, 'a particular part of the river' claimed by a small Indian band. The Victoria *Gazette* reported that 'Treaties were made with the Indian tribes on the river', and Marshall would like to believe that Douglas met Spintlum and 'promised to secure the traditional lands of the Nlaka pamux'.[31] But if so, the 'treaties' amounted to little more than the peaceful co-existence agreements reached with the miners. For though Douglas had concluded formal land purchase treaties on Vancouver Island, he did not do so on the mainland, where

---

[31] Douglas to Stanley, 27 Aug. 1858, and to Bulwer Lytton, 12 Oct. (*Despatches*); Marshall, *Claiming the Land* pp. 181-2

any reserves established proved subject to encroachment or curtailment when they conflicted with mining and other European development. Nevertheless, after 1858 there was only one serious outbreak. In 1864 Klatsassin's small Chilcotin band attacked road builders and other Europeans, killing nineteen, and then took to the hills. Punitive expeditions followed, and eventually those chiefly responsible were located (with the aid of a leading Chilcotin chief) and induced to surrender. Meanwhile 3,500 Fraser River Indians came to New Westminster to participate in the Queen's birthday celebrations.[32] From the perspective of the Indians, the great majority of the colony's inhabitants, the 1860s were, at least in the south of the Province, very bleak: they suffered from disastrous smallpox; and they moved from owning all the land to being assigned 'reserves' that would dwindle over time. But from the European viewpoint, there was substantial calm.[33]

At Yale Douglas assured a large gathering of miners that Britain's 'laws will be administered with justice and impartiality'. He had a 'long conversation' with Snyder, praising him for the course he had taken 'in restoring peace with the Indians', promising not to 'interfere with any rules and regulations ... the miners may have adopted',[34] and offering him a government post –

---

[32] *Dictionary of Canadian Biography*, Klatsassin, and Seymour, Frederick. Indian loyalty to the Crown was much strengthened by developments south of the border. 'There was one subject which especially preoccupied their minds', Douglas found, 'the condition to which the cognate Native Tribes of Oregon have been reduced', and his exposition of Her Majesty's Government's very different approach elicited assurances of 'boundless devotion to Her Majesty's person and Crown' (to Newcastle, 9 and 25 Oct. 1860 (*Despatches*)

[33] Between 1859 and 1871 Chief Justice Begbie hanged 22 Indians for murder, including Klatsassin and his associates, and reprieved a further 11; three Europeans were also executed – *Dictionary of Canadian Biography*, Begbie; see also the table of murders in Frederick John Hatch, *The British Columbia Police, 1858-1871* (University of British Columbia, M.A. thesis, 1955) Appendix C

[34] On arrival, miners had often turned to the common law mining code with which they were familiar – in July a meeting was convened at Fort Yale Bar 'to manage matters in California style, despite the regulations of government'; and several other bars plotted out mining claims 25 feet wide, though Douglas' first mining regulations had specified 20 (Marshall, *Claiming the land* pp. 101-3). Snyder claimed that Douglas now promised not to interfere, but Gold

which Snyder declined since on the current rates of official pay 'a man ... would starve'. Douglas did, however, appoint a Chief Constable (at $150 a month), 5 policemen (at $100), and 14 special constables, together with a few magistrates and other officers, and he exhorted the miners to support them as everybody should do 'who expects to receive their protection when he himself gets into difficulties'. He then returned home, leaving his appointees to cope. Snyder observed that

> 'All was peace whilst he was here, but as soon as he was gone the evil-minded commenced to do just as they pleased. He has no officers here to execute the laws; at least what few he has do not amount to anything ... They have a crown commissioner here, and a few policemen; but they do not amount to anything.'[35]

This left the then gold fields to some extent in limbo. Douglas had been well received by the Yale miners, and had managed to get them to give 'three cheers for the Queen, but evidently with a bad grace'. There was, he concluded, 'a strong American feeling among them, and they will require constant watching, until the English element preponderates in the Country'.[36] Meanwhile, as Snyder suggests, some people quite ready to ignore the British authorities were sometimes just ignored – by a 'set of men', the admittedly biased Gold Commissioner Hicks wrote, 'who are doing their utmost to treat the Authority with contempt and establish the same system as in California', with Ned McGowan angrily declaring that Governor Douglas 'had better mind his own business, for that he was the ruler of Hill's Bar, and that if the miners would only stand

---

Commissioner Hicks' attempts to do so would underlie some of his difficulties with McGowan at Hill's Bar

[35] Douglas to Lytton, 12 Oct. 1858 (*Despatches*), and his Yale speech (ed. Frederic W. Howay, *The Early History of the Fraser River Mines* (Victoria, 1926) pp. 1-3, 106, 185-6

[36] Douglas to Herman Merivale (Permanent Under-Secretary at the Colonial Office), 29 Oct. 1858 (*Despatches*)

by him he would put all Englishmen to defiance'.[37] By no means all miners were American – a Cornishman made a point of flying a home-made British flag, and a delighted Douglas then sent him an eighteen-foot Union Jack. But the names chosen for the first set of bars (those below Yale) are revealing: Cornish, Fifty-Four Forty, Canadian, Santa Clara, Eagle, American, Yankee-Doodle, Texas, Sacramento, London, Ohio, Wellington, New York, Trafalgar, Washington; and (inaccurate) reports that the Boundary Commission had found the Fraser to be south of the 49th parallel triggered American delight.[38] But there was little disposition to give the process a helping hand. That could most readily have been precipitated by trouble with the Indians, given the long-standing feelings that the HBC encouraged these in anti-American hostility. And the Fort Hope meeting called to respond to Indian shootings was told that 'Should the [HBC] authorities be found in any way conniving at the bloody deeds of the savages, this will result not only in the sacking ... of all their stockades and storehouses, but stripping this territory of every Vestige of British rule.' However such sentiments were stilled when the local HBC officers proved ready to cooperate; instead, the meeting's Secretary sent Douglas information and an appeal for help. Snyder, too, sent Douglas an account of his Fraser War doings, hoping that they would 'meet with your approval'. And even Hicks' Hill's Bar critics did not take unilateral action, but appealed in due form to the Governor to remove him.[39]

Douglas' belief that the miners would need watching was not unreasonable. For there were, as always, some annexationist proclivities in the American press. In much quoted doggerel the Olympia *Pioneer and Democrat* declared (admittedly rather late in the day) that

---

[37] Richard Hicks to Douglas, 26 and 28 Oct. 1858 (Howay, *Early History* pp. 8-11)
[38] Walkem, *Stories of Early British Columbia* pp. 124-5; Marshall, *Claiming the land* p. 194
[39] Marshall, *Claiming the land* pp. 162-4; Snyder to Douglas, 28 Aug. 1858; Howay, *Early History* p. 9n.

'Soon our banner will be streaming,
Soon the eagle will be screaming,
And the lion – see it cowers,
Hurray, boys, the river's ours.'

Similar sentiments can, unsurprisingly, be found in Californian newspaper correspondence: one letter held that 'Americans and Englishmen cannot mix, and but little would be needed ... on the Frazer River to provoke a crisis – a sort of independent California fight which would involve the two nations', while another looked to the Fraser-bound miners becoming 'the conquerors of Vancouver Island', following which Americans would 'thunder a welcome to the new State of Vancouver'.[40] But John Nugent, the special inquiry agent sent by the Buchanan administration in response to pressure from the former Governor of Washington Territory Isaac Stevens, concluded that while the American miners had 'at any time within the first six months' been numerous enough to seize 'the colonies, which fears of the authorities may have suggested as possible ... they entered the country with no marauding propensities'.[41] They had come to mine, and did not want unnecessary diversions. This had in fact been a major factor

---

[40] Margaret Ormsby, *British Columbia: a History* (Vancouver, 1958) p. 142; San Francisco *Bulletin*, 1, 10, and 21 June 1858, and 2 July ('Bow, Wow, Wow to John Bull'), quoted in Marshall, *Claiming the land* pp. 303-4, 353 n.

[41] Nugent to Cass, 8 Jan. 1859 (Manning, *Diplomatic Correspondence* iv pp. 774-5). Nugent was not the wisest choice for an agent. But I cannot accept Marshall's belief that he had been sent to see whether the British provinces were worth annexing, and that if, instead of assessing them as of little 'intrinsic value', he had 'known of the wealth of the Cariboo, perhaps things may have turned out differently' (*Claiming the Land* pp. 236-7). President Buchanan's administration was, as it showed during the 1859 Pig War, well disposed towards Britain, and the instructions given Nugent (by Cass, 2 Aug. 1858 – Manning, *Diplomatic Correspondence* iv pp. 169-72) were distinctly conciliatory: he should remind American citizens that 'so long as they reside in a foreign country, they must remember that they are subject to its laws and all lawful regulations of its authorities'; were these to prove onerous and oppressive, *Washington* would 'take the necessary steps to procure their modification' – and, by implication, should be left to do so without local attempts at direct action

in Snyder's case for a peaceful conclusion of the Fraser River war. The Indians, he wrote, were positioned to deny access to the upper Fraser; they *could* have been driven out, but this would have taken 'time and money ... The mining season was just commencing, and the object to be gained *now* was, to enable men to go up the river as soon as possible'.[42]

Such attitudes encouraged not conflict but cooperation with the British authorities. In mid-summer the Fraser rose, swamping many of the early gold workings. Some of the miners thus caught out were keen to transfer to the 'upper diggings' and start work there before winter set in. Douglas, for his part, wanted to enhance the Fraser's position as *the* route into the interior by linking its navigation with these diggings, reducing the astronomical cost of freighting in provisions and supplies, and so undercutting direct access routes from Washington Territory. Mutual interest produced a deal: 500 miners, enrolled in 'Companies' of about 20, volunteered to build a road bypassing the Fraser Canyon for no pay beyond their food and the supply of longer-term provisions at a reduced rate. The outcome was, in fact, only a qualified success.[43] But Douglas promised the Yale miners new ferries and roads, though only in general terms, and he would make similar promises two years later when confronting recalcitrant miners in Rock Creek.[44]

---

[42] 'Account of Capt. Snyder's Expedition', *Victoria Gazette*, 1 Sept. 1858 (quoted by Marshall, *Claiming the land* p. 236)

[43] Douglas to Stanley, 19 Aug. 1858 (*Despatches*). Douglas had difficulty in supplying enough mules and provisions, work took longer than expected, and this left the road-builders little time to establish themselves in the new mining district before the onset of winter (Marshall, *Claiming the land* pp. 127-34, which draws on petitions stating the road-builders' grievances). Also the route itself, a mixture of road and lake ferries, wore badly and proved costly since it demanded too much packing and repacking of goods. From 1860 work therefore turned to building a road through the Fraser Canyon

[44] Miners who had come in directly from Washington Territory refused point blank to take out licences or pay for the recording of claims. Douglas came over from Hope and addressed them with a mixture of compliments, basic civics instruction, and promises of a wagon road and bridge, as at Yale, but now also with the threat that he would return with marines if they did not 'comply with the law of this British country'. En route to Rock Creek he had encountered some

In the despatch reporting the completion of the road bypassing the Fraser Canyon, Douglas observed that a 'great number' of the miners had gone back to the United States for the winter. We have no real statistics. But Nugent reckoned that of the 30-33,000 on the Fraser at the peak of the 'gold excitement', the number there that winter 'probably does not exceed three thousand'.[45] Though not an unmixed blessing – the 'Pig War' would be set off by miners stranded in Victoria resettling as squatters on the HBC's San Juan farm (above, chap. 9) – the winter lull gave space for the British government's measures 'to relieve the country from its perilous state' to come into operation. In issuing his December 1857 Proclamation asserting the Crown's right to all gold on the mainland and promising mining licences, Douglas had acted on his own. The Colonial Office approved. But its Permanent Secretary Herman Merivale observed that the proclamation was 'wholly without legal force' since Douglas had 'no authority from the Crown beyond Vancouver's Island'. To give Douglas at least 'the semblance of authority', Merivale recommended sending him a commission as Lieutenant-Governor of New Caledonia (like his earlier one for the Queen Charlotte Islands). Fears of complications arising from the HBC's existing monopoly of trade with the Indians led to the taking of legal advice, and thence to deadlock as the Colonial Secretary Lord Stanley was confessedly too busy with India to take a grip on the problem.[46] But on 5 June Stanley was succeeded by Sir Edward Bulwer-Lytton, who promptly did so. Even Merivale had suggested only that Douglas be directed 'to let things take their course as regards the licenses & the gold diggings',

---

ninety other miners who wanted to overwinter but could not do so in the absence of supplies. These could, Douglas said, be obtained from Hope were a path cut to link with a horse-way already under construction; the miners 'at once volunteered … for the work', and a 'properly equipped' party turned up next morning to start on it – Robert Stevenson, 'A Pioneer of '59', in Walkem, *Stories of Early British Columbia* pp. 245-6, and Douglas to Newcastle, 25 Oct. 1860 (*Despatches*)

[45] Douglas to Lytton, 9 Nov. 1858, and Nugent to Cass, 8 Jan. 1859 (Manning, *Diplomatic Correspondence* iv pp. 756, 774-5)

[46] Colonial Office minutes on Douglas to Labouchere, 29 Dec. 1857 (received 2 March 1858) and 6 April (received 29 May) – *Despatches*

while trying to prevent 'any proceedings inconsistent with the assertion of British dominion in the territory'. Lytton instead decided to create a new Colony in order to establish 'a Government for a district which was threatened with great danger, and which ... had no legal Government at all'. In so doing, he terminated the HBC's legal privileges in the area, thus bypassing the problems that had stymied earlier action. The necessity for his measure, he told Parliament, 'had manifested itself a few days after' he took office: his first care had been to ask the Admiralty to send a 'Naval force ... sufficient to provide against lawless aggression', his second 'to frame a measure that should pass as rapidly as possible, and conciliate all opposition'.[47] In this he was successful. His bill had its First Reading on 1 July and became law on 2 August, the Queen having chosen 'British Columbia' as the new colony's name in place of the ambiguous 'New Caledonia'. One speaker would have preferred to sell the area to the United States to avoid future disputes, while another repeated his past attacks on Douglas and the HBC, but the Opposition spokesman, the Duke of Newcastle, was supportive.[48]

Lytton had asked for warships and had told Douglas that, should help be needed 'to maintain order among the adventurers resorting to the Gold Fields', they would make their crews and Marines as available as 'circumstances' and the fear of desertions would allow.[49] During the parliamentary debate he was pressed to go further. John Arthur Roebuck declared that he must also send soldiers. The colony's population was 'wild and vagabond', much of it from California 'where they had been living under Lynch law', so a militia on the New Zealand model 'would put down order instead of preserving it'; and were Lytton to install a Governor 'without the means of enforcing the law', he 'might as

---

[47] *Hansard*, 8 July 1858, 1101, 19 July, 1767
[48] Queen Victoria to Lytton, 24 July 1858 (J.H. Stewart Reid, Kenneth McNaught, Harry Crowe eds., *A source-book of Canadian history* (Toronto, 1964 edn.) p. 171); *Hansard*, 8 July 1858, 1119-1121, and *Hansard* [Lords], 26 July, 2100
[49] Lytton to Douglas, 1 July 1858 (*Despatches*)

well not have brought in this Bill'. Roebuck thought this view took Lytton aback.[50] If so, Lytton came round to it, and told Douglas on 30 July that he had arranged to send out 150 Royal Engineers.[51] However these did not begin to arrive until late October, and meanwhile Douglas bemoaned the absence of troops: government on the gold fields 'might be carried on smoothly with even a single company of infantry', but without one he could only deploy 'personal influence and management'.[52]

Still, control could be established over entrances to the Fraser, thanks to the fortuitous presence of naval survey ships, and with it came collection of customs duties (and, less reliably, of mining licences). Douglas also made some general appointments, and installed magistrates and Gold Commissioners in the mining districts. But Lytton clearly meant to manage the process. On hearing that Douglas wanted the Vancouver Island Surveyor-General to head a surveying department for 'the lands of Fraser's River', he wrote that he would himself send out 'a head of that department' – plus a Collector of Customs and a prospective Chief Justice. Moreover 'all legal authorities connected with the Government should be sent from home, and thus freed from every suspicion of local partialities', to which end he had enquiries made as to 'young lawyers' who might be 'glad' to go out. It was, too, Lytton later minuted, 'of great importance to the general social welfare & dignity of the Col[on]y that some gentlemen should be encouraged to come from England, not as mere adventurers, but professionally engaged – perhaps Stipendiary Magistrates or Gold Comm[issione]rs'. He conceded that HBC servants might have claims; yet 'great caution should be shewn, in not giving any appearance of undue favour' to them; and it was 'still

---

[50] Roebuck was promptly supported by Edward Ellice, another tough old man with Canadian connections – *Hansard*, 8 July 1858, 1109, 1114
[51] Lytton to Douglas, no. 5, 30 July 1858; on 2 Sept. (no. 6) Lytton added that H.M.S. *Tribune* had been ordered over 'with as many Supernumerary Marines as she can carry' and could be spared from her current station, while two further ships would come when they were no longer needed in Asia (*Despatches*). Such reinforcements explain the naval superiority Britain enjoyed around the island of San Juan in 1859 (see chap. 9 above)
[52] Douglas to Stanley, 26 July and 19 Aug. 1858 (*Despatches*)

more desirable that some appointments should be made from England'.[53] In due course Lytton's selections included, besides Colonel Moody of the Royal Engineers (who became Chief Commissioner of Lands and Works), the Chief Justice (Matthew Begbie), an Inspector of Police (Chartres Brew), a Harbour Master, a Collector of Customs, a Treasurer, a Colonial Secretary, and an Attorney-General.[54] Many other British immigrants also arrived, often presenting letters of recommendation and seeking administrative employment. One was shown a drawerful of such letters by Douglas and advised to go up country and get work on the roads.[55] More successful were John D'Ewes, who was recommended by Lytton and became Victoria's Post-Master, but absconded in 1861 with many of the takings,[56] and Joseph Trutch, a surveyor who became a large public works contractor in the 1860s, then, after British Columbia had joined Canada, its first Lieutenant-Governor.

The Colony of British Columbia was formally proclaimed in November 1858. But it must have appeared rather shaky when a letter arrived on 7 January from the Yale JP 'Captain' P.B. Whannell to the effect that, acting under a warrant issued by the Hill's Bar magistrate George Perrier, the 'notorious villain' Edward McGowan had come to Yale 'at the head of a lawless

---

[53] Lytton to Douglas, 14 Aug. 1858, no. 8, and his 15 Sept. minute on Douglas to Stanley, 26 July (*Despatches*). Douglas shared this view, asking in November for the immediate appointment of an Attorney-General, a Colonial Secretary, a Treasurer, and an auditor, with the three first posts 'filled by gentlemen of the best education and ability' to be paid accordingly; and both he and Lytton wanted to explore the possibility of offering former military and naval officers cheap purchases of land 'for the purpose of adding a respectable [and loyal] British element to the population' of British Columbia – Douglas to Lytton, 8 Nov. 1858, and Lytton to Douglas, 19 March 1859, no. 34 (*Despatches*)

[54] Ormsby, *British Columbia* pp. 156-7

[55] R. Byron Johnson, *Very Far West Indeed* (London, 1873), in *A source-book of Canadian history* p. 170

[56] Lytton tried to withdraw his recommendation on hearing of D'Ewes' questionable conduct in Ballarat, but mis-spelled his name (Lytton to Douglas, 29 Nov. 1858, and Douglas to Newcastle, 13 May 1862 – *Despatches*); Paul Parizeau, *Writing by the Steamer* Part 2, 'Stories from the early Mail Service of Victoria, Larceny in Victoria's Colonial Postal Service' (accessed 14/6/19)

band of ruffians, broke open the Jail, and liberated a Prisoner'. 'This town and district are in a state bordering on anarchy', with 'my own and the lives of the citizens ... in imminent peril.' Whannell besought Douglas' 'prompt aid', saying an 'effective blow must at once be struck on the operations of these outlaws, else I tremble for the welfare of the Colony'. Next day Douglas forwarded the letter to London, saying it 'correctly' portrayed 'the men we have to deal with ... reckless desperadoes requiring the strong arm to curb them'. He added that Lt. Governor Moody and Chief Justice Begbie had left for Yale with 25 Engineers and would be reinforced with marines and police.[57]

Moody and Begbie's steamer left Langley in haste at 11 pm. on 7 January but froze up for a day and only reached Hope on the 10th. *En route* they had learnt from the mail coach that Yale was quiet. At Hope, HBC factor Ogilvy confirmed this, but added that Whannell's character was such that 'an outbreak ... might take place at any moment' and he could easily be lynched. They were also met by Perrier, who had come to put his side of the case; and Begbie reported that all they had heard since leaving Langley had 'been on the side of what may be called Mr. Ned McGowan's faction'. Moody and Begbie decided on the low-key approach of leaving the troops at Hope, going on 'alone' to Yale, and trying 'to arrange matters in the ordinary way'.[58] This was wise. For while 'waiting the coming up of the troops', McGowan's party 'had arranged a plan, in the event of a collision with the troops [or if they 'adopted harsh measures towards us'], to take Fort Yale' and, though that might have proved more difficult, 'Fort Hope, and

---

[57] Douglas to Lytton, 8 Jan. 1859 (*Despatches* – Whannell's 31 Dec. 1858 letter is also in Howay, *Early History* pp. 56-7). See also Hauka, *McGowan's War* esp. chaps. 6 and 7 which draw on McGowan's 'Reminiscences' (San Francisco *Argonaut*, May-July 1878, esp. 1 and 8 June [now available online]), and on Moody's description of events to his Colonial Office friend Arthur Blackwood (Willard Ireland ed., 'First Impressions: Letter of Col. Richard ... Moody ... to Arthur Blackwood, February 1, 1859', *British Columbia Historical Quarterly* 15:1 (1951) pp. 85-107)

[58] Begbie to Douglas, 14 Jan. 1859, Moody to Douglas, 17 Jan. (both written from Yale) – Howay, *Early History* pp. 25-7, 33-4

retreat across country into Washington Territory – only twenty miles distant. This would, we supposed, bring on the fight and put an end to the long ... public clamor – that our boundary line must be "fifty-four forty or fight."' This, though, was a *dernier ressort*; and McGowan, who had heard well of Judge Begbie from the HBC's Allard, decided instead 'to stand trial, provided I was not sent [for this] to Victoria' (where the penalties would be higher).[59]

On arrival in Yale, Begbie and Moody were cheered; they returned thanks in the Queen's name, and then worked the crowd 'saying something friendly left and right'; and Begbie later conducted jail delivery hearings (jointly with the presumably reluctant Whannell), releasing people Whannel had arbitrarily detained by setting bail at astronomical levels. Whannell, McGowan would recall in a slightly confused passage, urged sending 40 soldiers to take and lodge him in jail pending trial; instead, McGowan sent Begbie a note promising to come voluntarily whenever wanted.[60]

However things then unravelled as a result of feuds from San Francisco. That city had been contested, sometimes violently, between the 'Law and Order' group and the 'Vigilance Committee'. People of both persuasions had come in 1858 to Yale (the drinking, social, and business centre) and its satellite the more purely mining Hill's Bar (one and a half miles downriver), with ex-Vigilance men more in evidence in the former, 'Law and Order' ones in the latter. Begbie wrote melodramatically that the life of none of the Hill's Bar leaders would have been 'worth an hour's purchase in ... San Francisco'. The Vigilante Dr. Fifer had backed Whannell in his row with Perrier. On Sunday the 16th, Perrier was told that he had been dismissed, and when this was made public there was what was euphemistically described as 'considerable excitement'.

---

[59] McGowan, 'Reminiscences', *The Argonaut*, 8 June 1878 p. 10. Moody would note that Hill's Bar was 'naturally a very strong place easily defended', especially as many of the miners had had earlier military experience, and had, when Whannell was taken to Hill's Bar, thrown 'out skirmishers' very professionally 'under a Major Dolan (a *real* Major)' - 'Moody to Blackwood' pp. 97-8)

[60] 'Moody to Blackwood' pp. 96-7; *The Argonaut*, 8 June 1878; Hauka, *McGowan's War* pp. 164-73

McGowan was in Yale (with Perrier), and that afternoon he encountered Fifer and called him out. Denouncing Fifer's 'slanderous tongue', McGowan 'commenced the affray', believing (Begbie thought) that he meant 'to construct something like a Vigilance Committee at Yale, directed' against Hill's Bar, 'and Dr. Fifer was rather roughly handled'.[61]

Moody decided that he should, after all, order up his Engineers from Hope and also send back to Langley for further reinforcements. The Engineers tried to avoid trouble by coming quietly by night, but they feared trouble – Ogilvy was given what Moody later described as 'the post of danger', being sent ahead to scout for ambush. As the party passed Hill's Bar, miners ran down to the river, shouting and firing their guns. This was probably 'only bravado', since the troops' commander heard no bullets, and instead of yielding to the temptation to return fire and very possibly provoking an incident, they pressed on regardless. Once in Yale they were given 'hot Coffee and breakfast' and paraded in full view of 'Heaps of Rowdies'. Everything then 'began to change ... Alarm vanished and Hill's Bar men were full of assurances ... that they were and always had been loyal men'. Indeed 200 staged a meeting in Yale that they pressed Moody and Begbie to attend. It opened with three cheers for the Governor, proceeded with an address 'pitching heavily into Whannell', followed by 'a very excellent (but superlatively humbugging)' speech, and concluded with three cheers for the Queen.[62]

Begbie thanked the speakers for their information but said he would be guided only by the facts. His conclusion was that Ikey Dixon had been assaulted at a Yale Christmas dance by two men,

---

[61] A leading member of the Vigilance Committee happened then to be in Yale, albeit on ordinary business - Begbie to Douglas, 3 Feb. 1859 (Howay, *Early History* pp. 37-9), Hauka, *McGowan's War* pp. 161-73

[62] Begbie to Douglas, 18 Jan. 1859 (Howay, *Early History* pp. 28-31); 'Moody to Blackwood' pp. 99-100; Hauka, *McGowan's War* pp. 174-6. Hill's Bar had earlier petitioned for Gold Commissioner Hick's dismissal, but as Whannell had (in his 31 December letter) ascribed the origin of the Yale disturbances to Hicks' acts in issuing gambling licences, it swung round to the only 'expressions of confidence' in him that Begbie ever encountered

Burns and Farrell. He complained to Whannell, who issued warrants for their arrest but also imprisoned Dixon to hold him as a witness. Burns and Farrell were apprehended in Hill's Bar and brought before Perrier, who sent Constable Hickson to Yale to fetch Dixon to give evidence. Whannell refused to release Dixon, instead ordering Hickson to bring Burns and Farrell to him. As Hickson would not do so without Perrier's authorisation, Whannell jailed him for contempt of court. On hearing this, Perrier issued one warrant for Whannell's apprehension and another demanding that Dixon be brought to Hill's Bar. To execute these, Perrier swore in McGowan and Kelly, 'the most noted men on Hill's Bar', and a dozen other special constables; they went to Yale 'fully armed', seized Whannell and his gaoler, and brought them before Perrier. The gaoler was discharged, but Perrier fined Whannell $25 plus costs for contempt of *his* court. Fifer, who had accompanied Whannell, paid and Whannell went home to appeal to Douglas for rescue. This was very much Perrier's version of events, and downplays (deliberately?) McGowan's role. He himself would recall that he had previously 'induced' Perrier to write a letter to Whannell. When Burns and Farrell fled to Hill's Bar, McGowan had gone to Whannell prepared to pay their fines, only to be rebuffed. Whannell later sought (through Fifer) to take up the offer. But McGowan changed his mind, persuaded 'his clients' Farrer and Burns to go before Perrier for trial, and took the opportunity 'to speak to the Judge about having Whannell arrested, brought down to ... [Hill's] bar and tried for contempt of [Perrier's] court', offering his services as constable. Perrier 'fell into the trap', then, when Whannell was brought before him, invited McGowan (much the better lawyer) to join him 'on the bench where I sat all the time while the trial was in progress'.[63]

---

[63] Perrier to Douglas, 4 Jan. 1859, and Begbie to Douglas 3 Feb. (Howay, *Early History* pp. 35-7, 52, 54-5); *The_Argonaut*, 1 June 1878 p. 10 – McGowan's 'Reminiscences' were written years later, probably exaggerate his own importance, and are at points chronologically confused, but should be taken seriously

Following the troops' arrival and good reception in Yale, Moody reported that 'the difficulties' there and at Hill's Bar 'are for the present settled'. A single constable was judged sufficient to summon McGowan to Yale for trial. To the charge of assaulting Fifer, he pleaded guilty, while descanting on his persecution in San Francisco and playing for sympathy with what he later admitted to have been 'bosh' about having sought 'protection under the British flag'; expressing regret, he promised 'to observe the laws strictly for the future', which, given 'his very considerable influence', Begbie thought would have more weight locally 'than any words of mine'. McGowan was duly fined $25 plus costs. Then, charged with arresting Whannell, he and Kelly contended that there was no case to answer, producing Perrier's warrant for Whannell's arrest, and calling Perrier to testify that they had only acted under his instructions. Concluding that no jury would convict, Begbie discharged them. Next day McGowan threw a huge Anglo-American-themed dinner at Hill's Bar for Begbie and the British officers.[64] But then, during a ball on Washington's birthday that the Hill's Bar leaders had promised would be trouble-free, McGowan smashed a plate over the head of someone who had insulted him. Duels were arranged (to be held, considerately, over the American border). McGowan's standing in Hill's Bar was undermined, and though the feuds were composed, he decided to sell up and return (with $4,700 in gold dust) to California, accompanied by two of his leading associates.[65] Meanwhile, Begbie reformed magistrates' selection and *modus operandi*, while Chartres Brew replaced Hicks as Gold Commissioner.

Moody had judged it prudent to leave troops in Yale, and Douglas believed this force – a hundred soldiers and marines – 'capable of overwhelming any factious opposition that may be offered to the enforcement of the Laws'.[66] 'McGowan's War' was over, to be remembered only as a curiosity. But things could have

---

[64] Begbie to Douglas, 3 Feb. 1859; Hauka, *McGowan's War* pp. 179-84, 189
[65] Chartres Brew to Douglas, 26 Feb. and 5 March 1859 (Howay, *Early History* pp. 84-7)
[66] 'Moody to Blackwood' p. 103; Douglas to Lytton, 22 Jan. 1859 (*Despatches*)

been different, and Douglas took the episode seriously. He did not want to have to rely on raising a local volunteer force, thinking it 'a most dangerous policy to put the sword in the hands of Aliens who have no love for British institutions, and who might turn it against Government whenever it suited their purpose.' He wanted instead a more professional force, and looked to recruit from the Royal Irish Constabulary. Whannell's original letter led Douglas to raise the number he was thus seeking from 60 to 150. But Lytton had already rejected a bid for £200,000 'to give the new Colony a fair start', and he was no more forthcoming now.[67] He felt B.C. should rely on its own resources (chiefly land sales), once observing, when criticised, that Merivale 'would sneer less at the economical system if he had to fight Estimates thru' the H[ouse] of C[ommons]'.[68] Lytton's Liberal successors were only a little more forthcoming, and the Colony's governance reflected this. Of the very small group of senior officials, most had several roles. Begbie was not only Chief – and itinerant[69] – Justice, but also on the Executive Council, and the drafter of the most important early legislation. And the same multi-tasking operated at a local level, much in the manner one associates with later colonial District Commissioners: on moving to a new area in 1871, the magistrate Peter O'Reilly indented for

'County Court Forms; Magistrates Forms; Treasury Forms; Mining Licenses; Leave of Absence Forms; Trade Licenses, Wholesale and Retail; Tape Line 100 feet; Gold Scales; one Flag and Halliard; two door locks and hinge; two press locks and hinges; four pairs of handcuffs; two pairs of leg

---

[67] Douglas to Lytton, 26 Oct., and Lytton to Douglas, 30 Dec., 1858); Douglas to Lytton, 27 Dec. 1858 enclosing Chartres Brew's letter dated 29 Dec., and Merivale's, Carnarvon's, and Lytton's March 1859 minutes on these; Douglas to Lytton, 2 July 1859 (*Despatches*)

[68] Lytton's 22 Jan. 1859 minute on Douglas' letter of 8 Nov. 1858 (*Despatches*)

[69] He is calculated to have ridden some 3,500 miles in 1865 – 'Begbie, Sir Matthew', *Dictionary of Canadian Biography*

irons; one tent; one axe; Brown's County Court Practice and
O'Keefe's Magistrates' Synopsis.'[70]

This style of government would give rise to problems. But, helped
by the fact that the European population was very low,[71] it
worked. In 1858 Douglas had had two main fears: of fighting
between Indians and the miners; and of a challenge to British rule
by American immigrants. Indian war had nearly come to the
Fraser Canyon in 1858. But thereafter the only one serious
outbreak was the small 1864 Chilcotin 'war'. As for the Americans,
Douglas' fears had proved groundless. They had come not as a
fifth column, but to make money, and McGowan's parting
assurance to Moody had been that

> 'the difficulties wd. Always be fr acts of violence arising fr
> personal quarrels only, never fr any opposition to the Govt.
> except what might arise on the spur of the moment & which
> some judgment on the part of the Magistrate might ...
> nearly always, avoid.'

Whannell and Perrier had not shown 'judgment', but other
officials were better – in May 1859 over 80 Hill's Bar miners
signed a testimonial to Chartres Brew, who had stepped in as their
temporary Gold Commissioner, praising his work and the way he
had 'retained the kind feelings and respect of all'.[72]

Still British fears remained. Douglas had originally meant to
build a capital for British Columbia near the HBC's existing Fort
Langley and had indeed already started selling plots there.

---

[70] Hatch, *British Columbia Police, 1858-1871* p. 40 – also pp. 7-8, 31
[71] In the absence of censuses estimates vary, but an 1861 petition alleging over-taxation put the total European population at 7,000, while Douglas said that (including the Chinese) it was really 10,000 (to Newcastle, 22 April 1861 – *Despatches*). In 1864 officials doubted whether the European population was much above 7,500 (Ormsby, *British Columbia* p. 209)
[72] 'Moody to Blackwood' p. 103; Margaret A. Ormsby, 'Some Irish Figures in Colonial Days', *British Columbia Historical Quarterly* 14:1 (1950) pp. 65-6

But early in 1859 Moody persuaded him that this would be too exposed to an American invasion, and that the town should be relocated to a position (New Westminster) further from the border that, shielded by the breadth of the Fraser, could be 'easily rendered unapproachable by the enemy'.[73] Later that year, during the 'Pig War' crisis, Moody dashed off a pessimistic military appreciation: he had not until recently been aware, 'I believe none of us were ... of the extremely small proportion of British subjects'. 'The vast majority' of the 'population in the mines are U. States citizens ready [in the event of an invasion] to rise and cooperate ... with their fellow countrymen.'[74] Actually, the population drawn in by the gold rushes was by now very mixed – American, British, other European, Chinese, and Hawaiian. The relative size of these groups varied with the seasons, since the British were more likely to settle permanently, the Americans to go south in the winter, returning again in the spring. And as time moved on the American element became less important. Even in 1858 the names of the diggings above Yale were less American than those along the original stretch below it. By 1860 the collection of customs duties had been sufficiently extended to discourage direct access from Washington Territory, while the outbreak of Civil War next year

---

[73] Moody to Douglas, 28 Jan. 1859, forwarded to Lytton on 4 Feb. (*Despatches*). Defence apart, Moody also felt Langley was so close to the frontier that, were it to be B.C.'s capital, it would become 'an American Town' using Bellingham just over the border as its 'Chief port' ('Moody to Blackwood' p. 104)

[74] Moody therefore regarded British Columbia as indefensible without substantial military reinforcements, though sea-power would enable Britain to hold Victoria – to Douglas, 8 Aug. 1859 (*Despatches*, forwarded to Lytton in an undated letter no. 9576, 2). Two years later, during the *Trent* crisis, Douglas was more optimistic. In the event of war, Puget Sound (from which US regulars had been withdrawn) should at once be seized, 'cutting off the Enemy's supplies by sea ... and entirely crippling his resources'; and were 'one or two Regiments' to be sent out, they could push overland to the Columbia, send a small naval force up it, 'and soon compel' the country 'to submit to Her Majesty's Rule' – thus recovering, though Douglas did not say so, the border for which Britain had contended before 1846. Douglas was 'firmly persuaded' that this would be practicable, and that it would require fewer troops than would defending B.C.'s long border (Douglas to Newcastle, 28 Dec. 1861– *Despatches*)

further restricted American immigration.[75] Also new gold strikes were further and further north; and by 1862, when miners converged on the Cariboo, Begbie could declare that it seemed 'as though every good family of the east and of Great Britain had sent' its best son there.[76] With such changes, and with the repeated demonstration that the Americans had come not to overthrow the government but to make money, the earlier fears of risings subsided – though the wider question of how British Columbia should relate to the US did not go away.

One drawback of the Cariboo discoveries was their remoteness. Road building had started in 1858, and it continued to follow the diggings. Two-thirds of the colony's taxes had, Douglas said in 1861, been spent on such works 'which have produced a reduction of not less than 100 per cent [sic] on the cost of transport, and nearly as great a saving in the cost of all the necessaries of life'; and when the Cariboo's potential was confirmed, he determined to 'push on rapidly with the formation of roads' 'to the remotest mines', so as 'to render travel easy, ... thereby securing the whole trade of the Colony for Frasers River, and defeating all attempts at competition from Oregon.' Any other course, he later wrote, 'would have brought the progress of the Colony to a standstill'.[77] So 'between 1859 and 1866' British Columbia 'completed, at a cost of nearly a quarter of a million sterling, more than 600 miles of waggon road' through sometimes very difficult country (blasting through the Fraser Canyon cost over £4,000 a mile).[78] Though financed, to a controversial extent, by tolls, it had required borrowing.

Douglas retired in 1864 in a well-deserved blaze of glory. Yet his administration bequeathed problems. British Columbia grew

[75] Marshall, *Claiming the land* pp. 134, 194-5
[76] Walkem, *Stories of Early British Columbia* p. 270
[77] Douglas to Newcastle, 22 April and 24 Oct. 1861, and 3 June 1863 (*Despatches*)
[78] Confidential Print, CO 880/5/10, '"British Columbia Finance". Memorandum by Sir Frederic Rogers, Permanent Under-Secretary ... and A.N. Birch' p. 11; Carrolyne Yardley, *The Cariboo Gold Rush Overview* (1998, accessed 21/10/15)

up as a colony distinct from Vancouver Island. But Douglas and other high officials lived in Victoria, making only occasional visits to the mainland. They were perceived, especially in New Westminster, as favouring Vancouver Island, and political antipathy between the two lasted for decades. Also administration was confined to a smallish group of Anglo-Irish or English officials. This was natural enough; government had had to be created largely from scratch, before the arrival of most of the settlers. Moreover Lytton had insisted that most of these officials should come from the UK. The group was neither static nor entirely harmonious – Douglas managed, eventually, to get rid of Moody and of Treasurer Gosset. But professional cooperation generated friendships, sometimes reinforced by marriages; and though well able to rough it upcountry, this group 'dearly loved social life and were punctilious in observing the niceties of the rules that prevailed at home'.[79] There thus developed an upper class of English officials, which tended to look down socially on the more middle-class Canadians.[80]

Douglas shared their disdain: he had, he wrote in response to a complaint, given offence by not cultivating 'the Canadian, in preference to the sound sterling English element in the Colony'.[81] In relation to the press, at least, this was understandable. Eastern newspaper editors (and more particularly Brown of the *Globe*) were first class political figures, and west coast activists had similar aspirations. The Nova Scotian Amor De Cosmos (né William Smith) arrived in Victoria in June 1858 and soon launched the *British Colonist* as the 'friend of reform' and scourge of what

---

[79] Margaret Ormsby gives brief accounts of such leading Anglo-Irish figures ('Some Irish Figures' esp. pp. 61-4); Hauka sees 'Begbie, Moody, Cary, Joseph Trutch and Joseph Pemberton' as heading a 'new elite' that sprung up in the early 1860s 'based on political power and legitimate connections to the Old Country' McGowan's War p. 214), a hostile view of which features in Trutch's *Dictionary of Canadian Biography* entry

[80] Governor Musgrave's 1869 choice of a Canadian-trained doctor after a riding accident made waves. His recovery was slow, and next July Attorney-General Crease's wife commented, 'Poor man! I feel so sorry he has such confidence in that Canadian doctor' (Ormsby, *British Columbia*, p. 234)

[81] To Newcastle, 13 May 1863 (ibid. p. 191)

he saw as 'family-company compact' government. Likewise, in New Westminster, the tone of John Robson's *British Columbian* is indicated by its 16 May 1861 spread, 'On the 3rd of March last, the serfs of Russia were emancipated. When will our time come?'[82] 'Emancipation' meant the 'responsible government' that was now general in the east, and its advocacy went with the intent that it should open the way to office for its promoters (as it eventually did), whereas in Vancouver Island, and even more in British Columbia, government was essentially the province of the Governor and his chosen advisers. Despite some movement in a more representative direction, the Legislative Council consisted (after the two colonies' 1866 merger) of 13 official and only 9 elected members; and all Governors shared the Duke of Newcastle's view that since British Columbia had too few people for 'responsible government', this would either give control to 'a small circle ... occupied by their own local personal or class interests', or place too much power in the hands of a purely transient population 'with no permanent interest in the prosperity of the Colony'.[83]

These cleavages, between Vancouver Island and the mainland, between the English and the Canadians, and between Government and political reformers, overlapped and were to prove important when the question of accession to Canada came to the fore. They were made more serious by economic depression. Douglas had ridden the gold boom. But in 1864 an important Cariboo bank failed, and next year the usual influx of miners did not come. British Columbia nevertheless decided to complete the Cariboo Road, and it also had to meet the £20,000 cost of suppressing the Chilcotin rising, while Vancouver Island pressed on with official buildings and public works, and found itself reduced to suing for a merger with British Columbia. London compelled a reluctant British Columbia to take it on, with substantial (though temporary) damage to the customs receipts. So when Governor Seymour

---

[82] 'De Cosmos, Amor', *Dictionary of Canadian Biography*; Olive Fairholme, 'John Robson and Confederation', in W. George Shelton ed., *British Columbia & Confederation* (Victoria, 1967) pp. 99, 101

[83] Newcastle to Douglas, 15 June 1863, 'Separate' (*Despatches*)

returned, in November 1866, from a visit to (and marriage in) Great Britain to head the now united colony, he was faced with a debt of $1.3 m. and a very serious situation. As the Colonial Office put it,

'In 1867 the growing indebtedness of British Columbia, and finally the refusal of the Bank of British Columbia to lend the Government any more money, obliged the Governor to arrest public works, to terminate the contract under which letters were sent to San Francisco, and to pray the Home Government to allow him to draw on them for 50,000l.'[84]

Seymour sought the aid in a telegram, declaring it 'Politically important ... Many officials must be dismissed if we get no help'; this, he explained in a supplementary letter, would jeopardise 'the conveyance of mails to Cariboo' and cause 'the most serious dissatisfaction amongst the miners'.[85]

Both the *British Colonist* and the *British Columbian* had from the outset given support to the idea of a federation of all Britain's North American colonies. But in 1864-7 the two west coast ones were chiefly concerned with their own affairs, their merger, and the highly contentious resultant choice of a capital. In March 1867 De Cosmos introduced a Legislative Council motion seeking B.C.'s inclusion in the new Canada. Only he and Robson, Helmcken remembered, 'knew much of this subject'. People were happy to join them in pressing Seymour to ask London to include, in the bill establishing Confederation, provision for British

---

[84] Margaret Ormsby, 'Frederick Seymour, the Forgotten Governor', *B.C. Studies* 22 (1974) pp. 10, 13; '"British Columbia Finance". Memorandum by Sir Frederic Rogers ... and A.N. Birch' p. 1

[85] Seymour's 28 Nov. 1867 cable and 13 Dec. explanatory letter (Confidential Print, CO 880/5/11, 'British Columbia. Copy of a Despatch from Governor Seymour to ... the Duke of Buckingham...' pp. 1, 3). In their responses to Seymour's cable, both Rogers and Birch advocated lending the £50,000 to preserve the Colony's credit; their analysis (CO 880/5/10) was printed for the Cabinet, 21 Feb. 1868, but the Cabinet ultimately refused the aid (Buckingham to Seymour, 13 July 1868 (*Despatches*)

Columbia's 'ultimate admission'. De Cosmos then tabled a motion seeking 'immediate entrance', but it was watered down into one approving the general principle of Confederation and asking Seymour to take steps to insure B.C.'s admission 'on fair and equitable terms'. Seymour had cabled London as requested, promising to write further, but did not do so; and the Colonial Secretary, the Duke of Buckingham, held off from replying in expectation of a fuller explanation of 'the reasons for this telegram'.[86] By September Seymour was deeply depressed both as to the province's finances (and their impact on his own salary), and as to the contrast people were drawing between Britain's stinginess and 'the energetic efforts now being made by the Americans to garrison' their recent purchase of Alaska 'and develop its meagre resources'. The 'main chance of keeping British Columbia English in sentiment', he suggested, 'is to furnish from home some pecuniary aid, some military assistance, or help its communications with the Dominion of Canada'. He therefore restated 'the wish of the people of this Colony and my own, for a fusion or an ultimate connexion with the Eastern Confederation', leaving it to Buckingham to decide whether 'that wish can be carried out'.

The Colonial Office had already been led to give the matter some thought by a panicky despatch in July forecasting a $223,000 deficit for the year. This had led the Permanent Undersecretary Sir Frederic Rogers to anticipate that 'high taxation, distress and want of assistance from home will probably cause ... [B.C.'s] American population ... to press for annexation – a pressure wh wd soon become irresistable (sic) except at a cost far greater than the fee simple the Colony'. Equally he feared that 'if the Colonists once find the annexation threat satisfactory in extracting money ... they will plunder us indefinitely by it'. So he posed the question whether, 'in the long run', B.C. was to 'form part of the

---

[86] Helmcken, *Reminiscences* pp. 239-40; J.W. Trutch to Acting Governor Philip Hankin, forwarded to Lord Granville, 19 July 1869, and Seymour's 11 March 1867 cable to Buckingham (*Despatches*). Provision had in fact already been made (British North America Act, Clause 146) for the future accession of other provinces including British Columbia

U.S. or of Canada; and if we desire to promote the latter ... what form of expenditure or non-expenditure is likely to facilitate ... it?' The Parliamentary Undersecretary C.B. Adderley thought it 'impossible that we should long hold B.C. from its natural annexation' and suggested that the minister in Washington 'should keep his ears open for any overtures of equivalents' for it. 'Still we should give ... Canada every chance, & if possible get Seymour to bridge over the present difficulties till we see what Canada may do.' But the Colonial Secretary, the Duke of Buckingham, had eschewed such speculation.[87] When Seymour himself raised the question of the Colony's 'ultimate connexion' with Canada, Buckingham's response was to postpone the question until the time 'when the intervening territory now under the control of the H.B.Co. shall have been incorporated within the Confederation'.[88]

Seymour therefore left the subject alone. Privately he sometimes remarked that he was 'by no means averse' to the measure.[89] But he left official members of the Legislative Council entirely free as to how they should vote, and he never raised the topic in the Executive Council. However De Cosmos went to Ottawa in 1867 to press the matter, and he was followed by a number of other Confederation advocates. Both Sir John Macdonald and his Customs Minister Leonard Tilley kept up a correspondence with the Canadian party. As in the Red River, this proved counterproductive. Telegrams were published, and

'the impression got abroad that secret negotiations ... were on foot ... of which the general public, the local Government and the Legislature were not cognizant.

[87] Minutes of 16 and 17 Sept. on Seymour's 15 July 1867 despatch to Buckingham, (*Despatches*)

[88] Seymour to Buckingham, 24 Sept. 1867 (explanation of the Legislative Council Resolution as a plea for assistance from 'either England or Canada towards the making of a road across the continent' and suggestion that this, or other 'pecuniary aid', afforded the best chance of keeping B.C. 'English in sentiment') and Buckingham to Seymour, 19 Nov. 1867 (*Despatches*)

[89] Collector of Customs W. Hamley to Hankin, forwarded to Granville 19 July 1869 (*Despatches*)

It was thought possible that ... the Colony ... might ... find itself actually landed in Confederation, before it had once had an opportunity of expressing its deliberate opinion as to the terms ... on which alone Confederation might meet with cordial concurrence.

The effect of these ... proceedings of unauthorized persons, on the public mind ... showed itself' in April 1868, when de Cosmos' address urging B.C.'s admission to Confederation on the basis of a detailed package of terms was stalled by 12 votes to 4, and then again in February 1869. A protest was then moved against a piece in the *Illustrated London News* implying that B.C. had 'pronounced in favor of Confederation'. Angered by abuse from R.W. Carrall, the 'Official Element' was, we are told, 'determined to put a final stop' to 'unauthorized negociation' with Canadian ministers, and Council resolved by eleven to five that, 'under existing circumstances', confederation with Canada 'would be undesirable, even if practicable'. One participant concluded that while there was a 'minority ... totally opposed to Confederation on any terms', the vote represented 'not so much ... opposition to the abstract idea ... of British Columbia eventually' joining Confederation 'as a conviction that any immediate steps would be premature'.[90]

It was, Dr. Helmcken later recollected, easy 'to get up public meetings'; and there were plenty. Dr. Carrall called a pro-Confederation meeting in Cariboo shortly after he arrived there in 1867. In January 1868 one was held in Victoria, presided over by the Mayor. A Confederation League was then established in Victoria in May, set up branches on the mainland, and in September staged a delegate conference in Yale. The Yale resolutions, Helmcken says, met with ridicule because one of the delegates was black. But they were taken seriously enough for 307 citizens of Victoria (headed by

---

[90] Letters to Hankin from Attorney-General Crease, J.W. Trutch, and Acting Colonial Secretary Good, all forwarded on 19 July 1869 (*Despatches*)

Helmcken) and 72 foreigners to sign documents of repudiation.[91] Ideas were of course fluid – Helmcken had favoured Confederation in 1867, but later turned against it. So perhaps the best indicators we have of the balance of opinion are the Legislative Council elections of 1868, in which Confederation was said to have featured as a 'test case': on Vancouver Island De Cosmos was defeated and four opponents of Confederation returned (their critics said with the support of Americans and annexationists), while the mainland elected four supporters (including Carrall and Robson) and one uncommitted candidate. There may, though, have been some subsequent decline in anti-Confederation sentiment – in July 1869 one official doubted whether any candidate 'would improve his chances by declaring himself opposed'.[92]

In Ottawa, Macdonald had recognised that nothing (beyond agitation) could be done till Canada had secured Rupert's Land: he wanted British Columbia, he told the owner of the *Colonist* in 1868, 'but policy was not to take it until H. B. Territory was had too ... Must have intervening territory'.[93] In April 1869 arrangements were at last made for Canada to buy Rupert's Land, and Ottawa again pressed the Colonial Office to get Governor Seymour to move for BC's accession. It was, Governor-General Sir John Young wrote, 'assumed that the great majority of the ... constituencies in British Columbia will be found well disposed to enter the Confederation', and in support he enclosed extracts from a letter of Carrall's to Macdonald.[94] A Colonial Office minute on this raised the question of whether, now that Canada would soon border on B.C., the London

---

[91] Helmcken, *Reminiscences* pp. 242-3, 246, 247; P.P. 1868-9 xliii pp. 357-66 (the Yale proceedings), pp. 366-8 (dissenting names); Ormsby, 'Frederick Seymour' pp. 16, 20

[92] Letters from Crease, Trutch, and Hamley to Hankin, all forwarded on 19 July 1869 (*Despatches*)

[93] Extracts from D.W. Higgins' lost Diary account of his Ottawa visit, printed in R.E. Gosnell, *The Story of Confederation...* (n.pl., 1918) pp. 85-6

[94] Sir John Young to Granville, 28 April 1869 (CO 42/675 fos. 403-4), enclosing extracts from Carrall's 2 April letter (fos. 411-16); Macdonald followed up on 25 May by urging Young to secure Seymour's recall (Ormsby, 'Frederick Seymour' pp. 20-1

Government should 'encourage or discourage [its] Confederation' with Canada. Comment, Rogers responded, was 'rather difficult' since the Home Government had 'not yet fully considered' the question. He presumed that Confederation 'would not be forced on BC – partly from respect to their feelings – partly from the doubtfulness of the scheme viewed as a matter of administration'. Equally, it would 'not be obstructed if both parties wished for it'. 'H M Govt influence' might be used, to a 'reasonable' extent, 'to favour it, if Canada wished it, and BC was doubtful.' But if the Canadians wanted Confederation, they should not rely on London but 'set their own shoulders to the wheel – and make the people ... of B.C.' their friends. Rogers placed 'very little reliance' on either Carrall's letter in favour of Confederation or the recent Legislative Council vote against it, but suggested telling Macdonald that 'at present' the latter 'must be taken as an expression of adverse opinion on the part of B.C.'. Governor Seymour should, though, be asked whether this just reflected hostile votes by the Official Members. In the meantime, London could not usefully interfere. Lord Granville approved, and on 2 June wrote accordingly to both Ottawa and Victoria.[95]

Granville soon changed his mind. On the 15th news of Seymour's death came by telegraph. The Queen was told that this was 'not a Matter of Regret as regards Your Majesty's service'. He should be replaced 'as soon as possible with the best man, for on the future Governor will much depend whether British Columbia will join the Canadian Dominion or become Americanized'; and Granville at once recommended Anthony Musgrave, 'an excellent man, and the person the Canadian Gov[ernment] desire to see' there. As Governor of Newfoundland, Musgrave had already negotiated terms for its adhesion to Canada (though they would in December be rejected by a general election), and Rogers later

---

[95] CO 42/675 fos. 405-6, Minutes (20-24 May 1869), fos. 407-10, Draft Letters (2 June). Asked how far the majority for Council's 'Resolution against Union' had been 'composed of public officers', Acting Governor Hankin got all the magistrates to comment, and forwarded the results to Granville (CO 60/36 fos. 234-81); they rather evaded the point by stressing that Seymour had left them completely free to decide on how to vote

minuted that his transfer 'to B.C. was at the desire of the Canadian auth[or]i[ti]es who thought themselves secure of Nfld, & wished to push on without delay'.[96] Musgrave was telegraphed to go at once to British Columbia, and told the question of Confederation was urgent: while the government did not want him to suggest that they meant to 'overrule' B.C.'s wishes, they attached importance to its 'early adhesion to ... the North American Confederation'; Musgrave should act accordingly, though without identifying himself 'with the views' of Confederation's 'more ardent' partisans.[97]

In writing to the Queen, Granville had suggested that if British Columbia did not join Canada, it would 'become Americanized'. Carrall's letter to Macdonald had observed that 'Yankee Emissaries [on Vancouver Island] are numerous and busily advocate' annexation to the United States. 'Many Englishmen', though no Canadians, 'are prepared to embrace that view'; and there was 'no saying what the annexationist leaven may effect', since 'the Hudson's Bay Factors' all favoured it in hopes that 'the real estate in which they have all invested will rise again on its accomplishment'.[98] Macdonald absorbed his correspondents' views, telling Musgrave 'letters from British Columbia show that things are in a bad way. The Government Officials, the Hudson's Bay agents and yankee adventurers have

---

[96] Granville to the Queen, June (probably the 15th) 1869 – Kent M. Haworth and Charles R. Maier, '"Not a Matter of Regret": Granville's Response to Seymour's Death', *BC Studies* 27 (Autumn 1875) p. 66. Musgrave had applied to succeed Seymour, whose term would be up next year (to Granville, 20 Feb. 1869 – CO 194/178 fos. 87-92, 135), and had also sought, and been given, Macdonald's support (Macdonald to Musgrave, and to Governor-General Young, 25 May 1869 (Libraries and Archives Canada, MIKAN 542084). Rogers' 15 Dec. minute that his transfer to B.C. was at the desire of the Canadian authorities is on Musgrave to Granville, 30 Oct. 1869 (*Despatches*)

[97] Granville to Musgrave, 17 June 1869 (CO 60/36 fos. 24-5)

[98] Carrall still held to this in 1876, telling the Canadian Senate that one of 'the strongest reasons' impelling 'loyal Canadians' in B.C. towards Confederation was that 'emissaries from the United States ... were pressing them' to join the Republic (Senate Debates, 3rd Parliament, 3rd Session: Vol. 1, 20 March 1876, pp. 152-3)

conspired together to defeat Confederation ... The consequence is great depression ... and increased feeling for annexation.'[99]

Whether Macdonald was right to believe this is less clear. Annexationist feeling had probably peaked in 1867 following news in April that the United States would be taking over Alaska and an (unfounded) report from New York that it was also negotiating to buy western British Columbia. In terms both of economics and of morale, the colony was then at a low ebb, and the news that it would soon be 'hemmed in' by American territory had, as Secretary of State Seward intended, made people 'feel more solitary and unprotected': 'How Cd. England let the States get Russian America?' asked Attorney-General Henry Crease. On Vancouver Island, the Victoria *News* and the Nanaimo *Tribune* came out for annexation, while the Victoria *Colonist* wavered before declaring in May in favour of Confederation 'as the only course that will preserve the loyalty of the people'. (Mainland newspapers, by contrast, all opposed union with the US, Robson's *British Columbian* protesting 'indignantly' 'against being sold ... to a foreign power like so many slaves'.)[100] American consuls were always given to detecting annexationist sentiment, and Allen Francis in Victoria was no exception. People, he told Seward, were urging annexation 'with great unanimity' as the only 'means of retrieving the Colonies from their present embarrassment and decline'. More observantly, a visiting American lawyer found that while 'all the Irish, Germans, and other naturalized subjects ... were most decidedly in favor of annexation', the 'English and Scotch' were 'extremely careful not to ... do anything which would subject them to imputations of disloyalty'. He did, though, believe they would mostly go for annexation if a vote 'could be called for with the consent' of the

---

[99] Macdonald to Musgrave, 25 May 1869; he also sent the Governor-General a letter 'from a newspaper man' to Tilley that 'corroborates' Carrall's statements (Macdonald to Young, 25 May 1869)
[100] Richard E. Neunherz, '"Hemmed In": Reactions in British Columbia to the Purchase of Russian America', *Pacific Northwest Quarterly* 80:3 (1989) pp. 103-6

British government.[101] In June Governor Seymour reported that there was 'a systematic agitation ... in favour of annexation. It is believed that money for its maintenance is provided from San Francisco.' Seymour was still fairly relaxed: 'We are not prosperous but there is no political agitation & the one paper specially employed to advocate annexation has ceased to exist.' Moreover, on 'the mainland the question of annexation' was 'not mooted', and during a recent tour he had been 'received everywhere with ... expressions of loyalty to the Government I represent.'[102] That said, Victoria, with a population of four to five thousand, was both B.C.'s largest town and something of a political hothouse; and, as HBC Chief Factor Tolmie reported, some people, particularly 'foreign-born residents', had succumbed to 'captivating assertions' that annexation would bring in investments and make it 'a city second only to San Francisco'. In July Francis was able to send Seward the draft of a petition asking Queen Victoria either to relieve B.C. of its debts and provide it with other assistance, or 'graciously permit' it 'to become a portion of the United States'. But its promoters were, American officers later reported, 'furiously assailed' with charges of disloyalty and treasonable conduct. Presumably for this reason, the petition attracted less support than its promoters had hoped. It was never formally presented, and the issue dropped out of the newspapers.[103]

It did, though, remain alive. In September a US fleet called in on its way to Sitka to receive the transfer of Russian America. This led Governor Seymour to fire off a series of pessimistic despatches on the colony's financial position, 'the total self-reliance imposed on us and the absence of all assistance from Home', and the

---

[101] Consul Francis to Seward, 23 April 1867, and W. Carey Johnson to Seward, 29 April (Neunherz, '"Hemmed In"' pp. 104-5)
[102] Seymour to Buckingham, 26 June 1867 (*Despatches*); Willard E. Ireland, 'The Annexationist Petition of 1869', *British Columbia Historical Quarterly* 4:4 (1940) pp. 268-9
[103] Tolmie did add that the controversy was largely fuelled by 'the discontent universally felt here with the form and manner of government in the Colony' – Neunherz, '"Hemmed In"' pp. 106-9; Ireland, 'The Annexationist Petition' pp. 268-9

danger that 'the annexationist feeling prevalent in Victoria' would be 'stimulated by the contrast' between this and 'the energetic efforts being made by the Americans to garrison [and develop] the miserable territory' of Alaska.[104] Two of the US officers stayed on in B.C. for a couple of months. They found a widespread feeling that annexation offered the 'only possible relief from the utter prostration of business'. This view, they claimed, was universal amongst the foreign population. It was, too, strongly held by HBC officers, though they preferred not to voice it in public. And even high 'colonial officials' told them that 'if it was for the best interests of the people, and their desire [was] that the colony should be ceded to the United States, such a cession should be made'. Many 'Englishmen' were admittedly 'so sensitive about their loyalties as British subjects' that they would 'vote against a cession even if a referendum were held'; but were 'the cession ... proclaimed as a fact', presumably with Britain's consent, 'rejoicings ... would be most enthusiastic and general'.[105]

All this suggests that much 'annexationist' sentiment was low key. Many people will have believed, with Helmcken, that joining the United States would eventually prove inevitable, without doing (or indeed wishing to do) anything to bring it about. The sponsors of the January 1868 Victoria Confederationist meeting were probably correct in observing that 'there is a small party in favour of annexation to the United States, and if it were practicable or possible their number would be largely increased.'[106] But it was not. Annexation was never raised at the official level, nor were there any British moves to sanction it.

That said, Macdonald was not alone in feeling concern. On 19 July 1869 a Colonial Office official minuted that he had been told the pro-Canadians were the larger party, but those for the United States the 'more stirring'. He suggested that a

[104] Seymour to Buckingham, 24, 25, and 28 Sept. 1867 (*Despatches*)
[105] Report by Lieutenant Scott and Major Hoyt, 20 Nov. 1867, forwarded by General Halleck to the US Adjutant General, 21 and 22 Nov. (Neunherz, '"Hemmed In"' pp. 109-10)
[106] P.P. 1868-9 xliii p. 346

pronouncement by the Home Government 'in favour of Union with Canada would not only instil energy into the ... [former], but would convert many of the latter.' Musgrave was accordingly sent a clear statement that Her Majesty's Government wanted B.C. to confederate with Canada, though it did not seek to prescribe the terms. Musgrave would have preferred to keep this quiet until he could lay it before his Legislative Council in December. But Canadian ministers leaked it to 'unofficial persons' in B.C.[107] Annexationists reacted by getting up a new petition. This declared (with some justice) that nearly 'all our commercial relations are with the United States ... They supply most of the necessities of life; They furnish us the *only* means of communication with the outside world; and we are even dependent upon them for the means of learning the events in the mother Country or the Dominion of Canada'. Confederation, the petition's bearer felt, 'would increase their burdens without affording them either political protection or material relief.'[108] Instead, President Grant was asked to procure, in his general negotiations with Britain, B.C.'s transfer to the United States.[109] However the petition attracted only forty-three signatures. Responding to enquiries from the British minister in Washington, Musgrave insisted that they were 'not those of British subjects or of persons of any standing or influence' and brushed the episode off as of 'no importance'.[110] The *British Colonist* opined that since

---

[107] Minute (approved by Granville), CO 60/36 fos. 26-7; Granville to Musgrave, 14 Aug. 1869 (P.P. 1868-9 xliii pp. 370-1); Musgrave to Granville, 30 Oct. 1869 (*Despatches*). Musgrave said that the leak and Canadian ministers' addiction to 'private correspondence with individuals here who have no official status and little social importance' had caused 'some little irritation'

[108] Ireland, 'The Annexation Petition' pp. 270, 273. In 1868-70 the US took between 41 and 51% of B.C.'s exports, and supplied from 54% to 64% of its imports; Britain accounted for most of the rest (Paul A. Phillips, 'Confederation and the Economy of British Columbia', in Shelton ed., *British Columbia & Confederation* p. 60

[109] Secretary of State Fish cited this when pressing Britain to quit North America; but there was no other response

[110] Musgrave to Edward Thornton (in Washington) and to Granville, 27 Feb. and 7 March 1870 (CO 60/38 fos. 242-3, 247-8). In Ireland's view, the petition's signatories were mainly Germans or Jews; in other respects, they represented 'a

'Annexation is impossible, even if it were desirable, and ... Confederation is inevitable, even if it were undesirable, would not all of us be more profitably employed in seeking to secure the best possible terms'?[111]

This was essentially what Governor Musgrave was doing. He toured B.C., and then put in a long report that played up his difficulties – probably to impress the Canadian government (to which it was copied).[112] Though it was 'believed in Canada' that there was 'a very general desire for Union', with opposition 'almost entirely confined' to the Officials on Council, there was, he said, 'a great diversity' of views; and it was by no 'means clear that the majority of the community are prepared for Union ... except on terms which are not likely to be possible...'. There were many foreigners who, 'though they live contentedly enough at present', 'would lean rather towards annexation to the United States, if there is to be a change'. Moreover, among people who had come from Britain, 'the feeling in favour of Confederation is not strong': with some notable exceptions, Canadians had not favourably impressed 'their fellow colonists', and this had left many disinclined 'to transfer the control of their affairs to Canadian authority'. Lastly, farmers feared that the Canadian tariff would give them insufficient protection.

Musgrave was scathing about the most prominent 'Agitators for Confederation', 'a small knot of Canadians' who hoped to make 'Responsible Government part of the new arrangements, and ... so place themselves in positions of influence and emolument.' They were allied with merchants looking to make Victoria a 'Free Port' again, chiefly to facilitate smuggling into the

---

fairly adequate sampling of the various elements' of Victoria's population. Nationality in the Victoria of the day was very fluid: most signatories remained there 'long after Confederation' and some rose to 'positions of considerable importance' ('The Annexation Petition' p. 281)

[111] 20 Nov. 1869 – ibid. p. 283

[112] Musgrave to Granville, 30 Oct. 1869. Granville was sufficiently concerned to tell Musgrave not to make any formal proposal to his Council unless he thought he could carry it (31 Dec. 1869) - *Despatches*

US.[113] 'From this combination the movement derives its greatest force', the remainder coming from people favouring Confederation 'partly from sentiment, partly from a restless desire for any change which they hope may improve their own prospects, without much thought as to how this is to be effected'. Musgrave had therefore 'taken the conduct of the matter into my own hands from those of persons [presumably like De Cosmos and Robson] who are not likely to carry it to a successful issue'.

Musgrave believed union 'to be possible', though far more difficult than it had proved in the East. He would exclude both 'Responsible Government'[114] and Victoria's conversion into a Free Port. That would dull the ardour of many who now clamoured for Confederation, but it would also remove 'a great deal of opposition' from what Musgrave later described as a 'sector of the Community having much' more 'at stake in its welfare'.[115] As for the Officials, he thought 'any personal motive for opposition' could be overcome by providing, in the terms of Union, that they should have the option of retiring 'on suitable Pensions'. But there would remain other difficulties, notably over finance and over the Colony's geographical position. The Rockies were a formidable barrier, and free 'commercial intercourse would be easier with Australia than with Canada'; so B.C. would probably demand at least a 'Waggon Road if not ... a Railway as a condition of Union'. He would, though, with the aid of his Executive Council, prepare 'some plan of Union' and put it to the next Legislative session.

Over the autumn, Musgrave worked on this, and, more generally, on his Officials. These constituted nearly half the legislature, and 'without the aid of the Official vote opinion' was 'so much divided' that the outcome would be 'very doubtful' – or

---

[113] A.N. Birch had observed that Victoria had, 'to a great extent, [been] sustained by the smuggling trade with the neighbouring American coast,' now largely 'destroyed by the abolition of the free port' ('"British Columbia Finance"' p. 10)
[114] With fewer than 10,000 Europeans, B.C. had hardly enough material even for the present 'imperfectly representative Legislative Chamber'
[115] Musgrave to Granville, 21 Feb. 1870 (*Despatches*)

so, at least, he told the Canadian Governor-General.[116] The Officials were English (or Anglo-Irish), and the idea of working to Ottawa not London did not appeal: 'Dear old Victoria will be sadly different in many respects', E.G. Alston wrote on the eve of Confederation; 'We are a conquered country & the Canucks take possession tomorrow.'[117] But their chief concern was with its likely effect on their own livelihoods. Confederation 'without conditions', Alston had written in early 1869 'would be a burning shame'; 'officials ought to combine & press our claims on the Govt. before such a catastrophe occurs, or we may be left out in the cold.' By September things had moved on, and O'Reilly wrote that since there was 'little doubt' Confederation would come 'sooner or later', 'our only chance is to work together, & battle against it until a satisfactory provision is made for us.'[118] Musgrave promised to insist on such provision. He also stressed, in private interviews, that 'HM Govt wish B.C. to come into Confederation' (albeit by an unforced vote of its legislature), as did the Canadian government, which was alarmed by 'the annexation cry' and feared that, 'if left alone, [B.C.] might choose to join the U.S.'[119] By January 1870 Musgrave was ready to come out formally for Confederation. And he could, where necessary, be firm, telling A.F. Pemberton that the proposals would be 'essentially a government measure'; 'I have therefore to request that you will afford them that support, in the Council, which it is usual to expect in these occasions from Officers of the Government.'[120]

---

[116] Musgrave to Young, 20 Feb. 1870 (copied to Granville, 21 Feb.)

[117] E.G. Alston to Crease, 26 June and 19 July 1871 (Ormsby, *British Columbia* pp. 250-1)

[118] Alston to Crease, 11 Feb., and O'Reilly to Crease, 16 Sept., 1869 – Susan Dickson Scott, 'The Attitude of the Colonial Governors towards Confederation', in Shelton, *British Columbia & Confederation* p. 148; Ormsby, *British Columbia* p. 228

[119] Helmcken's account of the way in which, even though he had been elected to oppose Confederation, Musgrave kept him working on the project (*Reminiscences* pp. 251-4). Helmcken was not an official, but he was on the Executive Council, and presumably his experience was not untypical

[120] Musgrave to Pemberton, 12 Feb. 1870 (Scott, 'The Attitude of the Colonial Governors' p. 157)

As to the terms to be demanded of Canada, Musgrave professed to find the financial ones the most difficult. For B.C.'s population was so low that the eastern provinces' 80 cents-a-head federal grant-in-aid 'would amount only to an insignificant sum'. But he seized on an article in which Helmcken had damned Confederation by arguing that the customs duties B.C. would lose were three times as high per capita as in the east. Inverting this, Musgrave determined to claim not for B.C.'s real (European) population (which he had put at under 10,000) but for a figure (eventually 120,000) that would supposedly produce the desired sum were the per capita duties the same. Beyond this, there was an extensive wish-list, including Dominion support for 'a first-class Graving Dock at Esquimalt', and for 'the speedy establishment of communication across the Rocky Mountains by Coach Road and ['at the earliest practicable date'] Railway', without which 'no real Union can subsist'.[121] The Legislative Council debated the proposed 'Terms' at some length, but suggested only minor changes. One of the most difficult demands, Musgrave had told Governor-General Young, was 'the construction of a Railway and Waggon Road'; but, 'so much importance is attached to the opening of communication that it would not have been politic to omit' it. Some 'of the other terms', too, 'may be thought by your Government to ask too much. But they must be prepared to be liberal if they desire Union': the Esquimalt Graving Dock would 'go far to obtain the suffrages' of Victoria's 'commercial community', while 'the Penitentiary, Marine Hospital, and Lunatic Asylum, will be regarded here as strong inducements.' Musgrave believed 'a large majority' of B.C. would cheerfully 'assent to the Scheme', but that 'any important modification' of the terms would be unlikely to 'obtain acquiescence'. So, he told Granville, the ball was in Canada's court, and it remained to be seen how far its Government 'can fulfil the expectations of this Colony.'[122]

---

[121] 'Proposed Terms of Union', British Columbia. Legislative Council, *Debate on the Subject of Confederation with Canada* (Victoria, 1912) pp. 162-5
[122] Musgrave to Young, 20 Feb. 1870, and to Granville, 21 Feb. (*Despatches*)

Everything went swimmingly. Musgrave had sent a balanced delegation to Ottawa to negotiate: Joseph Trutch, an official he had brought round to Confederation; Dr. Helmcken from Victoria, who doubted its feasibility; and R.W. Carrall, the Confederationist from Cariboo. On arrival in Ottawa, they were dined by the Governor-General, who whispered that the Canadian Government 'want you and British Columbia in very badly'.[123] Macdonald was ill, and negotiations were presided over by the ever-enthusiastic Étienne Cartier. They were not difficult. Over finance the Canadians said they could never take the bid for a notional population of 120,000 to Parliament, but they accepted that B.C. must have the $150,000 pa. it was designed to yield. The 'puzzle was how to get it', and Cartier came up with a 'brilliant' fudge.[124] The Canadians also agreed that displaced B.C. officials should, if necessary, be paid pensions, but they preferred to work out the details quietly with Governor Musgrave. 'Responsible Government' had not featured in the Colony's 'Terms'. But advocates had sent the journalist Henry Seelye to Ottawa to lobby for it. Parliament had just agreed that, on entering Confederation, Manitoba should have the same political institutions as other provinces. So it would have been odd to withhold them from British Columbia; and the upshot was the insertion into the terms of union of a clause noting that the B.C. legislature was about to be given an elective majority, and providing that it might, after Confederation, opt for 'Responsible Government'.[125]

This did not subsequently cause much trouble. But Dominion support for the Esquimalt Dockyard and arrangements to build the Railway would do so for the next fifteen years. Proper communication with Canada had always been regarded as a *sine qua non* of adhesion. But in drawing up 'terms' for union,

---

[123] Helmcken, *Reminiscences* p. 260
[124] B.C. would be allowed the (still excessive) notional population of 60,000 and be paid $100,000 pa. for land it had intended to let the railway have for nothing – Helmcken, *Reminiscences* p. 262, and its Appendix 3 ('Helmcken's Diary of the Confederation Negotiations, 1870') pp. 348-9
[125] 'Helmcken's Diary' pp. 345-6, 355-7

Musgrave's Executive Council had originally meant to ask only for a railway as far as Kamloops and a waggon road from there to 'Canada proper'. Trutch, an experienced public works contractor, instead insisted on a railway, without which, he thought, there would be 'neither physical nor sentimental Union'. Fears as to how it could be built then led Council to draw back and substitute the demand for the extension of B.C.'s Trunk Road to Fort Garry within three years of union, followed by the expenditure of a million dollars a year on building the 'initial sections' of a railway from the seaboard to connect, 'at the earliest practicable date', with the 'Railway system of Canada'.[126] Such scepticism as to the railway's practicability was widespread, and shared by Helmcken: the idea 'looked like an inflated balloon – I did not see how it could be built'. But as he went east to Ottawa on the newly opened railway from San Francisco, the journey 'opened my eyes not a little, for a railway had been built through a mountainous country quite as bad' as British Columbia. Helmcken was captivated. His diary records talking 'railway and confederation' to 'influential people' in Montreal and Quebec; and he later claimed to have told a sceptical Tilley that he too had doubted the project, but his 'eyes had been opened travelling through the Nevadas and Rocky Mountains. Anyhow it has to be built for the R[ail] R[oad] is a sine qua non – no R.R. no Confederation.'[127]

Macdonald had in fact already noted the successful building of the American Union Pacific Railway and hoped it would lead capitalists to undertake the construction of a Canadian counterpart.[128] B.C.'s delegation found Canadian ministers 'enthusiastically in favor. They do not consider that they can hold the country without it.' The Intercolonial had been a condition of union with the Maritimes, and Ministers were happy for it to 'be made a condition with us'.

[126] Helmcken, *Reminiscences* pp. 255-7, 344

[127] Helmcken *Reminiscences* pp. 257, 259, 261, 352; Brian Smith, 'The Confederation Delegation', in Shelton, *British Columbia & Confederation* p. 202

[128] Macdonald to Carrall, 29 Sept. 1869 (Libraries and Archives Canada, MIKAN 542724)

A railway to Red River would in any case be necessary, and one to British Columbia, they said blithely, would be only 'an extension'. There would, though, be no need for the preliminary 'waggon road'. The outcome was a promise (drafted by Trutch) in the terms of Union that, within two years of Confederation, construction would start at both ends of a line 'to connect the seaboard of British Columbia with the railway system of Canada' and be finished within ten years. Aid to the Esquimalt dock was more difficult, since Ministers feared that other provinces would want it too. But they were forced 'to give in', though they observed 'it was the hardest thing they had to swallow as it would open up *so many questions*' in Parliament.[129]

Earlier, Helmcken had warned that were Canada to offer only 'mean' terms, annexation to the US was bound to come up at the next elections.[130] Instead the terms were, in Musgrave's words, 'better than we had any right to expect'. Five hundred Victoria residents still sought to add a requirement that the Dominion build a Victoria-Nanaimo railway.[131] But Musgrave would not entertain their petition; and Confederation was endorsed, first in new elections, then by the resultant Legislative Council.

In Ottawa, things were different. The 'Terms' were presented to Parliament as a treaty that could not be amended. But the Liberals attacked them: Edward Blake labelled the railway clause a 'preposterous proposition' that would prove fatal to Confederation, while Alexander Mackenzie observed that to get 10,000 people into the Union they were 'agreeing to pay $10,000 a head', and that for 'thirty years to come it would be unnecessary to construct the greater proportion of the [proposed] line'.[132] Nor was concern as to cost confined to Liberals: 'so frightened were many of the ordinary Ontario' Conservative MP's, reported Trutch, that defeat seemed 'almost a certainty'. Some ministers wanted to qualify the

---

[129] 'Helmcken's Diary' pp. 344, 350-1, 353, 355-6
[130] *Debate on Confederation* p. 18
[131] F.H. Howay, 'Governor Musgrave and Confederation', Royal Society of Canada, *Proceedings*, 3rd series 15 (1921), Section 2 pp. 26-7
[132] Debates, 1rst Parliament, 4rth Session, Vol. 1 (28 March 1871) pp. 285-6 (Blake), (31 March) p. 310 (Mackenzie)

undertaking to build the line within ten years with the proviso, 'if the financial ability of the Dominion should permit'. Cartier (who was again running things while Macdonald was engaged on the Washington Treaty negotiations) ostensibly insisted that union with B.C. must go through 'on the terms arranged'. But he promised Parliament that building the railway would not entail any increase in taxation, and got Trutch (who was observing proceedings on the Colony's behalf) to assure the Conservative caucus that B.C. would not ruin 'them and ourselves together by insisting on the literal fulfilment of the bargain in the sense the Opposition had construed it'.[133] Parliament was reassured, and on 20 July 1871 British Columbia entered Confederation. But the next decade-and-a-half would see repeated crises over the implementation of the 'Terms' on which it had done so.

---

[133] Trutch to Helmcken, 17 April 1871 (W. Kaye Lamb, *History of the Canadian Pacific Railway* (New York, 1977) pp. 16-17). Trutch's assurances represented less of a climb-down than is sometimes suggested. For the 1870 delegates had been disposed to be flexible: what really mattered, they felt, was that railway construction in B.C. should be started; and rather than hedge this obligation round with penalties for non-performance, they preferred 'to rely on the honor of Govt. to fulfil the treaty' – and to leave the decision as to how to respond if it did not 'to the people of the time' (Helmcken's Diary p. 355)

CHAPTER 13

Consolidating Canadian Control; Manitoba under Canadian rule; the North West Mounted Police; treaties 'extinguishing' First Nations territorial ownership of the Plains (1871-7); the extinction of the buffaloes and its consequences; Cree resentment becomes organised in 1884; Riel's Rebellion and loosely associated Indian risings, 1885; railways (American aspirations; the 1872-3 'Pacific Scandal'; delays prompt British Columbian separatism; the Canadian Pacific escapes bankruptcy by rushing troops to suppress Riel's rebellion, and in 1886 opens transcontinental service)

In August 1870 Canada secured possession of Manitoba and, beyond it, of the 'North-West Territories', the 'great lone land' stretching to the Rockies and the Arctic. Next July British Columbia followed into Confederation. This, though, was only the start of a long process of settling, developing, controlling, and reconciling that would be bound up with the building, not completed until 1885-6, of a 'Canadian Pacific' railway through to the west coast. Manitoba itself could be reached by rail and steamer through the United States. But beyond it both settlement and control were, while not entirely dependent on the existence of a railway, at least far more secure once one had been built. 'In a year or two', Indian Commissioner Dewdney told Ottawa in 1881, 'with the Railway in the centre of the Continent we shall be in a position to dictate to the Indians. We are not so now, and any outbreak ... this year or next would be disastrous.'[1] No 'outbreak' came until 1885. By then the Canadian Pacific Railway was advanced enough to offer to move troops to Qu'Appelle in eleven days, thus providing a clear superiority of forces to suppress the risings. And Sir John Macdonald could tell Parliament, with some exaggeration, that the 'iron link' had so 'bound us together ... that we can now assemble ... at every point which may be assailed ... the whole physical force of Canada'.[2]

Riel's 1885 Rebellion proved the value of the railway. But it had been built less for the prairies than to secure British Columbia [B.C.] for the Confederation. For, as we have seen, the Canadian government had promised to start building lines 'within two years from the date of the Union' so as, 'within ten years', to connect 'the seabord of British Columbia' 'with the railway system of Canada'.[3] And though Joseph Trutch had promised unofficially that B.C. would not insist 'on the literal fulfilment of the bargain' should this appear financially ruinous, the city of Victoria, at least, often seemed disposed to do so – and B.C.'s charges that Ottawa was in wilful default, and moves to leave Confederation in

[1] 4 July 1881, quoted in Paul F. Sharp, *Whoop-up Country. The Canadian-American West, 1865-1885* (Minneapolis, 1955) p. 242

[2] House of Commons Debates, 5th Parliament, 3rd Session p. 2504 (12 June 1885)

[3] 'British Columbia Terms of Union – The Solon Law Archive' (https://www.solon.org/Constitutions/Canada/English/batu.html) Clause 11. The Dominion Government had also guaranteed 'for ten years' the interest (at 5%) on up to £100,000, the cost of building 'a first class graving dock at Esquimalt' (Clause 12)

response, raised political and constitutional questions that only subsided with the railway's completion.

* * * *

Actual possession of Manitoba came when Colonel Wolseley's force of British regulars and Ontario and Quebec militia reached Fort Garry in August 1870. Lieutenant-Governor A.G. Archibald followed in just over a week. But his troops were few. For after supposedly drinking Winnipeg's whisky supplies dry in three days, the regulars started to leave and, as had always been intended, were all gone by early September. That left two battalions of Canadian militia (771 men). Next spring they were reduced to about 80[4] – still a considerable force if compared to the position before 1869, but not enough to handle either a renewed Métis rising or a real Fenian invasion; and Archibald always felt he was walking on thin ice.

Cartier had told Archibald he had better not arrive before the troops (as he could have done had he taken the train to Minnesota); and Archibald soon wrote that he was glad he had instead 'come in by the lakes.' Had he arrived first (and alone), 'it would have injured me very much with that part of the settlement ['the English party'] whose violence it is at this moment of vast importance to be able to restrain.' There had indeed been talk, though J.H. McTavish (the HBC's chief clerk at Fort Garry) dismissed it, of an English rising against the outgoing Provisional Government; and some hoped that when the troops came they would proclaim martial law, 'to be followed by the hanging of a few of the French

---

[4] George F.G. Stanley, *Canada's Soldiers. The Military History of an Unmilitary People* (Toronto, 1960 edn.) pp. 237, 239; C.P. Stacey, 'The Military Aspect of Canada's Winning of the West, 1870-1885', *Canadian Historical Review* [hereafter *Can.H.R.*] 21:1 (1940) pp. 10, 12-13; 80 men available in July 1871 – Archibald's 'Memorandum connected with the Fenian Invasion of Manitoba in October, 1871' (*Report of the [Parliamentary] Select Committee on the Causes of the Difficulties in the North-West Territory in 1869-70* [hereafter *Select Committee Report*] (Ottawa, 1874) p. 139)

party'.[5] Archibald wrote that he had successfully preached 'conciliation' to the Anglophone leaders. But some of their followers wanted to pay Riel's party back for past repressions. And some of the militia were anxious to avenge the murder/ execution of Thomas Scott, saying (Archibald reported) that they had vowed 'before leaving home to pay off all scores by shooting down any Frenchman that was in any way connected with that event'.[6] Their bark was worse than their bite, but there was a good deal of brawling in the Winnipeg taverns, with marked men beaten up and even killed. Those responsible were generally unknown, but magistrates did identify the three who chased Elzéar Goulet (one of Scott's 'judges') into the river where he drowned. Yet for fear of inflaming the situation further, no prosecution was brought.[7] This did not go down well with the Métis. Riel, W.B. O'Donoghue, and Ambroise Lépine returned to conduct a protest meeting on 17 September that petitioned President Grant: 'coerced into a confederation with Canada, under false representations', they could only appeal to the United States, and so asked Grant to investigate their grievances, 'the pledges given to us and to your Government, and the extent to which those pledges have been violated, and to demand, on our behalf, that full reparation be made'.[8] The meeting's impact was blunted by a quarrel between O'Donoghue and Riel, probably over annexation to America, and both went back across the border. But the episode left the Métis in what Archibald later

---

[5] J.H. McTavish to Bishop Taché, 31 July 1870; Archibald's testimony and his 10 Sept. 1870 letter to Cartier – *Select Committee Report* pp. 36, 135, 137-8

[6] Archibald's 'Memorandum connected with the Fenian Invasion' (ibid. p. 140)

[7] George F.G. Stanley, *Louis Riel* (Toronto, 1963) pp. 160-1

[8] 'Memorial of the People of Rupert's Land and North-West', ed. George F.G. Stanley, *The Collected Writings of Louis Riel* i (Edmonton, 1985) pp. 110-19; Stanley, *Riel* pp. 161-3. The document (which survives only in a type-script copy) was taken to Washington by O'Donoghue; and some believe he spiced it up, adding the paragraph that, noting 'the vast extent of barren and impassable territory, that separates us from the Dominion of Canada', asks the President to take steps to 'enable us' either 'to enjoy a Government of our own choosing [independence], or to change our allegiance to some other Government of our choice [ie. the US]'

described as a 'sullen' mood. Even a year later Archibald could write of 'the persistent ill usage', by 'the disbanded volunteers and new comers who fill' Winnipeg, of Métis who had ventured into that town. Many had been 'so beaten and outraged that they feel as if they were living in a state of slavery'.[9]

In September 1871 there were rumours of a Fenian invasion, 'predicated', Archibald believed, on Métis discontent. In the event this proved a damp squib: O'Donoghue and 'General' O'Neill could muster only 70 men at Pembina; on 5 October they crossed, with half their force plus a constitution for the 'Republic of Rupert's Land', into what they thought was British territory, and recruited a few local Métis. But they were arrested by a US cavalry detachment.[10] Moreover all Red River turned out to oppose them, the 'English' at once, the Métis after initial hesitation. Riel, who had returned in May 1871, unobtrusively held meetings to encourage the Métis to reject O'Donoghue's overtures. But he worried that if he emerged openly, he would be arrested or murdered. However Archibald assured him, through Father Ritchot and others, that there would be no arrests, and was soon invited to review 200 Métis volunteers. He did so, being introduced to five or six people, among them Riel, with the anonymous formula, 'This is the captain the French half-breeds have chosen to lead them.' Archibald then shook their hands. As he later wrote, 'we presented externally' the aspect 'of a united people', but things were less good 'when the curtain is drawn aside and the whole truth displayed'. For his troops had to be hastily removed from Ritchot's St. Norbert to stop them committing 'an outrage'. And Archibald thought it too dangerous to bring the Métis volunteers over the river to Fort Garry, since a 'stray bullet would have undone the work ... now culminating in a united front'.[11]

---

[9] Archibald to Macdonald, 9 Oct. 1871 (*Select Committee Report* p. 156)

[10] The true line of the 49th parallel within Pembina was uncertain; the US cavalry believed the HBC post where it arrested them to be to its south

[11] Archibald's testimony and 'Memorandum connected with the Fenian Invasion' (*Select Committee Report* pp. 139-42); Stanley, *Riel* pp. 169-75; Ruth Swan & Edward Jerome, '"Unequal Justice:" the Métis in O'Donoghue's Raid of 1841', *Manitoba History* 39 (2000)

Archibald credited his 'policy of forbearance' with denying O'Donoghue the Métis support that would have enabled him to secure part of the Settlement and then pour in filibusters. But that was not how Ontario viewed his shaking hands with Riel and the increasing openness with which Riel subsequently moved around Manitoba. The Liberal party had latched onto the Scott case, with Ontario offering a $5000 reward for the arrest of his 'murderers'. And both Macdonald and Cartier, anxious to damp things down before what looked to be difficult federal elections, thought it would be best if Riel went back into exile. They managed to persuade Bishop Taché of this when he came to Ottawa in late 1871 to plead yet again for an amnesty; and $1000 was produced from secret service funds to support Riel and his family if he left Manitoba for a year. Taché returned to induce Riel to comply. At the last moment he was told to get Riel's military commander, Ambroise Lépine, to go too. Taché approached Archibald, who jumped at the idea. For, he wrote, news of the Ontario rewards had generated intense French excitement: even those who had not sided with Riel in 1869-70 saw 'punishment of the offenders' as a question of 'race, and would consider an attempt ... on any of these people as an attack on the whole'. Any attempt at arrest would therefore 'have led to serious bloodshed', but the 'lawless men, idlers and roughs' infesting Winnipeg's taverns might make one; some, indeed, had recently tried to break into Riel's house. The $1000 Ottawa had provided would not cover Lépine's exile as well as Riel's. So Archibald turned to the HCB's Donald Smith, telling him 'there was a danger of a rising of the French Metis', and Smith produced a further £600. Riel and Lépine then left for the border, by night and with police protection.[12]

---

[12] Stanley, *Riel* pp. 177-81; Archibald to Cartier, 24 Feb. 1872, and Smith's testimony (*Select Committee Report* pp. 93, 153-4). Gilbert McMicken also reported that the Métis were 'very uneasy' over 'the Lands not being given to them' and over the 'injustice' done to Riel, for whom 'they would do almost anything especially if incited to it on grounds affecting their common interest or ... feelings' (to Macdonald, 13 Jan. 1872, quoted by D.N. Sprague, *Canada and the Métis, 1869-1885* (Waterloo, Ont., 1988) pp. 100-1)

Perhaps Archibald worried too much. His position was strengthening steadily: 200 troops were rushed out in late 1871 in response to the Fenian scare, while next year 300 were recruited to garrison Manitoba.[13] Meanwhile there was appreciable immigration from Ontario. Riel returned after only four months of his covenanted year's exile; but though Macdonald continued to worry, the difficulties Riel caused were political only. In the federal constituency of Provencher he helpfully stood down in Cartier's favour in 1872, but after Cartier's death he was elected in 1873 and 1874. Riel felt it too dangerous to take his seat, but in March 1874 went muffled up after dark, was sworn in, and signed the roll as an MP. That April he was turned out of Parliament, with the Liberal Prime Minister Alexander Mackenzie forcing his Quebec colleagues to back expulsion. But Riel was then re-elected. The Governor-General, Lord Dufferin, told the Colonial Secretary that Riel would again be expelled, and that this would break up the government. For 'all the French members of the Cabinet' had said that this time they would have to vote against expulsion. The prospect led Dufferin to revive the thorny question of amnesty,[14] to which the trial of Lépine soon added a new dimension. In 1873 Manitoban 'Canadians' had secured a warrant for the arrest of both Riel and Lépine. Riel's friends spirited him away; and he would later claim that he had rejected an offer, made by Macdonald through a priest, of no less than $35,000 to go abroad for three years.[15] Lépine, though, was apprehended without incident.

---

[13] Stanley, *Canada's Soldiers* p. 239

[14] Dufferin's 'private' letters to the Colonial Secretary Lord Carnarvon, 12 Oct. and 8 Dec. 1874 – ed. C.W. de Kiewiet and F.H. Underhill, *Dufferin-Carnarvon Correspondence, 1874-1878* (Toronto, Champlain Society, 1955) pp. 82-92, 115-121. Two ministers had opposed expulsion in April

[15] Riel also claimed the offer had been twice repeated in 1874 by Prime Minister Mackenzie. There is no independent evidence to support these claims, made both in November-December 1884 and at Riel's 1885 trial; and $35,000 seems a lot. But Riel's biographer believes 'there is probably some truth in his statements, for Riel had an excellent memory for names, places, and dates' – Thomas Flanagan, *Riel and the Rebellion. 1885 Reconsidered* (2nd edn., Toronto, 2000) pp. 118, 124

He was tried in 1874, and 'to the astonishment of everybody' found guilty by a mixed 'English', 'French' and Métis jury, and sentenced to death. This generated a storm, with the Quebec legislature calling unanimously for Riel and Lépine to be amnestied. But to Dufferin it meant that 'instead of demanding reparation for a persecuted patriot', the Quebec clergy would now have to seek mercy for 'a convicted criminal'. The question, then, was how far Lépine's sentence should be reduced, and whether the same could be done for Riel. Action was postponed till after the Ontario elections. Then in January 1875 Dufferin, supposedly acting on his own initiative and citing Lépine's service against the Fenians, commuted his sentence to two years' imprisonment plus loss of political rights. Mackenzie followed up by persuading Parliament to recommend a general amnesty for actions 'in the North-West troubles', conditional in Riel's and Lépine's cases on five years' exile.[16] Riel took up this option, and this time really did stay away from Manitoba; his role in its politics, though not in those of the broader North-West, was over.

The chief duty of Manitoba's Lt.-Governors (initially Archibald, but from late 1872 Alexander Morris) was the preservation of order and Canadian control. But they had three further tasks: installing conventional elective 'responsible government'; keeping the Manitoba Act's promise to convey 1.4 million acres to the Métis and their children; and concluding treaties to extinguish the land rights of the various First Nations both within Manitoba and across the 'Fertile Belt' of the southern North-West Territories.

Archibald's government had been proconsular. He appointed a small Executive Council, gave it 'a memo. of 32 Bills which would be absolutely necessary ... and ... set them to work to get their hands in'. Over time Henry Clarke emerged as the Council's leading member; but the newly appointed Morris would not let Clarke become Premier, telling him 'he must be content with being the acknowledged leader of the Govt. in the House'. However

---

[16] See Barbara J. Messamore, *Canada's Governors General, 1847-1878: Biography and Constitutional Evolution* (Toronto, 2006) pp. 187-9

when the Legislative Council voted no confidence in July 1874, Morris urged not only Clarke but all the other ministers to resign. He then asked Marc-Amable Girard to form a government, 'thus introducing responsible government in its modern form into the Province – the previous ministry was selected personally by my predecessor and none of its members was recognized as first minister'.[17] Girard had to resign in December, observing that he had been 'the first French Premier of the Province' and would probably be the last. Ministries continued brief until late 1878, when the half-breed John Norquay became Premier and secured a comfortable electoral majority resting on both 'English' and 'French' support. Manitoban politics were always fractious, but Norquay governed for nine years, his Liberal successor for twelve.

Historians have been more interested in, indeed bitterly divided over, the fulfilment of the promise of land for the Métis. This had been central to the negotiations in Ottawa that gave rise to the 1870 Manitoba Act. Red River's emissaries, chiefly Father Ritchot, had represented the Métis as the real owners of the future province's lands and argued that (just as undeveloped land had been reserved to the HBC when Canada had bought Rupert's Land) a large grant should now be made to the Métis *and their children*. Eventually agreement was reached on a distribution of 1.4 million acres. Equally important was the question of how these should be assigned. Riel, whose ideal was always the creation of a Métis state, had finished by specifying that the country should 'be divided in two so that this custom of the two populations living separately may be kept for the safeguarding of our most threatened rights'. But he did this only after his emissaries had left for Ottawa, and Ritchot never pressed for it. Ritchot did, though, want the distribution to be under Manitoban control – preferably (as in other provinces) under that of the provincial legislature, but at least under the supervision of community leaders like Bishops

---

[17] Archibald to Macdonald, 16 Jan. 1871; Morris to Macdonald, Feb. 1873, and to Secretary of State Richard Scott, July 1874 – Archibald, Sir Adams George, Morris, Alexander, and Girard, Marc-Amable, *Dictionary of Canadian Biography*

Taché and Machray. However the words of the Manitoba Act reflected Macdonald's preferences and, probably, beliefs as to what the Canadian Parliament would wear. They gave considerable latitude to the Lieutenant-Governor, who should 'select such lots or tracts in such parts of the Province as he may deem expedient ... and divide the same among the children of the half-breed heads of families ... in such mode and upon such conditions ... as the Governor General in Council may from time to time determine.' And Macdonald explained privately to the HBC's Governor Sir Stafford Northcote that care would be taken 'not to put' the Métis 'all together'.[18]

An allocation of the 1.4 million acres to Métis children was undoubtedly made. However it was not, as they probably expected, immediate, but took seven to ten years. The process has been summarised thus:

a) the initial allotment of 1871 was based erroneously on all Métis as opposed to Métis children and thus had to be redone

b) in 1873, the government rectified the error and directed the allocation of land to Métis children only (though the heads of Métis families were in 1874 accorded $160 scrip redeemable in Dominion lands)

c) the second allotment to children started in 1875, but was aborted in 1876 because Canada underestimated the number of recipients;

d) the third and final allotment started in 1876 but took until 1880 to complete.[19]

---

[18] Cartier too had said that 'there would not be a block of land set apart for the half-breeds', but that anybody 'whose claim to land was recognised would receive an order entitling him to claim his allotment at any time' – Northcote's Diary, 2 and 4 May, 1870 (*Diaries 1869, 1870, 1871, 1875, 1882, of the First Earl of Iddesleigh* (privately printed, 1907) pp. 134, 142). Though Riel had envisaged a distinct block of land on which the Métis would live separately, Ritchot always said claimants should be able to select land wherever they pleased
[19] Sacha R. Paul, 'A Comment on Manitoba Métis Federation Inc v Canada', *Manitoba Law Journal* 37:1 (2013) p. 326

One school of thought, developed by the late twentieth century historian D.N. Sprague working for the Métis Federation Inc., held that the process was deliberately manipulated by Canadian governments to deprive the Métis of their land. This was opposed by Thomas Flanagan, who, working on behalf of the Canadian Justice Department from the official survey land records, argued that there were good reasons, including responsiveness to Métis demands, for many of the changes in regulations and processes. The lawsuit on which they were working eventually reached Canada's Supreme Court which in 2013, while rejecting the Métis Federation's more far-reaching claims, found that the ten-year delay in allotting the land meant that 'the federal Crown failed to implement the [Manitoba Act's] land grant provision ... in accordance with the honour of the Crown'.[20]

We should note that existing owners had their land holdings recognised. What is at issue is the additional 1.4 million acres that the Manitoba Act promised 'towards the extinguishment of the Indian Title to the lands in the Province' and 'for the benefit of the families of the half-breed residents'. The main allocation of this hitherto 'ungranted land', that made between 1877 and 1880, took the form of scrip or redeemable allotments. Recent experience of Russian and East European privatisations is that, when given scrip, most people promptly cash it in. This was the case both in Manitoba and (in the next decade) in the North-West Territories. Would-be purchasers accompanied the officials distributing the scrip and did a roaring trade. It does not appear that the Métis were cheated: the 50% of the land's face value they generally received without having to settle on and develop it was the price paid also to military and other scrip recipients. Some recipients no

---

[20] D.N. Sprague, *Canada and the Métis, 1869-1885* (1988); Flanagan, *Riel and the Rebellion. 1885 Reconsidered* chaps. 2, 3 (summarising his earlier findings). See also Brad Milne, 'The Historiography of Métis Land Disposal, 1870-1890', *Manitoba History* 30 (1995) pp. 30-41; Report of the Royal Commission on Aboriginal Peoples, Vol. 4, Appendix 5C 'Metis Nation Land and Resource Rights' (caid.ca/RRAP4.5C); Paul, 'A Comment on Manitoba Métis Federation Inc v Canada' esp. pp. 324-5

doubt had good economic reasons for selling, and some Métis proved well able to operate the new arrangements – Father Ritchot did so, making a fortune which he applied to Catholic and Métis charities. But most ended up with no new land, and a growing number left the province.

They had, of course, been doing so for some time, following the buffalo into the interior as they became less plentiful. The move to 'Métis wintering sites in the North West' had begun 'well before Manitoba's entry into Confederation'. It was an economically rational process, partially funded by the sale of the migrants' relatively minor Red River land holdings; and it paralleled a similar Métis departure from North Dakota that was clearly not a function of developments in Manitoba. But it was also encouraged by distaste for the new Canadian regime there. In 1871 the priest of St. François Xavier wrote that 'we are surrounded and swallowed up by *Protestantism and Orangeism*', with a number of his parishioners selling up and leaving; and (in what would become Saskatchewan) Father André reported next year that the Métis wintering near Carlton could not bear the thought of returning to Red River, where there had been too many changes at odds with their customs and morals.[21]

By the mid-1870s the boom in buffalo robes was played out. But the end of the decade saw a second peak in land sales and emigration, this time often by richer and more agriculturally settled Métis. As always, many factors will have been at work. Defeated in his bid to lead the francophone group in Manitoba's assembly, and burdened with debt arising out of the 1878 election, Charles Nolin left for Saskatchewan in 1879, and in 1883 settled near St. Laurent. Louis Schmidt, Riel's former Secretary, seems to have been trying to overcome his drinking habit. In 1880 he left for Batoche with financial aid from Bishop Taché, and in 1882 (he records) 'a strong emigration ... came to reinforce our groups',

---

[21] Erhard Ens, 'Dispossession or Adaptation? Migration and Persistence of the Red River Metis, 1835-1890', *Historical Paper/Communications historiques* 23:1 (1988) pp. 137, 141-4, citing Father Kavanagh to Taché, 14 Aug. 1871 and Father André in *Le Métis*, 3 April 1872; Flanagan, *Riel and Rebellion* p. 34

including that of Maxime Lépine (Ambroise's brother). Erhard Ens sees this emigration surge, while coincident with the decline of Métis political power in Manitoba, chiefly as a matter of people taking advantage of high land prices (stemming from the advent of a superior new brand of wheat) 'to establish themselves on larger farms elsewhere'. And he observes that the lists of 'claimants for "Halfbreed Scrip" in the settlements of St. Louis de Langevin, Batoche and Duck Lake in the mid-1880s read like the parish rolls of St. François Xavier'. In 1882, Father André estimated, fifty families had moved to the parish of Saint Laurent from Red River. But, as is so often the case, they had come at the wrong time.[22]

* * * *

Canada's strategy in the North-West Territories had four distinct, though inter-dependent, strands: the creation of an effective police force; the conclusion of treaties extinguishing the Indians' land titles; the building of a railway across to British Columbia; and agricultural colonisation. Macdonald had always meant to have a small force capable of protecting settlers from Indian attacks, and so forestalling the independent actions that had often led to wars south of the border. He was, he told its prospective commander in late 1869, thinking of a force of *Mounted Riflemen*. It 'should not be expressly Military, but should be styled *Police*, and should have the military bearing of the Irish Constabulary'. But since Manitoba became a Province, not a Territory, its policing was a local not a federal responsibility. So Macdonald looked instead to the Militia that went out with Wolseley. And though he accepted that a more mobile force would be needed to protect settlers further afield, he was in no hurry to meet the cost until these were more numerous.

[22] Charles Nolin, *Dictionary of Canadian Biography*; Raymond J.A. Huel, 'Living in the Shadow of Greatness: Louis Schmidt, Riel's Secretary', *Native Studies Review* 6:1 (http://iportal.usask.ca/docs/Native studies review/vi/issue1/pp16-27.pdf) p. 18; 'Les memoires de Louis Schmidt, 8 Juin 1911' (http://scaa.sk.ca/ourlegacy/permalink/25702) p. 98; Ens, 'Disposession or Adaptation?' pp. 141-2; Flanagan, *Riel and Rebellion* p. 44

Still, plans were drawn up in 1872, and legislation passed next May to authorise a force of 300. Even so, Macdonald would have preferred to recruit it gradually over the winter, and only send it out to replace the Militia in 1874.[23] But he came under pressure from Morris, who stressed that a force was needed to 'prevent the possibility of such a frightful disaster as befell Minnesota' – Indian wars.[24] Morris was also much concerned by the presence on Canadian soil, notably at 'Fort Whoop-up', of armed Americans whose whiskey sales were debauching the Blackfoot. Then in August 1873 news came of what appeared to be a 'horrible massacre' of Indians there. Actually this had been quite unconnected with the Fort Whoop-up traders.[25] But Morris attributed it to them, and warned that if 'the American borderers put the Indians to death in the summary manner described ... the Dominion Government will soon find itself involved in Indian difficulties of the gravest character.' It would be 'impossible to govern what is, in fact, almost half a continent without considerable force', and Morris kept pressing for one to be sent out before winter. Macdonald was far more relaxed and thought an Indian war 'in the winter months' unlikely. But he decided it would be politically dangerous to ignore Morris' warnings. In September he told the Governor-General that the government found it 'necessary' to send the Force out 'before

---

[23] S.W. Horrall, 'Sir John A. Macdonald and the Mounted Police Force for the Northwest Territories', *Can. H.R.* 53:2 (1972) pp. 180-91. Macdonald had originally envisaged 'a mixed' Force 'of pure whites & British & French Half-breeds, [but] taking great care that the Half-breed element should not predominate' (to McDougall, 12 Dec. 1869 – Libraries and Archives Canada [LAC], MIKAN 543527); later events may have fed fears of half-breed predominance, and the Force was at first recruited only from the east

[24] Alexander Morris to Macdonald, 16 Jan. 1873 (J.R. Miller, *Skyscrapers hide the heavens: a history of Indian-White relations in Canada* (Toronto, 2000 edn.) p. 208)

[25] 22 Indians had been killed, but by a mixed American-Canadian group of wolf-hunters in a conflict arising out of horse-thefts. Arrests were made. But witnesses contradicted each other, and courts north as well as south of the border discharged the defendants – Sharp, *Whoop-up Country* pp. 191-6

the close of navigation'; and 150 men managed to reach Manitoba just before the freeze-up, albeit without uniforms or supplies.[26]

At this point Macdonald's government fell. His Liberal successor, Alexander Mackenzie, a strong temperance man, was more concerned about Fort Whoop-up. But he saw it as a purely military problem; and when the United States suggested controlling the whiskey trade, he contemplated a joint expedition with the US providing most of the force – as the disgusted Dufferin put it, 'the police duties on both sides of the line were to be discharged by Yankee troops'. Dufferin saw this as endangering Canada's sovereignty. Also, since 'the Americans are abhorred by the whole Indian people', it might be unwise 'to become identified with them'. A purely Canadian expedition, though, would 'appear on the scene, not as the Americans have done,' to control the Indian tribes, but to ameliorate 'injuries inflicted on the red man by the white'.[27] Mackenzie was persuaded to mount an expedition. He would have preferred it to be military, since he did not relish a paramilitary police, but again he yielded, this time to the views of the Justice department. So Dufferin could tell the British minister in Washington in March 1874 that 300 'mounted riflemen' would be setting out in June. He added that 'though nominally policemen', they 'would be dressed in scarlet uniform'.[28] This was important: Morris had written that '50 men in red coats are better here than 100 in other colours'; and Canada's Adjutant-General, Colonel Robertson Ross, had been told by Indians, unhappy with the green of the Militia in Winnipeg, that 'we know ... the soldiers of our great mother wear red coats and are our friends'.[29]

---

[26] Horrall, 'Macdonald and the Mounted Police' pp. 191-6
[27] Dufferin to Sir Edward Thornton (the British minister in Washington), 13 Jan. 1874 (Horrall, 'Macdonald and the Mounted Police' pp. 197-8), and to the Colonial Secretary Lord Kimberley, 24 Dec. 1873 (R.C. Macleod, *The North-West Mounted Police and Law Enforcement 1873-1905* (Toronto, 1976) pp. 17-18)
[28] Dufferin to Thornton, 19 March 1874 (Horrall, 'Macdonald and the Mounted Police' pp. 198-9)
[29] However, though there was never any doubt that the Mounted Police would wear scarlet, the precise design of their iconic tunics may stem from the presence

The remaining recruits came out in June 1874, travelling to Minnesota by rail (for the United States warmly approved of this expedition); and the whole Mounted Police (hereafter NWMP) set out on 8 July on its celebrated 'Long March' west. This was almost a fiasco. Initially they meant to take the trade route along the North Saskatchewan and then go south to Fort Whoop-up. Later it was decided to move more directly along the international border, which was then being surveyed by a well-supplied joint Commission. But fears of an attack by American Sioux led the expedition to turn north and try to cut across country. Unfamiliarity with the Plains – the NWMP had all come from the east – and shortage of supplies nearly led to disaster, only averted by lucky purchases from Métis hunters and from the Survey Commission. The force had expected to have to fight on arrival, but by September was in no condition to do so. Fortunately, its commander called in on the American town of Fort Benton to pick up telegrams, and while there he was taken under the wing of its leading merchant, Charles Conrad.[30]

Fort Benton, at the head of navigation on the Missouri, despatched goods along several trails, including that to Fort Whoop-up where a major sale was whiskey. The trade had been restricted in American territory, but further north it was, in the absence of any governance, both easy and lucrative. Fort Benton men were happy to push the business, but they were at least equally happy to turn to something else. Conrad's firm, I.G. Baker, rushed supplies to the NWMP expedition; and a relationship was established that proved profitable to the firm – its sales to the NWMP averaged $122,400 in 1875 and 1876 – and indispensable to the Force's continuance in the area. Nor was the firm's support

---

in Manitoba, at the crucial time, of some 700 unwanted red Norfolk jackets – Macleod, *The North-West Mounted Police* p. 14; Stacey, 'The Military Aspect of Canada's Winning of the West' p. 17; Shane Peacock, '"Noble, Daring, & Dashing". The Image of the Mounties', *The Beaver* 78:3 (June/July 1998) p. 32 (citing a communication from the RCMP Museum in Regina)

[30] Garrett Wilson, *Frontier Farewell. The 1870s and the End of the Old West* (Regina, 2014 edn.) pp. 220-39

purely logistical. For Conrad introduced the half-breed scout Jerry Potts, whose guidance in Plains' ways proved invaluable. He soon escorted the expedition to Fort Whoop-up, which it found flying the American flag (as was quite common at the time, even outside the US) but otherwise inoffensive: the solitary occupant invited the policemen to lunch, and soon tried to sell them the premises for the exorbitant price of $25,000. Later that year Potts introduced Assistant-Commissioner Macleod to the great Blackfoot Chief Crowfoot.[31]

The meeting was a success, and in 1877 Crowfoot declared that 'The Police have protected us as the feathers of the bird protect it from the frosts of winter.' What Crowfoot really valued was the NWMP's ending of the whiskey trade: 'Bad men and Whiskey were killing us so fast that [but for its advent] very few ... of us would have been left here to-day.'[32] A purely military expedition, such as Mackenzie had originally wanted, would not have worked; for the traders, as some made clear, would simply have come back when it left. But the NWMP stayed, more especially in Fort Macleod (a substitute for Fort Whoop-up) and at Fort Walsh in the Cypress Hills. From there its officers maintained personal relations with the Chiefs, exerted a calming influence on Indian feuds, and spread a thin film of Canadian authority over the Territory. For a time their chief problem was the arrival in 1876-7 of some 5000-8000 Sioux, fleeing American vengeance for the defeat at Little Big Horn. They were, in the short run, far stronger than the 300 Mounted Police. So it was as well both that their leader, Sitting Bull, realised that Canada would respond to trouble by calling in the US army, and that he

[31] Sharp, *Whoop-up Country* pp. 86-95; Wilson, *Frontier Farewell* pp. 232-40. Potts' mother had been a Blood, and he had himself participated in the 1870 Blackfoot routing of the Cree (Potts, Jerry, *Dictionary of Canadian Biography*)
[32] Alexander Morris, *The Treaties of Canada with the Indians of Manitoba and the North-West Territories* (Toronto, 1880) p. 272 – also p. 270 for Button Chief's similar tribute

and Assistant-Commissioner Walsh quickly established good relations.[33]

* * * *

While explaining the arrangements required for Red River's entry into Confederation, Macdonald added that, beyond its immediate vicinity, 'the old Indian titles' had not been 'extinguished over any portion of this [recently acquired] country'. Between 1871 and 1877 seven treaties effected this peacefully throughout the 'Fertile Belt', all the land in which Canada was then interested.[34] Mackenzie (Macdonald's successor as Prime Minister) saw these as expensive, but 'nevertheless the cheapest [policy] … if we compare the results with those of other countries; and it is above all a humane, just and Christian policy'.[35]

Treaty negotiations, more especially the later ones, could be splendid affairs. Commissioners journeyed to a convenient venue (the choice of meeting place being often contested between different bands). They were accompanied by a Police or militia escort, sometimes with a band or cannons to fire in salute. This was largely ceremonial; but its 'moral influence' was said to have 'contributed most materially to the success' of the Treaty 3 negotiations, while in those for Treaty 4 it protected Chiefs anxious to negotiate from

---

[33] For the intense diplomacy relating to the Sioux until Sitting Bull's 1881 return to the US to surrender, see Sharp, *Whoop-up Country* chaps. 12-13. But for the collapse of the traditional Plains economy after 1879 Sitting Bull might ultimately have obtained sanctuary in Canada (as *eventually* did those Sioux who had fled Minnesota in the early 1860s)

[34] Macdonald later resisted humanitarian pressure to extend northwards; he meant to make no treaties 'until there is a likelihood of the country being requested for settlement purposes' – note of 27 May 1884, quoted by Dennis F.K. Mahill, *Treaty Research Report – Treaty Eight (1899)* (Treaties and Historical Research Centre, Indian and Northern Affairs Canada, 1986) note 12

[35] House of Commons Debates, 8 Feb. 1877 (quoted in Miller, *Skyscrapers hide the heavens* p. 211). Ged Martin notes that throughout the 1870s the annual US expenditure on Indian wars exceeded the entire Canadian federal budget ('The Department of Indian Affairs in the Dominion of Canada budget, 1882', *Martinalia* [2020, online])

warriors who sought to stop them.[36] Indians gathered in large numbers to meet the Commissioners, partly to make the treaty process as representative, and therefore binding, as possible, and partly because the cash and food incentives for attending were considerable. In 1874 nearly 500 lodges came to the Qu'Appelle Lakes, and the Commissioners had twice to send back for extra money ($6000, and then $15,000) to feed and pay them; and in 1877 nearly all the Blackfoot Chiefs were drawn up, with some 4,000 men, women, and children arranged in a semi-circle behind them.[37] There would be ceremonies of welcome, which in 1876 and 1877 included displays of military horsemanship and 'pipe stem dances'. The Commissioners understood their reception of the pipes as indicating that 'we had accepted the friendship of the Cree nation', and the Cree regarded treaties made under the pipe as particularly binding. Then, after orations – patronising on the part of the Governor, enthusiastic on that of most Chiefs – there followed bargaining, which could prove both difficult and protracted – the first four attempts to conclude Treaty 3 failed as the 'Saulteaux would not accept the terms offered' and successfully stood out for improvements.[38]

The treaties were broadly similar. Alexander Morris, who had been involved in most of the negotiations, gave a general summary. The Indians renounced 'all their right and titles to the lands' in question, apart from protected small reserves ('generally one section for each family of five'). It was hoped that they would gradually adapt to a settled life as farmers, and when they actually initiated cultivation there would be 'once for all' grants of tools, seed, and cattle to help them. Schools should be built, and agricultural instructors might be sent; and there would be an

---

[36] Morris, *The Treaties of Canada* pp. 52, 82
[37] Ibid. pp. 84-5, 267. In 1876 the Commissioners were allowed $60,000 for the treaty with the Plains Cree, though $12,731 was saved as many Indians preferred to continue with their buffalo hunt instead of coming to the Council (ibid. p. 95)
[38] John Leonard Taylor, 'Two Views on the Meaning of Treaties Six and Seven', in Richard Price ed., *The Spirit of the Alberta Indian Treaties* (Calgary, 1999) p. 15

absolute ban on the sale of alcohol ('fire-water') on the reserves. Equally, though, the bands might continue (as in fact most did) to hunt and fish as before, save on land that had actually passed into private occupation; and annual payments (of between $750, Treaty 4, and $2000, Treaty 7) for ammunition and netting twine were pledged to support this. A one-off gift (usually $12 a head) was made to those who attended the treaty-making Councils, and $5 a head would be paid annually to all bands who had taken the treaty, with Chiefs (whose role Canada sought to enhance) getting $25 and also uniforms, medals, and British flags.[39]

Different calculations are possible. But Ged Martin puts the capitalised value of these Canadian payments at some $7.4m. for 1.2m. square kilometres,[40] which he compares with the $2.7m. for which Prime Minister Mackenzie arranged in 1875 to buy the HBC's 27,000 square kilometres of unallotted land. The two transactions were not legally on a par; but Martin concludes that 'coming to terms with [the HBC's] Goschen [a banker and ex-minister] was a tougher proposition than buying off [the Blackfoot Chief] Crowfoot'.[41] Another comparison might lie with the 1867 US purchase of Alaska for $7.2m.

Their expense apart (and this did encounter criticism), Canada's gains from the treaties are clear: security that telegraph lines, railway construction, and, later, settlers would not be disturbed. Many Indians, though, also showed not merely readiness but eagerness to conclude treaties, if only to get things settled before worse befell. In 1869 Lake of the Woods Ojibwa

---

[39] The treaties' texts are printed in Morris, *Treaties of Canada* pp. 313ff.

[40] To which might be added some of the costs (far higher than was anticipated at the time of negotiation) of the pledge extracted from Canada by Treaty Six of assistance 'sufficient to relieve the Indians from the calamity' of 'pestilence' or 'a general famine'

[41] Ged Martin, 'How much did Canada "pay" First Nations for the Prairies?', *Martinalia*. Most Canadians believed, and in 1888 the Judicial Committee of the Privy Council would confirm, that what was being bought from the Indians was rights over the land, but not the fee simple freehold that the HBC would have been selling. From a very different mental background, Indians also believed in rights over land rather than absolute and exclusive possession of it

had warned officials not to 'bring Settlers and Surveyors ... [to] occupy our lands until a clear understanding has been arrived at as to what our relations are to be', while in 1871 a notice was posted in Portage la Prairie 'warning parties not to intrude on their lands, until a Treaty should be made'.[42] And in 1875 the Plains Indians were unsettled both by telegraph and railway surveys and by fears that Governor Morris might simply send people into their 'country until they outnumbered us'. So the missionary George McDougall was despatched to promise that Commissioners would come 'to negotiate a treaty with them, as had already been done ... further east'. On hearing this, one senior Chief, Mistawasis, responded, 'that is all we wanted'. But, McDougall reported, the Indians, though apologetic, were also 'unanimous in their determination to oppose the running of lines, or the making of roads through their country, until a settlement between the Government and them had been effected'.[43]

In 1870 Archibald reported that the Indians were in a 'state of considerable excitement' over Canada's purchase of Rupert's Land from the HBC, feeling that it was they, not the Company, who should have been 'treated with' and paid.[44] Red River's Swampies had also been deeply involved in its turbulent 1869-70 politics, and they resented Canada's concern with Métis land rights rather than their own. Moreover settlement was obviously coming soon – indeed in the 1871 negotiations, the Canadian side said that 'whether they wished it or not,' every year 'twice as many'

---

[42] Miller, *Skyscrapers hide the heavens* p. 209; Archibald to Ottawa, 19 July 1871, quoted in George F.G. Stanley, *The Birth of Western Canada* (London, 1936) p. 208

[43] Morris, *Treaties of Canada* pp. 172-5. Nevertheless, on his arrival in 1876 to negotiate this treaty, Morris still found the Indians upset by 'vague fears' that he was at pains to contradict (p. 183). The idea that he would just take the land he wanted was not that far-fetched, for mainland British Columbia resolutely refused to make land purchase treaties

[44] In 1874, after much circumlocution, Pisqua pointed to an HBC trader saying, 'You told me you had sold your land for £300,000. We want that money' – Carl Beal, *Money, Markets and Economic Development in Saskatchewan Indian Reserve Communities, 1876-1930s* (Ph.D. thesis, University of Manitoba, 1994) p. 112; Morris, *Treaties of Canada* pp. 97-106

immigrants as the thousand Indians there present 'would come in and fill up the country'. So 'now was the time ... to come to an arrangement' that would secure Indians and their children homes and annuities.[45] Treaties 1 and 2 represent a recognition of this. And when Morris encountered unexpected opposition in 1876, he reverted to this theme: unless arrangements were made to set specific pieces of land aside for the Indians, the country would be flooded with white settlers who would completely disregard them.[46]

But on the Plains the real problem was over-hunting, more especially of the buffalo. As early as 1871 some Cree Chiefs had written to Archibald to say that their country 'was getting ruined of fur-bearing animals, hitherto our sole support', and 'no longer able to support us'. So they asked him for 'assistance when we come to settle'.[47] This initiative led in 1874 to Treaty 4, followed two years later by Treaty 6, in the discussions surrounding which the grounds both for concluding the treaties and for reluctance to do so were clearly stated. While most Cree leaders were happy with Morris' reassuring letter and preliminary presents in 1875, Big Bear declared that 'when we set a fox-trap, we scatter pieces of meat ... [but] we want no bait'. Next year some Saulteux sought to block negotiations by stopping the Commissioners crossing the Saskatchewan; one explained that 'all along the prices have been to one side, and we have had no say. He that made us provided everything for our mode of living', with provision elsewhere for the maintenance of the white man; 'and now ... you come and stand on this our earth ... through what you have done you have cheated my kinsmen'. But the Métis would not help, while the Cree 'nation' offered the Commissioners a 'safe convoy' were this needed.[48] In the negotiations, though, divisions quickly became apparent. Some Chiefs, without actually rejecting the process,

---

[45] Morris, *Treaties of Canada* pp. 34-5

[46] Peter Erasmus, *Buffalo Days and Nights. As Told to Henry Thompson* (Calgary, 1999 edn.) p. 245

[47] Morris, *Treaties of Canada* pp. 169-71

[48] Morris, *Treaties of Canada* pp. 174, 176-7, 223-4

sought to stall it by making themselves scarce.[49] Others, Morris later reported, 'were either averse to make a treaty or desirous of making extravagant demands'.

Much time had therefore to be allowed for private Indian debates. In one of these, the interpreter Peter Erasmus remembered,[50] Mistawasis roundly asked his nephew Poundmaker, the Badger, and 'those others who object to signing this treaty',

> 'Have you anything better to offer our people? ... can you suggest anything that will bring ... [former conditions] back...?
>
> I for one think that the Great White Queen Mother has offered us a way of life when the buffalo are no more. Gone they will be before many snows have come to cover our heads or our graves...'

He then piled on the arguments. The 'Red Coats' Police had curbed the American whiskey traders who had destroyed the Blackfoot as 'all the Crees in the days of our fathers ... failed to do'; and Mistawasis looked 'to the Queen's law and her Red Coat servants to protect our people' against 'firewater' and to 'stop the senseless wars' among them. There really was no alternative. Past wars and smallpox had made the Indians too few 'to throw away the hand that is offered to help us, ... too weak to make our

---

[49] Beardy (of the Willow Cree) demanded an alternative venue on the ground that this had been pointed out to him in a vision, but meanwhile tried to induce the Fort Carlton Indians 'to make no treaty', urging them 'not to sell the land, but to lend it for four years' (ibid. pp. 188-9), while Sweetgrass simply stayed away hunting in the hope that nothing could be decided without him

[50] Erasmus, *Buffalo Days and Nights* pp. 246-50. Mistawasis (Big Child) and Ahtahkakoop (Star Blanket) had hired Erasmus as interpreter and insisted that he be allowed to attend the Chiefs' private discussions 'to keep us right on what was offered in the treaty terms'. His is the only eye-witness account we have of such Indian debates. It is, admittedly, oral history recorded more than four decades later, and, as an editor reminds us (p. xiv), it cannot be 'taken word for word as a source of precise factual information'. But on the public 1876 proceedings, it is very close to the official accounts (pp. xiv, xxv)

demands heard'; and in the 'Long Knives' country', the great Indian nations were 'being vanquished and swept into the most useless parts of their country.' Mistawasis' ally Ahtahkakoop then rubbed this in. With the buffalo gone,

> 'we will have only the vacant prairie which none of us has learned to use.
>
> Can we stop the power of the white man from spreading over the land like grass hoppers that ... consume every blade of grass ... in their path? I think not.'

The buffalo would 'soon be a thing of the past', and the people would die 'unless we find another way'. That 'new way' the 'Queen Mother' had offered them, and 'Surely we Indians can learn the [agricultural] ways of living that made the white man strong.'

Between them, Mistawasis and Ahtahkakoop largely got their way. For when talks with Morris resumed, people like Poundmaker did not oppose the projected treaty as such, but only questioned whether it offered enough to enable Indians to embrace this new way of life: 'I do not know how to build a house for myself...; again, I do not know how to cultivate the ground for myself'. On this basis some bargaining was possible, and the Indians at Fort Carlton both received Morris' proposals in writing and put written counter-proposals to him. A 'whole day was occupied with ... discussion of the food question, and it was the turning point with regard to the treaty.' The Indians pressed for assurances of support; Morris made it clear that Canada would not provide food on a permanent basis, but that in the event of 'pestilence' or 'a general famine' it would give assistance 'sufficient to relieve the Indians from the calamity'. This commitment had not figured in previous treaties, and Morris' superiors were not pleased. Also new was the pledge, once reserves had been surveyed, of $1000 for the first three years to buy provisions for those actually cultivating the land. More standard, though now on a more generous scale than in Treaty 4, were the 'once for all' grants of tools, seed, and stock to come when cultivation of the land actually started.[51] On all this Morris did make concessions. But he insisted that he would not haggle, and the stage was always reached when he tabled a take-it-or-leave it offer. Mistawasis had Erasmus check this to ensure that it contained everything that had been promised. He and Ahtakakoop then signed, the Fort Carlton Chiefs followed suit, and, this achieved, Morris soon persuaded Beardy's more reluctant Willow Cree and finally Sweetwater to come on board. Only Big Bear stood out. And next year Morris' successor as Lieutenant Governor, David Laird, completed the tally by concluding Treaty 7 with the Blackfoot Confederacy, probably the most powerful in the region.

Treaties 1 and 2 had had to be revised to incorporate promises made on the side during their negotiation. Thereafter Canadian negotiators were careful to give the Indians the text of the agreed terms in writing, and to have it explained by interpreters. But there is controversy as to whether the First Nations understood what they had promised. Mistawasis had the final draft of Treaty 6 checked, but 'the other chiefs' at the Fort Carlton talks took it on trust; and Sweetgrass and many others eventually deferred to their wisdom or authority, and accepted on behalf of their people.[52] How far the draft had really been understood, we shall never know. While stressing that the parties' very different cultural backgrounds will have coloured their interpretations of the treaties, J.L. Taylor concludes that the 'Treaty Six people believed they were giving up the surface rights or allowing the use of land to agricultural settlers'. Hence their efforts during the negotiation 'to get better benefits. In their view, the treaty benefits were, in part at least, compensation for what they were giving up or sharing.'[53] But a different picture came to be embedded in Indian tradition as recorded by oral historians in the late twentieth century:

---

[51] Morris, *Treaties of Canada* pp. 185, 332-3, 354-5; Stanley, *Birth of Western Canada* p. 212
[52] Erasmus, *Buffalo Days and Nights* pp. 254, 258-60
[53] Taylor, 'Two Views on the Meaning of Treaties Six and Seven' pp. 40-44. Treaty Seven had involved less negotiation for 'better benefits', and Taylor

an extreme version ran that when the treaty commissioners 'took the papers back to Ottawa, they made them so that the government could claim all of Canada. They did not ask permission here to do that.'[54] Perhaps this largely reflects ex-post disillusion with the eventual outcome. But two more contemporary contributory factors may be noted. One was, as a sympathetic journalist put it, that 'with the Indians any request which he makes, and which is not positively refused, he assumes to be granted.' Thus, as Chief Kitowehaw put it, 'When we asked for a yoke of oxen for each three families, although we were not told we should get them, we understood that we would. If we had been told that we were not to get them, we should not have complained.'[55]

Another factor shaping subsequent perceptions was the belief that the First Nations still had a decade to adapt to a post-buffalo world, and that there was therefore no immediate need to change.[56] There was enough concern over the buffaloes' durability to make farming on reserves seem attractive, at least as a fall-back for their future children. But there was no immediate need to

---

believes Indians tended to view it more purely as one of alliance and the Queen's protective care. See also Miller, *Skyscrapers hide the heavens* pp. 216-24

[54] Similarly for Treaty Seven, 'Tall White Man never mentioned land deal when he promised to pay twelve (sic) dollars every year as long as the sun shines...' – Taylor, 'Two Views' pp. 43, 44

[55] *Montreal Gazette*, 2 Sept. 1879 (reporting from Fort Carlton), cited in Deanna Christensen, *Ahtahkakoop. The Epic Account of a Plains Cree Head Chief, His People, and their Struggle for Survival, 1816-1896* (Shell Lake, Saskatchewan, 2000) pp. 379-80, 383. Similarly, despite Erasmus' cautions, Chief James Seenum took Morris' undertaking to pass his request for an unusually large reserve on to Ottawa as a promise that he would get it (*Buffalo Days and Nights* pp. 263-4, 269-70), while the more eminent Payipwat assumed acceptance of his 1875 demands since they had been referred to the government, and so 'maintained to his dying day that Ottawa had not fulfilled its promises' (*Dictionary of Canadian Biography*)

[56] Commissioner M.G. Dickieson hoped for this in 1876 (Beal, *Money, Markets and Economic Development* pp. 127-8); and to avoid scaring the buffalo from their feeding grounds, in September 1877 Treaty Seven banned development on the south side of Bow River for ten years – thereafter, it was feared, 'the buffalo will have become nearly extinct', but by then 'the Indians hope to have herds of domestic cattle' – Morris, *Treaties of Canada* pp. 261-2, 369

abandon traditional tribal hunting, and Morris sometimes played up to this. He told Sweetgrass that he accepted that 'not all' the Indians were ready to turn to agriculture; he did not want 'to take away the means of living that you have now'; and he saw Indians 'receiving money ... to purchase clothing for their children ... enjoying their hunting and fishing as before ... retaining their old mode of living with the Queen's gift in addition'.[57] From this perspective, nothing tangible had to be given up at once; yet concluding treaties yielded immediate cash payments plus the prospect of Canadian assistance if things did go wrong. So, while some leaders (and their bands) held out, most Chiefs signed fairly readily. As one oral tradition has it, 'The Indians had felt that they could go on living the way they used to. It was not until they were put on reserves that they realized they could no longer live the way they used to.'[58]

* * * *

In 1879 the buffaloes did not come north – Canadians believed the Americans stopped them – and the shock was enormous. At Blackfoot Crossing, the new Indian Commissioner, Edgar Dewdney, found 'about 1300 Indians in a very destitute condition, & many on the verge of starvation'. 'If you will drive away the Sioux and make a hole so that the Buffalo may come in,' Crowfoot told him, 'we will not trouble you for food, if you don't do that you must feed us or show us how to live.'[59] Dewdney arranged for the NWMP to distribute relief, but he also encouraged his Indians to go south of the border to hunt – in 1880 he reported that there were seven to eight thousand Canadian Indians around the Milk River just over

---

[57] Morris, *Treaties of Canada* pp. 231, 233; two years earlier he had told the Saulteux that it might be 'a long time' before there were many settlers, and until then 'you will have the right of hunting and fishing just as you have now' (p. 96)
[58] In specific relation to Treaty Seven, Taylor, 'Two Views' p. 44
[59] Dewdney to Macdonald, 2 Jan. 1880 (Christensen, *Ahtahkakoop* pp. 371-2)

the border.[60] Going south after the buffalo will have seemed fairly routine. For, as one Police Commissioner observed, the Indians on both sides of the 'International Boundary are one people, severed politically by an invisible line'.[61] However Canadian Indians were seen in America as a nuisance – at best unwelcome competition in hunting the dwindling buffaloes, at worst as responsible for an epidemic of horse and cattle stealing. US Indian agents and troops made periodic moves to expel them. In late 1879, and again in 1881, the Canadian government managed to secure grudging permission for their Indians to cross over to hunt. But in 1881, when the 'Young Dogs' stole horses and killed cattle, the American army disarmed and returned them, and in 1882 it spent the summer trying to drive Canadian Cree back across the border, often in a state of destitution.[62] The 'invisible line' was becoming real.

Meanwhile, Canada had promised the Indians assistance in the event of 'a general famine', and it did move to provide this: the cost of emergency provisions, $48,589 in 1878, rose to $563,150 in 1882 and 1883, and Indian expenditure became the third largest item in the federal budget.[63] Indians had congregated in the Cypress Hills where the buffalo had lasted longer than elsewhere in Canada, and sick and starving Indians clustered around the NWMP forts there, with Fort Macleod feeding 7,000 every other

---

[60] Sharp, *Whoop-up Country* p. 155, citing Dewdney's letters of Oct. 1880 and July 1881; Michael Hogue, 'Disputing the Medicine Line: the Plains Cree and the American Border, 1876-1885', in Carol Higham and Robert Thacker eds., *One West, Two Myths. A Comparative Reader* (Calgary 2004) p. 90

[61] Sharp, *Whoop-up Country* p. 133

[62] Payipwat, *Dictionary of Canadian Biography*; Hogue, 'Disputing the Medicine Line' pp. 89-100

[63] Martin, 'The Department of Indian Affairs in the Dominion of Canada budget, 1882', *Martinalia*; Beal, *Money, Markets and Economic Development* (to which Martin owes many of his figures) pp. 143-4. Martin puts the 1882 Indian expenditure (including the covenanted annuities and other payments) at $1.2m., overall debt service at $9.1m., and the provincial subsidies engaged for in Confederation at $3.5m.; emergency relief was cut back after 1883, but only to $478,038 in 1885

day in January 1880.[64] By 1882 few resources were left there beyond relief distributions, horse stealing, and the cross-border forays that had upset the Americans. In January Dewdney reported that some 4000 Plains Indians were in the US (and in some danger of expulsion) with 5000 around Fort Walsh. The government decided to move them to reserves well away to the north by withholding rations from those who would not go; Erasmus was employed to persuade 2000 to leave. But Plains Indians had not taken to living on reserves;[65] most simply trickled back to the Cypress Hills, and in December Fort Walsh gave out 44,800 lbs. of beef and 353,000 of flour by way of 'starvation allowances'. This Fort had always had water and sanitation problems, and bringing in supplies via Fort Benton was cumbersome, especially if the Missouri froze in winter. When the railway came to its vicinity in the spring of 1883, Fort Walsh could be closed, leaving the Indians little option but to return north.[66]

As early as 1879 Father Lestanc had written that all the Indians were 'in great want ... [and] consider the treaties of no value'.[67] The premises on which these treaties had been framed had proved flawed. As one historian puts it,

'When Ahtahkakoop and Mistawasis signed Treaty Six they believed they could support their early farming ventures by hunting and trapping. The change would be gradual and the hardship minimized ... [But] The buffalo had disappeared faster than anyone could imagine ... The Indian peoples' traditional economy had vanished ... Ahtahkakoop and a number of other chiefs were making a serious attempt to

---

[64] Stanley, *Birth of Western Canada* pp. 223-7; also over half the cases seen by the Fort Walsh NWMP surgeon were Indian (Jody F. Decker, 'Surgeons' Stories', *The Beaver* 78:3 (June-July 1998) p. 26)

[65] Dewdney had said that fewer than half of all North-West Territories Indians were on their reserves, with 11,600 moving about the Prairies (Stanley, *Birth of Western Canada* p. 231); *Buffalo Days and Nights* pp. 268, 323n.

[66] Stanley, *Birth of Western Canada* pp. 233-5; Parks Canada, *Fort Walsh National Historic Site* (accessed 7/4/20)

[67] Big Bear, *Dictionary of Canadian Biography*

farm, but just as they were starting to make some headway, drought, frost, and disintegrating tools dashed their hopes. In 1884 there would be no crops. The chiefs believed that the government had promised to look after their band members. This promise was not being kept...'[68]

This was not entirely fair. Canada had promised assistance in the event of 'a general famine', and it had moved to provide this. Still, the 1880s were marked by a string of Indian complaints. Many were reasonable, though not surprising for a large and new administrative programme: the agricultural tools supplied broke down (especially if misused); cattle (obtained on the cheap from the US) were substandard; farm instructors could be tyrannical and second rate, and in any case their numbers were reduced as the Canadian budget moved into deficit in 1884. There may, too, often have been chicken-and-egg situations, with bands finding cultivation impossible without tools, the Indian Department reluctant to provide these when work had not started. But by no means all complaints can be taken at face value;[69] and some requests reflected widely divergent understandings of the Treaties. Thus when Governor-General Lorne toured the Prairies in 1881, Ahtahkakoop asked for 'a thresher and reaper and the power to work them', Petihkwahakew for 'implements like the white man uses'. These were way beyond the written terms of Treaty 6, but would (in 1884) be represented as having been implicitly promised: the Indians had been told they 'would be taught to live like' the white man; 'he has threshing mills, mowers, reapers and rakes. As the Govnt. Pledged itself to put them in the same position as the white man, it should give them these things.' (The Indian Department did not accept this perspective, but it did, from 1883,

---

[68] Christensen, *Ahtahkakoop* pp. 481-2
[69] See Martin, 'M.C. Cameron's indictment of Canada's Department of Indian Affairs, 1885-91: the pitfalls of contemporary evidence', *Martinalia*

make some machines available, though even this was not without problems.)[70]

Overall, progress was slow. For while over 10,600 Indians were on the Reserves in southern Saskatchewan at the end of 1883, they had only 4143 acres (or 2 per family) under crop in in 1884, which left them still largely dependent on handouts. And in a desperate situation, many – probably most – Indians were looking for a new start. Big Bear, who had always distrusted the treaty process, could claim that 'a year ago, he stood alone in making these demands; now the whole of the Indians are with him.'[71]

During the Treaty 6 negotiations Morris had told the Indians to choose their reserves, taking 'a good place', and had assured them that they 'would not be held to their choice until it was surveyed', after which the reserves should have become unalterable without their owners' consent.[72] When the Plains Indians congregated on the Cypress Hills at the end of the decade, Piapot, Little Pine, and ten other bands ('most of the Assiniboine nation'), selected contiguous reserve sites. One was surveyed in 1880, with the expectation that the rest would follow next year. But the authorities became worried, partly because the area was not well suited to cultivation and might leave its occupants still dependent on handouts, but also because they did not like the idea of large contiguous reserves – Morris had seen a scattering of plots, each for 'one or more bands', 'as far preferable to the American system of placing whole tribes, in large reserves, which eventually become the object of cupidity to the whites, and the breaking up of which has so often led to Indian wars'. The system of band reserves would also 'diminish

---

[70] The reaper given to Ahtahkakoop came with no instructions, so it was fortunate that his local missionary was able to maintain it; and in 1883-4 much time was wasted waiting for the repeatedly delayed circulating thresher. Mitsawasis and Ahtahkakoop had themselves bought a thresher, but it broke down after one season – Christensen, *Ahtahkakoop* pp. 421-4, 427, 434, 442, 452, 478

[71] J.A. Macrae to Dewdney, 25 Aug. 1884 (Christensen, *Ahtahkakoop* p. 481)

[72] Morris, *Treaties of Canada* pp. 183, 218, 233, 241

the offensive strength of the Indian tribes, should they ever become restless'.[73] There were, too, rumours of plans for a revisionist First Nations Confederacy. The surveying of reserves was suspended, and in 1882 the Plains Indians were told they would receive rations only if they left the Cypress Hills. They soon trickled back, and on their return had again to be fed. So in 1883 Fort Walsh was closed, and the Cree were required to go north, sometimes under Police escort.[74]

They went remarkably quietly. But several Indians continued to seek some concentration of reserves, Piapot around Qu'Appelle, others in the general area of Battleford. Big Bear wanted 'one big reserve, or one part of the West, for the Indians' and talked of going to Ottawa to demand it; he also seems to have envisaged a system whereby one representative, chosen every four years, would deal with the government on behalf of all the Indian tribes. In this connection there were 'Thirst Dances' at which many Indians would congregate, followed by Councils. The best-known is that held in 1884 at Poundmaker's reserve, which nearly led to an explosion when the NWMP sought to make an arrest there. The eventual outcome was a Council of Chiefs, officially sanctioned and attended by people like Mistawasis and Ahtahkakoop, but convened by leaders who had either long held out against signing their original Treaty or had at least been dubious about it. Much was said of the Indian Department's backsliding on Canada's undertakings; and grievances were communicated to Ottawa with the warning that, while their 'young men' had thankfully not resorted to violence, 'it is almost too hard for them to bear' the Government's treatment 'after its sweet promises'. The Chiefs would wait only till next summer for a satisfactory reply, 'failing which they will take measures to get what they desire.' The nature of these "measures", J.A. Macrae reported, 'could not be elicited,

---

[73] Morris, *Treaties of Canada* pp. 287-8. Morris also thought small band reserves, within which each family should be assigned a section, were the best way of inducing the Indians 'to establish homes and learn the art of agriculture'
[74] John L. Tobias, 'Canada's Subjugation of the Plains Cree, 1879-1885', *Can.H.R.* 64:4 (1993) pp. 527-32

but ... the idea of war was repudiated.)'[75] The repudiation of 'war' is credible: impressed by what he saw while accompanying Lorne on his 1881 tour of the Plains, Poundmaker had told his followers that 'the whites will fill the country ... It is useless to dream that we can frighten them, that time has passed';[76] and both he and others had recently intervened to stop incidents exploding into violence. So the aim was presumably to stir up so great and so broad an opposition to the Treaties that Canada would renegotiate them.

* * * *

All this was far removed from mainstream Canadian politics, as indeed Westerners often ruefully observed. Much more attention was paid to the slow progress on the railway that had been so cavalierly promised to secure British Columbia. North American railways were then built by capitalists looking to profit from land sales on their completion. Their companies operated in a Hobbesian world, allying with (or taking over) some actors, attacking or impeding others, putting out propaganda, and seeking to enlist or buy useful politicians. In 1869 the Union and Central Pacific Companies had completed a line from Omaha to San Francisco Bay. Other entrepreneurs and companies had similar aspirations, and some were given to melding their own interests with dreams of national expansion. Thus in 1869, when Nova Scotia still resented its inclusion in Canada, R.J. Walker addressed the Nova Scotia League, inviting the province to accept the generous terms the US would offer for union, and blowing the trumpet for the Northern Pacific railroad. This would afford 'a grand route' from Nova Scotia, through Maine, Chicago, and St. Paul to 'the Red River ... and thence to the Pacific', whereas 'no continuous railroad route,

---

[75] Christensen, *Ahtahkakoop* pp. 470, 477-81; Big Bear, *Dictionary of Canadian Biography*; Tobias, 'Canada's Subjugation of the Plains Cree' pp. 535-9; Miller, *Skyscrapers hide the heavens* pp. 233-4; Stanley, *Birth of Western Canada* pp. 242, 275-6, 281-5, 289-94

[76] Poundmaker, *Dictionary of Canadian Biography*

entirely through British territory, can ever unite Halifax and Montreal with the Pacific.' 'Nature', Walker thought, 'forbids the bans',[77] but the Northern Pacific itself was less sure: the 1868 *Statement of its Resources and Merits* declared that 'a Pacific Railroad on British soil' would 'preclude the idea of political relations between that people and our own'. So it should be forestalled; and in 1869 a Senate Report duly concluded that the prior opening of a US North Pacific Railroad would seal 'the destiny of the British possessions west of' 91°. 'They will become so Americanized in interests and feelings that they will be in effect severed from the new Dominion and ... their annexation will be but a matter of time'.[78]

Among those who thought this way was the banker Jay Cooke, who in late 1869 invested $5m. in the North Pacific and took charge of its finances. He also funded the annexation propagandist James Wickes Taylor. That winter the Riel Rebellion seemed to offer a short cut to the takeover of the British North-West; and in January 1870 Taylor drafted, for Minnesota's annexationist Senator Ramsey, a bill authorising a land grant enabling the Northern Pacific's associate, the St. Paul and Pacific, to build to the border at Pembina. 'The measure will thus be seen to have a political significance', Taylor told the Secretary of State. If 'passed now ... it would exert a marked influence on' the Red River Convention then in session, and 'do more than all other agencies to determine the future relations of British North America.'[79] Cooke, too, looked to

---

[77] *Letter of Hon. Robt. J. Walker on the Annexation of Nova Scotia and British America* (Washington, 1869) pp. 13, 15-16

[78] W. Kaye Lamb, *History of the Canadian Pacific Railway* (New York, 1977) p. 12

[79] Leonard B. Irwin, *Pacific Railways and Nationalism in the Canadian-American Northwest, 1845-1873* (New York, 1968 reprint) pp. 128-34. Later Taylor used reports of a projected Canadian line to the Pacific (in connection with B.C.'s entry into Confederation) to again urge passage of 'Senator Ramsey's bill ... for aid to a railroad down the Red River': with this extension of the US system 'to Manitoba during 1871, no Canadian scheme could prevent the Americanization of the Northwest' – Taylor to Secretary of State Fish, 25 Jan., 16 Feb., and 27 June, 1870 (ed. Hartwell Bowfield, *The James Wickes Taylor Correspondence 1859-1870* (Vol. III, Manitoba Record Society Publications, 1968) pp. 135, 137-8, 178)

'the annexation of British North America northwest of Duluth ... This could be done without any violation of treaties' through the 'quiet emigration over the border of trustworthy men ... with a tacit (not legal) understanding with Riley and others there.'[80] 'Riley' (Riel) never entered into such an understanding, and Canadian rule came to Manitoba. But neither Taylor nor Cooke gave up. With Cooke's approval, Taylor became US Consul in Winnipeg, telling Representative Banks in November 1870 that he could 'advance the Annexation policy, with which you are identified, more effectually [t]here than elsewhere'. He drafted an annexation bill for Banks to introduce in a speech declaring that England was 'unwilling', Canada 'inadequate', to carry through the measures required to develop the North-West – 'Such guarantees can only be given by the United States, in connection with ... the Northern Pacific Railway.' Taylor also tapped into Manitoba's desire for a full rail connection with the US system, which he reported optimistically, 'every intelligent resident' saw as 'the sure precursor of a political connection with the United States'; and he 'encouraged' this by placing unsigned articles in local newspapers.[81]

At the same time, Taylor managed to strike up close relations with Manitoba's Lt.-Governor Archibald. 'I shall be consulted with regard to the railway system of North West British America', he boasted to Cooke's agent General Nettleton, 'and I am sanguine that it may be adjusted in accord with the interests of the Northern Pacific.' Archibald was soon suggesting that the North Pacific build from its Duluth hub both east to link with Canadian railways at Sault Ste. Marie, and west to Red River, down this to Winnipeg, and then across British territory to the Pacific – thus securing what he saw as an *international* line running 'from sea-bord to sea-bord ... by the shortest possible route'. Cooke responded by promising that the North Pacific would reach the Red River later that year and Pembina (using the St. Paul and Pacific) within the next two; later it

[80] Jay Cooke to General Sargent, 25 Feb. 1870 (Ellis P. Oberholtzer, *Jay Cooke. Financier of the Civil War* ii (Philadelphia, 1907) p. 296)
[81] Taylor to N.P. Banks, 24 Nov. 1870, and to J.C.B. Davis, 13 March 1871 (Irwin, *Pacific Railways* pp. 135, 137, 138, 165)

planned to build east from Duluth across northern Michigan.[82] The final piece of the jigsaw was legislation in Manitoba to permit the Governor to authorise 'any sufficient company' to construct railways within the province – in other words, to let the St. Paul and Pacific build from Pembina to Winnipeg. North Pacific boosters talked unwisely of 'innumerable lateral branches, penetrating ... the British Provinces ... whose people will thus be made tributary to us forever, or induced to unite ... under a common constitution and flag.' Macdonald 'disallowed' this Manitoba legislation.[83]

The North Pacific wanted to link with C.J. Brydges' Grand Trunk at Sault Ste. Marie; and its President, Governor Smith, seems to have talked rather too freely of its plans, 'in concert with certain parties at Washington', to build 'so near the boundary' that 'drop lines' could be run across 'to injure, if not prevent the construction of an independent line in British Territory'. Brydges told Macdonald that the US Government wanted to 'take advantage of the ... Northern Pacific Railway, to prevent your getting control, for Canada, of the Hudson's Bay Territory', and that 'the Minnesota people' were no doubt telling 'the insurgents in Red River that their only hope of getting Railway Communication, will be through United States sources'.[84] Macdonald agreed that 'the United States Government are resolved to do all they can, short of war, to get possession of the western territory.' But though he said immediate steps must be taken 'to counteract them' by showing 'unmistakeably our resolve to build the Pacific Railway', surprisingly little happened.

---

[82] Taylor to Nettleton, 24 Nov. 1870; Archibald to Taylor, 3 Jan. 1871, Taylor to Archibald, 25 Feb. (conveying Cooke's 'assurances') – Irwin, *Pacific Railways* pp. 137, 139-40, 144-5

[83] Ibid, pp. 149-50, 152-3

[84] Taylor approached Brydges on 12 Jan. 1870 (*James Wickes Taylor Correspondence* pp. 104-6); Brydges to Macdonald, 26 Jan. 1870 (Sir Joseph Pope ed., *Correspondence of Sir John Macdonald* (Garden City, N.Y., 1921) pp. 123-4). Brydges assumed that by 'certain parties at Washington' Smith meant President Grant's administration, but he probably meant figures like Senators Chandler, Howard and Ramsey, and Representative Banks – influential men, but not quite powerful enough to pass the legislation the North Pacific really wanted

Macdonald asked Brydges to 'work out a plan' that he and Cartier could then push through.[85] But nothing came of this. A year later the Montreal shipping magnate, Sir Hugh Allan, asked what was being done. Macdonald said the topic would come before the next session of Parliament; meanwhile he saw 'no objection to the capitalists of Canada or of England (or of the United States for that matter) joining together and making proposals for the construction of the road.'[86] Allan established contact with the North Pacific, and in the second half of 1871 American delegations came to Ottawa, saw Macdonald and the Finance Minister Sir Francis Hincks, and concluded that both were 'cordially *with us*'. 'This project', Cooke had been told, seemed 'to belong to the North Pacific' if financial steps could be taken 'to cooperate with or control' it.[87] The upshot, in December 1871, was agreement on a company to seek the contract; Allan would be the only major Canadian shareholder, and most of the capital would be held by Americans involved with the North Pacific, reinforced by Chicago entrepreneurs led by George McMullen. This, Cooke told a partner, 'is to be kept dark for the present ... [with] no hint of the Northern Pacific connection, but the real plan is to cross [from Allan's Canadian line] ... through Northern Michigan and Wisconsin to Duluth, then build from Pembina to Fort Garry and by and by through the Saskatchewan to British Columbia'. Though the prospective Canadian legislation would provide for a railway to Winnipeg along the 'North Shore' of Lake Superior, this was 'merely for [the sake of] public opinion'; the North Pacific's Michigan section would be 'blended' with the Canadian Pacific, 'and the bonds sold as such in London.' The North Pacific would thus clandestinely direct the railway that Macdonald hoped would consolidate Canada's hold on its newly acquired territory.

---

[85] Macdonald to Brydges, 28 Jan. 1870 (*Correspondence of Sir John Macdonald* pp. 124-5)
[86] Macdonald to Allan, 3 Feb. 1871 (Lamb, *Canadian Pacific Railway* p. 20)
[87] Jay to Henry Cooke, 8 Aug. 1871; W.B. Ogden to Jay Cooke, 17 June 1871 (Irwin, *Pacific Railways* pp. 148, 165)

Macdonald had some qualms about Allan's American associates: 'they are applying to build our Pacific Railway', he wrote as early as October 1871, 'You may depend upon it ... that no American ring will be allowed to get control over it.' So he encouraged the formation of an Ontario-based company to compete with Allan's, and by April 1872 he could write that there were three rival groups: 'the Hugh Allan ring, composed of Jay Cooke and Co., Scott of Philadelphia, and other millionaires'; Brydges and associated Montreal figures; and 'the Ontario Ring headed by D.L. Macpherson'. 'There will, I have no doubt, be a coalition between numbers two and three, and Allan will ... be obliged to abandon his Yankee confreres.'[88]

This was easier said than done. An act authorising the railway's construction was passed on 1 June. On the 19th Allan formed a new company with himself as President and various eminent Canadians as directors. He also stirred up political opposition to Cartier in Quebec until (as Allan put it to an American partner) Cartier 'agreed to give the contract as required'.[89] In return Allan offered electoral support, both personal and financial. Cartier put Allan's requirements to Macdonald, and Macdonald talked over possible merger terms with Macpherson, but found him reluctant to make concessions. Macdonald then offered Allan the presidency of any new merged company, with the other arrangements to be settled later. Allan wanted more, and wrote back saying he had arranged with Cartier that if the merger attempts failed, 'the construction of the railway should be confided' to his company. This Macdonald repudiated, refusing to go beyond the offer of the presidency. Matters were then postponed until 'after the [general] election'.[90]

---

[88] Macdonald to S. Bellingham, 10 Oct. 1871 (Lamb, *Canadian Pacific Railway* p. 26), and to Sir John Rose, 17 April 1872 (Irwin, *Pacific Railways* p. 178)

[89] Cartier's involvement in the Grand Trunk had led him to oppose a projected rival line to Ottawa, popular because it would go 'through the French country'. Allan stirred up public feeling, and worked the Quebec legislature until Cartier came to terms – or so he told Northern Pacific's President Cass, 1 July 1872 (Lamb, *Canadian Pacific Railway* pp. 29-30)

[90] Irwin, *Pacific Railways* pp. 212-13; Richard Gwyn, *Nation Maker. Sir John Macdonald: His Life, Our Times* ii (Toronto, 2011) pp. 212-13; Macdonald to

But Allan still seems to have been confident of success: he told McMullen the government had agreed to form a company in which he and his friends would hold 'a majority' of the stock, and to give it 'the contract for building the road'. The company was to be 'of Canadians only', but 'I fancy we can get round that one way or another'. Next day Allan was more explicit: 'the Government is obliged to stipulate that no foreigner is to appear as a shareholder, so as to avoid the former cry of selling ourselves to the North Pacific'; the Americans' shares would therefore have, ostensibly, 'to stand in my name for some time'.[91]

Allan's agreement with Cartier had noted that the 'Friends of the Government will expect to be assisted with funds in the pending elections', and here Allan was as good as his word. He was in any case a major Conservative donor; and, as Macdonald later argued, it was natural for him to assist the government that had promised him the Canadian Pacific's presidency against an opposition that would junk the project. The Canadians of the day were not squeamish. But Allan went over the top, or was taken there by a Cartier fighting desperately to retain his Montreal seat: $85,000 went to Cartier, $32,600 to his understudy Hector Langevin. More importantly, Macdonald also drew on Allan for $45,000 to help with key contests in Ontario – and on 26 August sent what would become the famous telegram: 'I must have another ten thousand. Will be the last time of asking. Do not fail me. Answer today.'[92]

After winning the election, Macdonald again tried to get Macpherson's 'Ontario Ring' to accept a merger. But Macpherson

the Governor-General, Lord Dufferin, 9 Oct. 1873 (Joseph Pope, *Memoirs of the Right Honourable Sir John Macdonald* ii (London, 1894) esp. pp. 180-4)

[91] Allan to George McMullen, 6 Aug., and to General Cass, 7 Aug., 1872 (Irwin, *Pacific Railways* pp. 184-5)

[92] Gwyn, *Nation Maker. Sir John Macdonald* pp. 212-13; P.B. Waite, *Macdonald. His Life and World* (Toronto, 1975) pp. 102-3. Allan would later claim to have spent nearer $350,000, but this may have included other expenses in politically promoting his company

suspected Allan's American proclivities, and his company chose to beat the nationalist drum:

> 'No more suicidal policy could be pursued by the people of Canada than to allow their [American] rivals to have such an interest in this national undertaking as would virtually transfer to them the ownership ... of 50 million acres of Canadian territory [the railway land grant] ... and grant them, in perpetuity, a monopoly of traffic over the Canadian, which is the shortest and best trans-continental route.'

On 24 October Allan at last accepted that he would have to shed his American partners. 'The opposition of the Ontario party', he now told McMullen, will 'have the effect of shutting out our American friends from any participation ... Public sentiment seems to be decided that the road shall be built by Canadians only.'[93] Cooke largely acquiesced in this dismissal, but McMullen did not.

In January 1873 a new company was formed to undertake the contract, with Allan as President, but with Directors carefully distributed across Canada's provinces. Allan left for London to raise money. He proved unsuccessful, partly because of rumours of an impending scandal.[94] There was, in any case, little European appetite for North American railway stocks – it was reported from Germany in August that an American bond 'even if signed by an angel of Heaven would not sell'. Understandably so; in September 1873 Jay Cooke and Co. suspended payment, brought down by Cooke's refusal to disengage from the North Pacific. The North Pacific had not been well run. But matters had not been helped by the Congressional investigation into the Union Pacific's 'Credit Mobilier' scandal.[95]

Canada, too, developed a scandal: the charges were that Allan had bought the transcontinental contract by contributing enormous sums to the Conservative election expenses of 1872 –

---

[93] Lamb, *Canadian Pacific Railway* p. 32; Gwynn, *Nation Maker* p. 216
[94] Gwyn, *Nation Maker* p. 233
[95] Oberholtzer, *Jay Cooke* ii pp. 394, 402, 418, 424

'the Government got the money and Sir Hugh Allan the Charter'; and Allan's concern had not, anyway, been Canadian, as it represented itself, but American. McMullen had called on Macdonald and produced his correspondence with Allan. He stressed that it was Allan who had initially approached the Americans, as they believed with government sanction; and he demanded either reinstatement of the original contract with Allan or Allan's exclusion from any connection with the new company. Macdonald could offer neither. He got Hincks to see Allan; a deal was apparently struck with McMullen, and Hincks reported that the matter had been 'quite satisfactorily arranged'.[96] But in April the Liberal MP Lucius Huntington levelled reasonably accurate charges, albeit with no supporting evidence. Things then went quiet until July, when Liberal papers published much of Allan's correspondence, and also Macdonald's killer telegram, 'I must have another ten thousand...'. McMullen had probably leaked or sold some of this material to the Liberals. They certainly paid the 'confidential clerk' of Allan's solicitor $5000 for a second batch of documents he had stolen.[97] And they made the most of their haul:

'Third Wizard (the *Globe*): Adjectives from Billingsgate,
      From my columns freely take,
      Add thereto McMullen's crams
      Stolen letters, telegrams,
      All these matters mix and mangle,
      To form a great Pacific Scandal.

      Double, double cauldron bubble
      Bring the Premier lots of trouble.'[98]

---

[96] Hincks apparently paid McMullen $20,000, with $17,500 to follow when McMullen returned the papers at the end of the parliamentary session – Gwyn, *Nation Maker* p. 223

[97] Lamb, *Canadian Pacific Railway* p. 30; Donald Creighton, *John A. Macdonald. The Old Chieftain* (Toronto, 1955) pp. 147-55, 161-3, 168

[98] *Canadian Illustrated News*, 3 Jan. 1874 – quoted by Waite, *Macdonald. His Life and World* p. 104

Macdonald manoeuvred to protect himself, and often seemed likely to survive. But with the return of Parliament in October, support peeled away. On 5 November 1873 his government resigned, to be succeeded by that of the Liberal Alexander Mackenzie.

The 'treaty' by which British Columbia joined Canada had stipulated that railway construction in the province should start by July 1873. Given the Canadian Pacific company's failure to raise money, this was, in any meaningful sense, impossible. Macdonald tried to make amends by arranging for a formal sod-breaking, and by appointing Esquimalt as the western terminus of the line – thus gratifying Victoria, B.C.'s capital and largest urban centre, but extending the Dominion's obligations well beyond the 'treaty' requirement of a line merely to the Pacific coast. That did not stop the provincial legislature protesting in July against the failure to make a real start. In Ottawa the protest was pigeon-holed. So in November the province sent a reminder, asking for 'a decided expression' of the Dominion's policy. This the new Prime Minister, Mackenzie, provided in his 25 November 'Sarnia' speech: Macdonald and Allan had intended to spend the enormous sum of $180m., but the Liberals meant to do things more cheaply, making interim use of the Great Lakes, of navigable waterways in the prairies, and of the American railway system.

B.C. was told the speech represented the government's probable future policy, but that a special agent might be sent to talk further. This agent, David Edgar, came to Victoria in March 1874. In the meantime, feelings had been stirred up by the federal election campaign. B.C.'s Premier, Amor De Cosmos, had been seeking reconstruction of federal support for the Esquimalt graving dock, and had asked his legislature for changes in the 'terms of union' to effect this. His opponents saw this as the prelude to backtracking on the more important railway clause. On 7 February a large protest meeting boiled over. Headed by Dr. Helmcken, and singing the campaign songs of the day –

'We'll hang De Cosmos on a sour apple tree,
We'll hang De Cosmos on a sour apple tree,
  As we go marching on'

– it marched on the legislature, drove the Speaker from the chair and De Cosmos into hiding, and set up a 'Terms of Union Preservation League'. Two days later the Legislature resolved that any change in the railway clause would have to be submitted to the people in an election. De Cosmos resigned, to concentrate instead on his position as an Ottawa MP, and his successor, George Walkem, aligned politically with Victoria to demand 'the terms, the whole terms, and nothing but the terms'.[99]

Edgar had been sent to tell 'leading men' in British Columbia that it was 'a physical impossibility to construct the [rail]road' by 1881 as 'provided in the terms of the union', and that attempting to do so could only result in 'useless expense and financial disorder.'. Mackenzie had every reason to believe this: surveys for the shorter and easier Intercolonial had started in 1864, but the line was still eighteen months from completion; and the respected engineer Sandford Fleming had told Allan's company in 1873 that were building 'pushed on … with undue haste', costs might more than double.[100] Edgar was to warn B.C. ministers that 'by insisting on the pound of flesh', they would only stimulate future disinclination to give 'anything but the pound of flesh'. But were the province ready to allow 'sufficient time', he should discover what it would like in return.

Bargaining followed. But by May Edgar believed the B.C. government was drawing back, not wanting to risk the elections any deal would require. He thought, though, that Canada could

---

[99] George Fletcher Henderson, *Alexander Mackenzie and the Canadian Pacific Railway 1871-1878* (Queen's University, Kingston, Ont., MA thesis, 1964) pp. 27, 37-41. On the dispute in general, see also Barbara J. Messamore, *Canada's Governors-General, 1847-1878: Biography and Constitutional Evolution* (Toronto, 2006) chap. 9, J.A. Maxwell, 'Lord Dufferin and the Difficulties with British Columbia, 1874-7' and Margaret A. Ormsby, 'Prime Minister Mackenzie, the Liberal Party, and the Bargain with British Columbia', *Can.H.R.* 12:4 (1931) and 26:2 (1945)

[100] Alexander Mackenzie to J.D. Edgar, 19 Feb. 1874 (Confidential Print, CO 880/7/5, 'Correspondence respecting the Canadian Pacific Railway Act so far as regards British Columbia…' pp. 3-4); Sandford Fleming's memorandum, Feb. 1873 (ibid. pp. 51-4). Fleming had suggested a scheme of work stretching to 1888

put it in the wrong by making a proposal that it would not dare submit to the electorate. In response B.C. refused to receive any proposal from Edgar until Canada agreed to be bound by it.[101] Mackenzie called Edgar home, and on 8 June responded curtly to a query from Lieutenant-Governor Trutch as to Edgar's precise status: he had presented his proposals 'on behalf of the Dominion Government', but they were now withdrawn. In reply, B.C. appealed, in June, to the Colonial Secretary, Lord Carnarvon, saying that Canada was in breach of the terms of union, as Walkem would come to London to explain. (He would depict Edgar's offer as one to finish work *within British Columbia* in 23½ years 'from the unknown period' of the completion of surveying, with nothing said of the remaining 2000 miles of line beyond the Rockies, and he demanded instead a guarantee of the railway's '"prompt commencement, continuous prosecution," and early completion'.)[102] Carnarvon declared his readiness to arbitrate, as, he told Dufferin privately, 'the only alternative to what may grow into a bitter quarrel'.[103] Mackenzie disliked the idea, but eventually agreed. So in August 1874 Carnarvon sent over recommendations, telling Dufferin to secure their acceptance. The Canadian Government feared trouble in Parliament, so Dufferin had 'a terribly hard fight'.[104] Eventually, though, both Canada and B.C. accepted the 'Carnarvon terms': the start 'as soon as possible' on the Esquimalt-Nanaimo line and its completion 'with all practicable despatch'; an annual 'minimum expenditure' on 'railway works' within B.C., once surveys were sufficiently advanced, of $2m., not the $1.5m. Edgar had offered;

---

[101] Dufferin summarised Edgar's proceedings in his 28 May 1874 letter to the Colonial Secretary Lord Carnarvon ('Correspondence respecting the Canadian Pacific Railway' pp. 81-3)

[102] Henderson, *Mackenzie and the Canadian Pacific* pp. 51-4; Walkem to Carnarvon, 31 Oct. 1874 ('Correspondence respecting the Canadian Pacific Railway' esp. pp. 171-5)

[103] 17 June 1874 (*Dufferin-Carnarvon Correspondence* p. 48). Dufferin and Carnarvon were friends, and relied heavily on their private correspondence

[104] Dufferin to Carnarvon, 11 Sept. 1874 (*Dufferin-Carnarvon Correspondence* p. 70)

and completion of the track by late 1890, with the railway opened next year 'to traffic from the Pacific seaboard to ... the western end of Lake Superior', where it would connect with existing lines through the United States and with 'the navigation on Canadian waters'.[105]

Despite some Liberal protests, all seemed set fair until April 1875, when the bill authorising construction of the Esquimalt-Nanaimo line was unexpectedly defeated in the Senate (by Liberal defections and 'adversary politics' Conservative votes). Mackenzie was then trying to strengthen his government by bringing back the leading Liberal Edward Blake. Blake had condemned, notably in his October 1874 'Aurora Speech', the building of what he saw as a ruinously expensive line through 'that "sea of mountains"' to propitiate British Columbia; and

'If under all the circumstances the Columbians were to say – "You must go on and finish this railway according to the terms [of union] or take the alternative of releasing us from the Confederation," I would – take the alternative! (Cheers.) I believe that is the view of the people of this country, and it may as well be plainly stated, because such a plain statement is the very thing that will prevent the British Columbians from making such extravagant demands.'[106]

Following the Senate defeat, Mackenzie initially wished to reintroduce the measure. But it became clear that this would split his party; and in May Blake was brought into the government on the 'understanding' that British Columbia would be offered a cash

---

[105] Carnarvon to Dufferin, 17 Nov. 1874 ('Correspondence respecting the Canadian Pacific Railway pp. 177-8). This precluded the reliance on waterways to cross the prairies that Mackenzie had originally advocated. But Carnarvon accepted the use of the Great Lakes, agreeing that there was at present no need to build 'the remainder of the railway ... northward of Lake Superior, to the existing lines' of central Canada
[106] ed. W.S. Wallace, 'Edward Blake's Aurora Speech', Can.H.R. 2 (1921) pp. 252-4

payment in lieu of the promise to build the Nanaimo line, while the 'obligations' to spend $2m. pa. on railway works within the province and to 'complete the line ... to Lake Superior by 1890' should be conditioned on their not requiring any increase in the rate of taxation.[107]

Blake's entry into the government went down badly in B.C.: 'it would be difficult', Dufferin observed after visiting the province in 1876, 'to describe the hatred with which ... [Blake] is regarded by all British Columbians'; 'nothing will induce them to forgive' his description of them 'as a useless incumbrance on the Dominion' and of 'their country as a "sea of mountains"'.[108] The government's policy was codified in a September 1875 Order-in-Council: the Esquimalt-Nanaimo line would not be part of the Canadian Pacific Railway, but only a local work that the Province might build, or not, as it pleased; and the Dominion would pay B.C. $750,000 compensation 'for any delays which may take place in the construction of the Pacific Railway'.[109] Things were not helped by a two-month delay in sending this to Victoria. But, Dufferin wrote, what brought 'discontent to a climax was the offer of $750,000 not as an equivalent for the loss of the [Nanaimo] Railway which the Senate had killed, but ... for delays which *may* occur in the construction of the main line ... it was regarded simply as a trap to induce British Columbia to forego her entire treaty rights'; 'this unhappy sentence has done more to destroy all confidence in Mr. Mackenzie than any other incident', confirming suspicions that he had engineered the Nanaimo Railway bill's defeat and that the mainland surveys were being 'needlessly multiplied in order to create new impediments'.[110] There followed

---

[107] Blake to Mackenzie, 19 May 1875 – Ormsby, 'Mackenzie, the Liberal Party, and the Bargain with British Columbia' pp. 156-8; Maxwell, 'Dufferin and the Difficulties with British Columbia' pp. 374-6

[108] To Carnarvon, 8 Oct. 1876 (*Dufferin-Carnarvon Correspondence* p. 289)

[109] Report of a Privy Council Committee, 21 Sept. 1875 (Confidential Print, CO 880/8/36, 'Further Correspondence relating to the Canadian Pacific Railway Act') pp. 2-3

[110] Dufferin to Carnarvon, 14 Sept. 1876 (*Dufferin-Carnarvon Correspondence* p. 268). There is a draft of the Order-in-Council in Blake's papers, and the usual

what Dufferin described as an exchange of 'recriminatory minutes' between the two governments, and another appeal from British Columbia to the Queen. Trutch observed privately that if Blake's policy came to prevail, 'Canada may say goodbye to B.C. and that means – as I see it – goodbye to Confederation and British Connection'.[111]

Dufferin volunteered to visit British Columbia in pursuit of 'an amicable arrangement'. Lord Carnarvon was enthusiastic, Mackenzie was not. And Dufferin's visit had to be neither one by 'an Imperial officer' nor a mission from the Dominion government, but only a Governor-General's 'progress'. Dufferin was greeted in Victoria not only by the standard welcoming arches but also by several bearing on the dispute with Canada: 'Union without Union', 'Our railway iron rusts', and a reference to Psalm 15, 'He that sweareth unto his neighbour, and disappointeth him not: though it were to his own hindrance ... Whoso do these things: shall never fail'; also by 'Carnarvon or Separation', under which Dufferin refused to pass.[112] Dufferin spent a month touring B.C. and talking to leaders and activists. He reported to Carnarvon that the agitation centred on Victoria. Most of Victoria's residents were from Britain, 'and like all middle class Englishmen, have a vulgar contempt for everything that is not English.' Popular sentiment there had always been 'very hostile to Canada'; and this feeling had grown since Confederation, Dominion officers being regarded much 'as were carpet baggers in the Southern States'. The 'one idea' was to make Esquimalt 'the terminus of a great transcontinental Railway'. For it

---

view is that he, if not Mackenzie, was aware of the ambiguity. In the spring of 1876 assurances were being given that the compensation related to the dropping of the Nanaimo railway, not to possible future delays on the mainland. But government policy had inclined towards the broader view in late 1875, and reverted to it during the November 1876 row with Dufferin (Ormsby, 'Mackenzie, the Liberal Party, and the Bargain with British Columbia' pp. 159-62; Messamore, *Canada's Governors General* pp. 204-5)

[111] Trutch to Macdonald, 3 March 1876 (Margaret A. Ormsby, *British Columbia: a History* (Vancouver, 1958) p. 269)

[112] William Leggo, *The History of the Administration of the ... Earl of Dufferin* (Montreal, 1878) p. 444

was upon this that 'the little town' of Victoria 'has to depend for its future'; and the hope was that building the Nanaimo railway would 'irretrievably commit the Dominion' to taking the transcontinental railway across the Seymour Narrows to Vancouver Island. Mackenzie's 'shilly-shallying' on this had not helped; and discontent had been brought to a climax by the wording of his $750,000 compensation offer and the further suspicion generated by Blake's return to the Cabinet. Admittedly the 'large majority of the mainland population' was 'strongly anti-Victorian', opposed to the Nanaimo Railway, and anxious that New Westminster should become the Canadian Pacific's terminus; but in the B.C. legislature Victoria could always command a majority in alliance with Nanaimo and Cariboo, both of which stood to benefit from the Seymour Narrows route.[113]

In his final speech in Victoria, Dufferin laid into the advocates of separation. He doubted whether they could persuade even Vancouver Island to 'so violent a course'. If they did, the mainland would stay with Canada. New Westminster would become its capital, with Canada building it up and diverting the railway to it. Burrard Inlet (the site of the modern Vancouver) would 'become a great commercial port', and Victoria 'would lapse for many a long year into the condition of a village'.[114] Dufferin had, though, hoped to add that the Nanaimo Railway dispute could be addressed in London by delegates from the province and the dominion under the Colonial Secretary's 'auspices'. Mackenzie barred this. But on his return to the east, Dufferin returned to the charge.

He warned Mackenzie that there was a real danger of B.C.'s secession. 'Of course you may say that their threats and menaces mean nothing and that they do no harm.' But at 'any day' 'the violent party and those ... most interested in property about Victoria' 'could carry almost any Resolution however extreme', and though 'a vote for the dissolution of the Union' might not,

---

[113] Dufferin to Carnarvon, 8 Oct. 1876 (*Dufferin-Carnarvon Correspondence* pp. 261-82)
[114] Leggo, *The Administration of the Earl of Dufferin* pp. 469-70

'in the last resort', be carried, its passage was 'a contingency by no means to be overlooked'. Dufferin therefore implored Mackenzie 'in the most earnest language to make any reasonable sacrifice ... for the sake of preserving intact the confederation of Canada'. Exclusion 'from the Western seaboard, and from all trade with the Pacific ports' would soon be felt 'as a most undesirable restriction, and so considerable a reduction of her "imperium" would infallibly damage ... [Canada's] "prestige"'. Moreover American 'statesmen would make great efforts to acquire the territory we should have so recklessly abandoned'. Nor would Dufferin wish to confess to the Queen that the Dominion, over which he had been sent to preside, had lost a Province, when it could have been prevented 'by a little good management, and ... a few hundred thousand dollars'. Mackenzie had now said it might prove impossible 'to float the contracts for [building] the Pacific Railway'; and should Canada then prove unable to meet its obligations to build the main line, 'a further negociation between the Dominion and the Province will have to be initiated'. It would be better to anticipate trouble by grafting 'this latter negociation' onto that over compensation for the dropping of the Nanaimo line, and getting 'Lord Carnarvon to assist us in inducing British Columbia to a reasonable compromise in regard to the whole affair'. Dufferin suggested that Carnarvon would increase the Nanaimo compensation from $0.75m. to $1m., but also that B.C. might then 'be brought' by pressure from England 'to acquiesce in an indefinite postponement of the western portion of the line'.[115]

Mackenzie was not unmoved by Dufferin's arguments, but they sometimes made him bristle. On one occasion he 'snorted ... and said that if an appeal was made to the Canadian people tomorrow they would vote British Columbia out of the Union with the greatest enthusiasm, for which statement [Dufferin observed] I am afraid there is considerable foundation'. Mackenzie

---

[115] Dufferin to Mackenzie, 9 Oct. 1876 (*Dufferin-Carnarvon Correspondence* pp. 284-9); Maxwell, 'Dufferin and the Difficulties with British Columbia' pp. 383-4; Messamore, *Canada's Governors General* pp. 202-3

was, too, subjected to counter pressures from within his Liberal party: the influential Nova Scotian Alfred Jones stressed the feeling against the railway in the Maritimes, and, 'looking to the future where you may have to rely mainly on us', hoped Mackenzie would 'let the B.C.'s know that we are not going to ruin the whole Dominion for their benefit!'.[116] Mackenzie's preferred course, he had told George Brown in January, was to 'go on the even tenor of our way, begin [the railway] as soon as we can, and let ... [B.C.] whistle.'[117] And despite several conversations with Dufferin, Mackenzie and Blake essentially decided to stick with this approach.

His government, Mackenzie had informed Carnarvon, had gone as far 'to satisfy British Columbia' 'as their hold on their followers will justify'. When told Carnarvon was waiting to reply to B.C.'s appeal to the Queen until he had heard what Ottawa intended to do, Mackenzie replied that there would be nothing new – he would simply continue to build the railway at the speed the country's resources would permit. Discussions climaxed in Dufferin's talks with Mackenzie on 16 November, and with both Mackenzie and Blake two days later. Mackenzie and Blake rejected 'anything like a conference ... in London', Mackenzie observing that the Colonial Secretary should not 'be too ready in interfering with questions having no bearing on Imperial interests', that Dufferin 'had nothing to do with it except as a constitutional governor, and that we had to be responsible to the people of Canada and no one else'. He would not again make the mistake of appearing before Carnarvon as before a judge; and he offered/threatened 'to retire at once and let ... [Dufferin] find someone else who might suit his views better'.

Mackenzie and Blake would have liked Carnarvon to tell B.C. that he backed their $750,000 compensation offer and the general

---

[116] Dufferin to Carnarvon, 9 Oct. 1876 (*Dufferin-Carnarvon Correspondence* pp. 282-3); Alfred Jones to Mackenzie, 10 Oct. 1876 (Dale C. Thomson, *Alexander Mackenzie. Clear Grit* (Toronto, 1960) p. 285)
[117] Mackenzie to Brown, 18 Jan. 1876 (Lamb, *Canadian Pacific Railway* p. 48). This approach was sympathetically depicted in a famous cartoon, 'British Columbia in a Pet'

Cartoon – British Columbia in a Pet

Uncle Aleck – don't frown so, my dear, you'll
have your railway by and bye
Miss B. Columbia – I want it now. You promised
I should have it, and if I don't, I'll complain to Ma.

approach of their Orders-in-Council, failing which he should keep quiet. On the 18th they added that 'they intended the phrase "delays which may occur" to cover [not just the abandonment of the Nanaimo railway but] all delays' present or prospective in the construction of the main line. 'This', Dufferin observed, 'is pretty much what the B.C. petition accuses them of doing'; and he 'completely lost my temper, and told them in very harsh terms what I thought of their principle of interpreting public documents' (by seeking 'surreptitiously to insinuate' into the Carnarvon Terms, as a 'controlling ... element', the 1871 Parliamentary Resolution that conditioned the building of the Railway on its not entailing any increase in taxation. Mackenzie's response was that

> 'Canada was not a Crown Colony (or a Colony at all in the ordinary acceptation of the term), that 4,000,000 of people with a government responsible to the people only could no t... be dealt with as small communities had been..., that we were capable of managing our own affairs, and that no government could survive who would attempt, even at the insistence of a Colonial Secretary, to trifle with Parliamentary decisions.'[118]

At this point everybody drew back. Dufferin wrote to Mackenzie suggesting that 'last night's discussion' had got off on the wrong foot by reason of a misunderstanding. He was ready to advise Carnarvon 'to postpone action for the present', while Mackenzie 'should make' Carnarvon 'feel that you are willing to help forward a more friendly settlement' than that implied by

---

[118] Next day Dufferin conceded this, but still insisted that 'within the walls of the Privy Council', he had 'as much right to contend for my opinion as any of my Ministers' and did not have 'to accept their advice merely because they give it' – Messamore, *Canada's Governors General* pp. 205-7; Maxwell, 'Dufferin and the Difficulties with British Columbia' pp. 385-7; Mackenzie's Memorandum on the conversations of 16 and 18 Nov. 1876, and Dufferin to Carnarvon, 20 and 23 Nov. 1876, and to Mackenzie, 19 Nov. (*Dufferin-Carnarvon Correspondence* pp. 309-10, 319, 410)

recent communications with B.C. 'The bargain that you have to make is a very simple one: to get British Columbia to recognise – upon conditions – the Resolution of 1871 as controlling the Carnarvon Terms. At present it does not'. Mackenzie replied that he would consult his colleagues. Next month he wrote that if Carnarvon postponed action but, in the event of Canada proving unable to let the contract and progress the railway, later summoned both parties to a conference to discuss 'some new solution which might be acceptable to both', Canada would comply (though 'I am the reverse of sanguine as to the results'). When reading this letter to Dufferin, Mackenzie sounded more forthcoming, and agreed that B.C.'s government might be told of his undertaking. Dufferin did so, adding unofficially that should railway building within the province not be started by the spring of 1878, there would be a general London conference in which 'the Secretary of State would ... prove a very powerful assistant in getting justice done to you'.[119] To secure such 'justice', Dufferin and Carnarvon were prepared to contemplate extreme measures. Among Dufferin's reasons for advocating an eighteen-month delay was that by then Mackenzie's 'Government would probably be weaker, the [Conservative] Opposition more formidable, and the Crown consequently stronger.' And if Mackenzie's government, having proved unable to keep its engagements, still refused 'satisfaction' or 'reasonable compromise, the renewal of an outcry for separation from B.C. might perhaps authorize a change of Ministry and a dissolution, or at least a strong hint of such an alternative'.[120]

---

[119] Dufferin to Mackenzie, 19 Nov. and to Carnarvon, 14 Dec. 1876, Mackenzie to Dufferin, 25 Nov. and 15 Dec. (*Dufferin-Carnarvon Correspondence* pp. 315-20, 323-8); Dufferin to B.C.'s Premier A.C. Elliott (private), 6 Jan. 1877 (Thomson, *Mackenzie* p. 292)

[120] Dufferin to Carnarvon, 23 Nov. 1876. Carnarvon signified general agreement, noting reports 'of a gradual recovery of strength by Macdonald and his party. I am satisfied that if we can adjourn the conflict – say for another ... eighteen months – we shall be, as you say, in a far better position to fight it' (to Dufferin, 13 Dec. 1876). Dufferin had on 8 October expressed fears that 'eventually you will have to put very strong pressure on Mackenzie to get him to do what is just and right', and had expressed his readiness at 'the proper time' and 'with your

'The great matter now', Dufferin had written, was to induce B.C. 'to wait patiently another year', and in March 1877 he praised its current Premier, A.C. Elliott, for allaying 'local impatience'. Things remained quiet even when Mackenzie announced that the railway would follow the Fraser River, not the northern route that had seemed likely in 1876. But in May 1878 the definitive elimination of Esquimalt as the Pacific Railway's terminus destroyed Elliott's popularity in his own riding of Victoria.[121] This enabled Walkem to campaign in the upcoming election under the slogans of 'Fight Ottawa' and of 'Secession'. He replaced Elliott as Premier, and in August persuaded the new legislature to call (by 14 votes to 9) for secession unless railway construction had started by May 1879.[122] But before this threat reached Ottawa, Mackenzie had lost office and Sir John Macdonald was again Prime Minister. He was far more acceptable in B.C. – indeed Victoria now provided him with a parliamentary seat since he had lost his long-standing one in Kingston. And Macdonald initially bought time by reinstating Esquimalt as the railway's terminus, albeit only to revert to Port Moody in October 1879.

By then the government had placed an initial contract for the building, by mid-1885, of a line from Yale up through the Fraser and Thomson canyons, and actual construction started in May 1880. But if this represented progress, it was still only limited.

approval – though without engaging your responsibility – to resort to the extreme tether of my constitutional responsibility for ... the maintenance of the integrity of the Dominion' (*Dufferin-Carnarvon Correspondence* pp. 278, 313, 322-3)

[121] Dufferin to Carnarvon, 18 Dec. 1876 (*Dufferin-Carnarvon Correspondence* p. 329); 'Elliott, Andrew Charles', *Dictionary of Canadian Biography*

[122] A British Columbia MLA, J.A. Mara, and his associates in Washington Territory allegedly contacted the House Foreign Affairs Committee with a scheme to divert the Ottawa government's attention by stirring Sitting Bull into a cross-border raid on the US, while B.C. moved via secession from Canada to 'separation from England, and its ultimate annexation to the United States.' When taxed with this, Mara roundly denied he had ever 'wrote a line nor spoke word in that direction' – Thornton (from Washington) to Lord Lorne, 15 March, and Mara to Dewdney, 3 April, 1879 (LAC, Macdonald Papers MG 26A Vol. 80, MIKAN nos. 489089 and 466992)

After Allan's withdrawal, no capitalists had been prepared to build the whole railway; and Macdonald, like Mackenzie before him, had initially been resigned to the state commissioning the work itself, piecemeal. Policy, Sir Charles Tupper wrote in April 1880, 'is to construct a cheap railway ... incurring no expenditure beyond that absolutely necessary to effect the rapid colonization of the country.' But in June Tupper persuaded the cabinet to authorise negotiation 'with capitalists of undoubted means' who might, for a cash subsidy and land grant, undertake 'the construction and operation of the [whole] line'.[123] He had in mind the group that, backed by the Bank of Montreal, had recently bought up the bankrupt St. Paul and Pacific line and built north to join the railway Mackenzie had built south from Winnipeg. The first through train ran in December 1878. Revenue boomed, and agriculture minister John Henry Pope drew attention to the group, supposedly advising 'Catch them before they invest their profits.' Economic conditions, depressed throughout Mackenzie's administration, were beginning to recover, and after further negotiations Tupper signed a contract with a 'syndicate' drawn from the backers of what was now called the St. Paul, Minneapolis and Manitoba.[124] The line was to extend 'from the terminus of the Canada Central Railway near Lake Nipissing ... to Port Moody', and was to be completed within ten years. In return the syndicate would receive $25m., 25 million acres of land, and some tax advantages. Also, to prevent the building of rival lines draining off potential traffic, and more especially lines linking with American ones across the border, the Canadian Pacific Railway [C.P.R.] was

---

[123] Lamb, *Canadian Pacific Railway* p. 66

[124] George Stephen (of the Bank of Montreal), James J. Hill (manager of the St. Paul and Manitoba), R.B. Angus, and Donald Smith (of the HBC), all participants in the rescue of the St. Paul and Pacific, each took up a fifth of the Canadian Pacific's initial stock issue, as did Duncan McIntyre, whose Canada Central Railway would feed into the projected line. Shares also went to New York and Paris bankers – Lamb, *Canadian Pacific Railway* chap. 4

(to Manitoba's disgust) accorded a temporary monopoly in its area.[125]

Parliament was convened in December 1880 to approve the deal. The Conservative caucus was at first 'shocked ... at the enormous concessions made by the Government'. But Tupper eventually persuaded it that 'the terms were reasonable' and that building the railway 'would give the party such éclat throughout Canada as would render it invincible at the next election.'[126] The Liberals were another matter. Since Blake had replaced Mackenzie as Leader of the Opposition, they had become even more hostile to undue railway expenditure for the sake of British Columbia – indeed Blake had, in April, moved a resolution that would have halted the construction there of the Pacific Railway.[127] Now the party bitterly opposed the contract. The parliamentary debate was lengthy and often very dull – Mackenzie went to sleep during Blake's five-hour speech, with a newspaper over his face. Over the

---

[125] Stoppage of the proposed South West Railway of Manitoba led the financier E.A.C. Pew in 1884 to devise a heroic remedy – raising $150,000 in cash to influence Winnipeg newspapers and, with a down-payment of $20,000, bring the Premier 'Honest John' Norquay to come out for North Western independence (followed by annexation to the US, when those involved in the plot would be *lavishly* compensated in bonds issued by the state of Manitoba). The idea was floated around Washington through S.J. Ritchie and G.W. McMullen (President and Vice-President of the Central Ontario Railroad) and their Ohio contacts, with Pew explaining that if the money was raised by November 'no interference from the Dominion or England [would] be possible until the opening of navigation'. But were this 'golden time' allowed to pass, 'the country will be lost to the United States for ever', presumably through the completion of the Canadian Pacific. On learning of the scheme, Macdonald investigated, but (rightly) did not take it very seriously –Carman Cumming, 'The Plot to Buy the Canadian Northwest', *Canada's History*, posted 17 Sept. 2014; Erastus Wiman to Macdonald, 6 Sept. 1884, and Macdonald's 11 Sept. reply (Pope, *Correspondence of Sir John Macdonald* pp. 322-4)

[126] The Liberal George W. Ross was given this account by a caucus member – *Getting into Parliament and After* (Toronto, 1913) p. 116; ed. W.A. Harkin, *Political Reminiscences of ... Sir Charles Tupper, Bart.* (London, 1914) p. 105; Pierre Berton, *The National Dream; the great railway, 1871-1881* (Toronto, 1970) pp. 364, 369

[127] Canada, Commons Debates, 4th Parliament, 2nd Session, Vol. 2 p. 1626 (cf. also Blake's comments, pp. 1467-8)

Christmas break many Liberal MP's held protest meetings, though the public response was not encouraging.[128] And in January they came up with a last-minute offer from a new Ontario syndicate, apparently offering better terms, but reserving the right to postpone the difficult sections of the line – those through the Canadian Shield north of Lake Superior, and through the B.C. mountains. Liberals saw the government proposals as financially disastrous: Blake thought their approval would 'be not merely injurious, but almost fatal to the future of my country'. But Macdonald said Blake's policy of stopping all work in British Columbia would drive that province out of the union, while his refusal to build the stretch of line north of Lake Superior would 'run off the trade into the United States' and destroy the policy of connecting the Dominion 'from sea to sea by one vast iron chain, which cannot and will never be broken'. Macdonald concluded, speaking with difficulty (and presumably the more impressively) because he was ill, by contrasting 'a Canadian road' connecting 'Halifax with the Pacific Ocean' and keeping 'the trade ... on our own side' with the Liberal line 'running from the United States and to the United States', by which the trade from both the east and the west would 'run into the States'; he wanted 'an arrangement which will give us ... a great, an united, ... a developing Canada, instead of making us tributary to American laws, to American railways, ... to American tolls, to all the ... tricks that American railways are addicted to for the purpose of destroying our road.'[129] Whether or not people found this convincing, Macdonald's majority was large, the question was one of confidence, and the act approving the railway contract was approved in February 1881.

The syndicate believed in getting on with the job. There were, Stephen had told Macdonald, two approaches: that of Allan and Jay Cooke involving a massive initial sale of bonds that then had to be serviced even though little income would come in until the

---

[128] Peter B. Waite, *Canada 1874-1896. Arduous Destiny* (Toronto, 1971) pp. 111-12; Ross, *Getting into Parliament* pp. 117-18
[129] Commons Debates, 4th Parliament, 3rd Session, Vol. 1 pp. 490, 493-4 (Macdonald), 496 (Blake)

line was completed; and that followed by the St. Paul and Manitoba of using the entrepreneurs' own capital, borrowing as little as possible, building quickly, and looking for a profit once construction had been completed.[130] In May 1881 the railway's 'Executive Committee' took the bold decision to abandon the easy Yellowhead Pass route over the Rockies in favour of the more southerly Kicking Horse Pass. Once over this, a long circuit around the Selkirks would be needed if they were unlucky. But they gambled on there being a practicable pass through these, and the American explorer Major Rogers duly found one.[131] This produced a considerably shorter route, and one in some ways easier to build. But it meant jettisoning many of the surveys conducted in the 1870s. Indeed 'the C.P.R. chose a new location for almost all the 1,900 miles ... that it constructed itself', which suggests that Mackenzie's long wait for the surveys' completion that had so angered B.C. may have been over-cautious.[132]

The next major decision was on the stretch of line to the north of Lake Superior. This was an integral part of Macdonald's vision, partly perhaps because of the difficulties he had encountered in 1870 in getting troops to Riel's Red River. But it was widely seen as impractical. In 1880 the President of the Grand Trunk had thought of taking on the C.P.R. contract, but only if the 'line around the north shore' was dropped; for otherwise his directors would just bin the idea.[133] Initially the C.P.R. syndicate was little more enthusiastic: Hill had described that stretch of the line as one 'that, when completed, would be of no use to anybody and ... a source of heavy loss to whoever operated it'. But were it not built, Stephen later observed, the C.P.R. would have 'terminated at Port

---

[130] Stephen to Macdonald, 9 July 1880 (Lamb, *Canadian Pacific Railway* pp. 67-8)

[131] Rogers' reward was the naming of the pass after him, plus a $5000 cheque (which he framed)

[132] Lamb, *Canadian Pacific Railway* pp. 52, 79-81, 91. The other major change of route was further east, between Callander and Thunder Bay

[133] Harkin, *Reminiscences of ... Sir Charles Tupper* p. 103. Tupper simply told him, 'We must have a through line'

Arthur in the summer', and in the other six months of the year have been 'simply an extension of the American line running up from St. Paul to the international boundary ... – in short not a Canadian Pacific Railway at all'. Stephen was here writing as a convert. He had, he told Macdonald in August 1881, at first shared Hill's 'misgivings', but had changed his mind. For without an all-Canadian line, the C.P.R. 'never could have become the property it is certain to be having its own rails running from sea to sea.' Macdonald would, he felt, 'be glad to hear this from me'. For, 'but for your tenacity on that point', Stephen did not think the line 'would *ever* have been built'.[134] The 'American line running up from St. Paul' was, of course, Hill's own; and Hill, like Jay Cooke before him, meant also to extend eastwards to Sault Ste. Marie and there pick up the Canadian traffic that a C.P.R. line north of Lake Superior would take directly to Winnipeg. The question seemed moot for much of 1881 and 1882, since little was done in the area beyond resurveying. But by 1883 it was clear that building north of Lake Superior would go ahead. So Hill reduced his C.P.R. holdings and left the syndicate: 'I saw that conflict was coming, and I said, "We will part friends."'[135]

Despite all this C.P.R. activity, British Columbia, and more especially Vancouver Island, continued to give political trouble. The Island was not pleased when railway work began at Yale even though De Cosmos had reported from Ottawa that it would start first on the Island. There were, too, other frictions, over the financing of the Esquimalt graving dock, over the location of the mainland lands B.C. was to contribute to support railway building and the work's need for large numbers of the Chinese labourers the province was trying to exclude, and over payment of the considerable Dominion subsidies to the province. Premier Walkem came to Ottawa in mid-1880 and again in December, to complain,

---

[134] James J. Hill to R.B. Angus, July 1880; Stephen to Macdonald, 27 Aug. 1881, and 10 Feb. 1884 (Lamb, *Canadian Pacific Railway* pp. 81-2, 113)
[135] Lamb, *Canadian Pacific Railway* pp. 106-7. They did, broadly, remain friends; but in later years, Hill, who had by then built out to Puget Sound, used that base to compete strongly with the C.P.R. for southern B.C.'s mining business

threaten, and lobby for the building of the C.P.R.'s 'Island section'. Macdonald was irritated, regretting in November that he had no artillery to turn on the 'bumptious Islanders'. Walkem's response was another petition to the Queen, demanding complete fulfilment of the Carnarvon Terms, and complaining that railway construction had started not on the seaboard but in what he termed the 'interior' of the province (the head of convenient navigation on the Fraser). New Westminster also resented being thus bypassed in favour of Yale, and the legislature approved the petition by 20 to 4, sending De Cosmos and Walkem to London to present it. The size of the vote seems to have rattled the Governor-General, Lord Lorne. He saw the C.P.R. as soon to provide a second British route to the Far East, a useful alternative to the less than secure Suez Canal; and he worried about the possible loss of the province, with its naval base and future dry dock, to the United States should B.C. break loose from Confederation. So, in the summer of 1881, he pressed its case on the Colonial Secretary Lord Kimberley, telling him that Macdonald could now afford further concessions. Kimberley shared some of Lorne's fears, and determined that B.C. should have the 'Carnarvon Terms' payout of $750,000, extension of the mainland railway to Port Moody (which was surely never in doubt), and a light railway to Nanaimo.[136] A *light* railway was not what Vancouver Island wanted, and it again lobbied Macdonald. He did indeed try to interest Stephen in building a proper line instead. But though Stephen had the route inspected, there was too much on his plate already, and in February 1882 he told Macdonald nothing could

---

[136] Ormsby, *British Columbia* pp. 279-83; W. Stewart MacNutt, *Impressions of a Governor-General. Days of Lorne* (Fredericton, N.B., 1955) pp. 106-8, 110). Canadian historians stress that Kimberley, as well as Lorne, saw the dispute as 'endangering the life-line of empire'. But this concern was not great enough to generate either British cabinet discussion or the circulation of a printed paper to cabinet members – for Gladstone's notes on cabinet meetings, see H.C.G. Matthew's volumes of *The Gladstone Diaries with Cabinet Minutes and Prime Ministerial Correspondence* (Oxford), for printed papers circulated, *List of Cabinet Papers 1880-1914* (London, H.M.S.O., 1964)

be done.[137] Later that year Walkem, damaged by the discovery that his estimate for the Esquimalt graving dock had made no provision for cement, left politics for the Supreme Court. But he was succeeded by his former lieutenant Robert Beaven.

Lord Lorne now decided to take a hand by visiting British Columbia, like Dufferin before him. He was accompanied by his wife, Queen Victoria's daughter Princess Louise, and the pair received a correspondingly warm welcome. The Princess enjoyed Victoria, and they stayed far longer than expected. One boy complained that Princess Louise was only a woman when he had expected a steamboat, but the general response to her unaffected strolling, shopping, and picnicking was very favourable. Meanwhile her husband joined Macdonald's agent, former Lt.-Governor Trutch, in discussions of possible political compromise, and also toured the province. While on tour he received a C.P.R. telegram to say that a route had been discovered through the Selkirks, and that the whole line would now be finished by 1887. Lorne hoped this would solve all difficulties, only to be told by Premier Beaven that there could be no permanent peace till Ottawa promised to build the Nanaimo railway as part of the C.P.R. main line. And when Lorne read the telegram out at a final dinner, Beaven countered by proposing that Vancouver Island be erected into a separate realm headed by Princess Louise.[138] Overall, though, Lorne's entourage saw the B.C. visit as a success – 'well worth the money', his secretary told Macdonald, 'for you won't have any trouble either there or from the home govt. for the next three years', Lorne having persuaded Victoria of Ottawa's sincerity and 'dampened down separatism'.[139]

In November 1882 Lorne told Macdonald that the entrepreneur James Dunsmuir was now ready to build the Nanaimo railway on better terms than before, and that the provincial government was

---

[137] Harkin, *Reminiscences of ... Sir Charles Tupper* p. 110; Ormsby, *British Columbia* p. 283

[138] MacNutt, *Days of Lorne* pp. 113-18; Robert M. Stamp, *Royal Rebels. Princess Louise and the Marquis of Lorne* (Toronto, 1988) pp. 195-7; Ormsby, *British Columbia* pp. 285-6

[139] Stamp, *Royal Rebels* p. 198

likely to accept an offer from Ottawa; and he forecast to Kimberley that a deal would be struck before the next session of the Canadian parliament.[140] Things should have been further eased when a 'peace party' government came into office in Victoria in January 1883. But it rubbed Macdonald up the wrong way by repeating the claim that the Nanaimo railway had been included in the original 'Terms of Union'. Moreover Macdonald had his own demands: given the C.P.R.'s path through the mountains, the 'railway lands' the province had provided along its route were almost valueless, and he wanted to exchange them for 3.5 million acres on Peace River. So, to Lorne's dismay, Macdonald played things long, forcing B.C.'s legislature ignominiously to amend the act it had passed earlier in the year. Eventually, though, everything was agreed: B.C. resumed the poor land in the south and instead granted the Peace River block; it received $750,000 to build the Nanaimo railway itself (and soon struck a deal with Dunsmuir); and Ottawa took over work on the Esquimalt graving dock (now clearly beyond the province's means), paying B.C. rather over $250,000. So Lorne could tell his successor that all grievances had been removed – though it was 1884 before the necessary legislation had been passed.[141]

* * * *

Things were different on the Plains. Arguably, discontent was endemic in that part of North America (on both sides of the border), flaring up periodically when conditions were bad, as they undoubtedly were along the North Saskatchewan. The C.P.R.'s decision to switch to a more southerly route had removed construction expenditure and cut both land values and future expectations. Nor were things helped by damaging frost in September 1883, a wet harvest in 1884, and generally falling grain prices. In the springs of 1883 and 1884 the poet and journalist

---

[140] MacNutt, *Days of Lorne* p. 117
[141] Ormsby, *British Columbia* p. 290; 'Smithe, William', *Dictionary of Canadian Biography*; MacNutt, *Days of Lorne* pp. 119-22

Charles Mair, who had been one of Riel's prisoners in 1870, trekked to Ottawa to tell the Interior Minister that 'there would be trouble' and urge concessions. Apparently getting nowhere, he moved his family back to Ontario in September 1884.[142] Ottawa seemed remote, and its appointees from the east were derided as 'carpet-baggers'. All this generated both rhetoric (the Edmonton *Bulletin* observing that 'without rebellion the people of the North-West need expect nothing'), and tangible organisation in the form of meetings in 1883-4 to form a Settlers' Union.

Among the Métis there were also special factors. The poorer ones were, like Indians, having to adjust to the disappearance of the buffaloes; and another staple source of income, cartage, had been much reduced by the spread of railways and steamers. Moreover all Métis, whether long resident in the North-West or more recently arrived from Manitoba, tended to consider themselves the original owners of the land, entitled to be bought out (as in Manitoba). There had been petitions to this effect since 1873, and in 1879 Macdonald had notionally gone some way towards meeting them by taking power to 'satisfy any claims ... in connection with the extinguishment of the Indian title, preferred by half-breeds resident in 1870 in the North West Territories' but outside Manitoba, 'by granting [them] land ... on such terms ... as may be considered expedient'.[143] 'Old Tomorrow' was, though, in no hurry to implement this: schemes for doing so were proposed in 1878-9, but they involved making the land non-transferable (to stop the recipients selling it on to speculators) and it was thought the Métis would not accept this; the claimants could, in any case, obtain Homestead land, and most applicants – nine-tenths, Macdonald told Parliament in 1885 – had already had scrip in Manitoba. The issue therefore continued to fester. It was, too, entangled with that of 'river lots'. For whereas Canadian surveyors were busily laying out land (58 million acres between 1879 and 1884) in rectangles, Métis settlers liked to take a narrow river

---

[142] Waite, *Canada. Arduous Destiny* p. 146
[143] Dominion Lands Act, 1879, clause 125e

frontage but extend it way back inland. Surveys of Edmonton accommodated this, and in 1883 the St. Albert Métis secured a promise that this would also be done for them. But the most purely Métis parish, St. Laurent, was more complicated. For it had already been surveyed, and the 1882 immigrants had then disregarded the existing survey lines. They felt, nevertheless, that the 1883 St. Albert promise applied to them too, while the Department of the Interior was reluctant to resurvey, and instead suggested complicated alternatives.[144]

Meanwhile the Settlers' Union had sought to join forces with Métis discontent in St. Laurent (cynics said with a view to buying scrip from them once they had obtained it); the upshot was a May 1884 meeting at which 'We, the French and English natives, being convinced that the government of Canada has taken possession of the North-West Territories without the consent of the natives', enunciated grievances, observed that Riel had 'made a bargain with the government of Canada in 1870', and sought his help in putting their complaints 'in a proper ... form before the government of Canada'.[145] A joint delegation, the Prince Albert half-breed James Isbister (of the Settlers' Union), Gabriel Dumont (the leader of the largest St. Laurent clan), and two other Métis, went to meet Riel in Montana.

* * * *

To the end of his life, Riel sometimes appeared normal and rational. But he had changed since leaving Manitoba in 1875. That December, a spiritual revelation, and an encouraging but anodyne letter from Archbishop Bourget of Montreal, had convinced him he had a personal mission as 'Prophet of the New World'. From then on, though he sometimes returned to Catholic

---

[144] Waite, *Canada 1874-1896. Arduous Destiny* pp. 146-52; Flanagan, *Riel and Rebellion* esp. chap. 2
[145] Flanagan, *Riel and Rebellion* pp. 11-12; John Hines, *The Red Indians of the Plains: Thirty Years of Missionary Experience in the Saskatchewan* (Toronto, 1916 edn.) p. 197

orthodoxy, Riel developed successive millenarian projections revolving around the belief that the Métis were a chosen people, and that God had either already taken the Papacy from Rome, conferring it upon Bourget (at his death on Bishop Taché), or that He would soon divide it in two, leaving Bourget as Pope of the New World.[146]

Riel had also lost confidence in Canada, and he revolved a variety of plans for re-installing himself in charge of Manitoba and the North West Territories and only returning them when his work was thoroughly done. In 1875 he first tried to interest President Grant's ally Senator Morton, then submitted a more fully worked out scheme directly to Grant. In 1878 he apparently approached the Fenians with a view to establishing, through 'the proposed war', 'a great northwestern republic'; and in 1879 he gave his fiancée to understand that he had gone back West 'not only to recover ... health but ... to create an Indian movement'. To this end he canvassed several Indian tribes then on the Montana-North-West Territories border, with a view to an attack on the NWMP in June 1880, the establishment of a provisional government, and the conclusion of a treaty with Ottawa. A few Chiefs nibbled, but most either remained aloof or informed the authorities.[147] Later, indeed, Riel married, took US citizenship, and settled down in Montana. But just as he periodically reverted to his eschatological ideas, so dreams of repeating his 1870 work and this time securing a real Métis state/province were never very far below the surface.

Riel accepted the Dumont delegation's invitation to come and help their 'political movement', but he made it clear that he did so also to pursue his own claims on the Canadian government. For several months his behaviour was ambiguous. He surprised people by his moderation and apparent caution; indeed in September 1884, Isbister suggested that both were being overdone and that

---

[146] Thomas Flanagan, *Louis 'David' Riel:'Prophet of the New World'* (Toronto, 1979) esp. chaps. 4, 8 and pp. 46, 49-50
[147] Flanagan, *Louis 'David' Riel* pp. 47-8, 104 (quoting Evelina Barnabé to Riel, March 1879), 105-9; Memoir to Ulysses S. Grant, Dec. 1875 (ed. Stanley, *Collected Writings of Louis Riel* ii (Edmonton, 1985) pp. 6-15, 18-19)

work on the petition to Ottawa was moving too slowly.[148] However some of the demands Riel put to Bishop Grandin during his visit to St. Laurent that month were distinctly ambitious: 240 acres each for the 'half-breeds of the North-west Territories', as in Manitoba; two million acres to be sold, with the proceeds invested to supply 'the destitute half-breeds' with ploughs and seeds, and to support schools and hospitals for them; a hundred townships 'in swampy lands' to be reserved for distribution to future half-breed generations over the next 120 years; and all this only as a down-payment until Canada could pay annual interest on 'the capital representing the value of our country, and ... public opinion consents to recognize our rights to land to their full extent'.[149] There seems to have been some resistance to the inclusion of these special land claims in the petition, but that for 240 acres, though not its more visionary companions, featured in the list of 'grievances' sent to Ottawa in mid-December.[150]

Riel's other purpose in returning from Montana was to pursue his own claims on the Canadian government; and the petition completed, it was natural that he should turn to these. He may too have feared (not unreasonably) that nothing would come of the petition and that there might then be an outbreak. On 12 December he approached Father André, saying that he could no longer control the Métis and that the Indians would support them if they rebelled. He wanted to leave, and asked André to get him some money. On the 23rd André and D.H. Macdowall (the district's representative on the North-West Territorial Council)

---

[148] Stanley, *Riel* p. 286
[149] Riel to Bishop Grandin, 7 Sept. 1884 (Confidential Print, CO 880/9/18, 'Correspondence respecting the Rising in the North-West Territory' pp. 15-16)
[150] Stanley, *Riel* p. 290; 'To his Excellency the Governor-General...', ibid. pp. 13-15. Flanagan contends that this petition was deliberately restrained but meant by Riel and W.H. Jackson to be the prelude to a Congress that would submit a far more radical 'Bill of Rights'. The two fell out in February 1885, with Jackson rejecting Riel's claim that the Métis still had title to the North West Territories and so were entitled to a seventh of its value. Riel then decided the Métis would have to go it alone, as in 1869 (Flanagan, *Riel and Rebellion* pp. 104-9)

had a long talk with Riel. He offered to leave, 'never to return'. But he expected 'some compensation, not as a bribe but as an indemnity for all the losses he had suffered' since 1870. 'His claims', Macdowall wrote, 'amount to the modest sum of $100,000, but he will take [as a down payment] $35,000 as originally offered [in 1873 – above, p. 848], and I myself believe that $3,000 to $5,000 would cart the whole Riel family across the boundary.' And though Riel had earlier repeated his fears of being unable to control the Métis, when the talk switched to his financial claims he declared, 'Mr. Macdowall, if I am satisfied the half-breeds will be satisfied.' That meant, André later wrote, that Riel would 'put all the influence he enjoys on the side of the government if he gets the help he requires'.[151] To Charles Nolin, though, Riel apparently said that if he got the money he would go to the US, start a paper, and with it 'raise the other nationalities in the States ... before the grass is high you will see foreign armies ... I will commence by destroying Manitoba, and then I shall destroy the North-West and take possession' of it.[152]

Riel probably fluctuated between the practical aspirations described to André and Macdowall and the millenarian ones recounted by Nolin. Father André had concluded as early as September 1884 that Riel was a disruptive figure; and in December-January he and others wrote urging that Riel be paid off and got rid of: 'The man is able to do a great deal of harm "s'il est poussé à la dernière extremité" ..., so I strongly advise not to look to some paltry thousand dollars when the peace of the country is at

---

[151] André to Father Coffee, 29 June 1885, and to Dewdney, December 1884; D.H. Macdowall to Dewdney, 24 Dec. 1884 (Flanagan, *Riel and Rebellion* pp. 122-5)

[152] Nolin's possibly self-exculpatory evidence at Riel's trial. Asked in prison about his bid for money, Riel initially said he had children to educate, but on being prompted about the newspaper, he switched to millenarian mode: 'Oh yes. This is my divine mission. I must establish a paper..., and with it I must raise an army of twenty or thirty thousand men to carry out my vocation as a Prophet and to reconquer the northwest which I have been chosen to govern' (Flanagan, *Riel and Rebellion* p. 126)

stake'.[153] Dewdney sent the letters on to Ottawa, but Macdonald had never liked Riel and was not forthcoming: 'We have no money to give Riel and would be obliged to ask for a Parliamentary vote. How would it look to be obliged to confess we could not govern the country and were obliged to bribe a man to go away?'[154] But in January 1885, whether in response to the uneasy conditions in the North West or more specifically to the December 1884 petition, the government did decide to start the process of making grants under the 1879 Dominion Lands Act by enumerating those Métis eligible to receive them. This decision proved of importance elsewhere, but it had no immediate impact in St. Laurent.

A meeting was held in Batoche on 24 February 1885 to consider the government's reply to the December petition. Riel had arranged to be driven to Winnipeg in mid-March, and he told the meeting he had now done his work and must return to Montana. But when his audience broke into shouts of dissent – the work Schmidt believed of a planted claque of supporters – Riel asked whether it would accept the consequences, and secured vocal support.[155] As early as September 1884, Bishop Grandin had noted, the Métis spoke of Riel with extraordinary enthusiasm. 'For them he was a saint; I would say rather a kind of God'[156] The process was fed by Riel's ostentatious piety, his periodic outbursts against the clergy, and, probably, by exposition to his intimates of his unorthodox religious doctrines. By December Father Végreville (a victim of one of Riel's outbursts) had concluded that 'the present movement is none other than that of 1870; to establish an independent nation of which L. Riel will be the royal autocrat, with his own religion of which he will be the supreme pontiff'.[157]

---

[153] Stanley, *Riel* pp. 284, 290; Flanagan, *Riel and Rebellion* pp. 127-9

[154] Macdonald to Dewdney, 20 Feb. 1885 (Flanagan, *Riel and Rebellion* p. 129)

[155] Father Végreville to Taché, 19 and 26 Feb. 1885; Schmidt's 'Notes on the métis movement at St. Laurent' (sent to Taché on 7 March 1885), and Nolin's more suspect testimony at Riel's trial (both cited in Stanley, *Riel* pp. 298-9, 411n.)

[156] Grandin to Taché, 8 Sept. 1884, and Amédée Forget to Dewdney, 18 Sept. (Stanley, *Riel* pp. 289, 299)

[157] Végreville to Taché, 16 Dec. 1884 (Stanley, *Riel* p. 294)

And following the 24 February 1885 Batoche meeting, this element became ever more pronounced.

On 1 March Riel declared that he had only to lift his finger 'and you will see a vast multitude of nations rushing here'. Next day several people, including Gabriel Dumont, undertook 'to save our souls by compelling ourselves ... to live righteously' and 'to save the country from evil government by taking up arms if necessary.'[158] Matters were delayed by a nine days' religious 'novena' to conclude on 19 March, the feast of the Métis' patron, St. Joseph. Some see Riel's declaration of a new order as the planned culmination of this process; others believe it was triggered by an HBC factor's bluster that 'the government were sending up five hundred men to take Riel'. Anyway, on 18 March Riel told a casual encounter that the Métis would 'strike a blow to gain their rights' and that he could bring hordes of half-breeds and Indians from the States in support. He would fill the government with 'God-fearing men' and open the West to good Catholic races (Poles, Bavarians, Italians, Germans, and Irish). The time had come 'to rule this country or perish in the attempt'. Later he told the horror-struck St. Laurent priests, Fourmond and Végreville, that a Provisional Government had been established; the '"old Roman" is set aside. I have a new Pope ... Mgr. Bourget. You will be the first priests of the new religion, and from now on you have to obey me.'[159] Next day at a mass meeting, Riel and Dumont appointed the Provisional Government's Council, the 'Exovedate' ('those picked from the flock'), which later acknowledged Riel

'as a prophet in the service of Jesus Christ ...; a prophet at the feet of Mary Immaculate, under the visible ... safeguard of St. Joseph, the beloved patron of the half-breeds...; as a prophet the humble imitator ... of St. John Baptist, the

---

[158] Stanley, *Riel* p. 302
[159] Dr. John Willoughby's deposition at Riel's trial (Stanley, *Riel* p. 305); Flanagan, *Louis 'David' Riel* pp. 135-6, citing J-V. Fourmond's MS. *Petite Chronique de St. Laurent*; Christensen, *Ahtahkakoop* p. 503

glorious patron of the French Canadians and the French Canadian half-breeds'.

It would be too much to say, with Riel's disgusted French Canadian Secretary that instead of making military preparations, the Exovedate 'stayed inactive, entirely taken up with religious discussions'. But it did pronounce that 'hell will not last for ever', and, to eliminate the relics of paganism, it changed the names of the days of the week. Not everybody was pleased: Isidore Dumont and Gilbert Breland told Riel that 'if we fight it's not for religion but for our rights. You came for our rights but now you only speak of religion.'[160]

Developments at St. Laurent are probably best seen as the forcible takeover by a local religious cult, the work of a charismatic leader backed by major local families. In the area's two other large Métis settlements, things were different. At Qu'Appelle the scrip enumerators were told that 'very little pressure would have been required to induce' the 'younger men' 'to throw in their lot with their rebellious brethren'; but pressure was all the other way, Qu'Appelle being both close to General Middleton's rail base and doing well from carting his military supplies. Likewise, though Prince Albert, the largest and oldest settlement, had been much involved in the 1880s land agitation, it had a substantial Anglophone component, and its local issues had been largely sorted out in 1884. When it came to the point, the town united in panic-stricken defence against 'the French and the Indians'.[161] So while individual Métis over quite a wide area corresponded with Riel's government and served as its agents, only in the Grandin district did they take up arms as a body.

---

[160] Stanley, *Riel* pp. 307, 319, 326-7; Flanagan, *Louis 'David' Riel* pp. 144, 148; MS. 'Mémoire de Philippe Garnot' cited by Jules Le Chevalier, *Batoche. Les Missionnaires du Nord-Ouest pendant les Troubles de 1885* (Montreal, 1941) p. 177
[161] Commissioner W.P.R. Street's account of his 1885 Qu'Appelle visit (ed. H.H. Langton, 'The Commission of 1885 to the North-West Territories', *Can.H.R.* 25:1 (1944) pp. 49-51); Flanagan, *Riel and Rebellion* pp. 43-4; Stanley, *Birth of Western Canada* pp. 323, 330-1; Hines, *Red Indians of the Plains* chap. 9

Initially they had some success. True, appeals to the 'English' half-breeds of St. Albert were politely turned down. But Riel nevertheless told Superintendent Crozier to surrender Forts Carlton and Battleford. Crozier refused, and instead of awaiting reinforcements, tried to repress the insurgency at the outset. On 26 March he was ambushed at Duck Lake, and might have fared worse had Riel not called off the pursuit to save bloodshed. Riel made much of this victory. But he had hoped 'to capture Major Crozier and his force and then say to the Canadian Government, consider the situation'. Instead the NWMP and associated Volunteers evacuated Fort Carlton (accidentally burning it down in the process) and withdrew to Prince Albert. Meanwhile, Riel's forces concentrated around Batoche, but took no further direct action.[162]

Insofar as Riel did not simply rely on celestial aid and imaginary allies from the United States, he looked to touching off Indian insurrections. As the 1884 Thirst Dance on Poundmaker's reserve and the subsequent councils showed, discontent had been dangerously high even before Riel's return to the North-West. Once back there, Riel had met Big Bear and other chiefs – Dewdney's informant Amédée Forget had noted the arrival of three from Qu'Appelle on 7 September. This process continued: in March 1885 an Indian sent Riel a list of chiefs who denied that they had bargained away their country by treaty, and asked for guidance as to 'which way you are going to commence'. Riel had also corresponded over the winter with the Métis schoolteacher at Bresaylor (north of Battleford), and no doubt with others. His Provisional Government now sent out mixed Métis-Indian parties with messages explaining its insurrection and appealing for support. After the victory of Duck Lake this was stepped up, with the circulation of fairly standard letters exhorting their recipients to seize local HBC or Government stores, provisions, and ammunition, and attack the NWMP, but not to kill civilians.[163]

---

[162] Stanley, *Birth of Western Canada* pp. 317-20, 324-32, 357-8
[163] Stanley, *Riel* pp. 282, 289, *Birth of Western Canada* pp. 322-4; texts of, and footnote comments on, many of the letters are to be found in Stanley ed., *Collected Writings of Louis Riel* iii pp. 62-85, a rather jumbled sequence of

Not all were well received: the letter sent to an Indian reserve near Fort Qu'Appelle was handed to the Farm Instructor, and the chief and his leading men called on the visiting Canadian scrip commissioner to parade their loyalty to 'the Great White Mother'; and at Lac la Biche, Alexander Hamilin replied that if any more couriers were sent, 'he, with two hundred men, would receive them with rifles'. By contrast, Charles Trottier brought to Riel's camp (from Prairie Ronde) a dozen Métis plus Chief White Cap and some sixty Sioux.[164]

Often Indians were exhorted only to local raids – 'Do not molest nor ill-treat anybody, but take away the arms' and ammunition 'from the Hudson's Bay stores at Nut Lake and Fishing Lake'; and there were many such raids on isolated stores and on farms and herds of cattle. But there were only two concentrations of Indian 'resistance' – those around the bands of Poundmaker and of Big Bear. After Duck Lake 'the Métis and Indians of Battleford and its neighbourhood' were asked to take and destroy Battleford, securing 'all the goods and provisions', and then send Riel a detachment of forty or fifty men. This letter was brought to Poundmaker's camp on 12 or 13 April, read aloud, and translated into Cree.[165] By then 200 Indians had already appeared at the town 'armed and in war paint'. Negotiations followed, and the Indians offered to go back to the reserve if their demands for supplies were met. The local Indian Agent was authorised to meet these demands and take Poundmaker to parley with Governor Dewdney.

Orders and letters of the Provisional Government's Council in Canada, Sessional Papers 1886, Vol. 19, Paper 43h pp. 12-14, 39-48. Both then and earlier, Gabriel Dumont also sent out envoys, messages, and symbolic tobacco 'on my own' (Stanley, 'Gabriel Dumont's account of the North West Rebellion, 1885', *Can.H.R.* 30:3 (1949) pp. 258-9)

[164] Langton, 'The Commission of 1885' pp. 52-3; W.J. McLean, 'Tragic Events at Frog Lake and Fort Pitt During the North West Rebellion', *Manitoba Pageant* 17:2 and 18: 1-3 (1972 and 1973), Part 2; Stanley, 'Dumont's account of the North West Rebellion' p. 258 (White Cap, like Trottier, was made an Exovede, but later successfully pleaded that he had acted under duress)

[165] Canada, 1886 Sessional Paper 43h p. 12; *Collected Writings of Louis Riel* iii pp. 79-80

But before anything could come of this, some Indians broke into the HBC store and started pillaging. They were then joined by Stonies who had already killed their Farm Instructor and another settler, and who now insisted on erecting the war tent that transferred control from civil chiefs to the warriors. Yet though there was a clear wish to take the stockade at Battleford, no actual assault was made; and on 24 April it was relieved by a column of Canadian troops.[166]

In the Fort Pitt area, an HBC agent thought he witnessed on 28 March some sort of compact between Wandering Spirit, a war chief, and Wood Crees from further south. It appears that next day two men arrived with a letter from Riel calling on the Métis to take up arms, seize ammunition, stir up the Indians, and put the police in an impossible position. Either then or on the 30th news of Duck Lake arrived, which led the small police force at Frog Lake to withdraw to Fort Pitt. On 2 April Indians led by Wandering Spirit sacked the HBC post at Frog Lake, making prisoners of its Agent and two women but shooting nine other Europeans. Big Bear had not been involved, but eleven days later he appeared before Fort Pitt with 250 men. A meeting was arranged with the HBC trader W.J. Mclean (whose past conduct had earned him Indian respect). There the chiefs

'referred to the extermination of the buffalo ... They said the government had made many promises to them that were not productive of any good, and that instead of their conditions improving they were becoming worse every year. Very much excited, Big Bear then said that they had now arrived at the determination to drive the government and the white people [though *not* the HBC] out of the country. In this they would get plenty of help, for they now had twenty ox trains loaded with rifles and ammunition, with

---

[166] Stanley, *Birth of Western Canada* pp. 334-6; Tobias, 'Canada's Subjugation of the Plains Cree' p. 544

ten thousand Americans coming to join them. They also had the half-breeds to fight with them.'

McLean warned them of 'the great forces' the government would bring against them. But this only prompted Wandering Spirit to declare that McLean

'had said too much about the government ... "We are tired of him and all his people, and we are going to drive them out of the country. Why do you want us to believe that the government has plenty of soldiers? Look at the Red Coats ... [NWMP] that you are keeping at the fort, is that plenty? Is that all the government can send? He has been trying to send more for two years to frighten us. We are not afraid of them."'

For good measure, Wandering Spirit added that the Indians had already taken Fort Qu'Appelle, Calgary, and Edmonton.[167]

Following such talks, the police garrison evacuated Fort Pitt by boat, while the civilians who had fled there surrendered to the Indians (who kept them as hostages). The Frog Lake 'massacre' remained untypical and one-off, but Big Bear's band sent out emissaries 'to stir up ... the tribes'.[168] Isolated HBC posts were pillaged, and cattle seized to feed the insurgents. However the band made no further strategic moves. Poundmaker invited it to join him, promising to provide carts and sixty fat oxen; this done, 'they would take Battleford with its large stock of provisions and then go on to join Riel at Batoche'. But the band were discouraged by reports that Poundmaker was retreating under attack. Big Bear's son, who (McLean says) had 'taken his father's place', then proposed joining Riel, but it was decided first to send couriers to

---

[167] Stanley, *Birth of Western Canada* pp. 338-42; *Collected Writings of Louis Riel* iii pp. 68-70; McLean, 'Tragic Events at Frog Lake', Part 1
[168] *Buffalo Days and Nights* chap. 15 tells of how these divided the band with which Erasmus lived; this was with difficulty instead persuaded to flee out of harm's way

check on his fortunes. On reaching Battleford, these reported that the earth there 'was trembling ... with soldiers and horses ... Nothing more was said ... about going to join Riel.'[169] Instead the band retreated north with its captives, pursued by General Strange, and gradually disintegrated. Big Bear finally surrendered on 2 July.

Poundmaker had been pressed by both his Stony allies and Riel to move down to Batoche. Instead he asked Riel on 29 April for both ammunition and news, including 'the date when the Americans will reach the [line of the] Canadian Pacific Railway'. Poundmaker added that he was still waiting for Riel to come to Battleford, since 'we are unable to take the fort without help'. He was, though, attacked at Cut Knife Hill by Colonel Otter's troops. This did impel him to move towards Riel at Batoche. But before he got there, it had fallen to General Middleton. So Poundmaker sought terms, then, when these were refused, surrendered unconditionally.[170]

Thus Riel cannot be said to have derived much help from either Poundmaker or Big Bear. For despite talk of driving 'the government and the white people out of the country', Indian insurgency had not really gone beyond pillage. And it had been limited. Its dimensions cannot be precisely stated, since some bands were divided and others, after an initial outbreak, got cold feet and drew back. But the Assistant Indian Commissioner Hayter Reed put the number of 'disloyal' bands at 28, while G.F.G. Stanley observes that although 'the rebels who took up arms numbered scarcely over 1,999, the number of Indians in Treaties 4, 6 and 7, totalled about 20,000'. The Department of Indian Affairs may have had an interest in playing down the trouble. But its 1885 Report praised the loyalty of eight named chiefs and their bands, 'whose reserves are situated in the [Battleford] districts affected by the late rebellion'. Three more chiefs in the area south of Edmonton were also singled out for praise. 'The other chiefs and bands ... adjacent to Edmonton, although they were considerably excited, committed' only two

---

[169] McLean, 'Tragic Events at Frog Lake', Parts 2 and 3
[170] Stanley, *Birth of Western Canada* pp. 363-8, 372-3

'overt acts', the damage from which they had since agreed to repay 'from their annuities'. In Assiniboia, south of the Saskatchewan district, 'the Indians were constantly besieged with messages from the ... [Métis] insurrectionists, urging' them to revolt, but only about twenty or thirty, 'who plundered the houses of a few settlers', did so. None 'of the Indians in the southern part of ... Alberta took any part in the rebellion'.[171] There had, though, been real fears that the Blackfoot might join in. Attempts had been made to enlist Crowfoot, who had adopted Poundmaker as a son. In 1885, Crowfoot's biographer says, 'his sympathies were with the Crees ... but he believed they could not win.' For some time, he remained non-committal. But the Blackfoot were the Crees' enemies, and one Blackfoot tribe even offered to fight for the government. Crowfoot eventually confirmed to a missionary, sent in haste to soothe him, that the Blackfoot would not rise; and when the Ottawa cabinet heard this, it burst into applause.[172] Had Riel enjoyed real victories, things might of course have been different; and the Governor-General wrote that 'but for the success of the Canadian forces ... I have little doubt that there would have been a general [Indian] rising'.[173] As it was, once Riel's forces disintegrated, Indian resistance collapsed. Poundmaker and Big Bear surrendered, while other and more militant leaders fled. In all, 81 Indians were brought to trial. Some (including White Cap) were acquitted. But eight (including a penitent Wandering Spirit) were demonstratively hung for the 'Frog Lake massacre' and three other killings. Poundmaker and Big Bear were imprisoned, and though soon released, they died shortly thereafter. Big Bear's band was dispersed, and there was no further question of a large

---

[171] Gwyn, *Nation Maker* p. 489; Stanley, *Birth of Western Canada* p. 353; *Report of the Department of Indian Affairs for the Year ended 31st December, 1885* pp. 10-12

[172] Crowfoot, *Dictionary of Canadian Biography*; Crowfoot to Macdonald 11 April 1885 (Pope, *Correspondence of Sir John Macdonald* p. 343)

[173] 13 Nov. 1885 – Confidential Print, CO 880/9/19, 'Canada. Case of Louis Riel. Despatch ... stating the reasons for the non-commutation of Riel's sentence' p. 3

autonomous Cree reserve. Rather, with the more recalcitrant leaders removed, Commissioner Dewdney took the opportunity of establishing a tighter grip on the existing reserves, and used the supply of food 'rations' to pressurise the Indians to switch to agriculture – beginning, as a hostile historian puts it, 'the process of making the Cree an administered people'.[174]

* * * *

Canada owed the speed of its success to the Canadian Pacific Railway, the C.P.R. company its survival to Riel's insurrection. By 1883 it had accumulated an impressive team of American managers, under the overall direction of Cornelius Van Horne. New construction went well. But that meant high expenditure, which George Stephen had to meet through financial engineering and repeated attempts to raise money.[175] By late 1883 a crisis was clearly approaching, leading Macdonald to summon Tupper, the contract's original sponsor, back from his post as High Commissioner in London: 'Pacific in trouble. You should be here.' Tupper recalls that on arrival he 'found everybody in despair'. Stephen wanted a $22.5m. loan, secured against the C.P.R.'s land holdings. Macdonald was minded to refuse, but was dissuaded – by one account roused from his bed and dissuaded – by J.H. Pope, who told him that 'the day the CPR busts, the Conservative party busts the day after'. 'It was', writes P.B. Waite, 'perhaps the only argument that would have influenced Macdonald.' Tupper had government accountants go over the C.P.R.'s books, reassured the Bank of Montreal (which had extended temporary credit), and recommended asking Parliament to authorise a four-year loan. 'Don't call it a loan', Blake said. 'You know you will never see a

---

[174] Tobias, 'Canada's subjection of the Plains Cree' pp. 546-8. In 1885 Indians from the 'disloyal' bands were barred from leaving their Reserves without official permits. This Pass System came to be generalised by extra-legal administrative action, and in places survived into the 1940s
[175] These can be followed in Lamb, *Canadian Pacific Railway* chaps. 8, 9

918

penny of the money again.'[176] Debate was intense, and Maritimers and Quebeckers both demanded pork-barrel before they would support the government. The Quebeckers, indeed, stayed ostentatiously outside the Chamber on the final day, only trooping in to vote when the division bells rang about midnight. But the loan went through in March 1884; in return, Tupper soon proposed subsidies for the 'Short Line' across Maine and for railway building in Quebec.[177]

Unsurprisingly, Macdonald told Stephen in July that he must not look for 'any more legislative assistance'. But in January 1885 Stephen said it 'must go down unless sustained.' Three ministers opposed relief, and Macdonald said he shared the *Week*'s view 'that, however docile our majority, we dare not ask for another loan.'[178] 'Old Tomorrow' took refuge in indecision. C.P.R. directors Stephen and Smith pledged all their possessions to raise funds and just kept things going. But on 18 March their formal application for money brought things to a head. There were pressures on both sides. Tupper, from London, and the powerful Ontario Catholic Senator Frank Smith both argued that to let the company fold would precipitate financial, national, and party disaster. But Finance Minister Sir Leonard Tilley seemed fairly relaxed. The C.P.R.'s failure was widely anticipated, and its rival the Grand Trunk (whose President had crossed the Atlantic to be in Ottawa) stood ready to pick up the pieces.[179] Stephen believed

---

[176] Harkin, *Reminiscences of ... Sir Charles Tupper* pp. 114-15; P.B. Waite, 'Pope, John Henry', *Dictionary of Canadian Biography*; Gwyn, *Nation Maker. Sir John Macdonald* pp. 403-5; Lamb, *Canadian Pacific Railway* pp. 109-11

[177] Waite, *Canada 1874-1896. Arduous Destiny* pp. 132-5. Pope had an interest in the 'Short Line'

[178] Lamb, *Canadian Pacific Railway* p. 128; Macdonald to Tupper (now back in London), 24 Jan. 1885 (Pope, *Correspondence of Sir John Macdonald* p. 332)

[179] Besides building to the west, the C.P.R. had acquired lines around Montreal to generate traffic, which the Grand Trunk saw as 'aggression'. In 1882-3 Sir John Rose got the two concerns to work out a co-existence deal, but the C.P.R. would not ratify it. So the Grand Trunk lobbied against the 1884 loan to the C.P.R., and some of the latter's 1884-5 money market difficulties have been attributed to Grand Trunk opposition – Lamb, *Canadian Pacific Railway* chap. 7; *Correspondence of Sir John Macdonald* pp. 294-5

that the Council meeting on 26 March would reject his application. There is some dispute as to whether it actually did.[180] But whatever the truth, things were drastically altered by news of Riel's rebellion.

This began on 18 March and routed a small NWMP force at Duck Lake on the 26th – a timing so convenient for Macdonald and the C.P.R. that conspiracy theorists have held that he deliberately provoked the rising. One of the strengths of railways was their capacity to move troops; and Stephen had told Macdonald the previous August that should there be Fenian trouble in Manitoba, troops could be sent out 'any time that winter', using sleighs to bridge the gaps in his line.[181] The idea had come up again in 1885, and Van Horne had talked to the Minister of Militia. He had moved soldiers by rail during the American Civil War, and had made some contingency preparations. So he now offered, in the face of much incredulity, to get troops out in eleven days. The first party left on 28 March; they reached Winnipeg seven days later, using sleighs where rails had not been laid but also making two twenty-mile marches on the frozen lake. Meanwhile work on the line continued; in all, over 3000 men were sent out, with horses and equipment; and the final party travelled all the way by rail.[182]

With these forces, General Middleton could not lose.[183] Gabriel Dumont later said he had wanted to harass Middleton's advancing troops by night to stop them sleeping but had been over-ruled by Riel: 'mine was the better plan, but I had confidence

---

[180] Stephen to Macdonald, 26 March 1885 (*Correspondence of Sir John Macdonald* pp. 338-9). Waite, *Arduous Destiny* p. 139 believes the application was rejected, Lamb, *Canadian Pacific Railway* p. 130 that Senator Smith had managed to keep the decision open

[181] Waite, *Arduous Destiny* pp. 137-8

[182] Waite, *Arduous Destiny* pp. 137-8, 140; Lamb, *Canadian Pacific Railway* p. 130; Pierre Berton, *The Great Railway 1881-1885. The Last Spike* (Toronto, 1971) pp. 357-60

[183] Riel supposedly had 475 men at the outset (including 58 Indians) – information collected from Michel Dumas by Father Cloutier (ed. Lawrence Barkwell, 'Dumas, Michel (Le Rat or Watchekon)', *www.metismuseum.ca/resource.php/07259*; 60 Sioux and a dozen Métis later came in with White Cap and Trottier. But Dumont makes it clear that actual combatants, even in the final defence of Batoche, were many fewer

in his faith and prayers, and that God would listen to him.' But the Exovedate minute book casts doubt on this. What Riel was seeking was another 1870-style deal with Canada – he prayed for 'the grace to make as good a treaty [for the Métis and the Indians] as Your charitable and divine protection and the favourable circumstances permit. Make Canada agree [also] to pay me the indemnity which is my due, not a little indemnity, but one just and equitable before you and before men.' And the strategy adopted was that of fighting only when the enemy entered the Métis settlements.[184] It was executed with tactical skill, while Riel prayed – once with two people supporting his raised hands as Aaron and Hur had those of Moses during the defeat of the Amalekites [Exodus 17: 11-13]. But after an initial clash on 24 April, Middleton continued his ponderous advance, and on 9 May opened his attack on Batoche. By then Métis morale was low, largely, Dumont says, because the Catholic priests refused 'all religious aid' to 'soldiers' and their families. There had never been much ammunition – Michel Dumas put the initial stock at twelve powder barrels and about a thousand assorted cartridges – and much had by now been used up. Four days of skirmishing consumed most of the remainder, and when the Canadian militia lost patience and launched a frontal attack, the Métis force was overrun and disintegrated.[185] After some debate Dumont fled to the United States, while on 15 May Riel surrendered to Middleton. Though the other insurgents were treated rather gently, Riel was tried for high treason, and on 16 November executed.[186]

---

[184] Stanley, 'Gabriel Dumont's account' [dictated in 1888] pp. 256-7; Dumont, Gabriel, *Dictionary of Canadian Biography*; Riel's Diaries, 29 April 1885 and undated, *Collected Writings of Louis Riel* iii pp. 403-5

[185] Barkwell, 'Dumas, Michel'; Macleod, 'Dumont, Gabriel'; Stanley, 'Gabriel Dumont's account' esp. pp. 265-7, and *Riel* pp. 331-9. The insurgents were not absolutely out of powder – after taking Batoche, General Middleton reported that 'in spite of what has been said to the contrary ... we found large quantities of powder and shot' (14 May 1885 – 'Correspondence respecting the Rising' p. 21) – but presumably short supply was exacerbated by difficulties of distribution

[186] Though Riel's rebellion had been generally disliked in the east, Ontario and Quebec took predictably different views as to whether he should be executed;

With troops being railed west, there was, as Van Horne wrote, 'no more talk [in Ottawa] about the construction of the Lake Superior line having been a useless expenditure'.[187] But Macdonald still took things down to the wire before he felt it safe to provide the C.P.R. with adequate financial backing – on 16 April Van Horne was reduced to wiring, 'Have no means of paying wages … and unless we get immediate relief we must stop … Do not be surprised … if an immediate and most serious catastrophe happens' when the workforce, marooned in the middle of nowhere, was left unpaid. On 1 May the cabinet did authorise a loan to enable the railway to meet a bond payment.[188] But it kept Parliament busy with a complicated, and in no way urgent, bill on the federal franchise. This was to gain time to square Conservative MP's. For, as Macdonald told Stephen when he complained once too often, 'The majority of our friends in Parlt. and *all* our & your foes were in favour of the Govt. assuming possession of the road [when it went bankrupt], and [only] my personal influence with our supporters and a plain indication of my resignation … got them into line – This was done by personal communication with every one of them'.

---

and McDougall warned that 'Canada cannot afford to have her future content disturbed by any portion of her population believing that Riel died as a martyr.' Riel had strange views, and often little contact with reality (on 16 July he wrote of securing full rehabilitation from the Supreme Court, with 'the hand of God' bringing him out of prison to become Premier of Manitoba and continue his work of 1870 – *Correspondence of Macdonald* pp. 348-50); and though it is unclear whether this met the legal test for insanity, his execution could have been prudentially commuted on these grounds. In one of his most controversial decisions, Macdonald chose not to (Gwyn, *Nation Maker. Sir John Macdonald* chap. 29). The London government was told that Riel 'must have known what kind of events were certain to result' from his actions. Also, were his sentence commuted, so must have been those of the Indian murderers 'whose culpability is beyond question less than that of the men who instigated their crimes'; this would demoralise existing, and deter future, 'white settlers', and lead 'the Indians generally' to believe that the Government 'did not dare to hang' them ('Canada. Case of Louis Riel' pp. 3-4)

[187] Berton, *The Last Spike* p. 385

[188] Van Horne's 16 April 1885 wire to Stephen, passed on to J.H. Pope (*Correspondence of Sir John Macdonald* p. 345); Gwyn, *Nation Maker* pp. 485-6

Also, Macdonald might have added, by further railway promises and subsidies to Quebec and the Maritimes. So it was not until July that the Commons finally voted support for the C.P.R., one hour before its bank credit was due to expire.[189]

That, however, represented a turning point, unblocking the London money market. On 7 September 1885 Donald Smith drove in the 'last spike' at 'Craigellachie'[190] near Revelstoke, B.C., where the line built west from Winnipeg met that constructed up from the Pacific coast. On 4 July 1886 the first through train from Montreal crossed the continent to Port Moody (at some 21 miles per hour). Sir John and Lady Macdonald soon followed in a more leisurely fashion; through the Rockies and the Fraser canyons, Lady Macdonald rode above the engine's cowcatcher to enjoy the views, even persuading her more elderly husband to join her for a time. And in August Sir John drove in the last spike on Dunsmuir's Esquimalt and Nanaimo railway, thus finally putting Ottawa's controversy with B.C. to bed.[191]

The original purpose of the Canadian Pacific had been to tie British Columbia to Canada; and Trutch, who had pressed for the line at the outset, could now write that 'with its accomplishment a new era' had opened up. 'The railway will at once Canadianize the Province.'[192] That sort of thing does not happen 'at once'. But there were many signs of change. Canadian coins now came into common use, whereas previously US currency had circulated at par while Bank of Montreal notes were at a discount.[193] And Victoria lost its economic and demographic dominance to the city of Vancouver that after 1886 sprung up around the C.P.R.'s new

---

[189] Macdonald to Stephen, 26 May 1885 (Waite, *Arduous Destiny* pp. 142-3); Berton, *The Last Spike* pp. 402-3; Lamb, *Canadian Pacific Railway* p. 132
[190] The rallying point of Clan Grant in Scotland. C.P.R. directors invoked the name as a symbol of determination
[191] Ormsby, *British Columbia* p. 304
[192] Trutch to Macdonald, 9 Feb. 1886 (ibid. p. 291)
[193] Walter Sage, 'The Critical Period of British Columbia History, 1866-1871', *Pacific Historical Review* 1:4 (1932) p. 430

terminal (and port) on Burrard Inlet.[194] Many 'British' and 'English' features remained, especially on Vancouver Island. But time altered perspectives: 'While you or I talk of the Old Country as "Home"', wrote Judge Crease, sometime Attorney-General of the Crown Colony of British Columbia, 'all our children call Canada "Home".'[195]

---

[194] Chartered in April 1886, Vancouver burnt down in June. But in 1891 it had a population of 13,709 to Victoria's 16,841, in 1901 26,133 to Victoria's 20,816
[195] Ormsby, *British Columbia* p. 329

CHAPTER 14

Alaska: Russia's sale, 1867; 'Pelagic sealing'; settling the Alaska boundary, 1898-1903; mudflats in Passamaquoddy Bay, 1910

The 1825 treaty defining the border between British and Russian America had given the latter a narrow mainland lisière to serve as a buffer between the Russian American Company [RAC]'s island headquarters at Sitka and the expanding Hudson's Bay Company [HBC]. But in 1839 an agreement between the two companies ended their competition by leasing most of the lisière to the HBC (above, p. 446). Over time the rent changed. But the lease was continued, and the arrangement so clearly benefited both parties that during the Crimean War they agreed (with government blessing) that Sitka should not be involved.[1]

In terms of territorial occupation, the lease did not amount to much. The HBC had envisaged establishing trading posts throughout the leased area, taking over the Russian Fort Dionysius and starting to build two others. But in 1843 Governor Simpson decided to close them and substitute visits, usually only one a year, by steamers like the *Labouchere*, to buy furs from the Tlingits,

---

[1] Nikolay Bolkhovitinov, 'The Crimean War and the Emergence of Proposals for the Sale of Russian America, 1853-1861', *Pacific Historical Review* 59:1 (1990) pp. 19-21; Donald C. Davidson, 'The War Scare of 1854: The Pacific Coast and the Crimean War', *British Columbia Historical Quarterly* 5:1 (1941) esp. pp. 243-4, 246-8, 252; J.S. Galbraith, *The Hudson's Bay Company as an Imperial Factor* (Berkeley, 1957) pp. 165-8

who, in turn, imported them from tribes beyond the Rockies.[2] These cruises seem to have been profitable – in 1843, to the tune of some £4750.[3] This did not stop the HBC trying for a lower rent in 1849, but the lease was fairly readily renewed until 1859. It was then extended until January 1862, though with changes to cover the RAC's growing trade with California. But there followed a return of private trader 'interlopers', partly resulting from the 1858 Fraser Valley gold rush. In July 1861 Governor Berens asked the RAC either to control them or to cut the rent from £1500 to £1000 pa. This must have seemed only a negotiating tactic, especially when the HBC agreed to continue the lease on the existing terms until 1863. But there were real fears that the 'interlopers' would make the trade unprofitable, and in June 1862 the RAC was told the lease would not be further renewed. That autumn, though, London learnt that the *Labouchere's* cruise had been so profitable that it had gone north a second time, eventually making $14,106 on the 1861-2 'Outfit'. The HBC reversed course, and the lease was renewed until 1865.[4]

Meanwhile the RAC's income plummeted,[5] and in January 1865 it offered the HBC all Alaska, islands as well as lisière, up to Mount St. Elias, either through a lease for £3000 a year 'or by the

---

[2] Donald C. Davidson, 'Relations of the Hudson's Bay Company with the Russian American Company on the Northwest Coast', *British Columbia Historical Quarterly* 5:1 (1941) p. 49; Galbraith, *The Hudson's Bay Company as an Imperial Factor* pp. 158-9, 451n.

[3] Galbraith, *Hudson's Bay Company* p. 161; Davidson, 'Relations' p. 49 suggests a rather lower annual profit of $8-10,000

[4] C. Ian Jackson, 'The Stikine Territory lease and its Relevance to the Alaska Purchase', *Pacific Historical Review* 36:3 (1967) pp. 292-4, 297-8, 300; Galbraith, *Hudson's Bay Company* pp. 170-1

[5] In the late 1850s the RAC had prospered by using its American furs to buy tea in China and selling this in Russia. But the price of tea collapsed, with losses to the Company in 1863-4 of 797,000 roubles against a total 1865 income of 706,000 – Aleksandr Iu. Petrov, 'The Activity of the Russian American Company on the Eve of the Sale of Alaska to the United States (1858-67)', *Russian Studies in History* 54:1 (2015) pp. 61-90, which looks far more closely at the Company's finances than have earlier historians

purchase of the Territory' (for which no price was suggested).[6] However the HBC, now under new ownership, was seeking to realise value for its shareholders by selling Rupert's Land. It was not in the business of buying new territory, nor, indeed, had it ever done so. So the purchase suggestion, if indeed it was genuine, was not followed up. For the expanded lease, however, the HBC offered £2000 a year. This was declined. Instead, a one-year renewal of the existing lease was arranged. On the British side this was partly to gain time for advice from Victoria. In May 1865 Chief Factor Tolmie responded at length to Rutkovski's memorandum, doubting whether the expanded lease was worth even £2000 pa. But he observed that to preserve 'international peace ... it would be desirable that our Government' buy from Russia the 'strip of territory south of Mount St. Elias', 'as verbally proposed [sic – 'suggested' might have been a better word] to me' by the Governor of Russian America, when last in Victoria. For 'Should the British Government decline' Rutkovski's 'offer', 'it might be tendered to and accepted by the United States' and perhaps cause 'future complications.'[7] This advice was prescient, but of no effect. The existing lease was again renewed for one year in 1866. Then in January 1867, buoyed by recent good trading, the HBC proposed a further three-year lease. In February the RAC agreed, subject to the Tsar's approval.[8] But by then Tsar Alexander II had decided to sell to the United States.

* * * *

The idea that the United States 'will inevitably spread over all of North America' and that 'sooner or later' Russia's 'American possessions will have to be ceded to them' antedated the Crimean

---

[6] A. Rutkovski's proposal was that the Russians should stay in Sitka and keep control of the California ice trade, but otherwise operate only as the HBC's agents – Jackson, 'The Stikine Territory Lease' pp. 301-2

[7] Chief Factor Tolmie to HBC Secretary Fraser, 3 May 1865 (quoted by Jackson, 'The Stikine Territory' p. 304)

[8] Jackson, 'Stikine Territory' p. 305; Galbraith, *Hudson's Bay Company* p. 173

War – the Governor-General of Eastern Siberia had invoked it in 1853 to argue that Russia should move likewise to secure 'sway over the entire' Asiatic Pacific seaboard.[9] But it was the War that first sparked any tangible moves. News that the RAC's American posts had been neutralised (and were therefore safe) was surprisingly slow to reach either the Russian chargé in Washington, Eduard De Stoeckl, or the vice-consul in San Francisco, Pyotr Kostromitinov; and Secretary of State Marcy apparently told Stoeckl the British would attack as soon as war had been declared. So a backdated document purporting to sell all the RAC's possessions to the San Francisco American-Russian Commercial Company was concocted. This 'sale' was dropped as soon as news of the neutralisation agreement arrived. But it had given the Americans ideas; and both Marcy and California's Senator William Gwin asked Stoeckl whether the Russians were 'seriously disposed' to sell their colonies – for which the United States would pay well. Stoeckl replied that 'we had never had such an intention.'[10]

But after the war the idea of a sale was raised by no less a person than the Tsar's younger brother, Grand Duke Constantine. He needed to make drastic economies in the Navy, and in April 1857 suggested taking 'advantage of the excess of money at the present time in the Treasury of the United States' by selling them colonies that 'bring us very little benefit'. Finance apart, this was only realistic; for 'we must see that the United States, which … wants to have unbroken sway over North America, will take the … colonies from us, and we will not be able to recover them.' Constantine therefore suggested ascertaining the colonies' value. The Tsar felt the idea 'worth considering'. So former RAC Governors were consulted, and Wrangell suggested that 7.4 million roubles could probably be obtained, though twenty million might be the proper figure were it not for *future fears*. The Foreign

---

[9] Bolkhovitinov, 'The Crimean War and the Sale of Russian America' pp. 17-18
[10] Stoeckl to L.G. Senyavin, 24 Aug./5 Sept. 1854 (ibid. p. 27). This contemporary report is probably more reliable than Gwin's 1878 statement that Stoeckl tried to effect a sale, that Gwin secured President Pierce's agreement, but that Marcy insisted that the proposal be turned down (ibid. p. 26)

Minister Prince Gorchakov proposed to ask Stoeckl to sound out the US administration, but Tsar Alexander decided to wait until after the renegotiation of a war-time contract that might reduce the colony's value.[11]

Later that year, though, there were worrying rumours that large numbers of Mormons might move into Alaska, leading the Tsar to observe that it was 'necessary to resolve the question of our American possessions'. Constantine renewed his pressure for an amicable sale 'ahead of time', since 'following the natural order of things' the United States 'must strive to possess all of North America', and 'sooner or later ... they will seize our colonies'. Gorchakov was in less of a hurry, but Stoeckl was told in late 1858 to report any indications of American readiness to buy. In late 1859 his friend, the Western booster Senator Gwin, surfaced the idea of a purchase, saying President Buchanan was interested. Unobtrusive discussions followed. But they did not get far, the question of price being raised only with Gwin, who suggested $5 million (6.5m. roubles). Stoeckl was asked to find out whether Russia was really prepared to sell, in which case Buchanan would take the matter to his cabinet. Stoeckl reported to Gorchakov, adding lengthy arguments for selling. But the Tsar commented that further thought would be necessary. Gorchakov told Stoeckl it would need more money to tempt him – $5m. did not represent Alaska's 'real value'. When this was put to Gwin, he said that while West Coast men might be prepared to pay more, he doubted whether the rest of Congress would. He also thought that in view of the dissatisfaction with the Buchanan administration, the matter would have to wait till the meeting of the next Congress in December 1861. Before then the Civil War had supervened. Stoeckl commented that the only option left was 'to renew the

---

[11] Bolkhovitinov, 'The Crimean War and the Sale of Russian America' pp. 29-35; Oleh W. Gerus, 'The Russian Withdrawal from Alaska: the Decision to Sell', *Revista de Historia de America* 75-6 (1973) p. 165. The renegotiation for which Tsar Alexander had decided to wait was completed in 1859

[Russian American] Company's charter, limiting somewhat its monopoly', and the Tsar recorded his agreement.[12]

Renewal would be debated at length, with the RAC damaged by the resultant delays. But in April 1866 Grand Duke Constantine signed, and the Tsar approved, a revised version of the Charter. Nevertheless there had been further talk of selling, encouraged by the RAC's financial difficulties. Hit by the collapse of its chief source of income, sales of Chinese tea, the Company had, in September 1865, secured a state grant of 200,000 roubles a year towards its costs in administering the colonies (together with forgiveness of debts of 725,000). In past controversies, the Finance Ministry had generally supported the RAC. But in September 1866 the reforming Finance Minister, Count von Reutern, mentioned this grant in a memorandum to the Tsar warning that, even with drastic expenditure cuts, Russia would have over the next three years to find 45m. roubles in 'extraordinary resources' and foreign loans.[13] Reutern now talked to Stoeckl (who was in St. Petersburg *en route* to a new posting) and to Duke Constantine, and both Reutern and Constantine wrote to Gorchakov. Reutern observed that in seventy years the RAC had failed either to 'Russify' the local population 'or to contribute in any way to our merchant navigation', and that it could 'only be sustained by considerable' government assistance. The colonies could not be held in a war with a naval power; and even in peace they might generate clashes with 'American traders and sailors', requiring the maintenance there of 'costly land and naval forces'. Constantine reiterated his long-standing views, adding a reference

---

[12] Stoeckl to Gorchakov, 23 Dec.1859/4 Jan. 1860, translated in Hallie M. McPherson, 'The Projected Purchase of Alaska, 1859-60', *Pacific Historical Review* 3:1 (1934) pp. 80-7; Stoeckl to Gorchakov, 4/16 July 1860 and 9/21 July 1861, Bolkhovitinov, 'The Crimean War and the Sale of Russian America' pp. 44-5, 49

[13] Nikolai Bolkhovitinov, 'How it was decided to sell Alaska', *International Affairs* (Moscow) August 1988 pp. 117, 125n.; Andrei V. Grinev, 'Russia's Emperors and Russian America...', *Russian Studies in History* 54:1 (2015) pp. 26-7, and Petrov, 'The Activity of the Russian American Company on the Eve of the Sale of Alaska', ibid. pp. 74-8

to 'the exceptional benefits close alliance with the North American States would' bring, and to 'the need to eliminate everything that could lead to a disagreement' with them. Both men stressed that 'the future of Russia in the Far East' lay rather in the 'Amur Territory' acquired from China in 1858-60. Gorchakov favoured a sale, but asked that this be first discussed in the Tsar's presence 'in a narrow committee (because of the need for secrecy)'.[14] The 'narrow committee' (Constantine, his subordinate Navy Minister Krabbe, Reutern, and Gorchakov, with Stoeckl in attendance) all sought a sale; and the meeting proceeded on the basis of a summary of Constantine's and Reutern's opinions and of Stoeckl's reports, with the suggestion that the United States be induced to renew the 1859 purchase offer. A brief meeting was scheduled for 16/28 December (the Tsar had another engagement an hour later). Reutern gave further details of the RAC's poor financial condition; all joined in the discussion; and it was decided to sell. The Tsar then asked Stoeckl to return to Washington to try to arrange things. Over the next month he was given a description and map (approved by the Tsar) of the proposed new Russian-US boundaries, and a Finance Ministry instruction that the price should be at least $5m. in cash.[15]

Countries then only very rarely sold their colonial possessions. Denmark and the Netherlands had done so on the Gold Coast, and in 1867 Denmark was prepared to sell its West Indian islands. But Russia was both a far greater and, in other directions, an expansionist Power, so this decision was remarkable. There was no direct compulsion to sell, and many of the arguments advanced for so doing were questionable. The soundest, probably, were the

---

[14] Reutern to Gorchakov, 2/14 Dec. 1866, and N.K. Krabbe to Gorchakov presenting Constantine's views, 7/19 Dec. (Bolkhovitinov, 'How it was decided to sell Alaska' pp. 117-18); Gorchakov to Tsar Alexander, 12/24 Dec. 1866, and Gorchakov's draft memorandum of 15/27 Dec., which may or may not have been sent to the Tsar (ibid. pp. 119, 121, 126n.)

[15] Bolkhovitinov, 'How it was decided to sell Alaska' pp. 119-120, 122-3; Frank A. Golder, 'The Purchase of Alaska', *American Historical Review* 25:3 (1920) pp. 417-18

financial. For though the RAC's position may have been slightly better than Reutern suggested,[16] a sale would bring in some money; and the state will have benefitted more from the railways in which (in accordance with Constantine's wishes) this was invested than it had from its American possessions. As a junior Asiatic Department official, Baron F.B. Osten-Saken, observed, the prevalent discussion featured the colonies' 'negative qualities', with their '*positive* advantages' belonging 'only to the future'.[17] Assessing these takes us into the realm of 'might-have-beens', where we cannot penetrate far – certainly not to the transformative oil developments of the 1970s. The only definite 'advantage' Osten-Saken alluded to, the prospective Collins 'Overland Telegraph' (to Europe through Alaska and Siberia), never materialised, being overtaken by a line under the Atlantic. To this should be added the 100,000 seal skins taken each year from the Pribilof Islands, and the harvest of other furs which the Company had by 1867 managed to increase. But all further 'advantages' were problematic. There was fishing; but Russia was worse placed than the US to develop this, and in any case progress proved slow until the advent of salmon canneries after 1878.[18] There was also gold; this had produced $14.4m. for the US by late 1896, but as a result of individual prospecting and gold rushes that the RAC would not have relished and of the subsequent heavily capitalised mines that

---

[16] The Director of the State Bank thought it could continue without any new government donations, and that its prospective income had been 'very conservatively' stated (Director of State Bank to Reutern, 8/20 Dec. 1866 – Bolkhovitinov, 'How it was decided to sell Alaska' p. 120)

[17] Osten-Saken was so upset by the prospect of a sale that, too late to have any effect, he penned a memorandum contesting the arguments advanced for it (Hunter Miller, 'Russian Opinion on the Sale of Alaska', *American Historical Review* 48:3 (1943) pp. 524-5)

[18] For the seals, see John W. Foster, *Diplomatic Memoirs* ii (Boston, 1909) p. 22. Fishing, at first only undertaken by a few ships, was transformed after 1868 by salmon canneries (produce in 1878 $59,400, in 1889 $2.8m.) on a scale that could not have been effected under Russian rule – Ernest Gruening, *The State of Alaska* (New York, 1954) pp. 74, 88; C.L. Andrews, *The Story of Alaska* (Calwell, Idaho, 1938) p. 150; Alaska Humanities Forum, Alaska's Heritage, 'Fishing and Sea Hunting' (accessed 3 May 2017)

it could not have established. These sectors apart, the United States, too, found Alaska largely unprofitable: in 1890 the 'Permanent White Population' was only 2021, with a further 2277 cannery workers and ships' crews 'Employed in Summer Only'.[19]

Grand Duke Constantine, however, was looking less to economic calculations than to prospective diplomatic gains, notably a 'close alliance with the North American States'. Such an alliance was, in fact, unlikely. For despite much American goodwill towards Russia, the US still had no intention of engaging in 'entangling alliances', or even in Great Power politics outside its own hemisphere; and when it did start to join in the latter, this was in many ways more consonant with British than with Russian interests. The US apart, the only other conceivable buyer of Alaska was Britain; and it was to its long-standing British partner, the HBC, that the RAC looked. But though Tsar Nicholas had had warm feelings towards Britain up to the early 1850s,[20] these were overturned by the Crimean War and the later British sympathy for the 1863 Polish rising. No Russian government figures ever suggested offering to sell Alaska to Britain. Indeed one benefit of selling to the US was that it would give the British 'uncomfortable and dangerous neighbours in the north as they now have in the south of their [American] possessions'. 'This', Gorchakov observed, 'may perhaps be our motivation for selling'. It was something Stoeckl repeatedly invoked. Sale to the United States, he had reported with relish in 1859, 'would displease the

---

[19] Department of the Interior, *Report on the Population of the United States ... 1890, Part 1* (Washington, 1895) Appendix, 'Statistics of Population. Alaska'; Gruening, *The State of Alaska* pp. 73-4; Andrews, *Story of Alaska* p. 175

[20] In 1841 Tsar Nicholas had, in connection with the McLeod affair, called Britain 'his ally' and reproved the US for endangering peace – Nesselrode to Alexander De Bodisco, 18/30 March 1841 (ed. Kenneth Shewmaker, *The Papers of Daniel Webster. Diplomatic Papers Vol. 1 1841-1843* (Hanover, N.H., 1983) pp. 52-3). In 1852 he promised Britain armed support in the event of a French attack on Belgium, and next January he talked with the British ambassador in hopes of updating earlier loose agreements on Near Eastern cooperation (M.S. Anderson, *The Eastern Question 1774-1923* (London, 1966) pp. 111-13, 117-19)

British Government to the last degree.' For 'British Oregon' would then be 'crowded' on both sides 'by the Americans and [would] escape with difficulty from [their] aggressions.'[21] Alaska's sale did indeed unsettle British Columbia in 1867 (above pp. 824, 830-1); and following the Klondike Gold Rush, it landed Britain, Canada, and America with an awkward border problem. But its impact was overcome, partly because the United States was a less predatory power than the Russians imagined.

Russian leaders had always stressed their colonies' vulnerability, talking in the 1850s of the impossibility of preventing their direct seizure by the United States (Britain would have found the operation easier). In 1866-7 their fear was less of direct US action than of the 'American buccaneers who have become bolder in raiding our shores after' the recall of 'our naval squadron'. As the HBC observed, American ships did indeed conduct some 'interloping' trade with the local Indians; and if Russia acted to protect the RAC's trade monopoly, clashes were possible. These, it was said, might damage relations with the US and require the maintenance of 'costly forces ... to protect the rights of the company'.[22] Such fears, if perhaps exaggerated, were not unreasonable. But the 'buccaneers' were also seen as agents of the United States' 'Manifest Destiny' to take over all North America, something Constantine and Stoeckl repeatedly cited (though in which Osten-Saken did not believe).

In American eyes, Stoeckl explained,

'this continent is their patrimony. Their destiny (our manifest destiny as they call it) is to expand continuously, and in this expansion ... adventurers have more than once played the role of pioneers. It is they who, little by little, invaded Texas

---

21 Gorchakov's 15/25 Dec. 1866 memorandum (Bolkhovitinov, 'How it was decided to sell Alaska' p. 121); Stoeckl to Gorchakov, 22 Dec. 1859/4 Jan. 1860 (Hallie McPherson, 'The Projected Purchase of Alaska, 1859-60' p. 86)
22 Reutern to Gorchakov, 2/14 Dec. 1866, Gorchakov's 15/25 Dec. memorandum, and the summary of the opinions of Duke Constantine, Reutern and Stoeckl sent to the Tsar in preparation for the 16/28 Dec. conference (Bolkhovitinov, 'How it was decided to sell Alaska' pp. 118, 121-2)

which later became a State of the Union. New Mexico and other parts of the South were acquired in the same way.

It might have been hoped that the limited resources of our colonies would have shielded them from the rapacity of the filibusters, but not so...'

To any complaints, Stoeckl said, the US government replied that it could do nothing to restrain its citizens; 'it is for you to defend your territory.' And this could only be done by keeping a sizeable fleet on the Coast. Even Britain with its Pacific fleet, he continued, had found its possessions exposed to the filibusters' depredations. A few weeks after news of gold finds on the Fraser,

'four or five thousand Americans were digging on the spot. Unable or afraid to send them back, the English Governor let them stay on the condition that they submit to the laws of the colony. The Americans refused, declaring that they recognised no authority except that of the United States and formed a provisional government. England let them do so. Happily for it, the gold ... was soon worked out and the Americans scattered. Otherwise British Columbia would now be a territory of the United States.'[23]

Stoeckl meant this despatch to provide material for newspaper articles defending his treaty, and might be thought to have exaggerated accordingly. But he wrote in a private letter that it 'was a matter of either selling' the colonies 'or seeing them taken from us'.[24] For the most part his argument is weak: the ninety-plus American whalers in the North Pacific[25] had been coming for a

---

[23] Stoeckl to Gorchakov, 12/24 July 1867 – the French text is in Hunter Miller, 'Russian Opinion on the Sale of Alaska' pp. 529-30 (but with what must be the misprint of 'prisonniers' for 'pionniers')

[24] Stoeckl to Baron Westman, July 1867 (ibid. p. 531)

[25] Howard I. Kushner, '"Seward's Folly"? American Commerce in Russian Alaska', *California Historical Quarterly* 54:1 (1975) pp. 7, 13

long time and were not now going to take up residence in Russian territory and then rebel, like the Texas settlers. Would-be gold miners represented a more likely danger. Stoeckl's account of the Fraser River events was clearly wrong, and since then the smaller 1863 rush (of some 5-800 people) up the Stikine had been handled quite smoothly. Still, there were concerns in London in the 1860s as to *British* ability to cope with the consequences of a gold strike on the Saskatchewan, where there were no armed forces; and St. Petersburg might have had legitimate concerns as to its colonial authorities' ability to manage any major rush without the naval resources that had enabled Governor Douglas to control access to the Fraser in 1858. But that said, it is hard to see the Russian Empire losing Alaska had it resolved to keep it, though who can say what might have happened after 1917 (White Russian control, pre-emptive anti-Bolshevik annexation by either Canada or the US...)?

Anyway, Russia took a pre-emptive decision to sell, and sent Stoeckl back to Washington to secure an offer. Since Seward had already once tried to start up talks, this was unlikely to prove difficult.[26] Stoeckl and Seward soon met, probably on 11 March. On the 15th Seward secured Presidential and cabinet authorisation to buy Russian America for 7 million gold dollars.[27] Seward then offered $5m. to $5.5m., while Stoeckl hoped to get another million. In the event, Seward let himself be pushed up to the authorised $7m., and on 25 March a draft treaty was wired to St. Petersburg for approval. Two very minor changes were requested. Seward refused both, but, Stoeckl wrote, 'by way of compensation' raised the price to $7.2m. 'without consulting the Cabinet'.[28]

---

[26] Kushner, '"Seward's Folly"' pp. 13-15

[27] To put this figure in perspective, the price agreed later that year for Denmark's two Caribbean islands was $7.5m.; the 1872 British payment to the US in settlement of the Alabama claims was $15.5m.; and total federal spending in 1867 was $376.8m.

[28] Stoeckl to Gorchakov, 6/18 March 1867 (ibid. p. 209); David Hunter Miller, *The Alaska Treaty* (Kingston, Ont., 1981) pp. 72-3, 88-95 (drawing on Stoeckl's three despatches to Gorchakov of 7/19 April 1867)

The increase may have been meant to provide a slush fund. Certainly this was how Stoeckl took it: he accompanied his report (to von Reutern) of the $7.2m. price with a private letter, in response to which the Tsar authorised 'the necessary personal expenditures in the matter of the cession of our North American colonies'. Next year Stoeckl complained that 'the treaty affair' had already

> 'swallowed up the greater part of the two hundred thousand dollars that were given to me after the signing to cover secret expenditures, not touching the seven millions. I warned Mr. Reutern about this at the time.'[29]

Such was Seward's haste that the treaty was signed at 4 am. on 30 March. Seward had hoped for ratification before the Senate adjourned later that day, but instead the treaty went in the usual way to the Senate Foreign Relations Committee. Seward's unpopularity rubbed off onto it – the treaty's strongest opponent in that Committee, William Fessenden, said he would change his mind over Alaska if Seward were 'compelled to live there'; and the Chairman, Charles Sumner, thought the treaty could not pass.[30] But most Senators quickly came round. Seward had mounted a skilled public relations operation, obtaining supportive references from experts and planting them in newspapers. After some initial bewilderment, most came out in support, the main arguments for the purchase being (in descending order) the likelihood of economic benefit, the possibility that it would

---

[29] Stoeckl to von Reutern, 7/19 April 1867 (though, sadly, the surviving copy of the personal letter is illegible); von Reutern to Stoeckl, 'absolutely secret', 28 April/10 May 1867, conveying the Tsar's authorisation; Stoeckl to Gorchakov, 30 April/12 May 1868 – N.N. Bolkhovitinov, *Russian-American Relations and the Sale of Alaska, 1834-1867*, ed. and tr. Richard Pierce, (Kingston, Ont., 1996) pp. 304-5. Golder's misreading of Stoeckl's 1868 complaint as referring to expenses for the 'Perkins' not the 'Treaty' affair has occasioned some confusion ('Purchase of Alaska' p. 424n.)

[30] Lee A. Farrow, *Seward's Folly. A New Look at the Alaska Purchase* (Fairbanks, Alaska, 2016) pp. 65-6; Stoeckl to Gorchakov, 7/19 April 1867 (Miller, *The Alaska Treaty* p. 111)

facilitate the acquisition of British Columbia and promote the United States' predestined expansion over all North America, and the desirability of maintaining Russian friendship.[31] Seward supplemented this by more direct lobbying, with dinners for Senators where (as the New York *Herald* put it) 'terrapin and Château Margau[x] will doubtless assist in the elucidation' of the subject. And when the treaty came before the full Senate, another paper reported that 'Seward had his messengers in the lobby all afternoon, carrying letters to and fro, and distributing gorgeous invitations to his fourth Russian dinner' that evening. All this, and Sumner's powerful support for a measure that would help 'squeeze England out of the continent', secured comfortable ratification on 9 April.[32]

Legally, the United States acquired Alaska on the exchange of treaty ratifications in June 1867, and a handover ceremony was staged at Sitka in October, though the Russian flag stuck and proved hard to lower. But payment could not be voted until the House of Representatives re-assembled in December. This was not initially seen as an obstacle – on first hearing of the treaty, Sumner said breezily that the necessary appropriation would pass in twenty-four hours, and that was also the view of Thaddeus Stevens, the Appropriations Committee Chairman.[33] By the autumn things seemed more problematic, partly by reason of the engagement that summer to buy Denmark's Caribbean islands. Alaska generated fewer reservations, but some people felt that expansion would have to be stopped (especially when it transpired that Seward had contemplated rounding off his Danish purchases by buying Iceland and Greenland).[34] By then, too, Washington was well down the

---

[31] Richard E. Welch, 'American Public Opinion and the Purchase of Russian America', *American Slavic and East European Review* 17:4 (1958) esp. pp. 492-3

[32] Walter Stahr, *Seward. Lincoln's Indispensable Man* (New York, 2013 edn.) pp. 486-7, 489-91; Farrow, *Seward's Folly* pp. 64-6

[33] Stoeckl to Gorchakov, 7/19 April 1867 (Bolkhovitinov, *The Sale of Alaska* p. 221)

[34] Stahr, *Seward* p. 516

road that led to President Johnson's impeachment in February 1868. There was also the Perkins case. During the Crimean War, Stoeckl had arranged for an American entrepreneur to supply Russia with munitions, carrying the risk that Britain would seize them as contraband but making a profit of over 100% if successful. The war ended before the munitions could be supplied, but Benjamin Perkins claimed $373,613 for those he had already bought. A New York court was unsympathetic, but American diplomats pressed Russia for payment. By 1867 the cause had been taken up by influential figures: in July the Chairman of the House Foreign Affairs Committee, Nathaniel Banks, and Senator Henry Wilson presented a petition from Perkins' widow, asking that 'a sum sufficient to pay' her husband's claim be held back from the moneys due to Russia. The movement was well organised, with advice from Thad Stevens' nephew Simon and (Seward believed) Banks. Its backers, Stoeckl wrote next March, included Representative Butler (who 'had a thirty thousand dollar interest'), 'Senators, lawyers, newspaper editors' and others. Their target was $800,000, with the backers getting $600,000, the Perkins heirs the remainder. Initially they hoped to get a favourable ruling from the Judiciary Committee on the claim and then deduct the sum awarded from the Alaska payment to Russia. Later they instead tried demanding that the case go to international arbitration, with money – Butler moved for $500,000 – withheld from the payment to cover its award.[35]

Seward kept reassuring Stoeckl that the appropriation would eventually pass with no deduction, a view shared by other professionals (though Banks did say that its opponents 'were at first a majority').[36] But Stoeckl's nerves were not good. Already by

---

[35] Bolkhovitinov, *The Sale of Alaska* pp. 292-4, 309, 351-2; Miller, *The Alaska Treaty* pp. 163, 167-70; Golder, 'Purchase of Alaska' pp. 422-3; Paul S. Holbo, *Tarnished Expansion. The Alaska Scandal, the Press, and Congress, 1867-1871* (Knoxville, Tennessee, 1983) pp. 15-16, 47-8
[36] Seward to Stoeckl, 11 Sept. 1867 and 20 April 1868 (Holbo, *Tarnished Expansion* p. 16); Robert J. Walker to Seward, 9 Feb. 1868, and Nathaniel Banks to Seward, 20 March and 13 May (Miller, *The Alaska Treaty* pp. 163, 171-2)

December 1867 he seemed 'very, very anxious', and by the end of March he thought the situation hopeless and asked Russia for further instructions.[37] These two mind-sets converged in a resort to corruption, to be paid for out of the $200,000 slush fund. Congress had changed little, if at all, since the early 1850s (above pp. **), and Seward was well aware of how it operated. When he sought advice on influencing the Senate during the 1868 Impeachment proceedings, he was supposedly told by the lobbyist Cornelius Wendell, 'Buy your way out'.[38] In the Alaskan context, Wendell's counterpart was Robert J. Walker, the former member of the 1850s 'Organization'. Walker was a convinced expansionist who undoubtedly supported the Alaskan purchase on its merits. But he was also a professional agent. By April 1868 Stoeckl had hired him for the sum (later increased) of $20,000; and Stoeckl reported that Seward was (cautiously) working 'with Walker' and employing 'all means by which to attract members of the House to our side'.[39] Seward's version, as later told to the President, was that Stoeckl had said 'there was no chance of the appropriation passing' unless 'influence was brought to bear in its favor'. So various sums, which Seward enumerated, 'were paid by the Russian minister directly and indirectly ... to secure appropriation'.[40]

After a nerve-wracking delay, due chiefly to President Johnson's impeachment, the appropriation act finally passed on 27 July, and on 1 August Stoeckl received his 7.2m. gold dollars. $7,035,000, it later transpired, went to the Russian government,

---

[37] Simon to Thaddeus Stevens [no relation], 2 Dec. 1867 (ibid. p. 170); Golder, 'Purchase of Alaska' p. 423

[38] To that end, he and his New York ally Thurlow Weed helped raise $150,000 (Stahr, *Seward* p. 510)

[39] Stoeckl to Gorchakov, 18/30 April 1868 (Bolkhovitinov, *The Sale of Alaska* pp. 303-4)

[40] President Johnson's note of his 6 Sept. 1868 conversation with Seward – Miller prints both this and John Bigelow's MS. diary account of what Seward told him on 23 Sept. of 'how the treaty was consummated' (*The Alaska Treaty* pp. 182-3)

while $26,000 was paid to Walker, and $139,000 (in four tranches) to Stoeckl. On 13 December Reutern reported on this to the Tsar, and on the 23rd (Old Style) he sent Stoeckl 'the Emperor's ukaz' classifying 'as actual expenditure the sum of 165,000 dollars retained by Your Excellency for use known to His Majesty out of the' $7.2 million dollars 'due the Russian government by treaty'.[41] This 'use' clearly included payments to lobbyists, Congressmen, and newspaper owners/editors. Suspicions were fanned when Walker was pick-pocketed in August of $16,000 worth of gold certificates. A telegram then arrived from London recording a $5m. transfer to the Russians (in fact in connection with a railway investment), which led to claims that over $2m. had been kept in America for purposes of corruption. The issue was worked up by two lobbyists, whom Walker accused of blackmail,[42] and hit the press. Congress had to mount an inquiry. But, as the Russian chargé noted, it did not really grill its own members, instead asking the Russian legation for an explanation it knew 'would be refused'.[43] So not much was revealed. There are inconsistencies between Seward's account to the President and that which he gave shortly thereafter to John Bigelow; and historians have argued as to precisely who was paid and how much. Bolkhovitinov's reconstruction is:

$21,667 – the Tsar's reward to Stoeckl and the legation secretary Bodisco for negotiating the treaty

$10,000 – cost of telegraphing the draft treaty to St. Petersburg

---

[41] Reutern to Stoeckl, 23 Dec. 1868 (Old Style) – Bolkhovitinov, *The Sale of Alaska* p. 321. Reutern's 13 Dec. report has unfortunately not come to light

[42] During the appropriation's passage, Walker told the Russian chargé, they had promised that if he 'gave them money they could guarantee the vote of nine representatives'. Later they said 'they knew that Seward, Banks and Butler had been bribed by the Russian government and that if they did not receive hush money, they would reveal all. Again they were sent packing' – V.A. Bodisco to Gorchakov, 10/22 Dec. 1868 (Bolkhovitinov, *The Sale of Alaska* p. 316)

[43] Bodisco to Gorchakov, 10/22 Dec. 1868 (ibid. p. 316); Holbo, *Tarnished Expansion* chap. 3, which suggests that, for a quarter of a century, the affair went far to associate expansionism with corruption (p. 92)

$26,000 – to the agents R.J. Walker and F.P. Stanton

$34,000 – to newspapermen ($30,000 to John W. Forney, of the Washington *Morning Chronicle*, $3,000 to his junior partner D.C. Forney, and $1,000 to M.M. Noah)

$73,333 – to ten members of Congress, and a further $6,667 that Seward was about to give Thaddeus Stevens when the latter died (total $110,000 in paper dollars)

Total: $165,000 gold dollars.[44]

* * * *

Having got Alaska, Washington did little with it – in 1879, indeed, the army was pulled out, forcing Sitka to appeal to the Royal Navy for protection against the encircling Tlingit.[45] The exception was the management of the 4.7 million seals that bred on the Pribilof Islands in the Bering Sea. Under the Russians, these had been sustainably 'harvested'. With the change of rule came the competitive short-term exploitation that had in North America virtually extinguished the buffalo, in the southern hemisphere most of the fur seals.[46] Some 250,000 seals were killed in 1868, but this prompted Congress to a most untypical intervention. It halted the next year's killing, and in 1870 gave the politically well-connected Alaska Commercial Company a twenty-year monopoly over the islands with the maximum seal take set by the US

---

[44] Bolkhovitinov, *The Sale of Alaska* p. 322-3, which takes account of the fact that some payments are recorded as made in gold dollars, some in depreciated paper 'greenbacks'

[45] In response H.M.S. *Osprey* spent a month off Sitka until replaced by an American warship – Gruening, *The State of Alaska* p. 39; Part 2 of that book is entitled 'The Era of Total Neglect (1867-1884), Part 3 'The Era of Flagrant Neglect (1884-1898)'

[46] Rudyard Kipling's 'The White Seal', written when the survival of the Pribilof herd was itself threatened, contains an elegiac list of now desolate southern rookeries (*The Jungle Book*, London, 1894)

Treasury, originally at the Russian level of 100,000 a year.[47] Since the seals killed were *holluschickie* – adolescent males relatively few of whom were needed to mature and mate with the harems of females – this might well have proved sustainable. But seals could also be hunted at sea, more especially (during the breeding season) in the waters around the Pribilof Islands. As males generally stayed ashore throughout the season, most of those killed at sea were females going out to feed while suckling young. Killing a mother also cost the life of her child, and, if she was already mated, that of next year's embryo. Moreover wounded seals might break away and die without their skins being recovered. So 'pelagic sealing' was indubitably wasteful, though quite how wasteful became a matter of international dispute.

A precedent was set in 1876 by the seizure of an American sealer twenty miles from land, under the act banning killing 'within the limits of the Alaska Territory, or in the waters thereof'. In 1881 the Acting Secretary of the US Treasury defined these as covering everything between the Aleutian chain and the Bering Strait. Since only US vessels were involved, the State Department was not consulted.[48] But as whaling declined in the 1880s, schooners – chiefly but not exclusively American and Canadian – turned to the Pribilof seals, first as they swam up the coast in the spring, and then, from 1885, within the Bering Sea during the June-September breeding season. The Alaskan Commercial Company, concerned about the impact on seal numbers and hence its own profitability, pressed for action. In 1872 Treasury Secretary Boutwell had felt the US did not have 'the jurisdiction or the power to drive off' British sealing parties unless they operated

---

[47] The rent was set at $55,000 pa., plus $2.625 a skin and a levy on seal oil. The Company was also to provide the islands' Aleut inhabitants with food, fuel, and schooling – James Thomas Gay, *American Fur Seal Diplomacy. The Alaskan Fur Seal Controversy* (New York, 1987) pp. 21-4

[48] Gay, *Fur Seal Diplomacy* pp. 25-6; see also the map Secretary of State Blaine sent to the British on 30 June 1890 (*Papers relating to the Foreign Affairs of the United States, transmitted to Congress* (hereafter FRUS), 1890 facing p. 439)

'within a marine league of the shore'.[49] But in 1886 US revenue cutters started to seize Canadian-flagged ships and take them to Sitka for trial. The judge appears to have followed a brief prepared by the American Commercial Company in instructing the jury that 'the waters of Alaska' comprised all those 'within the boundary set' by the 1867 treaty as far as 'the western end' of the Aleutians; and the ships were duly condemned. A State Department official later told General Foster that this had all been the work of subordinate officials and of the Commercial Company's Washington lobbyist: 'the subject was never considered by the Secretary of the Treasury, the Secretary of State, the Attorney-General, or the President'.[50]

Canada was upset. The *Victoria Daily Times* satirised US jurisdictional pretensions by reporting that, a seal having been shot near Montreal, it would 'now be in order for the Alaska Fur Company to arrest someone, on the ground that the mammal must have wandered away from the Behring Sea.'[51] And in the autumn of 1886 the British government, which still handled Canada's foreign relations, duly lodged complaints against the apparent US claim to 'sole sovereignty' over 'a stretch of sea extending in its widest part some 600 or 700 miles'. The US administration released the seized Canadian ships but gave no assurances that arrests would not resume – as indeed they did next year, when six more ships were seized. A further protest followed. Secretary of State Bayard turned to seeking an international arrangement whereby the contracting parties would 'prevent' their nationals 'from killing seals in Behring Sea' in ways that 'threaten the speedy extermination of those animals and

---

[49] However in 1888, after trouble had arisen, Boutwell sought to explain this away by saying that his letter had referred only to 'the Pacific Ocean south of the Aleutian Islands' – ed. John Bassett Moore, *History and Digest of the International Arbitrations to which the United States has been a Party* i (Washington, 1898) pp. 768-9

[50] Gay, *Fur Seal Diplomacy* pp. 27-8; Foster, *Diplomatic Memoirs* ii pp. 22-4, 26-7

[51] *Victoria Daily Times*, 2 Oct. 1886, quoted in *Fur Seal Diplomacy* p. 28

consequent loss to mankind'. Privately, the British Prime Minister Lord Salisbury accepted that if hunting at sea continued indefinitely, 'the seal must disappear';[52] so he asked for detailed proposals. Talks in 1888 broke down, the Americans blaming Canada's obstruction, the British the onset of American elections. Meanwhile the operations of the US revenue cruisers had been suspended; and since Canada did not comply with Salisbury's request to keep the sealers in port, they made hay. Partly as a result, the outgoing Congress passed a law asserting the 'dominion of the United States in the waters of the Behring Sea', and called for a Presidential Proclamation promising to arrest all vessels violating US laws there. This the incoming President Harrison duly issued, and in 1889 seizures resumed.[53]

The 'Behring's Sea matter' was, Salisbury felt, 'the only really black point on the Anglo-American horizon'; but he feared 'we may have trouble any day, because the views of the two parties [the US and Canada] ... are so far apart.'[54] For years he and Secretary of State Blaine debated the American claims, and negotiated, sometimes angrily, over ways of resolving the situation. Neither had an entirely free hand. The North American Commercial Company, which secured the Pribilof Islands lease in 1890, was run by important Republicans and enjoyed substantial influence over the Harrison administration. Equally, the interests Salisbury and his Washington minister Sir Julian Pauncefote were defending were largely Canadian; and the Governor-General warned that, while there seemed to be no 'growth of opinion either in favour of annexation to the States or of Independence for Canada, ... if we are forced to believe that our interests ... are not

---

[52] Bayard to US ministers in Britain, Russia, Japan, Germany, France, and Sweden, 19 Aug. 1887, and E.J. Phelps to Bayard, 12 Nov. (FRUS 1888 pp. 1824, 1827); Salisbury to the British minister in Washington, Sir Julian Pauncefote, 26 June 1889 (Lady Gwendolen Cecil, *Life of Robert Marquis of Salisbury* iv *1887-1892* (London, 1932) pp. 346-7)
[53] Charles C. Tansill, *Canadian-American Relations, 1875-1911* (New Haven, Conn., 1943) chaps. 10, 11; Gay, *Fur Seal Diplomacy* pp. 28-35, 43-5
[54] Salisbury to Pauncefote, 26 June 1889

considered of any importance to the Home Government, we furnish to those who desire separation from England a very dangerous weapon…'.[55]

In 1890 Salisbury's immediate problem became the likelihood that the US would resume its arrests of the previous year: if it did, 'the news is grave indeed, for my colleagues are all of opinion that we cannot tolerate a renewal of the captures.' His judgment 'of opinion here' was that

> 'we shall not be allowed, even if we were inclined, to permit United States cruizers to treat Behring Sea as if it were their private property.
>
> I confess that the attitude, both at Washington & at Ottawa, makes me somewhat apprehensive… If both sides push their pretensions to an extreme, a collision is inevitable.'[56]

Fortunately, Washington did not do so. Salisbury let it be known that he had readied four warships to protect British vessels in the Bering Sea (much as the US had often done for its ships fishing around or in Canadian waters). Unofficial reassurances were given, the American cruisers did not go north that year, and discussion moved on to possible arbitration.[57]

Next spring the United States offered two versions of a *'modus vivendi'* arrangement to cover the 1891 season: either non-interference with British sealers, provided they stayed twenty-five miles from the Pribilof Islands; or a complete ban on killing, by land as well as by sea, pending arbitration. This last represented a major diplomatic departure, since the US had previously targeted

---

[55] Unsigned letter to Pauncefote, 12 March 1890 (Charles S. Campbell, 'The Anglo-American Crisis in the Bering Sea, 1890-1891', *Mississippi Valley Historical Review* 48:3 (1961) p. 395)

[56] In May the Cabinet unanimously told the Queen she could not, 'without a serious loss of reputation and power', submit to the US claim 'to treat Behring's Sea as if it were their own territorial water' – Salisbury to Pauncefote, 28 March, and to the Queen, 24 May, 1890 (Cecil, *Life of Lord Salisbury* iv pp. 350-1)

[57] Campbell, 'The Crisis in the Bering Sea, 1890-1891' pp. 399-402

only pelagic sealing, keeping its property on land unimpaired. The North American Commercial Company was furious and managed to persuade the US Treasury to give it secret authorisation to kill its now usual 60,000 seals. At this point the administration was taken aback by British acceptance of the second, broader, *modus vivendi* offer. It decided to rescind the secret authorisation, only to be further embarrassed when this was discovered and published by its leading conservation expert, Henry Elliott. Tortuous further negotiations led first to the conclusion of a revised *modus vivendi* for 1891, then in February 1892 to the signature of an arbitration treaty.[58]

Everything nearly came unstuck over the need for a further *modus vivendi* to cover the period of arbitration. The United States wanted this to be on the same basis as before, only 'more effectively executed'. But Canada was sore over having been deprived of its 1891 sealing without compensation, and British experts did not anticipate 'any serious diminution of the fur-seal species' if hunting resumed. So Salisbury offered no more than a ban on pelagic sealing within thirty miles of the Islands, with land killing limited to 30,000.[59] This occasioned 'stormy debate' in the Senate, and Pauncefote telegraphed that it was hardly worth holding out on so small a point and endangering 'the settlement of the whole question'. The difficulty, Salisbury then explained, was 'the necessity of consulting the wishes of the Dominion'. Canada was unlikely to 'endure a simple renewal of that agreement' unless the London Government promised to compensate the pelagic sealers itself – something the British House of Commons would not permit. So, after consulting Canada, the British cabinet instead suggested a resumption of sealing provided every vessel gave

---

[58] Campbell, 'Crisis in the Bering Sea, 1890-1891' pp. 404-14. Elliott had, in 1890, produced a report on the catastrophic decline of the seal herd (to 960,000 from the 4.7 million of 1874). He had agreed to its suppression provided the US offered to end killing by land if Britain abandoned pelagic sealing. He was later dismissed, and retaliated by publishing some of his report

[59] Blaine to Pauncefote, 24, and Pauncefote to Blaine, 29, Feb. 1892 (FRUS 1891 pp. 614, 619-20)

security for the payment of damages should arbitration uphold US claims to the Bering Sea.[60] President Harrison was angered, and, despite Blaine's warning that 'If we get up a war cry and send naval vessels to Behring Sea it will re-elect Lord Salisbury', he insisted on a firm response: should Salisbury insist on 'free sealing for British subjects', the question would become 'no longer one of pecuniary loss or gain, but one of honor and self-respect'. An aide felt the letter meant 'a backdown on the part of G.B. or war ... This may be the beginning of a "War" diary.'[61] The Canadian government thought Harrison was bluffing, and that there was not 'the least possibility of an appeal to arms'. But Pauncefote was warned that the US Senate, too, might cause trouble, while the Chairman of its Foreign Relations Committee indicated a possible compromise on compensation provided Britain renewed the *modus vivendi*. Salisbury had left himself wiggle room, and he offered to renew the *modus* on these terms if the Senate ratified the arbitration treaty.[62] This opened the way for arbitration in Paris by a 'Tribunal' of two American and two British judges, one French judge, one Italian, and one Swede.[63]

---

[60] Pauncefote to Salisbury, 10 March, and Salisbury to Pauncefote, 11 and 18 March, 1892 (ed. Kenneth Bourne, *British Documents on Foreign Affairs ... from the Foreign Office Confidential Print,* Series C North America, 1837-1914, 10 *Expansion and Rapprochement 1889-1898* (University Publications of America, 1987) pp. 117-18)

[61] Blaine to Harrison, 6 March 1892 (referring to the upcoming British general election), and Everard Tibbott's diary, 22 March (Charles S. Campbell, 'The Bering Sea Settlements of 1892', *Pacific Historical Review* 32:4 (1963) pp. 360, 362); Acting Secretary of State Wharton to Pauncefote, 22 March 1892 (FRUS 1891 pp. 625-8)

[62] Governor-General to the Colonial Secretary, 16 and 24 March 1892 (Campbell, 'Bering Sea Settlements' p. 364); Pauncefote to Salisbury, 24 and 25 March 1892, and Salisbury to Pauncefote, 26 March (*British Documents* 10 pp. 120-1)

[63] There was one final obstacle: France's Foreign Minister bristled at the request to provide an English-speaking judge – French was the language of diplomacy! So, though the Tribunal's proceedings were conducted in English, proprieties were preserved by the rendering of its protocols and award in French, with an English translation (Foster, *Diplomatic Memoirs* ii pp. 33-4, 44)

Possession of the Pribilofs had occasioned a marked shift in the United States' international posture. Previously, Washington had always held that it neither could nor wished to control the activities of its vessels on the Northwest Coast; and this had, as we have seen, been an important factor in Russia's decision to sell Alaska. But in 1887 Washington proposed to Britain, Russia, Japan, France, Germany, and Sweden, individual agreements whereby both they and the US would stop their citizens killing seals in the Bering Sea in the ways that now threatened 'the speedy extermination of these animals'.[64] More generally, Secretary of State Bayard, perhaps reluctantly,[65] and his successor Blaine with far more enthusiasm, were seeking to protect the sovereign rights over the greater part of the Bering Sea that concern for the Pribilof herd had now led the US to claim. Of this new position Pauncefote later observed that hitherto the United States had been regarded as

'the first nation to vindicate the freedom of the sea in respect of this very portion of the Pacific Ocean by the vigorous

---

[64] Russia asked that the area covered should also include the waters around its own rookeries in the Commander Islands and the Sea of Okhotsk. Secretary of State Bayard readily agreed (even though, as his successor later noted, this would have required US legislation) - Bayard's letters to these six countries, 19 Aug. 1887, and to the US minister in St. Petersburg, 9 and 18 April 1888; Acting Secretary of State Francis Wharton to Pauncefote, 4 June 1891 (FRUS 1888 pp. 1824, 1839, 1891 p. 560)

[65] Tansill shows that, after examining the archives and asking in St. Petersburg as to any pre-1867 Russian claims in the Bering Sea, Bayard concluded in early 1887 that the arrests of British sealers were unjustified, and advised President Cleveland that Bering Sea was 'part of the high seas', with US jurisdiction extending no further there than on its Atlantic coast. But in August Acting Attorney-General Jenks argued that America was entitled to protect the seals there since they had 'no other habitat than upon the public domain of the United States'; and State Department Solicitor Wharton, reversing his previous advice, now held that 'wherever a sovereign has property' he has 'sufficient police control over the [adjacent] waters ... to enable him to protect it ... As far as I recollect, the three-mile rule has never applied to the North Pacific ... [and does not bind] the seal fisheries.' In 1889 this view was, Tansill believes with Cleveland's encouragement, fastened by law onto the incoming administration (*Canadian-American Relations, 1875-1911* pp. 272-5, 291)

protest of Mr. J. Q. Adams against ... the claims ... asserted by the ... famous Ukase of 1821.

I think it will be a matter of general surprise to learn that, in the view of the United States' Government, that protest was not intended to apply to the claims of Russia in Behring's Sea. But, whatever opinion may be formed on that point, it is certain that the principles of the law of nations invoked by Mr. Adams apply with equal force, whether to the north or the south of the Aleutian Islands, and that the millions of fur-seals which migrate annually to Behring's Sea do not, on entering its waters, become the exclusive property of the United States.'[66]

When these questions finally came before the Paris Arbitration Tribunal, Pauncefote's confidence was fully justified. All the points of international law were determined against the United States: though Russia had by the 1821 ukase claimed jurisdiction up to 100 miles offshore, it had admitted in the subsequent 1824 and 1825 negotiations that jurisdiction should 'be restricted to the reach of a cannon shot from shore'; Britain did not, by the 1825 treaty, 'recognize' any Russian claim 'to exclusive jurisdiction as to the seal fisheries in the Behring Sea outside of ordinary territorial waters'; nor had Russia, after the 1825 treaty, held or exercised 'exclusive rights as to seal fisheries therein' beyond its 'ordinary territorial waters'. These findings were all carried by six votes to one, that of Senator Morgan (who, like his Canadian counterpart Sir John Thompson, resolutely voted the national line). Slightly, but only slightly, less clear was the question of whether the United States had 'any right ... of protection or property' in the Pribilof fur seals 'outside the ordinary three-mile limit'. Blackstone could be quoted to the effect that there was property in bees when they left the hive, but the counter was that there was none in pheasants when they left one's property. In the event, Morgan's formula – that

---

[66] Pauncefote to Salisbury, 24 July 1890 (*British Documents* 10 p. 33)

the US had over the seals outside the three-mile limit 'the rights that all nations have, under international law, in respect of self-protection and self-defense' – drew the support of the other American, Justice Harlan, and the abstention of Baron de Courcel, but was voted down by the four remaining arbitrators.[67]

However the Tribunal had been asked not only to pronounce on questions of law but to recommend regulations to conserve the seals. This enabled Morgan and Harlan to counter-attack, moving that no 'pelagic sealing should be allowed which would seriously endanger' the preservation of the herd. This was defeated, and instead the three neutral arbitrators submitted alternative proposals: no sealing within 60 miles of the Pribilofs (Thompson failed to substitute 30); a close season in May, June, and July (dates adopted after a long tussle); pelagic sealing to be conducted only by unpowered boats, with nets, explosives, and firearms banned; and exemptions for Indians. It was then agreed, against Thompson's wishes, that these regulations should remain in force until amended by 'agreement between the Governments of the United States and Great Britain'. These governments should also decide on ways 'of giving effect to the Regulations', and add others governing killing on land. Finally, in view of the 'critical condition to which ... the race of fur seals is now reduced', both were asked to prohibit any killing for at least a year.[68]

Temporary restrictions on pelagic sealing were duly introduced. But the United States continued to urge, with reason,[69] that they were insufficient, and to press for further limitations, preferably

---

[67] *History and Digest of International Arbitrations* i pp. 914-20, and the English-language text of the Award (pp. 945-55). The US arrests of Canadian seal ships were therefore illegal. Britain sought $542,169 compensation, but in 1894 settled for $425,000. However, Senator Morgan defeated the appropriation, so the issue went to a mixed Commission. This awarded $473,151, which was paid in mid-1898 (Gay, *Fur Seal Diplomacy* pp. 95-6)

[68] *International Arbitrations* i pp. 925-9, 956-7 ('Declarations ... referred to the Governments of the United States and Great Britain for their consideration')

[69] By 1911 the Pribilof herd had fallen to 100,000, though illegal land killing as well as pelagic sealing was to blame (Tansill, *Canadian-American Relations* pp. 364-5, 371n.)

also involving Russia and Japan. Canada, and therefore Britain, proved very reluctant. But by 1897 the idea had surfaced of buying out the Canadian interest: US Treasury Secretary Lyman Gage privately believed Canada should be paid $500,000. Talks started on revising the Tribunal regulations, with Canada's new Liberal Prime Minister, Sir Wilfrid Laurier, and his Minister of Marine visiting Washington in November 1897.[70] Hitherto Laurier's premiership had been chiefly notable for maintaining tariff protection against the US while giving Britain a degree of preference, and for his enthusiastic participation in the British celebrations that accompanied Queen Victoria's diamond jubilee. But he had told his cabinet at the outset that 'the establishment of close and friendly relations with the United States must be a cardinal feature of Canadian policy', to which end 'Canada must more and more take negotiations with Washington into her own hands'.[71] He now floated the idea of a joint commission to consider all Canadian-American problems; President McKinley was enthusiastic. Matters were delayed by the American wish for a moratorium on all sealing while talks were in progress. But by mid-1898 revision of the Paris sealing regulations had been included in the Commission's wide-ranging agenda. The Commission's British side was led by the former Lord Chancellor Lord Herschell, but his colleagues were the Newfoundland Premier, and four Canadians (including Laurier himself and two other ministers) in whose hands the outcome was left.

The Commission met first in Quebec in August 1898, and in November adjourned to Washington. The atmosphere was one of remarkable goodwill. President McKinley had been well-disposed even before the outbreak of the Spanish American War in April 1898. British and Canadian sympathy for the United States in that war, a marked contrast to the general European attitude, had then

---

[70] Robert Craig Brown, *Canada's National Policy 1883-1900. A Study in Canadian-American Relations* (Princeton, N.J., 1964) pp. 330-1
[71] Laurier cleared this with the Colonial Secretary, Joseph Chamberlain, when in London in mid-1897 – O.D. Skelton, *Life and Letters of Sir Wilfrid Laurier* ii (London, 1922) pp. 123, 126

produced a surge of anglophilia, reinforced by a number of myths (notably that the Royal Navy had interposed in the Philippines to shield the American from the German fleet). Nevertheless, the Commission's actual operation reflected the principle later encapsulated in Speaker Tip O'Neill's celebrated dictum that 'All politics is local'. Laurier himself had commented that 'The Commission is bounded on the east by Gloucester cod and on the west by Indiana lambs, no, sometimes on the west by Seattle lions.' Canada too had its local interests, notably those of Ontario lumber and of the Maritimes' wish for tariff-free fish export to the US. But in Secretary of State Hay's view the real difficulty was the involvement of its Canadian members in 'their own party and factional disputes': 'Sir Wilfrid Laurier is far more afraid of [the Conservative Opposition leader] Sir Charles Tupper than he is of Lord Salisbury and President McKinley combined.'[72]

Progress was in fact made on several topics, and 'it was decided from the very first' to seek 'the cessation of pelagic sealing'.[73] Not all Canadian ministers were happy about abandoning 'a sovereign right'. But Laurier's reply was that they might thus secure compensation for 'our sealers': 'You know as well as I do that if pelagic sealing is allowed to continue for two or three years more, it will then come to an end by the gradual destruction of the herds. Then the sealers would be left without any compensation, but with a fleet on their hands.'[74] Negotiations proceeded for a Canadian surrender of the right to pelagic sealing, with the US in return

---

[72] Hay to Joseph Choate, 28 April 1899 (William Roscoe Thayer, *The Life and Letters of John Hay* ii (Boston, 1915) pp. 205-6

[73] See W.C. Cartwright's 25 March 1899 Foreign Office 'Memorandum showing the Positions before the Anglo-American Commission ... when the last meeting took place...' (Confidential Print, FO 881/7135, 'Correspondence respecting the... Joint Commission for the Settlement of Questions pending between the United States and Canada, Part 1', p. 132)

[74] Laurier to David Mills and to Clifford Sifton, 28 Jan. 1899 (Brown, *Canada's National Policy* p. 375). Canada's average annual take (albeit quite largely from Asian as distinct from North American waters) had fallen from 62,500 in 1891-6 to a little over 30,000 in 1897-8 (Alvin C. Gluek, 'Canada's Splendid Bargain: the North Pacific Fur Seal Convention of 1911', *Canadian Historical.Review* [hereafter *Can.H.R.*] 63:2 (1982) p. 182)

The Alaska Boundary Dispute

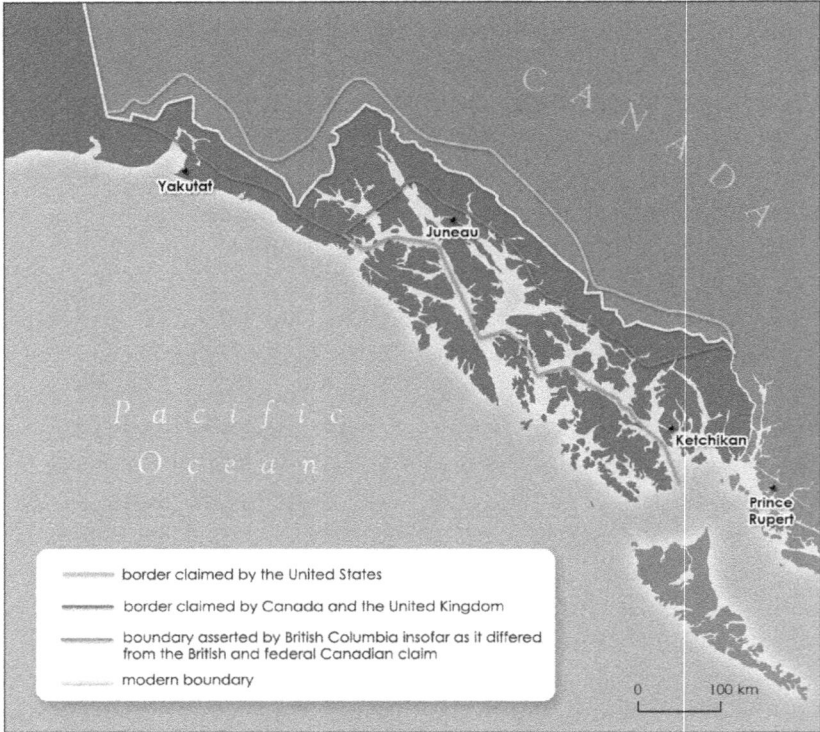

Border claimed by the United States – right hand line
Modern boundary – next line from the right
Border claimed by Canada and the United Kingdom –
next line from the right
Boundary claimed by British Columbia insofar as
it differed from the British and federal
Canadian claim – left hand line
Source – William R. Shepherd, User: 1926: AnonMoos,
Rudyologist – redrawn version of 1926 Canada-Alaska 1903
boundary-map.jpg [PD-US], Rudyologist declares
modifications to be also PD

buying the sealing fleet (supposedly for between $0.5m. and $0.75m.) and paying Canada a percentage of the receipts from the killings on land. Also included in the package, if we can believe a later letter of Laurier's, was Canada's acquisition of an Alaskan port from which to service the Klondike gold rush.[75] But, as we shall soon see, negotiations over the port ran into the sands, and Laurier pulled the rug from under the Commission, insisting that 'there will be an agreement on Alaska, or none at all on any of the subjects in dispute'.[76]

* * * *

It 'seems too bad', wrote General Foster (one of the US Commissioners), 'that such a useful herd of animals should be gradually destroyed because of a failure to agree about the ownership of some glaciers.'[77] But the Klondike Gold Rush had converted what had previously been a minor issue, not worth spending money on,[78] into one of high national feeling that might, as Lord Herschell put it, 'at any time occasion acute controversy and even conflict'.[79] The gold rush up the Fraser River in 1858 had been followed by others all the way north. By the 1890s prospectors were trying their luck on the Yukon; in 1896 significant deposits were found in Canadian territory at Rabbit – renamed Bonanza –

---

[75] Herschell to Salisbury, 7 Feb. 1899 ('Joint Commission Correspondence, Part 1', pp. 155-6); Senator Fairbanks to Secretary of State Hay, 25 March (Brown, *Canada's National Policy* pp. 376-8); Laurier to Governor General Earl Grey, 29 Sept. 1906 (Libraries and Archives Canada, Albert Henry George Grey, 4th Earl Grey fonds: héritage [hereafter Grey Papers] – Film c.1358 image 624-5)
[76] Réal Bélanger, *Wilfrid Laurier, quand la politique devient passion* (Quebec, 1986) p. 237; also Laurier to Principal Grant, 27 Feb. 1899 (Skelton, *Life and Letters of Laurier* ii pp. 131-2)
[77] *Diplomatic Memoirs* p. 189
[78] Experts talked and border surveys were periodically proposed, but it was not until 1893 that a joint US-Canadian survey of the stretch from Portland Canal to the line of 141° West was actually mounted (Norman Penlington, *The Alaska Boundary Dispute: a Critical Reappraisal* (Toronto, 1972) pp. 30-2)
[79] Herschell to Salisbury, 21 Feb. 1899 ('Joint Commission Correspondence, Part 1', p. 162)

Creek, and by the end of the year most of what became the town of Dawson had been staked out; then in July 1897 one ship reached San Francisco with $400,000 worth of gold, another Seattle with $700,000. The Klondike 'stampede' of would-be miners followed. It brought the rapid establishment, in what had previously been almost uninhabited land at the head of the Lynn Canal, of the American towns of Skagway and Dyea.[80]

Previous access to the Klondike had been largely by boat up the Yukon River – the route taken by the North West Mounted Police (NWMP) when first sent there in 1895 to symbolise Canadian sovereignty.[81] But in a gold rush time is crucial, since otherwise the best claims will all have been staked. Shorter routes – up the Lynn Canal, over the mountains at its head to Lake Bennett, and then by water to and down the Yukon – had already been surveyed, and most stampeders went this way. There were in fact three passes over the mountains: the White from Skagway; the Chilkoot from the neighbouring Dyea; and the flatter, but longer, less direct, and less popular Chilkat from Pyramid Harbor (near the modern Haines). Much, perhaps even most, of the profits of a gold rush come from supplying the miners, so ownership of these departure points was seen as crucial. Were they American, miners would most naturally fit out in Seattle and ship from there; if Canadian, Vancouver and Victoria could more easily compete. A formal diplomatic settlement was not reached till 1903, but it largely reflected developments on the ground in 1897-8.

From August 1897 'stampeders', mostly American, poured off the ships at Skagway, establishing a great tent camp. Many stayed on, over-wintering before attempting the onwards journey into the interior, or simply servicing other would-be miners as they prepared to cross the passes; and by October there was, according to the NWMP, 'a fair-sized town with ... a population of about

---

[80] David Wharton, *The Alaska Gold Rush* (Bloomington, Indiana, 1972) pp. 25, 43, 79-82, 84-6, 283n.
[81] Norbert MacDonald, 'Seattle, Vancouver, and the Klondike', *Can.H.R.* 49 (1968) pp. 237-8

20,000'. This was a considerable over-estimate, but later that year the same process had produced another mushroom town at Dyea.[82] In theory, the Canadian government claimed ownership of the heads of the Alaska inlets, but in practice it was quick to accept American *faits accomplis*. For, as Interior Minister Clifford Sifton told a critic in August 1897, with the boundary still in dispute Canada's access to the Yukon depended on US goodwill. Hence the decision in July to seek Washington's consent 'to our sending goods in bond from the head of the Lynn inlet', paying 'the cost of sending an American [customs] officer with every transport until they reach ... undisputed Canadian territory'. Similarly in September Canada secured President McKinley's consent to the building of a telegraph line inland from Skagway.[83]

There was, though, no meeting of minds as to where 'undisputed Canadian territory' started. The United States tended to believe that the 1825 Anglo-Russian treaty entitled it, as Russia's successor, to a lisière extending '10 marine leagues' (34.5 miles) inland from tidewater. To avoid provocation, Canadian police and customs posts had initially been established inland on Lake Bennett. But the US Customs Commissioner for Dyea and Skagway claimed yet further; and early in 1898 an American party 'went just below the Police Station, where the Union Jack is floating, and hoisted the Stars and Stripes. The police immediately ... demanded an explanation, and after some parleying the flag was lowered and an apology tendered.' 'I fear', continued our NWMP source, 'there will ultimately be trouble there...'[84] Sifton

[82] Another estimate of Skagway's population in the spring of 1898 was 8,000, with 1000 stampeders passing through every week; Dyea was a little smaller – National Park Service, *Klondike Gold Rush, Dyea* and *Determining the Facts 2*; Explore North, *The History of Skagway, Alaska* (all accessed 11/9/17). By 1900 Dyea had vanished, and Skagway had fallen to about 3000

[83] R.W. Scott to Laurier, 23 July 1897, on his, Paterson's and Sifton's decision (in the absence of other ministers) to approach Washington for customs concessions; Sifton to H. Bostock, 3 August 1897 – D.J. Hall, *Clifford Sifton i The Young Napoleon, 1861-1900* (Vancouver, 1981) pp. 166-7, 170

[84] F.W. Turner to George F. Stelly, 4 Jan. 1898 (Confidential Print, FO 414/158, 'Part X. Further Correspondence respecting the Boundary between the British

agreed. 'In another ten days', he later wrote, the Americans 'would have been in possession of the territory down to Lake Bennett, and it would have taken twenty years of negotiating to get them out, in fact I doubt whether we would ever have' done so. He accordingly over-rode Police caution, and insisted that Canadian posts be established at the summits of the White and Chilkoot passes.[85] This took effect in February. The US Customs Collector at Juneau later reported that he had told the Canadian in charge at the summits that he 'was required... to establish Customs offices on the frontier of each trail' and 'intended to locate them at the lakes'. But 'the Canadian police would not permit me to do so'. 'Owing to the serious International question relating to the boundary', and the atrocious weather conditions on the summits, Collector Ivey deferred action until he heard from Washington. But on 26 March the commander of the newly arrived US troops in Dyea requested the Canadian officers, in writing, 'to cease exercising jurisdiction at the summits of Chilkoot and White Passes and at Lake Lindeman'. This drew a firm British protest to Washington against 'action of this kind ... by officers necessarily unacquainted with the present position of the controversy', and it seems not to have been repeated.[86] The Canadian posts stayed put; and the iconic image of the Gold Rush is of a string of laden people staggering up the snow-covered slope to encounter, at the top, Canada's 'peace, order and good government' in the form of red-coated Mounties – who insisted that the miners bring enough food for a year, and who would, in the coming months, shepherd them down through the white water of the Yukon and its tributaries.

Possessions in North America and the Territory of Alaska. February to September 1898' [hereafter 'Further Correspondence 10'] p. 22)

[85] Penlington, *Canada and Imperialism 1896-1899* (Toronto, 1971 reprint) pp. 84-5; Sifton to Major Walsh, 1 April 1898 (Hall, *Sifton. The Young Napoleon* pp. 181-2)

[86] J.W. Ivey to the US Treasury Secretary, 23 March 1898 (US National Archives, RG 76 E 340); Governor-General Lord Aberdeen to Chamberlain, undated, Salisbury to Pauncefote, 9 April, and Pauncefote's 20 April 1898 Memorandum to the State Department ('Further Correspondence 10' pp. 70, 82)

The Canadian government had thought of improving the route up from Skagway. But during his inspection tour in the autumn of 1897, Sifton switched to favouring a narrow-gauge railway running entirely through Canadian territory, initially from the head of navigation on the Stikine River to Teslin Lake on a Yukon tributary. One of the reasons, the Colonial Secretary Joseph Chamberlain was told, was 'the difficulty of obtaining bonding and other ... privileges from United States' authorities'.[87] But the choice of route was made as much for strategic as for commercial reasons: 'Canada must have a [rail] road available ... for military and police purposes. Unless provision previously granted by United States authorities, Lynn route could not be used for taking troops in[to] Yukon, whilst the character of the Yukon population requires a route available at any moment'.[88]

There had been a surprising amount of speculative interest in constructing railways into the North-West Territory; and in January 1898 a deal was struck with a reputable contractor to build the Teslin line by September. 'You will' then, Sifton told Major Walsh, be able to come out of the Klondike 'by railway and steamboat like a Christian'. But it did not happen. For though the Opposition's leader Sir Charles Tupper had promised parliamentary support for the line, party pressure turned him round. It is not clear why the Conservatives opposed the project. Objection could be taken to the land grant and other incentives offered to the contractors. But a more likely explanation is adversary politics: Conservatives fought the measure just as they had destroyed Mackenzie's railway bill in 1875, some fearing (the civil servant Joseph Pope was told) that were it passed, 'the contractors would

---

[87] 'I am', Sifton had written on 26 January 1898, 'having a tremendous amount of trouble with Customs officials in Alaska'; and indeed, though Washington authorised a major alleviation of bonding arrangements in February, local officers managed on various pretexts to delay implementation until May (by which time that season's Klondikers were over the passes) - 'Further Correspondence 10' p. 180, also pp. 72, 80-2, 85, 175-6)

[88] Aberdeen to Chamberlain, undated telegram (April 1898) – 'Further Correspondence 10' p. 74

have given the Liberal Machine such a large "rake-off" as to have secured them power for 20 years. That [Pope commented] may be so.' The Senate, whose membership still reflected the long Conservative ascendancy, threw the bill out on 30 March.[89]

There was, in any case, little chance of completing the line in 1898. For though it would later have been extended back to a Canadian harbour, it was initially to run from the upper Stikine River, to reach which everything had to be transferred at the American port of Wrangell from sea-going to river vessels. Congress seized on this as a diplomatic lever, moving to bar such transfer unless Canada conceded a whole Christmas tree of special interest demands. Such interference with Canada's right, under the 1871 Washington treaty, to navigate the river across the American lisière was probably illegal. But by the time the US could be brought to accept this (if indeed it could), the Stikine would long since have frozen over. The Canadian Senate's rejection of the railway bill thus saved much trouble and hard feeling. Equally, the Congressional move was more limited than had first appeared, being intended (Pauncefote was told) only to stop Canada conferring a monopoly on the new line and so blocking the projected railway inland from Skagway. The way was now free for that line; construction started in June 1898, reached Lake Bennett a year later, and Whitehorse (on the Yukon) in 1900.[90]

Talks had been underway for some months; and after the Teslin railway bill's rejection everything rapidly fell into place – as the *Washington Post* put it, 'the friction which had been expected over the Klondike Regulations has been removed, mainly on account of the friendliness shown to this country by Great Britain in the war with Spain'.[91] Canada dropped its policy (never actually enforced) of restricting gold prospecting in the North-West to British subjects, and agreed to issue mining licences at the most

---

[89] Hall, *Sifton. The Young Napoleon* pp. 182-4, 186-7. Earlier the Canadian Pacific had repaid Conservative support with large financial contributions.
[90] Pauncefote to Salisbury, 26 March 1898 ('Further Correspondence 10' p. 38); http://wpyr.com/mcclures-magazine-article-march-1900 (accessed 31/8/17)
[91] *Washington Post*, 28 April 1898 ('Further Correspondence 10' p. 83)

convenient location, the head of the Lynn Canal. The United States finally implemented the relaxation, promised in February, of the arrangements for customs transit in bond. And it agreed to a *provisional* boundary at the summits of the three passes up from the Canal. (This was immediately implemented at the more important White and Chilkoot Passes, though the precise border on the Chilkat was not agreed until 1899.[92]) The underlying issue, the conflicting Canadian and American territorial claims, was referred to the Joint High Commission that would meet later in the year.

The Canadian claim was very weak. In negotiating the 1825 Treaty defining Alaska's land borders, Russia had insisted on a continuous strip sufficient to keep the HBC on the far side of the coastal mountains. It had then published maps displaying its understanding of the result. These were not challenged: indeed, British maps broadly followed them. And when questioned in 1857, Sir George Simpson explained that the 'British territory runs along inland from the coast about 30 miles', and submitted a map that depicted the border as some way inland from the heads of the coastal inlets, curling around that of the Lynn Canal before turning west to Mount Fairweather and then up to Mount St. Elias.[93] This was still the Canadian government's understanding when the question of a border survey came up in early 1886: Sir John Macdonald told the Governor-General the line should run from the 'northern extremity of the Portland Canal until the 141° of west longitude'; and as it should never 'exceed 10 marine

---

[92] W.R. Day (of the State Department) to Pauncefote, 9, and Pauncefote to Salisbury, 10, May 1898 ('Further Correspondence 10' pp. 84, 88-9). Canada would not accept a border on the Chilkat summit as this was more than 30 miles, the maximum American claim, from tidewater. It took further bargaining before the line of the Klehini river was substituted

[93] 1827 Russian map – Penlington, *Alaska Boundary Dispute* p. 13; Simpson – *Report from the Select Committee on the Hudson's Bay Company* (P.P. 1857 (Session 2) xv) esp. questions 1026-31 and Map on p. 569

leagues from the ocean', it could 'easily be obtained at any point by a measurement with a surveyor's chain from the ocean.'[94]

This consensus came under increasing pressure. British Columbia had never liked the Alaskan border. The first difficulty – over its precise location on the Stikine river – had been resolved in 1878 by agreement on a *provisional* border 25 miles upstream from the coast.[95] But the province saw the US claim to islands at the entrance to the Portland Canal as a threat to its utilisation of Observatory Inlet; by 1884 it was contending for a line up not the Portland Canal but the more northerly Clarence Strait; and there followed a series of maps that eventually reduced the American lisière to discontinuous sections divided by the deep coastal inlets. A further impetus was contributed by the nationalist geologist Dr. Dawson, when negotiating informally with his equally nationalist US counterparts.[96] The most important change, though, came in 1888 when it seemed that the Joint Commission on Atlantic Fisheries might also address the Alaska boundary. General Cameron, who had participated in past border surveys and who enjoyed influence as Tupper's son-in-law, then produced a reinterpretation of the 1825 treaty. This had said the border should not be more than 10 marine leagues from the 'Ocean'. And whereas Americans equated 'Ocean' with 'tidewater', Cameron saw it as ending where inlets became so narrow (six miles across) as to be territorial waters. If so, the head of the Lynn Canal, more than ten leagues past this point, was Canadian.[97] The Canadian government duly adopted this

---

[94] However since the coast was irregular, it might be well for a Commission to suggest an alternative line 'correcting' rather than following 'some of the greater irregularities' – Macdonald to Lord Lansdowne, 9 March 1886 (Tansill, *Canadian-American Relations* pp. 144-5)

[95] A criminal escaped while being conveyed downriver, and question arose as to whether his recapture had been on American territory and so illegal (Tansill, *Canadian-American Relations* pp. 137-8)

[96] See the sequence of maps in Penlington, *Alaska Boundary Dispute* pp. 26-9, and those in John A. Munro ed., *The Alaska Boundary Dispute* (Toronto, 1970) pp. 168-9

[97] Cameron's undated (1888) Memorandum (*Alaska Boundary Tribunal* [hereafter A.B.T.] iii (Washington, 1904) pp. 339, 345). In 1875, though, Cameron had assumed that the line to be marked was inland of the head of Lynn

principle.[98] But, as both Laurier and Sifton admitted in Parliament in 1898, there remained the difficulty that the United States had, without any British protest, exercised sovereignty in the area since 1867, establishing the towns of Skagway and Dyea in 1897.[99]

Nevertheless, the British side began at the Joint High Commission with a maximalist claim. Though this was unsurprisingly rejected, the American commissioners were, in Laurier's words, 'at first and almost to the last disposed to come to a reasonable compromise.'[100] Serious bargaining did not start until 14 December, when Senator Fairbanks offered Canada free access to the Lynn Canal ports, plus transit 'across the intervening territory of Alaska without the payment of duty'.[101] This would have met the Dominion's commercial needs. But Canadian Ministers wanted an alternative all-British route to the Klondike – 'one of the ports on the shores of the Lynn Inlet', as their Privy Council had specified in July - in case the Americans imposed 'differential or exorbitant railway rates' on the route via Skagway.[102] Lord Herschell duly suggested the unpopulated Pyramid Harbor. He also warned President McKinley that 'unless the attitude of the United States' Commissioners greatly altered, a Treaty would be impossible'. McKinley graciously declared that a treaty was required by the 'highest interests of the two countries'; and, when Herschell asked for a port, he said, 'You must have *something* you want', and promised to talk to the American Commissioners.[103] Possibly as a

---

Canal, and had in 1885 advocated trying to buy the whole lisière (for £300-350,000) to acquire control of both sides of Portland Canal/Observatory Inlet (Tansill, *Canadian-American Relations* pp. 153-4)

[98] Tansill, *Canadian-American Relations* pp. 156-7; A.B.T. iii pp. 344-6

[99] Tansill, *Canadian-American Relations* pp. 165-6. Canada had, once, pushed for a protest (in 1888), but this was delivered in Washington in so vague a form as to be legally valueless (ibid. p. 157; A.B.T. iii pp. 346-8)

[100] 27 Feb. 1899 (Skelton, *Life and Letters of Laurier* ii pp. 131-2)

[101] 'Joint Commission Correspondence, Part 1', p. 132

[102] 'Confidential Memorandum by Mr. Cartwright [Herschell's Foreign Office Secretary] ...', 27 March 1899 (ibid. p. 216); Report of a Committee of the Privy Council, 4 July 1898 (*British Documents* 10 p. 420)

[103] Herschell's 16 Dec. 'Memorandum respecting the Lynn Canal', and Herschell to Fairbanks, 21 Dec., to Salisbury, 22 Dec., 1898 ('Joint Commission Correspondence, Part 1' pp. 123-4, 130, 132)

result of this, possibly as part of the prospective deal on pelagic sealing, on 24 December Fairbanks offered a fifty-year grant of shore frontage at Pyramid Harbor with a strip of territory running up the Chilkat river to the border; this would be subject to Canadian law and administration, though US 'citizens and vessels' should have equal treatment and the area should not be used for military purposes. The offer, Fairbanks wrote, 'embraced all but the sovereignty of the soil ... It grants all that is of commercial or practical value, to-wit port, customs and transit privileges, and avoids the rock upon which the treaty would undoubtedly suffer shipwreck in the ... Senate.'[104]

Canada should have snapped it up. But there were fears that with so short a lease people might hesitate to build a railway under a Canadian charter.[105] Instead, the delegation asked that Canada should hold Pyramid Harbor for as long as it kept a customs house or police force there, and also that US, Canadian, and British-registered ships should have equal rights not only there but also at Skagway and Dyea.[106] Meanwhile 'the proposed surrender of Pyramid Harbour leaked out and gave rise to a violent agitation in the Western States': on 2 February 1899 the impressively organised Seattle Chamber of Commerce sent telegrams 'to men whose influence may count with the commission', and promised that 'no stone will be left unturned to prevent the concession of Alaskan territory which would be

---

[104] 'American Proposition as to Grant of Port and Strip of Territory', 24 Dec. 1898 (Tansill, *Canadian-American Relations* p. 176n.); Fairbanks to Herschell, 24 Dec. 1898 (US National Archives, RG 76 E 337 'Fairbanks-Herschell Correspondence 1898-1899')

[105] Hall, *Sifton. The Young Napoleon* pp. 200-1. The danger may have been exaggerated: dispute as to Skagway's ownership had not stopped the building of the White Pass and Yukon Railway, which had merely secured charters from all three of the countries involved

[106] 'Draft Article respecting the Alaska Boundary...', 2 Feb. 1899, and Herschell to Salisbury, 7 Feb. ('Joint Commission Correspondence, Part 1' pp. 155, 156-7). Later, Foster would also claim that whereas the Canadians had initially asked for a connecting strip two miles wide up the Chilkat river, 'when they came to lay it down upon the map it broadened out to about twenty miles' (to Secretary of State Hay, 25 July 1899 – US Archives, RG 59 E 927)

disastrous to the shipping interest of the coast'.[107] There may have been no connection with the American Commissioners' discovery next day that their offers would advantage British over American shipping, and their consequent insistence that Pyramid Harbor would have to observe US navigation laws.[108] But the agitation stymied Herschell's wish instead to return to the US offer of 14 December. He felt it was now too late, 'especially as the American Commissioners could not be persuaded to take a strong line against an organised body of ship-owners'.[109] The alternative seemed to be arbitration. Its terms were debated amid growing irritation, and the British side produced convoluted schemes whereby, whatever the findings, the United States should keep Skagway and Dyea and Britain Pyramid Harbor. But to no effect. The British cabinet left to the four Canadian Commissioners the decision on breaking off or continuing the talks, and they were suspended on 20 February.

The US had thus made what Herschell's Secretary W.C. Cartwright later described as 'two very substantial offers'.[110] That

---

[107] 'Confidential Memorandum by Mr. Cartwright' ('Joint Commission Correspondence, Part 1' p. 215); *Seattle Post Intelligencer*, 3 Feb. 1899, cited by William A. Harper, 'The Alaska Boundary Question: the Seattle Commercial Interest and the Joint High Commission of 1898-99', *Journal of the West* 10 (1971) p. 266. Congressmen would be told that cession 'of any portion of Alaska ... means [electoral] death to us in this section in 1900', while President McKinley would receive about a hundred telegrams, some even threatening secession in the event of such concession. However the agitation was largely confined to Seattle, backed by the state of Washington (ibid. pp. 266-71); Charles S. Campbell, *Anglo-American Understanding, 1898-1903* (Baltimore, 1957) pp. 110-112. Surprisingly, 146 'american residents and property holders of Dyea' (which was already in decline) petitioned the Commission for the port's transfer to Canada, and for 'free [Canadian] access to Lynn Canal equally with Americans' (undated, U.S. National Archives RG 76 E 336)

[108] For otherwise British ships would become able to carry goods there from US ports, while American ones could not do so from Canadian ones

[109] Campbell, *Anglo-American Understanding* pp. 111-112; Cartwright's 25 March 1899 'Memorandum showing the Positions before the Anglo-American Commission ... when the last meeting took place...' and his 'Confidential Memorandum' ('Joint Commission Correspondence, Part 1' pp. 212-13, 215)

[110] 'Confidential Memorandum' (ibid. p. 215)

for a fifty-year lease of Pyramid Harbor would have outlasted any likely gold rush and have given Canada ample time to build an alternative route into the Yukon from its own territory. Professor Penlington suggests that Laurier was attracted, and that he long remained reluctant to break off talks.[111] If so, his cabinet saw things differently. The Justice Minister told him that 'A concession which falls short of sovereignty is not worth taking ... I am sure that in Ontario the public will be much better satisfied if you stand for your rights, than if you make what they regard as undue concessions for the sake of obtaining a treaty'.[112] On 4 February five ministers rushed down to New York to stiffen the Canadian Commissioners; and Herschell's attempts to get these 'to follow ... their own judgment' in the face of 'unreasonable pressure' from their Cabinet colleagues proved unavailing. When it was all over, Sifton saw things as 'in a very satisfactory shape, and the best evidence of that is the furious wail from [Opposition leader] Tupper whose campaign thunder is entirely destroyed.'[113]

As Sifton's biographer observes, Canada lost little, even along the border, from the Commission's breakdown. There were occasional scares, and Canada continued to pay lip service to the danger of trouble should gold be found in a disputed area. But 200 troops had been sent to the Yukon in 1898 to support the hundred Mounted Police. Moreover the miners had gone to the Klondike, as to the Fraser in 1858, to make money, not trouble. And though no permanent border agreement could be reached, the United States had accepted a temporary frontier at the summits of White and Chilkoot Passes, with further negotiation in 1899 agreeing another on the Dalton Trail Chilkat Pass route. W.C. Cartwright, indeed, felt Canada was lucky *not* to have acquired Pyramid Harbor. For though a Chilkat railway could certainly be built, the progress already made on the White Pass line rendered

---

[111] Penlington, *Canada and Imperialism* pp. 127-8
[112] Mills to Laurier, 25 Jan. 1899 (Tansill, *Canadian-American Relations* p. 178)
[113] Herschell to Fairbanks, 24 Jan. 1899, and to Salisbury, 7 Feb. ('Joint Commission Correspondence, Part 1' pp. 156, 198); Hall, *Sifton. The Young Napoleon* pp. 203-4; Brown, *Canada's National Policy* pp. 384-5

this unlikely. If so, 'after incurring considerable expense' in setting up Pyramid Harbor, 'the Canadian Government would find it impossible to divert the trade from Dyea and Skagway', leaving Pyramid a 'white elephant'.[114] Nor did Canada in fact need possession of a Lynn Canal port to get back 'the trade of the Yukon District'. In 1898 three-quarters of the goods entering the Yukon had indeed come from the US; but by 1900 more relaxed US customs regulations, the White Pass railway, and the shift from individual stampeders to larger-scale capitalised mining had so changed things that the same proportion was now sourced from Canada.[115] Canada, then, could afford to wait.

But the London government did not wish to; and in April 1899 Chamberlain asked Ottawa 'what concessions to the views of the United States' it would be prepared to make 'to obtain a settlement'. By June Chamberlain had concluded that little would come from 'further telegraphic correspondence' and asked Ottawa to send 'some responsible officer' to London to see 'whether some understanding can be reached' by direct talks.[116] Ottawa dragged its heels. But Lord Salisbury took advantage of the presence in London of the Public Works Minister Israel Tarte to develop another proposal for Pyramid Harbor. He now suggested to the American ambassador that Canada might accept 'a perpetual lease' of a small, fenced area: US laws and customs regulations would apply there; but a railway might be built thence to the Yukon, with goods sent on in bond 'without intervention of United States officials'. The idea was passed to Washington, and the British chargé reported that Secretary of State Hay thought the scheme promising, while the press was 'on the whole favourable'

---

[114] 'Confidential Memorandum' ('Joint Commission Correspondence, Part 1' p. 216)

[115] Hall, *Sifton. The Young Napoleon* p. 200; MacDonald, 'Seattle, Vancouver, and the Klondike' pp. 241-2, 244-5

[116] Chamberlain to Governor-General Lord Minto, 28 April 1899 (*British Documents … from the Foreign Office Confidential Print*, 11 *Expansion and Rapprochement, 1899-1905* [hereafter *British Documents* 11] p. 39); Colonial to Foreign Office, 13 June 1899 (ibid. pp. 62-3)

(perhaps more accurately, acquiescent) to what they were told of it. Chamberlain pressed the scheme strongly on Governor-General Minto, observing that if the US administration accepted, 'they would be making a substantial concession'. For 'whatever arguments may be based on letter of Treaty of 1825, careful examination of United States' case ... based on continuous uncontested jurisdiction ... shows that it is unassailable.' So he was sure 'your ministers will not wish to sacrifice only chance of obtaining an all-British route to Yukon' and 'would acquiesce in action of Her Majesty's Government.'[117] Minto put this to Laurier, saying that 'if the conditions suggested' enabled Canada to secure a communication from the Lynn Canal, 'it might be better to accept them at once, rather than wait' for an arbitration that might prove 'of very doubtful advantage'. But Tarte had already wired Laurier to ask whether the scheme would be acceptable, and had been bluntly told, 'No. Leave matter altogether to us here.' And Minto found Laurier 'absolutely decided not to accept the proposal'; for 'even if it gave satisfactory communication [to the Yukon], it would not settle the boundary difficulty' elsewhere.[118]

In relation to Alaska, the British hand was weak. There were, though, hopes of strengthening it through linkage with the negotiations over the building of a 'trans-Isthmian' (later

---

[117] Salisbury to the British chargé in Washington Reginald Tower, 12 July, and to the US ambassador in London Joseph Choate, 18 July, 1899; Tower to Salisbury 28 July; Chamberlain to Minto, 21 July – *British Documents* 11 pp. 71, 72, 73-4, 82. The difficult former Commissioner General Foster told Hay the proposal might do - though he feared the Canadians would seek 'an exclusively British port' and the perpetual lease of a strip of land (rather than simply the right to build a railway) between Pyramid Harbor and the Yukon, and would himself like to limit the lease to 99 years – Foster to Hay, 25 July 1899 (US Archives RG59 E927)

[118] Minto to Chamberlain (private), 24 July 1899 (ed. Paul Stevens and John T. Staywell, *Lord Minto's Canadian Papers* i *1898-1904* (Toronto, Champlain Society, 1981) pp. 107-8); Brown, *Canada's National Policy* pp. 395-6. Laurier later secured cabinet endorsement of his objections – Confidential Print, FO 414/161, 'Boundary between the British Possessions in North America and the Territory of Alaska. Further Correspondence XI', 'February to December 1899' pp. 102-3

'Panama') Canal. To reach the Caribbean from San Francisco during the Spanish war, the U.S.S. *Oregon* had had to make a 66-day dash around the Horn. Congress wanted a Canal to secure a short cut. But to preclude a clash of interests in Central America, the United States and Britain had, by the 1850 Clayton-Bulwer treaty, jointly engaged *not* to 'obtain or maintain' exclusive control over any future 'trans-Isthmian' canal. Legally, this treaty could only be revised with British consent, and the US administration duly sought this, though many in Congress would have been happy to charge ahead regardless. When the American diplomat Henry White first approached Lord Salisbury in late 1898, the latter was relaxed. But as the Joint Commission faltered, the British cabinet came to fear 'there would be serious dissatisfaction' if they yielded 'a point so obviously to the advantage of the United States, without some diminution at least of the causes which might bring the two countries into conflict'. Both Salisbury and Chamberlain made this point to White.[119] And Salisbury had asked Pauncefote whether 'the Alaska boundary question' could be 'settled in the same Treaty' as the de-negotiation of Clayton-Bulwer. Hay, who strongly rejected Canada's Alaskan claims, deplored Britain's bid to make 'the Clayton-Bulwer matter depend on the successful issue of the Canadian negotiations'. And he convinced Pauncefote, and through him the Foreign Office, that trying to combine the two questions in the Canal treaty 'would arouse the violent hostility of the Extremists', against whom it was 'all the [US] Government can do to maintain the "general [Clayton-Bulwer] principle"' of the Canal's neutrality. Any American concession, Pauncefote advised, would 'only be given separately, and in recognition of the friendliness of British policy.'[120]

---

[119] Salisbury to Pauncefote, 26 Jan., 3 and 15 Feb., 1899 (*British Documents* 11 pp. 2-3; 'Joint Commission Correspondence, Part 1' p. 153); White's 4 February account of an interview with Chamberlain (Allan Nevins, *Henry White. Sixty Years of American Diplomacy* (New York, 1930) p. 147)
[120] Nevins, *White* p. 146; Pauncefote to Salisbury, 6 Feb. 1899 (*British Documents* 11 p. 16)

This made linkage more difficult. But Chamberlain still hoped for parallel negotiations 'to secure ... a reasonable adjustment of the other questions' in return for concessions on the Canal. In April 1899 he 'strongly urged' deferring Clayton-Bulwer discussion until Washington was 'prepared to agree a reasonable arrangement for settling the Alaska Boundary'; and in May he told the Canadian Government that 'up to the present the Foreign Office have accepted this view'.[121] That, though, must be doubtful: a draft Convention revising Clayton-Bulwer was indeed pigeon-holed; but a senior Foreign Office official had told White in February that Britain 'would give way', though if the Joint Commission failed 'we must adhere to diplomatic forms and allow a certain time before doing so.'[122] By May, even the Colonial Office felt that 'we can hardly postpone a [Clayton-Bulwer] settlement ... indefinitely in order to gain concessions for Canada in Alaska' that 'they would not have required' but for their own 'supineness' in not protesting at the proper time against American settlement of Dyea and Skagway.[123] By the end of the year Congress had become impatient, and seemed likely to vote to build the Canal regardless both of Clayton-Bulwer and of the multi-lateral safeguards it enshrined (which the Administration wished to preserve). By now, too, Britain was internationally isolated over the South African War. America, observed Pauncefote, 'seems to be our only friend just now & it would be unfortunate to quarrel with her' over 'Canadian negotiations which are of a purely local character.'[124]

London accordingly put it to Ottawa that only signature of the pigeon-holed Convention revising Clayton-Bulwer could prevent the passage of much worse Congressional legislation and an 'affront' to President McKinley, 'whose friendly attitude is in

---

[121] Colonial to Foreign Office, 13 March and 11 April 1899 (*British Documents* 11 pp. 9, 23); Chamberlain to Minto (*Lord Minto's Canadian Papers* i p. 65)
[122] White to Hay, 17 Feb. 1899 (Campbell, *Anglo-American Understanding* p. 135)
[123] Sir John Anderson's 15 May 1899 minute (cited in ibid. pp. 144-6)
[124] Pauncefote to Salisbury, 19 Jan. 1900 (Campbell, *Anglo-American Understanding* pp. 189-90)

the present condition of public affairs of great importance'; and Ottawa duly waived its objections.[125] But though Britain thus accepted the Convention, Congress did not, insisting instead that the United States must be allowed to fortify the Canal. So Anglo-American negotiations resumed, with Hay also offering a treaty on Alaskan arbitration. Once more Britain sought to link the two issues, telling the Canadian government in July 1901 that it hoped to get better terms on Alaska if the two issues 'were treated at the same time'. But the linkage was now quite as much to pressure Ottawa as Washington. For Britain went on to stress that 'if boundary question further delayed, we may lose advantage that our readiness to settle the canal question gives us', while in October the Governor-General was asked to tell his ministers that the Canal negotiations were 'proceeding quickly, and that if we are to have any indirect advantage therefrom we' needed to have 'their views on draft Treaties at earliest possible date'.[126] There was no move to condition the Canal talks on a satisfactory Alaskan settlement; in November all was agreed, and in January 1902 the Hay-Pauncefote treaty signed. The Alaskan issue now stood alone.

The other notable development of late 1901 was the discovery of a plot by the picturesquely named 'Order of the Midnight Sun' 'to take possession of the Yukon Territory' once the river froze. The Yukon Field Force troops had been withdrawn in 1900, and the plotters supposedly calculated that new 'troops could not reach them over the ice for at least six weeks'. Meanwhile they planned 'to rush [the NWMP barracks in] Whitehorse, take the smaller detachments along the' Yukon, and then seize Dawson; once there, they would establish a 'Republic of the Yukon' and

[125] Chamberlain to Minto, 30 Jan. 1900, and Minto's 1 Feb. reply (*Lord Minto's Canadian Papers* i pp. 256-9)
[126] British despatch of 2 July 1901, quoted in Laurier to Minto, 14 August (*Lord Minto's Canadian Papers* ii p. 55); Chamberlain to Minto, 8 Oct. 1901 (*British Documents* 11 p. 202)

raise money by issuing promissory notes.[127] In preparation, a Manifesto announced the intention to 'establish a republic', listing grievances against 'the present corrupt and incompetent rule of British Columbia and North-West Territory governments'; and a supplementary June 1901 'Letter to the Citizens of Skagway' warned of the danger of being bypassed by a Canadian port elsewhere on the Lynn Canal or by an all-Canadian railway, whereas Skagway would almost certainly become the state capital should the Yukon be 'annexed to the United States'. Meanwhile the Order's two founders travelled around trying to raise money. On 16 September 1901, the ice seller and gambler H. Grehl left his papers at a Canadian-run store, which turned them over to the Mounties. Grehl then fled. And though his partner Clark stayed on for a time in Skagway, he too left in November.

Subsequent investigation showed that there was very little to the affair. Despite promises of over $25,000 'from the most prominent man in Skagway', and later claims of support from 'many influential people' including two US Senators, only $2,400 was actually contributed (with a further $1000 advanced by Clark). No arms or ammunition were secured; and when the NWMP contacted the US troop commander in Skagway, he was shocked and promised 'he would not permit any such organization to exist' there.[128] The NWMP were fairly relaxed – this may not have been the first mare's nest they had encountered.[129] Sifton and

---

[127] Inspector Staines (Dawson) to Superintendent Primrose (Whitehorse), 20 Sept. 1901; Fred White (Comptroller, NWMP) reporting the results of later investigation to Sifton, 1902 – David Ricardo Williams, *Call in Pinkerton's: American Detectives at Work for Canada* (Toronto, 1998) pp. 126, 134-5. Fred Clark to the *Poverty Bay Herald* (San Francisco), 30 Dec. 1901 (accessed 3 Aug. 2017), and Pinkerton's report of May 1902 conversations with Clark (*Call in Pinkerton's* pp. 32-3)

[128] Scott Dumonceaux, *The Conspiracy; the Canadian Response to the Order of the Midnight Sun and the Alaska Boundary* (University of Saskatchewan, M.A. thesis, Sept. 2013) esp. pp. 10, 21-2, 30-1, 38-9, 89-91; Williams, *Call in Pinkerton's* pp. 126, 132-4

[129] For plans in 1897/8 'to overpower the NWMP and officials and ship them down the Yukon ... so that the conspirators could take over the country', see Dumonceaux, *The Conspiracy* pp. 17, 80. Three 'things', observed the Yukon

Laurier were less so. Their response did not go beyond standard precautions. But, Scott Dumonceaux suggests, the episode may have led them to take the possibility of future trouble seriously.[130] Though they had adopted an inflexible negotiating line, they had always *talked* of the danger of trouble with America were gold to be found in a disputed area. And in 1902 there do seem to have been real fears that such trouble might trigger intervention by the headstrong new President, Theodore Roosevelt.

* * * *

In January 1902 Roosevelt had told his ambassador in London to 'Let sleeping dogs lie'.[131] He did not want to act on Alaska till Britain had concluded its South African War (as was done on 31 May). But the British Military Secretary in Washington, Colonel Kitson, repeatedly warned that 'the longer we wait, the worse terms we shall get.'[132] And the diplomat Cecil Spring-Rice, who had been staying with his close friend the President, came to Ottawa to relay Roosevelt's views: while Roosevelt, Hay, and Senator Lodge were

> 'personally friendly to Canada and care little about the boundary question *per se*, they cannot avoid recognising the feeling in the United States, especially among the foreign element, grows more hostile to England every day, and more adverse to any … compromise… in the face of this animus,

---

Census Commissioner (in connection with 1898) 'held the conspirators back: the fear of the police, the want of a bold leader, and the knowledge that a force of Canadian regulars [the Yukon Field Force] … was advancing into the country'

[130] The Canadian government's response is discussed in Dumonceaux, *The Conspiracy* chap. 3. Lord Minto shared these fears, despite reassurance from the US commander in Skagway (Carmen Miller, *The Canadian Career of the Fourth Earl of Minto* (Waterloo, Ont., 1980) p. 164)

[131] Nevins, *White* p. 192

[132] Col. Gerald Kitson to Lord Minto, 13 May 1902; also Kitson to Pauncefote and Minto, 26 and 28 March, and Kitson to Minto, 24 May – *Lord Minto's Canadian Papers* ii pp. 139-40, 155, 161

Roosevelt dare not risk in arbitration an inch of territory in Alaska. Apart from this ... the President personally is of opinion that ... the overwhelming strength of the United States' case ... render[s] it impossible for them to agree to arbitrate... every day lessens our chance of securing an arrangement even seemingly defensible..., and yet to a settlement we must come if we wish to avert rupture and possible war ... Mr. Spring-Rice urges that we should look the question squarely in the face, even though ... we should be obliged to forego our claim to the heads of the inlets... perhaps this might be done at least sacrifice of our dignity, by extending the present provisional boundary, and by having it ... marked on the ground throughout the entire _lisière_. He says the game of the Democratic party is to keep this question open as a running sore, hoping for an opportunity of bringing about a collision in the disputed territory of which no man may see the end.'[133]

Minto showed his correspondence to Laurier, who said 'Kitson's opinion entirely tallied with the information' 'from his own private agent in Washington'. The 'pith of it is that the President is expecting a strong anti-British movement with which it will be difficult for him to deal – & which might complicate any Alaskan frontier proposals.'[134]

This was, perhaps, not good advice. Roosevelt had long thought that 'we might as well let the _modus vivendi_ be ... it would be best when we have reached a settlement not to disturb it'. The Senators he consulted in early 1902 agreed. And he later

---

[133] Pope to Laurier, 21 May 1902 (_Minto's Canadian Papers_ ii pp. 159-60n.) Pope felt Spring-Rice looked at the question 'exclusively from an Imperial point of view' as something 'it would be convenient for England to have ... out of the way', but also that he thought Roosevelt and his friends wished 'it disposed of, more from a desire to preserve the English alliance, than from any material advantage the United States might obtain over Canada in Alaska'

[134] Minto's Journal account of his 3 June 1902 talk with Laurier, and his 4 June letter to the Foreign Secretary Lord Lansdowne (ibid. pp. 165-6, 168)

wrote that he had told both Pauncefote and Kitson they should 'let the thing rest'. For 'if they persisted in taking the thing up it would make it necessary for us to finish it.'[135] What Laurier wanted, he told Minto in June 1902, was 'a modus vivendi frontier in extension of the present one, to be drawn along the whole line of frontier - ... if this was done a frontier line would at any rate be created ... which though nominally temporary, might continue indefinitely.' If so, the two men's wishes for the foreseeable future were not that far apart. But instead of letting things be, Laurier looked to inconspicuous talks while he was in London for the Coronation festivities, hoping to pre-empt trouble from hypothetical future gold finds by agreeing a line in areas where there had, as yet, been no occasion to do so. This inevitably involved what Roosevelt had wanted to avoid, 'taking the thing up' – especially if, as Minto told the Foreign Minister Lord Lansdowne, 'in deference to Canadian public opinion we must do something to save our "amour propre"' (probably at the southern end of the 'debatable land', 'where American claims are not near so strong').[136]

Deeply 'impressed with the gravity of the Alaska problem', Lansdowne agreed to see Joseph Choate, the US ambassador, unofficially to get things moving.[137] Laurier, though, did not stick to his extended *'modus vivendi'* idea, but instead surprised Henry White by saying that 'what he would like is an arbitration in order to "save his face" ... vis a vis his [own] people'. Later he told Choate that the Canadian government 'would probably not object

---

[135] Roosevelt had, he said, also repeated this to Pauncefote's replacement, Sir Michael Herbert, in the 1902-3 winter – Roosevelt to Arthur Hamilton Lee, M.P., 24 April 1901, and to Elihu Root, 8 Aug. 1903 (ed. Elting Morison, *The Letters of Theodore Roosevelt* iii (Cambridge, Mass., 1951) pp. 66, 546; Pauncefote to the Foreign Secretary Lord Lansdowne, 28 March 1902 (*British Documents* 11 pp. 263-4)

[136] Minto's account of his 3 June 1902 talk with Laurier, and his 4 June letter to Lansdowne

[137] Lansdowne to Spring Rice, 6 June 1902 (FO 800/144 fo. 156); Minto's 'Conversation with Laurier and Lansdowne, 24 June 1902 (*Lord Minto's Canadian Papers* ii pp. 170-1)

to an arbitral tribunal composed of six members', an American requirement the Canadians had always rejected on the grounds that it would end in a three-on-each-side deadlock.[138] Roosevelt's response was unenthusiastic. He did not take the possibility of trouble very seriously, believing he had sufficient troops in the area to control the miners; and he felt 'the Canadians have no right to make a claim based on the possible effect of their own wrong-doing' in advancing 'this wholly false [territorial] claim'. He was prepared for further talks. 'But really it is difficult for me to make up my mind to any kind of arbitration.' What he would do was to 'appoint three commissioners to meet three' of theirs 'if they so desire', but only 'to try to fix the line', 'not to yield any territory whatsoever.'[139]

Back in Canada, Laurier secured his cabinet's acceptance of a three-a-side Commission, a concession he had, before leaving for Britain, promised not to make.[140] And Lord Pauncefote's newly appointed successor, Sir Michael Herbert, made it his mission to secure a Commission. At first Hay talked only of one whose members would 'place their reasoned opinions on record'. But in December, as he later wrote, he managed to persuade Roosevelt to accept one whose majority decision should be final, because 'I felt sure that we could convince any great English lawyer that our contention was just'.[141] The British government jumped at this prospect of finality, insisting only that the terms of reference should not prejudice the issue (as, in the Canadian view, all

---

[138] White to Hay, 28 June 1902 (Nevins, *White* pp. 192-3); Lansdowne to the British chargé in Washington, Arthur Raikes, 16 July 1902 (*British Documents* 11 pp. 270-1)

[139] Roosevelt to Hay, 10 and 16 July 1902 (Roosevelt, *Letters* iii pp. 286-8, 294-5)

[140] John W. Dafoe, *Sir Clifford Sifton in relation to His Times* (Toronto, 1931) p. 217. The cabinet was then tied up by an unconnected political crisis

[141] Herbert to Lansdowne, 17 Oct. 1902 (*British Documents* 11 pp. 276-7); Hay to White, 20 Sept. 1903 (Nevins, *White* p. 198). Though the US had bombastically pressed Britain in 1895 to arbitration over Venezuela with a neutral umpire, it had resolutely refused to try this over Alaska, Hay observing that 'we know enough of arbitrations to foresee the fatal tendency of all arbitrators to compromise' (to Whitelaw Reid, 27 July 1899 (Thayer, *Hay* ii p. 207)

previous US drafts had done). So, on 24 January 1903, after a last pro-forma Canadian bid for genuinely neutral arbitration, the Hay-Herbert treaty was concluded, providing for 'six impartial jurists of repute [three from each side] who shall consider judicially the questions submitted to them'. Roosevelt relied on his friend Senator Lodge to see the treaty through the Senate. As Lodge later recalled, North-Western Senators said they would support it only if they were happy with the choice of US Commissioners. Lodge revealed that these would be himself, Senator Turner (Washington), and the War Secretary Elihu Root – all men fully committed to the American claim. Lodge then pushed ratification through on a voice vote, thus circumventing the constitutional need for a two-thirds majority.[142]

Roosevelt later said he had asked two Supreme Court justices to serve. Both had declined - which was just as well since (as one of them had confirmed) had they served, they would have felt 'that judicially the case did not admit of a compromise' and stood out 'for a decision on every point in favor of the American view', thus ensuring deadlock.[143] At the time, though, what was clear was that Roosevelt's Commissioners were not 'impartial jurists of repute', and Canada was shocked. Its cabinet had not liked the Hay-Herbert treaty, and many ministers now wanted to drop it. Laurier and Minto both tried, indirectly, to get Washington to reconsider the choice of Lodge and Turner, prompting Foreign Office fears that they might thereby derail the whole process. So, though London had asked the Canadian government for comments, it then decided not to wait, and, in what Laurier termed 'a slap in the face for Canada', cut things short by ratifying

---

[142] Lodge's 1925 recollections, reprinted in James White, 'Henry Cabot Lodge and the Alaska Boundary Award', *Can.H.R.* 6:4 (1925) p. 334; Herbert suspected that Lodge had bought the retiring Senator Turner's vote by promising him appointment as Commissioner (to Lansdowne, 24 Feb. 1903 – FO 800/144 fo. 296); Penlington, *Alaska Boundary Dispute* pp. 71-2

[143] Roosevelt to Arthur Hamilton Lee, 7 Dec. 1903 (*Letters* iii pp. 665-6); Hay spent an hour trying to get Justice White to reconsider his refusal to serve (Herbert to Laurier, 23 Feb. 1903 – FO 800/144 fo. 286)

the treaty.[144] The Colonial Office was not happy; but Chamberlain eventually replied to a Canadian complaint by saying that had Britain refused to ratify, the 'United States would have taken the law into its own hands, and Canada as well as we would have found ourselves face to face with a most critical situation which I believe it was the intention and interest of the Canadian government to avoid'.[145]

This reading of Roosevelt's likely reaction was correct. He stated his basic position, in typically strong language, on several occasions. Thus, in a July 1903 letter meant to be shown to Chamberlain, he declared that:

> 'Nothing but my very earnest desire to get on well with England and my reluctance to come to a break made me consent to the appointment of a Joint Commission ... However, there were but two alternatives. Either I could appoint a commission and give a chance for agreement, or I could do as I shall of course do in case this commission fails, and request Congress to make an appropriation which will enable me to run the boundary on my own hook.

> ...I earnestly hope the English understand my purpose. I wish to make one last effort to bring about an agreement through the commission ... But if there is a disagreement I wish it distinctly understood ... that in my message to Congress I shall take a position which will prevent any possibility of arbitration hereafter ... [and] render it necessary for Congress to give me the authority to run the line as we claim it ... without any further regard to the attitude of England and Canada. If I paid attention to mere abstract right, that is the position I ought to take anyhow. I

---

[144] Miller, *The Canadian Career of Earl Minto* pp. 166-7

[145] Penlington, *Alaska Boundary Dispute* pp. 73-81; Laurier to Herbert, 20 Feb. 1903 (FO 800/144 fo. 291); Minto's notes of conversations with Laurier, 26 Feb. and 7 March, and Minto to Chamberlain, 8 and 9 March, 1903 (*Minto's Canadian Papers* ii pp. 261, 271-3); Chamberlain to W.S. Fielding, 2 April 1903 (cited by Penlington, p. 81)

have not taken it because I wish to exhaust every effort to have the affair settled peacefully and with due regard to England's dignity.'

Again in October, 'I do wish' the British 'could understand that this is the last chance, and that though it will be unpleasant for us, if they force me to do what I must do in case they fail to take advantage of this chance, it will be a thousandfold more unpleasant for them.'[146]

These letters, and still more Roosevelt's sending instructions to his own Commissioners and attempts to push the British government into leaning on theirs, have played badly with many historians: Penlington referred to 'a jingoist mood that apparently possessed Roosevelt [from June] until the boundary was settled', while to Tyler Dennett it seemed 'as though in the entire boundary matter the President was delivered into the possession of his most evil genii'.[147] But this has been challenged. David Haglund and Tudor Onea contend that Britain (a fellow Great Power) 'was handled with kid gloves throughout the dispute', unlike the lesser Canada; Roosevelt's 'refusal to back Britain into a shameful corner was part and parcel of his diplomacy of honour, buttressed as this was by an operational code that would not countenance causing a peer state to lose face.'[148] Probably they protest too much – in later life Roosevelt remarked that while Hay 'was a fine

[146] Roosevelt to Oliver Wendell Holmes, 25 July, and to Elihu Root, 3 Oct., 1903 (*Letters* iii p. 529-31, 613) – cf. also Roosevelt to Root, 8 Aug., to Hay, 29 June, 29 July, and 21 Sept. (ibid. pp. 507, 532-3, 546, 603), and to Lodge, 29 June, 1903 (H.C. Lodge ed., *Selections from the Correspondence of Theodore Roosevelt and Henry Cabot Lodge* ii (New York, 1925) [hereafter *Roosevelt Lodge Correspondence*] p. 37, and the June meeting described by Howard K. Beale, *Theodore Roosevelt and the Rise of America to World Power* (Baltimore, 1956) p. 130
[147] Penlington, *Alaska Boundary Dispute* pp. 88-9; Tyler Dennett, *John Hay. From Poetry to Politics* (New York, 1937) p. 357
[148] David G. Heglund and Tudor Onea, 'Victory without Triumph: Theodore Roosevelt, Honour, and the Alaska Panhandle Boundary Dispute', *Diplomacy & Statecraft* 19:1 (2008) pp. 20-41, esp. pp. 33, 37

Secretary of State, he was much too gentle a person to handle the kind of big stick that was necessary' in the Alaskan connection.[149] But Roosevelt's dictum was 'Talk softly', as well as 'Carry a big stick'; and his Alaskan warnings to Britain were all delivered in a quiet and genuinely friendly fashion – unlike Grover Cleveland's 'twisting of the lion's tail' over Venezuela in 1895.[150] Also, provided the Tribunal awarded Roosevelt the main point, the Lynn Canal and other inlets, he was much readier than is commonly stated, indeed rather readier than the American Commissioners, to bargain over what he saw as lesser matters. There were, said the letter to Holmes that was to be shown to Chamberlain, points like 'the islands in the mouth of the Portland Channel' 'which the commission can genuinely consider', and 'a chance for honest difference and honest final agreement' in regard to the supposed line of mountains along the coast. Indeed Roosevelt told Hay he would be 'glad to use' 'those little [Portland Channel] islands' 'as a makeweight in the Alaska boundary matter'.[151]

After the usual written submissions, the Commissioners (on the US side, Root, Lodge, and Turner, on the British, Baron Alverstone [Lord Chief Justice of England], Sir Louis Jetté [Lt.-Governor of Quebec, and a former Judge], and Allen Aylesworth [a leading Ontario barrister]) started to hear oral argument in London on 15 September 1903. This had its moments: when the United States' David Watson was brandishing a cane to illustrate points on a map, he speared his glasses, and they flew under the British side's tables. 'With an "Oh! Lord!" the American orator came to an abrupt stop, while ... Counsel of His Britannic

---

[149] Mark Sullivan to White, 6 Oct. 1925, quoted by Tansill, *Canadian-American Relations* p. 263

[150] Similarly, though there is debate over Roosevelt's handling of Germany during the 1902-3 Venezuelan debts crisis, Beale concludes that he probably did, as he later claimed, quietly threaten naval intervention, and then publicly praise the Kaiser's apparently unprompted change of course and proposal of arbitration (*The Rise of America* pp. 396-401)

[151] Roosevelt to Holmes, 25 July 1903, and to Hay, 15 Sept. (*Letters* iii pp. 530, 601)

Majesty scrabbled about on the floor in search of the missing eyes!'[152] Lodge and Root were impressed by Sir Edward Carson's oratory and disappointed with Watson's presentation. But, as Lodge observed, 'so far as effect on the decision of the Tribunal goes it makes no earthly difference. That decision will be reached by the Commissioners and it does not depend on the arguments.'[153]

Things seemed promising. Herbert heard that the American Agent, General Foster, was 'in favour of a compromise according to which the Canadians should be given their claim in the South the Americans getting their own way in the North.' And on 19 September White wrote that Alverstone had been talking 'quite freely' to Lodge and Root, and had 'intimated that he is with us on the main question'. Equally there 'seems to be unanimity in thinking that the Canadians have a good case upon the Portland Canal', with Root saying that Senator Turner would 'give way' on this 'and on Prince of Wales Island'.[154] Lodge reported to Roosevelt that Alverstone 'feels bound on the law and the facts as at present advised to hold that the [boundary] line goes round [not across] the heads of the inlets, which is, of course, the main contention.' On the Portland Canal he 'takes very decisively the British view.' On question 7, 'What, if any exist, are the mountains referred to [in the 1825 treaty] as situated parallel to the coast?', Alverstone wanted to pick 'out a series of mountains' that would reduce the lisière 'to as narrow bounds as possible, his idea being, I presume to try to let the Canadians down as easily as possible.' After discussion with Ambassador Choate,

> 'We are all agreed that if Alverstone decided in our favor on ... the heads of the inlets ... we could afford, with a slight modification, to accept their Portland Channel; but we were also agreed that we could come to no definite

---

[152] F.M. Carroll, 'Robert Lansing and the Alaskan Boundary Settlement', *International History Review* 9:2 (1987) p. 285
[153] Lodge to Roosevelt, 29 Sept. 1903 (*Roosevelt Lodge Correspondence* ii p. 61)
[154] Herbert to Lansdowne, 10 Sept. 1903 (FO 800/144 fos. 332-4); White to Hay, 19 Sept. 1903 (Nevins, *White* p. 197)

conclusion ... until we saw what line he proposed to make under question 7.'[155]

The Commissioners became stuck over this line. The Americans sought to expedite things by getting the British government to lean on Alverstone. White had just received a tough letter from Hay warning that if the Tribunal did not reach agreement, Roosevelt would 'hold the territory' and 'emphasize ... our sovereignty in a way that cannot but be disagreeable to the Canadians'.[156] White asked Root whether he should show this to the British Prime Minister, Arthur Balfour, with whom he was about to spend a weekend. On 2 October Lodge and Root told White the Tribunal was 'in danger of breaking' as a result of *Canadian* pressure; he should urge Balfour to tell Alverstone the British government would support him in taking a stand against this.[157] White duly talked to Balfour. He 'never heard directly' whether Balfour did anything in response. But Balfour's secretary, J.S. Sandars, 'let me know very confidentially that he had two interviews with Lord Alverstone'.[158] And on 9 October White arranged a meeting between Balfour and Lodge, who repeated much the same message, 'only manifesting more anxiety than I should as to the probability of failure.'[159]

---

[155] Lodge to Roosevelt, 24 Sept. 1903 (*Roosevelt Lodge Correspondence* ii pp. 57-9). Lodge asked Roosevelt to cable if he disapproved. Instead Roosevelt wrote (on 5 October) that he was happy to leave decisions on the mountain line to the Commissioners, and that 'Of course, we can yield on the Portland Canal Islands, if Alverstone goes with us on the main contention' (ibid. pp. 66-7)
[156] Hay to White, 20 Sept. 1903 (Nevins, *White* p. 198)
[157] Root to White, 2 Oct. 1903, and Lodge to White (two letters), 2 Oct.– Tansill, *Canadian-American Relations* pp. 254-5; Nevins, *White* p. 200
[158] White to Hay, 20 Oct. 1903 (Nevins, *White* pp. 200-1). White also showed Sandars Roosevelt's 26 September letter (ibid. p. 199) reiterating his intention, absent a Tribunal agreement, of treating the disputed territory 'as ours' and reducing 'to possession' that part of it he did not already control – White to 'My dear Arthur' [Balfour], 8 Oct. 1903 (John Satterfield Sandars Papers, Bodleian Library, Oxford, X Films 2/8, MS Eng. Hist. c. 745 fo. 48)
[159] White to Hay, 20 Oct. 1903

Oral pleading before the Tribunal ended on 8 October, and tension mounted. Deadlock over the mountains continued, and on the 14th Choate told Lansdowne that 'now or never is the time to save the situation', and that they must talk confidentially. 'The upshot of our conversation', Choate later wrote,

'was that the Commissioners, or four of them [the Americans plus Alverstone], must agree on the drawing of the line, and that ... we might ourselves agree on what would be a satisfactory line, and perhaps, if necessary, advise the Commissioners what we thought ... I left satisfied that he and Mr. Balfour would, if they had not already done so, tell Lord Alverstone what they thought as to the necessity of agreeing upon that line, and that the present chance of settling the controversy ought not to be lost.'[160]

Lansdowne's version was less dramatic. Choate was indeed 'very solemn over the consequences of failure'. He had been 'surprised when I told him that Alverstone was not "riding to orders" and would certainly resent a suggestion that he decide the questions referred to him otherwise than according to the evidence. But he evidently wished me to understand that the U.S. government was favorable to the idea of compromise' - with the American view prevailing on the 'main point (as to inlets)', the British winning on the Portland Canal, and with 'a transaction over the ... mountains parallel to the coast. I expressed myself strongly in favour of a reasonable give and take settlement as between the two governments, but stuck to my opinion that it was impossible to press our Commrs.'[161]

---

[160] Choate to Hay, 20 Oct. 1903 (Tansill, *Canadian-American Relations* pp. 258-9n.). Later, however, Choate back-tracked, first asking that the letter be destroyed, then cabling that 'These were only my conclusions not from anything said' by Lansdowne 'but from the necessity of the situation as it then appeared' (Campbell, *Anglo-American Understanding* p. 338n.)
[161] Lansdowne to Balfour, 16 Oct. 1903 (Add. MS. 49,728 fos. 71-3)

Earlier, though, Lansdowne had written that 'if there is to be any discussion as to ... bringing about' a 'compromise', 'the F.O. had better not be officially concerned ... For there are other means of arriving at the desired result & I have already taken steps to ensure that they shall not be neglected.'[162] He now repeated 'what had passed to Alverstone', and believed him 'disposed to accept a compromise' on the mountains 'if we get our way as to the Portland Channel. I made no secret of our great desire for a settlement and I have no doubt that he will do his level best not to let the tribunal separate without effecting one.'[163] Sandars too had 'a long talk' with Alverstone, who said 'that he is now in a very tight place.' He was 'very much annoyed' with the Americans, but was straining 'every nerve to bring about a decision, and the matter is not quite hopeless.'[164]

Three questions were at issue: on the islands in the Portland Canal, Alverstone expected American concession; on the most important issue, US ownership of the land immediately above the Lynn Canal and other inlets, he endorsed the American position; but the reason he chose for doing so (not the only possible one) required a mountain line close to the shore. Accordingly, he asserted that his two last positions stood or fell together, and between Portland Canal and White Pass held out 'stiffly' for a line following the mountains 'nearest the shore' as against one ten leagues inland. Most of the Commissioners' time was spent on this topic, which was discussed on 5, 8, 12, and 14 October.[165] For the Americans felt that even if they won over the heads of the inlets, they could not afford to have the lisière 'cut down too much', and that (as Senator Turner insisted) they would have to rest whatever

---

[162] Lansdowne's 14 Sept. 1903 reply to Herbert's 10 Sept. letter about Foster (FO 800/144 fo. 336)

[163] Lansdowne to Balfour, 16 Oct. 1903

[164] Sandars to Balfour, 14 Oct. 1903 (the date of Lansdowne's talks with Choate and Alverstone) – Add. MS. 49,761 fos. 112-14

[165] Lodge to his daughter Constance Gardner – John A. Garraty, 'Henry Cabot Lodge and the Alaska Boundary Tribunal', *New England Quarterly* 24:4 (1951) pp. 485, 488, 490, 491

line they conceded on 'a *tenable* theory on which we can stand at home'. Things were not helped by the absence of reliable maps, which led Alverstone to consider reaching a decision 'on the Lynn Canal and the Portland Canal', and declaring that on the mountains between them there was too little evidence to come to a decision.[166]

Root, too, felt that 'the insufficiency of the surveys was such' that the mountains question could not be answered 'on any judicial grounds'; and on the 15th the Americans sent 'a long despatch ... laying the situation before the President and asking his opinion'. Alverstone, they said, 'stands stiffly for line following mountains nearest the shore around heads of inlets, and giving us a strip only a few miles wide along the shore ... To stand on the ten marine leagues throughout would in all probability involve a disagreement on all but the' inlets 'question and possibly on that'. Past surveys were so incomplete that it was impossible (save perhaps near Mt. San Elias and around the Lynn Canal) either to identify the appropriate mountains for any boundary differing 'from ten marine leagues line' or to show that Alverstone's 'proposed line near the coast cannot be the true line'. So one possibility was a year's adjournment to permit a proper survey, even though this might neither alter Alverstone's views nor provide any objective answer. The President was asked whether this would be preferable to 'an immediate vote which would result in a disagreement on all but the [inlets] question and possibly on that.'[167]

When the Commission resumed on Friday the 16th, Alverstone carried Lodge off to his own room in the Foreign Office, saying 'matters were reaching a crisis & something must be done'. Lodge replied that he had been unable to come up with a mutually acceptable line, but Alverstone repeated 'that we must reach a decision, that he would make great sacrifices'. So the Americans

---

[166] Lodge to Roosevelt, 24 Sept. 1903 (*Roosevelt Lodge Correspondence* ii pp. 57-9; Sandars to Balfour, 14 Oct. 1903

[167] Choate to Hay, 15 Oct. 1903 (Tansill, *Canadian-American Relations* p. 257 n.), and Lodge to Constance Gardner, 19 Oct. (Garraty, 'Lodge and the Alaska Boundary Tribunal' pp. 491-2)

recessed, and 'after some hours got a line out'. Then, on Saturday morning, Washington's reply to their 15 October query arrived. The administration 'evidently did not like the idea of an adjournment, & it was also evident, were ready to take less than we really hoped to get', provided they could announce a favourable decision on the inlets. In this context, the Commissioners were authorised to accept the 'English contention' that the Portland Canal ran 'north of Pearse and Wales Island'. After reading this, Lodge told his daughter, he and Root showed Alverstone their line, 'which with a modification which we expected to make for him at the Stikine he accepted substantially as we had drawn it.' Then, when all the Commissioners had assembled, 'we produced our line & fell to on the maps, Lord Alverstone repeating there his substantial agreement, the Canadians holding sullenly aloof.'[168]

Aylesworth later gave a more dramatic account. When the Canadian Commissioners arrived, they found Root and Turner in the room. Lodge came in and whispered to Root, who went out through the door Lodge had come by. Root then came back to talk to Lodge. Lodge left and then returned. Finally 'Lord Alverstone entered by the door through which Lodge and Root had passed.'[169] Presumably something was being stitched up. There followed a vote on the Portland Canal: the American Commissioners agreed that this ran north of Wales and Pearse Islands; but to the Canadians' horror, Alverstone then joined the Americans in leaving the islets of Sitklan and Kannaghunut to the United States. He also, as expected, sided with them in according the US a continuous lisière 'separating the British possessions from the ... waters of the ocean.' That done, the Commissioners returned to the mountains line, with a 'Final struggle over one or two points'

---

[168] Lodge to Constance Gardner, 19 Oct. 1903 (Garraty, 'Lodge and the Boundary Tribunal' pp. 491-3)
[169] Aylesworth's 1942 recollections – Douglas Cole, 'Allen Aylesworth on the Alaska Boundary Award', *Can.H.R.* 52 (1971) p. 48

before this too was settled on Monday 19 October.[170] Alverstone proudly told Balfour,

> 'I have settled the Alaska Boundary with one slight exception ... I have had a tremendous fight for 6 days and it has been one of the hardest of the many hard jobs I have had. I have had to yield certain minor matters on which I pressed for a decision more favourable to Great Britain, had I not yielded I should not have got a settlement at all...
>
> I have much to tell you when you come to town which I cannot put in a letter.'[171]

In forwarding this to Balfour, Lansdowne noted that the 'Canadians are undoubtedly much upset by the decision';[172] and their anger would assume huge dimensions. Minto and Laurier both thought that 'probably Canada's realest loss has been in the Klehini and Porcupine Creek district' (on the Dalton trail to the Chilkat Pass) that had passed to Canadian control in 1899. Laurier told Minto 'he could not understand why the [*modus vivendi*] frontier there ... had not been confirmed.'[173] There is a Canadian tradition that, in drawing his line there, Alverstone simply forgot the *modus vivendi*, and 'his United States colleagues did not feel it was incumbent on them' to remind him. This seems unlikely. Aylesworth recalled that all the Commissioners had been present when this section was agreed, and that he had himself

---

[170] Lodge to Constance Gardner (Garraty, 'Lodge and the Boundary Tribunal' pp. 493-4)

[171] Alverstone to Balfour, 20 Oct. 1903 (Add. MS. 49,728 fos. 78-9). The 'slight exception' was a gap in the mountains line from north of the Stikine River to south of White Pass (see the map in Penlington, *Alaska Boundary Dispute* p. 101), which was left to be filled (as it proved amiably) by Commissioners in 1905 (ibid. pp. 115-16). Alverstone told Balfour he had 'fought for hours' over this, chiefly against Senator Turner

[172] Lansdowne to Balfour, 20 Oct. 1903 (Add. MS. 49,728 fos. 75-7)

[173] Minto to Colonial Secretary Lyttelton, 25 Oct. 1903 (*Minto's Canadian Papers* ii p. 357)

intervened to ensure that the boundary should touch Mt. Fairweather. For the most part, though, it was a matter of Alverstone doing 'what he could with Root and Lodge', saying 'that the line had gone out too far at one place and ought to come in at another and so on' – in short, bargaining.[174] And the new line on the Dalton trail probably took account of the fact that American miners on Porcupine Creek had been upset by the *modus vivendi*, 149 of them protesting to President McKinley.[175] But whatever the reason, and whatever the degree of Canada's 'loss' there, the 'value of the district', as Minto put it, 'luckily has not been so far impressed on the Canadian public'.

The islands in the Portland Canal were quite another matter. On 12 October Alverstone had, Lodge wrote, 'read an opinion against us on the Portland Canal', and this was copied to all the Commissioners.[176] The topic was not discussed again until Saturday the 17th. By then the Americans had been authorised to accept the 'English contention as to North Channel of Portland Canal', and they struck a deal with Alverstone covering both this and the general course of the mountain line. The Portland Canal Islands had always been discussed as a unit, and the 'English contention' would have given Canada all four; but there was a Canadian belief, though no hard evidence, that the Americans first conceded it, then at the last moment drew back and refused to sign unless they got the two small islands, Sitklan and Kannaghunut. Be that as it may,[177] Alverstone used his position as

---

[174] White, 'Lodge and the Alaska Boundary Award' pp. 345-6; Cole, 'Aylesworth on the Alaska Boundary Award' pp. 475-6. An American assistant supposedly secured the inclusion in the boundary line of 'Kate's needle', the mountain named after his wife

[175] Dumonceaux, *The Conspiracy* esp. pp. 23-6

[176] Lodge to Constance Gardner (Garraty, 'Lodge and the Boundary Tribunal' p. 490); Alverstone to Minto (in Lyttelton to Minto, 17 Nov. 1903), and to Anderson, 17 Nov. – *Minto's Canadian Papers* ii p. 368, 368n.

[177] Aylesworth's 1942 interview (Cole, 'Aylesworth on the Alaska Boundary Award' pp. 476-7); White, 'Lodge and the Alaska Boundary Award' p. 346. When Lodge told Roosevelt on 24 September that if Alverstone backed the Americans on the inlets, they could afford to accept British views on the Portland

Chairman to call for separate votes on the two groups: the Americans then conceded Wales (on which there was an American cannery and some US War Department sheds) and Pearse; but Alverstone joined them in awarding Sitklan and Kannaghunut to the US. He then revised his 12 October paper accordingly, but in a slapdash way, altering the conclusion but not the argument.

* * * * *

Though Alverstone felt the 'two tiny islands' were 'of absolutely no value', he feared he would be 'howled at by Canada' for his decision. He was. No sooner had the Tribunal's Award been signed than the Canadian Commissioners told the *Times* that the lost islands commanded 'the entrance to Portland Canal, to Observatory Inlet, and the ocean passage to Port Simpson', destroying 'the strategic value to Canada of Wales and Pearse Islands'.[178] Minto had written earlier that Wales and Pearse Islands 'give command of Observatory Inlet, & therefore Port Simpson' where 'three trans-continental railways' were 'all planning to have their Pacific Terminus'; and Lansdowne had duly noted 'the increasing value of Port Simpson'.[179] But the Governor-General and the Canadian government had both vetoed the suggestion that the topography should be quietly examined 'from a military standpoint ... with a view of deciding if the Alaska boundary affects it'.[180] And it was not until Minto was taken aback by the scale of resentment against the Award that he really looked at the map. He then told Laurier the idea that 'the islands allotted' to the US affected Port Simpson was 'completely ill-founded'. They were 14 to 15 miles away, and their strategic value

Canal, he had added 'with a slight modification'. This may indicate that he still meant to try for Sitklan and Kannaghunut
[178] *The Times*, 21 Oct. 1903 p. 7
[179] Minto to Lansdowne, 23 Jan. 1903, and Lansdowne's 21 Feb. reply (*Minto's Canadian Papers* ii pp. 252, 258)
[180] Col. R.E. Foster (British military attaché) to the Washington chargé A.R. Raikes, 1 July 1903, and Raikes to Lansdowne, 5 Aug. (*British Documents* 11 p. 327)

was in any case 'cancelled by the far greater importance of Wales and Pearce ... The whole position appears to me to be completely misunderstood by the Canadian public.'[181] Next month Laurier admitted privately that the islands' value was 'very much exaggerated'. But he tried to discourage investigation by the Canadian militia's Commander, Earl Dundonald. And though Dundonald's report amply confirmed Minto's view, Laurier relocated the projected railway terminus and port to Prince Rupert, thirty miles back from Port Simpson (actually a far better site).[182]

In 1902 Laurier had revived the Alaska question in hopes of extending the *modus vivendi* line to the foot of the panhandle and placing it on a permanent (if professedly 'provisional') basis. Lord Alverstone largely delivered this, though now *de jure*. Laurier had also gone for an even-numbered Tribunal, something Canada had previously always vetoed, with its 'British' side consisting of two Canadians and one senior U.K. judge (Laurier had initially suggested the Lord Chancellor). It was entirely predictable that the US Commissioners, whether 'jurists of repute' or not, would back the American case, just as their Canadian counterparts would go the other way. As the Colonial Office appreciated, this would expose Britain 'to a great risk. It is quite possible that the English jurist might take the view of his American colleagues ... and unless he succeeded in converting ... the Canadians – which is not likely – Canada would certainly complain that she had lost her case through the presence of a British jurist on the Commission'.[183] That was, of course, what happened.

---

[181] Minto to Laurier, 22 Oct. 1903 (*Minto's Canadian Papers* ii pp. 351-3)

[182] Minto's 17 Nov. Conversation with Laurier (*Minto's Canadian Papers* ii p. 370); Minto to Lyttelton, 24 and 29 Dec. 1903 (CO 42/893 fos. 377, 394); Dundonald to Militia Minister Sir F. Borden, 8 March 1904 (*British Documents* 11 pp. 338-9 – and p. 327 for the similar views of British Naval and Military Intelligence); G.R. Stevens, *Canadian National Railways* ii (Toronto, 1962) p. 124

[183] Sir Montague Ommany (then in temporary charge of the Colonial Office) to Lansdowne, 7 Jan. 1903 (cited in *Minto's Canadian Papers* ii p. 275n.)

In October Laurier had told Pope that 'he would be satisfied to get Wales and Pearse islands, but that if' the Tribunal 'went against us on that he would feel we were badly used'. And on the 18th Minto could write that what he and Laurier hoped for was 'to lose in the North' on the Lynn, and to 'gain in the South' on the Portland, Canal.[184] But in writing to the Canadian Commissioners, Laurier had laid down a marker in case things went wrong. If they could not 'get our full rights' [that is, if they lost 'in the North'], they should 'fight for our contention on the Portland Canal ... that point must be decided in Canada's favour. If we are thrown over by Chief Justice, he will give the last blow to British diplomacy in Canada.'[185] Lord Alverstone did secure Wales and Pearse, and it was open to Laurier to declare victory (as indeed Minto urged on 20 October). But by then Laurier had lazily accepted the Canadian Commissioners' view that Sitklan and Kannaghannut 'command entrance to [Portland] canal and destroy strategic value Wales and Pearce', and had wired back that abandoning them was 'one of those concessions which have made British diplomacy odious to Canadian people': the Commissioners should 'protest in most vigorous terms'.[186] Chamberlain's take on all this was that Laurier wanted to settle Alaska 'at almost any price, but he wanted at the same time to throw the blame of any concession on to ... [Britain's] shoulders'.[187]

This interpretation may be too Machiavellian. But it was certainly convenient for the Laurier administration to have

---

[184] Pope's paraphrase of Laurier's letter, which reached London on 13 October (*Public Servant: the Memoirs of Sir Joseph Pope* (Toronto, 1960) p. 298); Minto to Arthur Elliott, 18 Oct. 1903 (*Minto's Canadian Papers* ii pp. 347-8)

[185] Laurier to Sifton, 8 Oct. 1903 (Dafoe, *Sifton* pp. 228-9)

[186] Minto to Laurier, 20 Oct. 1903 (*Minto's Canadian Papers* ii p. 351); Laurier to Clifford Sifton (in his capacity as the British Agent), 18 Oct. (Dafoe, *Sifton* p. 233)

[187] Chamberlain to Minto, 28 Dec. 1903 (*Minto's Canadian Papers* ii p. 403). Chamberlain believed that had he not been in South Africa at the crucial time, he would not have let the Lord Chief Justice serve as Commissioner, and would have put Britain in a position to make it clear that 'every step was taken in concurrence with Sir Wilfrid'

scapegoats. For Canadian anger was genuine. The Commissioners' experience in London had been unfortunate: they 'did not meet with the high official recognition they expected', and their 'wives were not sufficiently taken care of!'. More seriously, Alverstone 'did not understand the calibre' of the Canadians, and treated them 'as juniors'; and he had been 'too friendly to the Americans'.[188] The last straw was the way in which, on 17 October, Alverstone caballed with the Americans while leaving his colleagues to kick their heels, and then, with no prior notice, reversed his 12 October opinion on the Portland Islands so as to award two of them to the US. Aylesworth, Jetté, and Clifford Sifton (now the British Agent) had already contemplated pulling out and had had to be told not to by Laurier. Their feelings now bubbled up again, and, this time encouraged by Laurier, they let fly in the *Times*: there was 'no process of reasoning whereby' the Tribunal's line between the two groups of Portland Islands 'can be justified'; 'our observation of the discussions ... has led us to the conclusion that, instead of resting upon any intelligible principle, the choice' of line along the mountains 'has been a compromise between ... entirely irreconcilable views of the true meaning of the ... treaty'. They did not consider the Tribunal's findings on either the islands or the mountain line judicial, and had therefore 'declined to be parties to the award'. The 'course the majority determined to pursue ... ignored the just rights of Canada', and they had had 'to witness the sacrifices' of Canada's interests, 'powerless to prevent it'.[189] Alverstone drafted a reply, but was persuaded by Lansdowne not to plunge into 'a newspaper controversy'.[190] So the Canadian Commissioners' version held the field.

---

[188] Minto to Lyttelton, 19 Nov. 1903, and his 11 Nov. Conversation with Sifton (*Minto's Canadian Papers* ii p. 363, 376); Lansdowne to Balfour, 20 Oct. 1903, summarising his talk with Pope (Add. MS. 49,728 fo. 76)
[189] *The Times*, 21 Oct. 1903 p. 7
[190] Lansdowne to Balfour, 23 Oct. 1903 (Add. MS. 49,728 fo. 80). Lansdowne thought Alverstone's rejoinder 'effective', but the private explanations Alverstone later sent to Aylesworth and Laurier failed to convince

The Award, wrote Sifton's *Manitoba Free Press*, 'will take its place with the [1842] Ashburton Treaty as damning evidence of Great Britain's subserviency to the United States, where the latter's interests conflict with those of Canada',[191] a subserviency caricatured next day in the *Toronto News*:

'LORD ALVERSTONE (to Canada): Is there anything more I can do for you?

CANADA: We would like to go on drawing breath.

LORD ALVERSTONE (to Messrs. Root, Lodge and Turner): Any objection to our young friend continuing to use the atmosphere?

MESSRS. ROOT, LODGE and TURNER (cheerfully): None at all just now.

LORD ALVERSTONE (with a judicial air): My decision is that you are entitled to the temporary use of all air not required for United States purposes.'

Lord Minto thought that a mountain was being made out of a molehill, and that Laurier would have been 'quite prepared to welcome' the Tribunal's decision had it 'not been for the loss of the two small islands'.[192] But, as Sir Richard Cartwright said, 'the actual award of the Tribunal was not the most important point, he was much more impressed with the manner the decision had been arrived at and the general effect the whole history of the negotiations would undoubtedly have on Canadian public opinion'. It was, Minto told his wife, 'impossible to exaggerate the angry feeling here – open talk of separation &c. &c. – ... Alverstone is accused ... of having after he had agreed with the Canadian Commissioners on the boundary, changed his mind

---

[191] 22 Oct. 1903 – Munro, *The Alaska Boundary Dispute* p. 92 – and pp. 88-93 for further press comment
[192] Minto to Lyttelton, 23 Oct. 1903; Conversation with Cartwright, 13 Nov.; Minto to Alverstone, 8 Dec. – *Minto's Canadian Papers* ii pp. 357, 367, 386

owing to pressure' from the American Commissioners, a charge that had 'set the whole of Canada on a blaze of indignation.'[193] The agitation was, though, largely a newspaper storm – the only direct actions that historians cite are the Toronto Board of Education's flying the Union Jack at half-mast on Trafalgar Day, the booing of 'God Save the King' in Victoria, and the Mayor of Vancouver's statement that he would not be surprised if the outcome was 'a strong and widespread movement looking towards ... Canadian independence.'[194]

Such a movement did not emerge. No serious effort was made to fan the flames. Sifton told Lord Minto 'he certainly was not going to make any remarks in public.'[195] And when the issue was brought up in Parliament, Laurier declined to attack Alverstone. Instead he took up one theme of the press campaign by saying that the real trouble was that Canada lacked 'the treaty-making power which would enable us to dispose of our own affairs', and that they would 'ask the British parliament for more extensive powers'. But his colleague Cartwright spoke both of this, and of his own proposal for a Canadian agent in Washington, 'as a red herring which he hoped might be very advantageously used to draw the attention of the public from the embittered pursuit of the Alaska argument'. Nor, after things had settled down, was any demand for treaty-making powers in fact pressed.[196]

---

[193] Conversation with Cartwright; Minto to Lady Minto, 30 Oct. 1903, to Chamberlain, 14 Dec. – ibid. pp. 358, 365, 392

[194] Penlington, *Alaska Boundary Dispute* p. 106; Munro, *The Alaska Boundary Dispute* p. 9

[195] Conversation with Sifton, 11 Nov. 1903 (*Minto's Canadian Papers* ii p. 363)

[196] Laurier's speech – Canada, 9th Parliament, 3rd Session, Vol. 6, 14810-18 (23 Oct. 1903); Cartwright – *Minto's Canadian Papers* ii pp. 365-6 (13 Nov.) Similarly, nothing was done to build the direct railway line 'upon Canadian territory' to the Yukon, the need for which had been another theme of Laurier's speech

Commissioner Aylesworth, the person perhaps best placed to translate anger over the Alaska Award into a popular movement, had no intention of doing so. Some expected his reception by the Toronto Canada Club to generate a storm. But at the close of his speech there, Aylesworth pulled out all the stops. There had been concerns that the meeting would be one of 'resentment' –

'I felt that could not be so.

I am proud ... that the halls of these rooms are adorned with Union Jacks. (Applause)

I am proud that the people of Toronto still sing 'God Save The King' ... (Applause)

It would be a sad day if after losing ... [over Alaska], we should say that this shall be a weakening of the ties that bind us to the Mother Country. (Applause)

In the words of Burke ... 'Those ties, though light as air, are still as strong as iron.' (Loud applause)

Those ties can surely still stand the strain of many Alaska awards. (Loud cheers)

Two thousand years ago it was a man's proudest boast to be able to say "Civis Romanus Sum". Is it not now a matter of equal pride to be able to quote the words of a noble Canadian [Sir John Macdonald], 'British subjects we were born, British subjects we will die.' (Tremendous applause, the audience rising and cheering vociferously)

...Whatever is the result of the Alaska award, this much is certain, we believe that Canada is for England, and that Canada is part of the great and grand British Empire. (Loud applause and cheers)'

Had Aylesworth 'told the whole story', observed the *Globe*, 'such a fire would have been kindled as neither imperialistic exhortation nor trade preferences would soon put out. That Mr. Aylesworth understood is plainly the secret of his restraint and moderation.'[197] Perhaps. But as John A. Munro observes, 'for want of a leader the protest stultified'.[198] By December Minto could tell the King that the Alaska issue had 'for the time disappeared'; and a Colonial Office official observed that 'to judge from the newspapers' it 'has been only a 9 days wonder & has fallen much into the background – at least in Eastern Canada'.[199]

However Minto also wrote that the award would be 'hoarded up with other supposed grievances, such as the Maine frontier story &c. &c.'. It was: Lord Alverstone came to be coupled with Lord Ashburton in giving away Canadian interests to appease the United States.[200] Attitudes softened over time. But a fully revisionist account had to wait until 1972, when Norman Penlington wrote to liberate Canada from the 'hang-up ... of a bitter experience': "The truth shall make you free", and that 'truth' was that though, in the 'Great Evasion', Canada blamed Britain, it was Laurier who 'was chiefly responsible for the Alaska Award'.[201] In one respect, indeed, regret over Alaska bit deeper than that over Maine. There had been no attempt to seek revision of the Maine border. But in 1919, at the Paris Peace Conference, Prime Minister Borden was induced to suggest to Lloyd George and the Colonial Secretary Lord Milner that the United States

---

[197] *Toronto News*, 3 Nov. 1903 – CO 42/893 fo. 213; The *Globe*, 3 Nov. 1903 (Skelton, *Life and Letters of Laurier* ii p. 154)

[198] Munro, *The Alaska Boundary Dispute* p. 95

[199] Minto to the King, 18 Dec. 1903 (*Minto's Canadian Papers* ii p. 396); minute on Minto's 29-30 Dec. telegram (CO 42/893 fo. 394)

[200] Minto to Chamberlain, 14 Dec. 1903 – also his similar remark to Sifton (*Minto's Canadian Papers* ii p. 364, 392). In 1907 Governor General Grey thought of asking the members of the recently appointed Historical Manuscripts Commission to review the 'negociations between the U.K. and U.S. re Canada' with special reference to the Ashburton Treaty and Alaska. 'A statement ... signed by these impartial non-political Canadian historical scientists, will prick the bubble that at present fills the Canadian horizon. The idea that Canada has been sacrificed again and again by John Bull in his desire to cultivate the friendship of Uncle Sam is rooted so deep ... that ... nothing any Englishman can say will uproot it. Our only chance is to get the pickaxe into Canadian hands', 8 April 1907 (Grey Papers, Film c.1358 images 775-6)

[201] Penlington, *Alaska Boundary Dispute* pp. viii, 117

should cede the Alaska Panhandle, perhaps in return for British Honduras, perhaps simply to demonstrate its own devotion to idealism at a time when it was calling on Italy to give up Dalmatia. Unsurprisingly, nothing came of the idea.[202]

The Alaska Award had undoubtedly been viewed as a loss throughout English-speaking Canada (Quebec was less concerned). It had, in Minto's words, 'focussed much that was [previously] indistinct'; and it had emphasised, even among enthusiasts for the British connection, the feeling that Canada had interests distinct from, sometimes even in contradiction to, those of the Empire as a whole. But Minto was mistaken in believing that the consideration of its future relations 'with the Motherland' 'now appear[s] likely to be forced upon us'.[203] Such an evolution in fact proved very gradual. Perhaps the most that can be claimed is that the Award 'halted any rising imperial tide in Ontario', and so 'strengthened Laurier's hand in opposing the movement for closer [proto-federalist] imperial relations'. For 'English-Canadianism and ... full Canadian Autonomy, the First World War was the most important ... event', with Ontario's reaction to the Alaska boundary decision merely 'an important prelude.'[204]

A more immediate effect was to help turn Canada towards the Arctic. US action, hard on the Tribunal decision, to detach Panama from Colombia (in order to build the Canal) was seen as alarming: a Montreal *Star* cartoon, 'American Aggression', depicted the eagle asking, after eating bones marked 'Alaska' and 'Panama', 'Let me see; what else is there right now?'[205] The Canadian government

---

[202] Milner told Borden he favoured the scheme; but they should first get 'from some authoritative American source an intimation, however informal, that they really would be prepared to give up that strip of coast, or at any rate the bulk of it, in exchange for British Honduras' (Gaddis Smith, 'The Alaska Panhandle at the Paris Peace Conference, 1919', *International Journal* (Toronto) 17 (1961-2) esp. pp. 25-9)

[203] Minto to Lyttelton, 18 Nov. 1903 (*Minto's Canadian Papers* ii pp. 371-2)

[204] John A. Munro, 'English-Canadianism and the demand for Canadian autonomy. Ontario's response to the Alaska Boundary decision, 1903', *Ontario History* 57:4 (1965) esp. pp. 198-9, 203

[205] Penlington, *Alaska Boundary Dispute* pp. 113-14

fully shared this concern, and sought to remove what might otherwise have proved tempting morsels. In 1880 Britain had in theory transferred to the Dominion all its northern territory except Newfoundland and Labrador. But few steps had been taken to actualise Canadian control, and most exploration of the far north had been done by foreigners. In late 1903 the government decided the time had come for 'some system of supervision and control', and despatched the *Neptune* 'for the purpose of patrolling, exploring, and establishing the authority of ... Canada in the waters and islands of Hudson bay, and the north thereof'. Though the Colonial Office asked for a statement of Canada's claims (and anticipated that the waters of Hudson Bay would prove 'a very nice question to arbitrate about'), this was essentially a Canadian domestic matter.[206]

But, as a newspaper report from Ottawa put it, 'The Alaska Commission Award has set the [Canadian] Government thinking'.[207] US press reports and Senator Lodge's speeches on his return home prompted fears of American encirclement, and led Laurier to believe that the United States sought to acquire the French islands of St. Pierre and Miquelon. 'As these islands are contiguous to British territory [Newfoundland] and opposite to the entrance to the River St. Lawrence ... they are of more importance to Canada than to any other country'.[208] More generally, a Privy Council Memorandum observed, 'It has long

---

[206] Morris Zaslow, *The Opening of the Canadian North 1870-1914* (Toronto, 1971) esp. pp. 251-4, 259-6, 264-5 (citing the instructions given to the six-man police force sent out on the *Neptune*); minute on Minto to Lyttelton, 17 Nov. 1903 (CO 42/893 fo. 180)

[207] Ottawa Correspondent of the *Standard*, 21 Dec. 1903 (CO 42/898 fo. 325)

[208] Minto to Lyttelton, 25 Nov. 1903 (*Minto's Canadian Papers* ii p. 377); Canadian Government Memorandum enclosed in Minto to Lyttelton, 3 Dec. (CO 42/893 fos. 316-18). Privately, 'in answer to Minto's skeptical inquiry Laurier [even] reaffirmed his belief that the United States might seize Newfoundland' (Penlington, *Alaska Boundary Dispute* p. 134n.); on 8 Jan. 1907 Laurier told the Governor General of information that the US had approached France to buy St. Pierre and Miquelon ('which goes to show that the americans are trying to put their hands on everything available around Canada') and urged counter-measures (Grey Papers, Film c.1357 image 315-16)

been apparent ... that the most popular policy in the Republic is the extension of its territory', and that American 'public men and the press' see absorption 'as the natural destiny of Canada. In view of these sentiments it is obviously in the interests of the Empire' that the US should gain 'no additional territory ... in or adjacent to the northern half of North America.' It had recently tried to buy Denmark's West Indian islands; and 'as American whalers and fishermen frequent the waters opposite to the west coast of Greenland, it is not improbable that ... a proposal might be made to acquire Greenland from Denmark'. To obviate this, Canada proposed itself to buy both St. Pierre and Miquelon and Greenland, and asked Britain to set this in motion.[209] Nor was this entirely paranoia. Lodge firmly denied having talked of St. Pierre and Miquelon, and anyway the Colonial Office was sure France would never part with them – they were too valuable for both fishing and smuggling. But Greenland seemed another matter. Seward had been attracted by the idea of acquiring it (above p. 938), and Lodge had wanted to try for its inclusion in the purchase of the Danish West Indies. The British Ambassador Sir Mortimer Durand had been uncomfortable about Canada's actions in the north, forecasting that if 'anything high handed' was done to American fishermen, 'no one' would be 'more ready to fight than our friend Lodge'. And in 1905 Lodge was indeed telling Roosevelt he did not care for Laurier's language about Baffin Bay. 'What our rights there may be or what our trade amounts to I do not know but Laurier's tone is offensive ... What we ought to do is buy Greenland of Denmark ... it would end Laurier's talk about Baffin Bay', and, he later added, 'save trouble with Canada'. The Senate, Lodge believed, would back the purchase.[210] However Greenland

---

[209] Minto to Lyttelton, 25 Nov. and 3 Dec. 1903 (*Minto's Canadian Papers* ii pp. 377-8, 381-2); Canadian Memoranda, 1 and 3 Dec. (CO 42/893 fos. 315-18, 322-3)

[210] Durand to Lansdowne, 8 Jan. 1904 (FO 800/144 fos. 364-5); Lodge to Roosevelt, 12 May and 10 June, 1905, and Roosevelt's 24 May reply (*Roosevelt Lodge Correspondence* ii pp. 120, 125, 136). Lodge thought the Kaiser 'would make Denmark sell [Greenland] to us', and that it would prove 'profitable in

was not sold either to Canada or to the United States. Nor did the process of gradually pushing Canadian posts north,[211] and of demanding small licence fees from those whalers and explorers that Canadian cruisers managed to encounter, prove any bar to the settlement of the outstanding US-Canadian issues.

The moment the Alaska issue that had blocked progress in 1898-9 was resolved, Secretary Hay tabled another offer on pelagic sealing. This was premature, but by 1905 people were talking of reviving the Joint High Commission. However the US Senate did not like the idea, and Hay's successor, Root, instead sought to 'clear the slate' through 'Treaties on all outstanding questions'. Laurier's reaction to Root's June 1906 list of fifteen topics was that almost all could 'be easily disposed of', but that pelagic sealing and Atlantic fisheries presented real difficulties. Root had offered individual compensation for Canadian sealers, but not 'a national compensation in return for the relinquishment of a national right'. 'In 1899', Laurier said, 'we asked [in this connection] the use of a harbour in Alaska'. 'No Canadian government could carry their people in such a surrender ... unless it is accompanied by a satisfactory quid pro quo.' And for this Laurier required the ending of US tariffs on Canadian fish, offering in return 'free fishing in our waters' – in effect a return to the arrangements under Reciprocity and the 1871 Washington treaty (both abrogated by America).[212] The Foreign Secretary would have liked Laurier to be more forthcoming, adding alternative demands that the US Executive might be 'able to accept and get through the Senate', and there was some talk of trade reciprocity

---

minerals like Alaska'. Roosevelt was in less of a hurry, but did ask whether 'we could get the people to back us in buying Greenland as well as the Danish Islands'

[211] This process extended until Norway's 1930 relinquishment of its claims to Ellesmere Island (with Hans Island formally in dispute between Canada and Denmark/Greenland from 1973 until it was partitioned in June 2022)

[212] Laurier's position is most clearly stated in his 29 Sept. 1906 letter to Earl Grey and Grey's 25 Oct. letter to Foreign Secretary Sir Edward Grey that Laurier approved as 'a correct account of my position' (Grey Papers, Film c.1358 images 624-5, 630-7)

in coal and lumber, and of a US cession of its Roberts Point enclave south of 49°.[213] But Laurier continued to insist on 'free fish for free fishing' until it became quite clear that the Senate (led by Lodge) would never accept it. This made for a very awkward position, since the alternative to 'a free fish for free fishing arrangement and a settlement of all outstanding questions' seemed to be Canada's 'eventual withdrawal ... of all privileges enjoyed by American Fishermen' under the current 'modus vivendi', reversion to the legal position under the 1818 Anglo-American Convention, 'and the risk of a new Dogger-Bank incident in Canadian Waters!'.[214] A further difficulty was that the two sides had different views as to their rights under that Convention. But this may in fact have helped them to move towards a solution: over the course of 1907 support grew for referring these differences to arbitration by the Permanent Court at The Hague, thus decoupling them from Pelagic Sealing (on which Canada continued to negotiate toughly until 1911[215]). An Anglo-American General Arbitration Treaty was finally concluded in April 1908 providing for reference to The Hague of differences in the interpretation of treaties; the requisite Special Agreement defining the points at issue and the arbitrators' powers followed in January 1909; and when the case was heard in 1910, Canada's Aylesworth was the British Agent. The Tribunal's award was a compromise, but one broadly favouring the British. The British and Canadians ascribed this outcome to the merits of their case and the quality of its presentation. Root felt the judges had decided against the US 'before the argument began', the Austrian Professor Heinrich

---

[213] Sir Edward to Governor General Grey, 12 Jan. 1907, and Grey to Sir Richard Cartwright, 11 April (Film c.1358 images 702-4, 778)

[214] Earl Grey to Winston Churchill, 22 April 1907 (ibid., images 782-3). Newfoundland had already illustrated the danger. For when Lodge killed the 1902 deal that traded fishing rights for access to US markets, Newfoundland had responded with such tough fishing laws and regulations that Britain had had to intervene to arrange successive *modus vivendi* compromises. (In 1904 a panicky Russian fleet had shot up British trawlers on the North Sea's Dogger Bank, taking them in the fog for Japanese torpedo boats.)

[215] Gluek, 'Canada's Splendid Bargain', *Can.H.R.* 63:2 (1982) passim

Lammasch being particularly predisposed towards Britain by reason of its friendly attitude during the 1908 Bosnian crisis. Either way, a settlement was reached that had eluded so many previous attempts.[216]

The process of conciliation had been helped on by changes in personnel. Lord Minto had not much liked Americans and had been wary of the pro-American feeling prevalent in Britain. The next Governor-General, Earl Grey, aimed at settling 'every outstanding question between Canada and the United States'.[217] This was also the intention of Elihu Root, who became Secretary of State in 1905 on the death of the ailing Hay. Root felt the Joint High Commission's failure had left 'affairs with Great Britain in a mess', and he hired the Commission's former Secretary 'to work out... a statement of every question... and the causes of the failure to agree'. Building on this, he arranged for Grey to visit Washington to see the President and talk; he then sent Sir Mortimer Durand a draft pelagic sealing treaty and a 'general statement' of his views on other outstanding matters. A further impetus came in 1907, when Durand was replaced by James Bryce, who proved an outstanding Ambassador. In 1909 Bryce remarked that Canadian-American relations took up three-quarters of his embassy's attention; and he was always careful to keep Canada on-side, visiting Ottawa each year.[218] The outcome was impressive, 'eight different treaties and agreements', ranging from arbitration over the fishery question and 'Canada's Splendid Bargain', the 1911 US, British, Russian, Japanese pelagic sealing treaty, through the important 1909 treaty establishing a Joint US-Canadian Committee to manage water levels in, and extraction from, the

---

[216] Tansill, *Canadian-American Relations* pp. 94-119

[217] Grey to the Colonial Secretary Lord Elgin, 8 Feb. 1906 (Alvin C. Gluek, 'The Passamaquoddy Bay Treaty, 1910: a Diplomatic Sideshow in Canadian-American Relations', *Can.H.R.* 47:1 (1966) p. 7)

[218] Gluek, 'The Passamaquoddy Bay Treaty' pp. 7-9; Neary, 'Grey, Bryce, and the Settlement of Canadian-American Differences', *Can.H.R.* 49:4 (1968) pp. 358-9, 364; John Herd Thompson, 'Canada and the "Third British Empire", 1901-1939' in Phillip A. Buckner ed., *Canada and the British Empire* (Oxford, 1908) p. 93

Great Lakes and other Boundary Waters, to numerous less spectacular agreements. 'Bryce, Grey, Root, and Laurier', it has been observed, 'all had reason to be proud of their work'[219] – though Laurier's 1911 commercial Reciprocity Treaty proved a bridge too far and was repudiated by the Canadian electorate.

* * * *

Of these treaties, that most relevant to this book was the relatively minor 1908 Boundaries Treaty. This provided for marking or re-marking the boundary from coast to coast. But its chief purpose was to settle the line from the mouth of the St. Croix through Passamaquoddy Bay to the open sea. In 1817 the Commission under Article 4 of the Ghent Treaty had determined the ownership of the Bay's islands (above pp. 164-6) but had not sought to fix the water line. Uncertainty as to the border's precise course permitted 'for many years an easy liberality among the [local Lubec] people, whose occupation at one time was largely smuggling'. There was also, in Canadian eyes, progressive encroachment on their waters both by American fishing vessels and by the setting of fishing weirs on some disputed shallows. So in 1891 a Canadian cruiser seized seven US fishing boats.[220] Trouble was avoided through diplomatic discussion, and an 1892 convention provided for Commissioners to determine the water line. The US appointed Thomas Mendenhall, Canada W.F. King. (They were also to discuss the borders of the Alaska panhandle, which probably did not help their relationship.) They quickly agreed on most of the line, and, in the summer of 1893, marked it with stone pillars and buoys. But they disagreed over two points. One was an islet off Eastport called Pope's Folly. A literal reading of the 1817 award, as favoured by King, would have made it British. But this would have required an awkward kink in the natural boundary

---

[219] Neary, 'Grey, Bryce, and the Settlement of Canadian-American Differences' esp. pp. 379-80; Brown and Cook, *Canada 1896-1921* esp. pp. 174-7

[220] Thomas C. Mendenhall, *Twenty unsettled miles in the northeast boundary* (Worcester, Mass., 1897) pp. 13-14

channel, and Mendenhall produced a variety of reasons why the islet should be American. Then below Lubec there were two possible channels. Mendenhall had originally meant to accept the more westerly one. But that would have placed American fishing weirs in Canada; their Lubec owners protested; and Mendenhall had instead to demand the smaller and more crooked easterly channel that ran close by Campobello. Unable to resolve these differences, the Commissioners were in 1895 reduced to submitting separate reports. People had long lived with the uncertainty, and could continue to do so. Moreover, for most of the line, the Commissioners' markers survived, and, at least according to Mendenhall, were 'quite generally accepted as authoritative'.[221]

The dispute might well have been resolved had the 1898-9 Joint High Commission not been cut short by Alaska. Afterwards it had to wait till US-Canadian relations again improved. A 1908 treaty then directed that most unresolved Anglo-American border disputes should go to arbitration. Accordingly, the April 1908 Boundaries Treaty reconvened the 1890s Commission, with arbitration to follow in the event of disagreement. Each side submitted copious testimony, and, this proving mutually incompatible, negotiation followed. King, for Canada, offered to relinquish Pope's Folly, provided the boundary below Lubec followed the western channel. But talks broke down, as the division the US side offered of the shallows between the two channels proved, on inspection, to keep most of the fishing weirs and other assets in American hands.

To salvage things, Bryce visited the area. He concluded that while Pope's Folly might once have been valuable as a site for a fort, it was now only worth a couple of hundred dollars as a 'summer cottage or ... afternoon tea house'. Nor was the disputed fishing worth much. He therefore tried to persuade Laurier to accept the American offer. But Laurier refused. So Bryce pressed the United States to accept King's offer, stressing that the alternative, arbitration, would cost it $15,000. Eastport wanted to

---

[221] Mendenhall, *Twenty unsettled miles* esp. pp. 17-18, 23-5; Gluek, 'The Passamaquoddy Bay Treaty' pp. 2-4, and Map (p. 11)

agree; but there were fears that Lubec interests would then cause trouble, as they had when Mendenhall had contemplated accepting the western channel. The only solution was to buy them up. So four dilapidated fishing weirs were acquired with $4003 diverted from the moneys the US had appropriated to meet the costs of arbitration. Lodge and the senior Maine Senator were squared, and in May 1910 a treaty was formally concluded. That summer the corpulent President Taft drove out to view the waters in question. A Canadian gibed that if he meant to take possession of Pope's Folly in person, the US would have either to expand the island or shrink its President. But Taft himself commented that 'all the controversies between Great Britain and the United States ... are now settled or are in the course of settlement by arbitration and ... this is the first time in the history of the two countries when that could be said.'[222]

---

[222] Gluek, 'The Passamaquoddy Bay Treaty' pp. 10-21. The settlement was taken as ending all US-Canadian disputes over borders on land. A miniscule one has since cropped up over Machias Seal Island, ten miles south-west of Grand Manan, nine miles off the Maine coast. In 1832 New Brunswick established a lighthouse there, which is now maintained by, significantly, Canada's Department of External Affairs, with a bird sanctuary and attendant access controls attached. But Seal Island has not been mentioned in any treaty or Commissioners' award; and a Maine family claims to have acquired it in 1865. A more official US claim materialised in the 1970s, and was incorporated into US law by a Fisheries Proclamation in 1977. The area was not included in the zone of off-shore rights submitted to the International Court of Justice for judgment in 1981. It has occasioned little concern, but dove-cots were fluttered when, in 2018, US Border Patrol vessels stopped Canadian fishing boats. Elsewhere, the two countries have a number of conflicting claims to off-shore waters (David H. Gray, 'Canada's Unresolved Maritime Boundaries', Geography Dept., Durham University, IBRU *Boundary and Security Bulletin* 5:3 (1997) pp. 61-70): in view of global warming and the forthcoming carve-up of rights under the Arctic Ocean, the most important are over the Northwest Passage (an 'international strait' or as Canada maintains 'internal waters') and the projection into the Beaufort Sea of the Yukon-Alaska land border (which turns on the proper interpretation of the words *jusqu'à* in the 1825 Anglo-Russian treaty)

CHAPTER 15

Concluding Thoughts

Mexico was not Canada, and the story of the United States' southern border differs greatly from that of our present concern, its northern. So, of course, does that of other borders (the long Russian-Chinese border, the Polish-German border, France's eastern border...). 'International relations' theories stumble on the fact that most major happenings are quite largely sui-generis. They are also multi-causal. Probably the most studied historical event is the outbreak of the First World War. It was once depicted as the explosion of the 'long fuse', the inevitable result of the Great Powers being divided into two rival alliance systems. But so they were, and for a longer period, during the Cold War, which ended peacefully. Other commonly invoked explanations of 1914 include: Serbia's shift from Austrian client to the 'Piedmont of the South Slavs', and the Great Powers' eventual inability any longer collectively to control the young Balkan states; perhaps too readily perceived Austro-Hungarian fragility; exaggerated fears generated by Russia's rapid recovery from its 1905 disasters; a climate of exuberant nationalism, sometimes by way of escape from internal problems; military plans geared towards the offensive (when technology in fact favoured the defensive); the 'Anglo-German naval race' and the broader competitive military build-up after 1912; even the love life of Conrad von Hötzendorf. No one or two of these factors would by themselves have caused the War; it came from their inter-connected multiplication. Even so, 'what if' questions arise, including what Sir Adam Roberts has called the chauffeur's eye view of Sarajevo: what if Franz Ferdinand's car had taken a different route, or Gavrilo Princip had been as ineffective or inhibited as the other conspirators?

The story of the US-Canadian border is less complicated, as well as happier. But no single explanation governs all points of its evolution over the century-and-a-half here treated. So we shall first view it from some of the main 'international relations' perspectives, and then note outcomes that might well have been different.

The influence of law is clear from the outset. On 30 October 1782 the British Peace Negotiators brought over 'Books, Maps, and Papers, relative to the Boundaries' and John Adams 'all the essential Documents relative' to the boundary of Massachusetts. They had, Adams reported, to

> 'search, the Boundaries of Grenada the two Floridas, ancient Canada according to the Claims of the French, Proclamation Canada, Act of Parliament Canada &c and the Bounds of Nova Scotia and most if not all of the thirteen States'.

These 'documents' were, of course, mostly used as weapons, but they might also constrain their own side's claims: Adams later recalled that one American Commissioner pushed for a border further east, 'but his Colleagues observing, that, as the St. Croix was the River mentioned in the charter of Massachusetts Bay, they could not be justified in insisting on St. John's ... he agreed with them to adhere to the charter'.[1] The St. Croix was duly adopted.

---

[1] Adams' documents (which he took the unfortunate Comte de Vergennes through in detail when he asked after Sagadahoc) were: Governor Pownall's 'act of possession in 1759; the Grants & settlements of Mont Desert, Machias & all the other townships East of the Penobscot River: the orig[inal] Grant of James 1rst ... of Nova Scotia, in which it is bounded by the St. Croix River, ... the dissertations of Govrs. Shirley & Hutchinson, & the Authority of Governor Bernard' – Adams to Livingston, 31 Oct., 6 and 11 Nov., 1782 (ed. Mary A. Giunta, *The Emerging Nation. A Documentary History of the Foreign Relations of the United States under the Articles of Confederation, 1780-1789* i (Washington, 1994) i pp. 631, 639, 655-6), and Adams' 15 Aug. 1797 evidence to the Boundary Commissioners under the Jay treaty (*Second Statement on the part of Great Britain according to the Provisions ... for regulating the Arbitration ... under the Fifth Article of the Treaty of Ghent* (London, 1829), Appendix no. 4 pp. 6, 8)

But, as Jay's 1794 treaty put it, doubts arose as to 'what River was truly intended under the name of the River st Croix mentioned in the ... Treaty of Peace', and Commissioners were appointed 'impartially to examine and decide the ... question according to such Evidence as shall be laid before them'. The experiment was a success (though in identifying the river's 'source', mutual convenience was allowed to replace the Commissioners' legal judgement). Later, the treaty of Ghent concluded a second Anglo-American war on the basis of the status quo ante, and provided for Commissions to decide various disputed questions 'in conformity with the true intent of the ... [1783] Treaty of Peace'. In the first of these Commissions, that on the Passamaquoddy Bay islands and Grand Manan, the American Commissioner's wish to finish in time to take up his seat in Congress led him to accept their former division between the two countries. But his British opposite number, Thomas Barclay, had been brought to make this offer, despite his belief that the 1783 treaty entitled Britain to *all* the Passamaquoddy islands, by growing doubts as to Britain's claim to Grand Manan and worries as to how it might be handled by an arbiter.

The second (the most important) Commission was instructed, inter alia, that the 'point of the Highlands ... designated in the former Treaty of Peace ... as the North West Angle of Nova Scotia' had not 'yet been ascertained', and charged with identifying it 'in conformity with the provisions of the said Treaty'. This involved determining 'the boundary line which extends directly North to the ... North West angle ... [and] thence along ... the Highlands which divide those Rivers that empty themselves into the River St. Lawrence from those which fall into the Atlantic Ocean'. But it soon became apparent to the British Agent, Ward Chipman a New Brunswicker, that a due 'north line' from the St. Croix would cut across the strategic British winter route up the St. John to Quebec before it reached the watershed above the River St. Lawrence (or even that between the Restigouche and the St. John). So he developed a legalistic argument[2] to justify his

---

[2] This ran that the language used elsewhere in the 1783 treaty showed it did not regard either the Gulf of St. Lawrence or the Bay of Fundy as forming part of the

contention that the border should instead turn left at Mars Hill, a mere 40 miles north of the St. Croix, and run along the ridge he believed extended west from there. This became the British position; deadlock ensued; and eventually King William of the Netherlands was asked to arbitrate. He wanted to make a compromise award, giving Britain just room enough for its strategic route, and allowing the United States to keep the fort it was building on land the Commission's survey had shown to be north of the 45th parallel and therefore in Canada. The eminent Dutch jurist Cornelis van Maanen assured him that this was within his legal powers as arbiter. But both English and American lawyers, operating within a common law system, disagreed, and William's findings (prefaced by the words 'Nous sommes d'avis – Qu'il conviendra d'adopter') came to be taken as no more than recommendations. This mattered. For, as Secretary of State Livingston explained, had William simply declared even a perverse line to be that 'intended by the Treaty of 1783', the United States would have accepted it, and Maine could not have objected since the territory beyond the line could not, under the treaty, 'be within the state'. But mere *recommendation* of a 'convenient' border did not alter the legal position under the treaty, and Maine's consent would be needed for any change, since the United States had no power 'to circumscribe' a State's 'limits without its assent'.[3] It would be a decade before this difficulty was overcome – by inducing Maine to send, to participate in the negotiations with Britain's Plenipotentiary Lord Ashburton, a delegation empowered to give the state's assent to their outcome. Daniel Webster did this, in part, by secretly showing Maine's leaders (and its delegation) two maps apparently bearing boundary lines drawn by the American negotiators of 1782 that were consonant with the current *British* claim, and warning of the consequences should such maps come before a future arbiter. This prospect, together with the general wish

---

'Atlantic Ocean'; if so, 'Highlands' (watershed) between the River St. Lawrence and that Ocean could only be found well west of the 'north line' from the St. Croix

[3] Livingston to the British chargé Charles Bankhead, 21 July 1832 (Parliamentary Papers 1837-8 xxxix p. 17)

in Washington for a settlement, eventually led Maine's delegation to give the state's reluctant consent to the deal worked out between Webster and Ashburton – one broadly along the lines the King of the Netherlands had recommended (and that Britain had long been prepared to offer).

Soon afterwards, contention over Oregon became acute. Though there was no authoritative treaty to refer to, the formal negotiations of 1844-5 took the form of rival statements and justifications of the two sides' claims. These statements would, presumably, have proved useful had the issue been sent to arbitration as the British wished but the United States would never allow. As it was, the 1846 treaty was reached by other than legal means. It resolved the main issue, but its drafting proved to have been careless in not specifying the route the water border should take through the Gulf of Georgia. This would in 1859 occasion the briefly dangerous 'Pig War'; and though that was quickly damped down, it was 1872 before the issue reached the arbitration of the German Emperor. He found the channel favoured by the United States better fitted the terms of the 1846 treaty.

Further north, the borders of Russian America had already been settled by the US-Russian treaty of 1824 and the Anglo-Russian one of 1825. This latter reserved to Russia a strip (lisière) along the coast of what is now the Alaskan panhandle but permitted the British to cross it by river. In 1834 the Russian American Company (RAC) stopped the Hudsons Bay Company (HBC) from doing so, and was hit by a claim for damages (backed by the British Government). In 1838 the Russian government told the RAC it would have to settle, and this brought the two Companies to agree next year on a durable and mutually advantageous relationship. That ended with Russia's 1867 sale of Alaska to the United States, after which a number of Anglo-American frictions developed there. The first one of importance stemmed from the United States' wish to protect its Pribilof Island seals (a significant economic resource) from Canadian ships hunting them on the high seas. American cruisers arrested these, and to justify their actions the United States was reduced to claiming 'sole sovereignty' over much of the Bering Sea. This Britain could not accept, and the claim eventually went to a Tribunal of multinational judges meeting in Paris. In 1894 this first found against the United States, and then laid down 'conservation' rules governing the hunting of seals at sea. (These soon proved insufficient, and negotiations over 'pelagic sealing', increasingly on a multilateral basis, continued until 1911 when the issue, as far as it concerned Canada, was resolved by a US-British-Russian-Japanese treaty.)

The mid-1890s gold strikes in Canada's Klondike prompted a rush of would-be miners. Access usually ran via the head of the Lynn Canal, possession of which secured the United States, at least initially, most of the profits from outfitting them; and Canada's wish for an access that would be entirely within its own territory made the Alaska boundary a major Anglo-American issue from 1898 to 1903. But since that boundary was governed by the 1825 treaty, Canada's claim had to take the form of a rather strained interpretation of the treaty.[4] It was at first pursued through the diplomacy of the 1898-9 Anglo-American Joint High Commission, and later Canada hoped Britain could secure it as the price of its consent to revision of the Clayton-Bulwer treaty barring construction of a canal across the Panama isthmus. But when nothing came of this, Canada's Prime Minister Sir Wilfrid Laurier pressed for a final solution; this was delivered by at least a kind of legal arbitration. The Tribunal's composition cannot be said to have met the highest judicial standards, but it is hard to fault its decision on the Lynn Canal, the only really important issue. And while Roosevelt privately emphasised his readiness, in the event of any other outcome, to use the United States' locally overwhelming power, the Tribunal process did to some extent mask this, and would more successfully have built a golden bridge for Canadian withdrawal but for its handling of two insignificant islets in the Portland Channel further south.

---

[4] The 1825 treaty had said the border of the (now American) lisière should not be more than 10 marine leagues from the 'Ocean'. And whereas Americans equated 'Ocean' with 'tide-water', Canada saw it as ending where inlets became so narrow (6 miles across) as to be territorial waters, more than ten leagues below the head of the Lynn Canal

But if determination of the boundary's line was repeatedly framed, or at least influenced, by considerations of law, geographical determinism was much less in evidence. Admittedly this might be seen both in the 1782 adoption of a clear water boundary in the form of the Great Lakes, and in US acceptance in 1846 that Britain had to have the southern tip of Vancouver Island to avoid exclusion from meaningful access to the mainland coast. But though the 'Disputed Territory' between Maine and New Brunswick was best accessed via the latter's St. John River and depended on this to export its produce, law in the form of the 1783 treaty trumped geography, and most of it went to Maine. Further east, British North America's Maritime provinces had, in winter, no direct communication with Canada except by the route up the St. John, which though strategically important was *not* an artery of commerce. Indeed, as opponents of Confederation observed, Nova Scotian ships were more likely to be found in Calcutta than in Canada.[5] Nevertheless Nova Scotia and New Brunswick joined Canada in 1867, with Confederation bringing the Intercolonial Railway. West of Montreal, one can indeed talk, with many Canadian historians, of the early 'Empire of the St. Lawrence'. But its water communications lost their unique advantage with the United States' westward growth and its construction first of the Erie Canal in 1825 and then of railways. Beyond Upper Canada, North West and later Hudson's Bay Company traders were indeed serviced in summer from Montreal by water and from Britain by sea via Hudson's Bay. But by the later 1860s the combination of steamers on the Red River and railways to Minnesota had diverted the ordinary trade of the Red River settlement. And the inhabitants of St. Paul looked on Red River and the Plains beyond as natural dependencies, first economic and then hopefully political, until these were torn from them by the completion (in defiance of the Canadian Shield barrier) of the Canadian Pacific Railway. Building this had been the price of British Columbia's entry into Confederation. HBC posts on the West Coast had, despite their

---

[5] McLelan, Archibald Woodbury – *Dictionary of Canadian Biography*

river-and-portage communications with Montreal, essentially been serviced from the Pacific. From their outset, the colonies of Vancouver Island and British Columbia [B.C.] had depended largely on Californian trade. Rapid communication with Britain ran via San Francisco, and then overland; and Governor Musgrave observed that 'commercial intercourse would be easier with Australia than with Canada'.[6] The Canadian Pacific changed this, as it was meant to, and for the first time Canadian coins circulated freely in B.C.[7] Though the United States remained (as it had become in mid-century) Canada's chief trading partner, the Dominion was constructed, largely in defiance of geography, on an East-West axis; and later developments like the 1897 Crowsnest Pass rail freight Agreement further reinforced this.

But law and geography are only two factors in the composite of a state's interaction with the external world that, reified as the 'international system', largely (extreme neo-realists would say entirely) determines its international position and actions. Without US independence, North American borders would have been no more than provincial and would have been settled in a different way.[8] Without French intervention in the Revolutionary War Britain might still have been unable to subdue the majority of the Thirteen Colonies. But the United States would have been severely squeezed financially, and under intense pressure to reach some accommodation with the power that held New York city and looked to extend its coastal and peripheral occupations. As it was, the surrender at Yorktown, brought about by the partnership of a French fleet and an American army, broke Britain's will to continue the colonial war. In 1782 new governments switched to seeking a

---

[6] Governor Musgrave to Lord Granville, 21 Feb. 1870 (CO 60/38 fos. 153-4)

[7] Walter Sage, 'The Critical Period of British Columbia History, 1866-1871', *Pacific Historical Review* 1:4 (1932) p. 430

[8] The Canada-New Brunswick boundary dispute was eventually referred to Imperial arbitration, with an award in 1851. That between Ontario and Manitoba went to the Judicial Committee of the [Imperial] Privy Council, with an award in 1884; and in 1927 this similarly decided the case between Canada and Newfoundland over Labrador (A.F.N. Pole, 'The Boundaries of Canada', *Canadian Bar Review* 42 (1964) pp. 100-139)

pre-emptive peace with the United States, at first the better to fight their remaining wars, later to avoid becoming too dependent on France in the making of the general peace. Accordingly, as the Comte de Vergennes said when he saw the Anglo-American terms, Britain bought peace rather than made it.[9] The infant United States thus secured, at least on paper, far more of the 'old north-west' than either its military position or French wishes would have accorded. Also, though US envoys would in 1782 have welcomed the British recovery of West Florida that seemed likely to emerge from the Anglo-French-Spanish peace negotiations, the actual outcome, Spanish acquisition of all Florida, meant that on its southern border the United States had only to deal with powers that (unlike Britain) were soon much weaker than itself.

A decade later came other, longer, Anglo-French wars from which the United States would derive many benefits, most notably Louisiana. Though lacking the naval capacity to defend this, France had foolishly taken it from Spain; it extricated itself by selling to the United States. Previously, the US had stretched only to the Mississippi; now it reached the Rockies and could envisage extension to the Pacific. The 1803 King-Hawkesbury treaty would have taken the US-British border south from the Lake of the Woods to the Mississippi, but acquisition of Louisiana led President Jefferson to switch to an entirely new and more northerly claim, the 49th parallel. Though Britain rejected this, it would, four years later, have been conceded as part of a deal to keep the United States, while formally neutral, within the British trading sphere.[10] However, Jefferson refused to submit the Monroe-Pinkney treaty to Congress for ratification; and thereafter Anglo-American relations worsened rapidly until the United States

---

[9] Vergennes to de Rayneval, 4 Dec. 1782 (Giunta, *The Emerging Nation* i p. 706)
[10] In 1793-5 the United States had been bitterly divided over whether to join its former ally France in the war. Instead, John Jay and President Washington steered it into a deal whereby the United States secured, inter alia, the northern forts Britain still occupied despite the 1783 treaty, Britain an American alignment that morphed into the 1798-1800 US naval 'Quasi-War' with France. Monroe and Pinkney had in 1806 negotiated an updating of the Jay treaty

declared war in 1812. It did so for many reasons. But resentment over the seizures of US ships to enforce Britain's continental blockade and the pressing into the Royal Navy of the many crew members still viewed as British subjects was, if not a sufficient condition for American entry into the war, at least a necessary one; and the 'War of 1812' was to that extent a product of the wider European conflict.

The United States joined this just as French power started to crumble. Napoleon's unexpected collapse in 1814 enabled Britain to transfer some (though only a minority) of its forces to America, and to try what one year's campaign could do to achieve its maximum war aims. But its only really tangible military achievement was occupation of the Maine coast. The American peace negotiators proved remarkably stubborn; and by the autumn a mixture of international and domestic considerations inclined the British government to call it a day. 'We do not', wrote Lord Bathurst in September, 'think that the Continental Powers will continue in a good humour with our Blockade of the whole Coast of America beyond' the current campaign, while 'the prosecution of the War will not be popular here much longer'; and in November 1814, the Prime Minister explained that the government had been led to try to end the war 'by the consideration of the unsatisfactory state of the [European peace] negotiations at Vienna ... by the alarming situation in the interior of France', and by the political 'difficulties we shall have in continuing the property tax'.[11] International developments had that spring left the US dangerously isolated, but in the autumn they were working the other way. The upshot was the Anglo-American Treaty of Ghent which, when ratified in Washington, ended the fighting, though it did no more than prescribe ways of settling the most salient boundary disputes and left many other issues unresolved.

---

[11] Lord Bathurst to Henry Goulburn, 12 Sept. 1814 (W.L. Clements Library, Goulburn Papers); Lord Liverpool to Viscount Castlereagh, 18 Nov. 1814, and his similar explanation of 28 December to George Canning (C.D. Yonge, *The Life and Administration of Robert Banks, Second Earl of Liverpool* ii (London, 1868) pp. 73, 75)

Thus far the impacts of the 'international system' have been readily apparent. Thereafter they are less clear. Eighteenth century colonies had been caught up in European wars, and even US independence did not wholly disengage North America from this framework. However in 1815 a European balance was established that averted wars between Great Powers for decades, general war for a century, while leaving Britain broadly unchallenged outside Europe. A side effect was that the US and Britain were mostly left to work out their mutual relations between themselves.[12] Admittedly British ministers long doubted whether this could continue. In 1824 Liverpool and Canning, who had both been in office during the Napoleonic Wars, reminded their colleagues that 'peace, however desirable..., cannot last for ever. Sooner or later we shall probably have to contend with the combined maritime power of France and of the United States.'[13] In 1845, Peel, Wellington, and the War Minister Lord Stanley all saw a war with the United States as likely to lead to one with France, especially if anything happened to King Louis Philippe.[14] Even as late as 1869, the Foreign Secretary warned the Queen that were the treaties with Portugal or Belgium 'to lead us into war in Europe, we should find ourselves immediately called upon to defend Canada from American invasion'.[15] But the United States derived little benefit from these fears: Liverpool and Canning were advocating recognition of the newly independent South

---

[12] In 1870, though, both were nudged towards a settlement by the Franco-Prussian War, which left London the only place where the US could borrow to support its debt conversion programme, while the possibility of Britain becoming involved in continental hostilities added to the attractions of a deal to prevent its opponents building *Alabama*-type commerce raiders in America

[13] Yonge, *Life and Administration of the Earl of Liverpool* iii pp. 297-304

[14] Wellington's Memorandum, 1 March 1845, and Peel to Aberdeen, 17 Oct. (ed. Arthur Gordon, Baron Stanmore, *Selections from the Correspondence of George Earl of Aberdeen 1845* (privately printed, 1885) pp. 71, 390); Stanley to Canada's Governor General Sir Charles Metcalfe, 16 Sept. 1845 (Kenneth Bourne, *Britain and the Balance of Power in North America* (London, 1967) pp. 146-9)

[15] Lord Clarendon to Queen Victoria, 16 April and 1 May 1869 (ed. George Earle Buckell, *The Letters of Queen Victoria. Second Series ... between the Years 1862 and 1868*, i (London, 1926) pp. 590, 594)

American states in order to draw them into the British orbit and exclude US influence; Wellington and (more cautiously) Peel were advocating measures of British rearmament that, though designed to deter a sudden French attack, would in 1846 rattle the Polk administration.

Still, US hopes of profiting from British entanglements sometimes resurfaced. In mid-1859 the British minister Lord Lyons stressed the need to convince Americans 'that they cannot take advantage of the State of Affairs in Europe to obtain undue advantage in matters affecting British interests'; and in 1870 such hopes rose far higher: 'What a time this would be', wrote Under Secretary Bancroft Davis on hearing of Russia's repudiation of the Black Sea's 1856 demilitarisation, 'to strike in London for the independence of Canada and the settlement of the Alabama Claims.'[16] Though no war with Russia transpired, the international situation did impact on British policy. For, as the then Colonial Secretary Lord Kimberley later wrote, 'it was the general opinion ... that the other nations of Europe would in all probability sooner or later be drawn into' the Franco-Prussian War, and 'it seemed dangerous to leave the Alabama question unsettled.' Earlier in the year, Secretary of State Hamilton Fish had indeed warned that Europe might 'at any time' become convulsed, and that, should Britain become involved, 'the ocean will swarm with Alabamas' unless Anglo-American differences had first been resolved.[17] Such considerations were not strong enough to secure the United States' chief wish, Britain's abandonment of Canada. But they were among the factors that led London to seek reconciliation through a qualified apology, and to accept international

---

[16] Lord Lyons' briefing of the incoming Foreign Secretary Lord John Russell, 11 July 1859 (Lord Newton, *Lord Lyons. A Record of British Diplomacy* (London, 1917) p. 16); Bancroft Davis to Secretary of State Hamilton Fish, 13 Nov. 1870 (Adrian Cook, *The Alabama Claims. American Politics and Anglo-American Relations, 1856-1872* (Ithaca, N.Y., 1975) p. 135)

[17] ed. Ethel Drus, 'A Journal of Events during the Gladstone Ministry 1868-1874 by John, First Earl of Kimberley' 13 June 1871, *Royal Historical Society, Camden Third Series* 90 (1958) p. 23; Fish's diary record of his 24 March 1870 conversation with Sir Edward Thornton (Allan Nevins, *Hamilton Fish. The Inside History of the Grant Administration* i (New York, 1957 edn.) p. 410)

arbitration (and the probable award of *Alabama* damages) on the basis not of the 'principles of International Law … in force at the time', but of three new rules that 'the High Contracting Parties agree to observe … as between themselves in future' and to press on 'other maritime Powers'.[18]

We cannot test the proposition that British involvement in major war would have drawn in the United States, for Britain's only war with a Great Power during the long nineteenth century was the limited Crimean one with Russia, fought far from the Atlantic and with France as an ally. Anglophobes in both the US and France often stated that were Britain ever at war with either power, the other would come in. But one wonders. In the 1845-6 Oregon crisis, the French government sympathised with Britain, and would certainly have tried to remain neutral. During the 1861 *Trent* affair, the French minister in Washington told Secretary of State Seward 'to dismiss all idea of assistance from France, and … the vulgar notion that the Emperor would gladly see England embroiled with the United States in order to pursue his own plans in Europe'; later Paris declared that Britain was legally in the right and advised release of the Confederate diplomats taken from a British mail steamer on the high seas.[19]

By the 1920s relations between the US and Canada were running well, with pride in the then internationally unusual 'undefended border'. The Canadian Liberal leader Mackenzie King credited this to arms control, declaring, on the eve of the great 1921-2 Washington Conference, that 'If on the Pacific they will agree to do what we a century ago did so successfully on our Great Lakes … Europe and Asia alike may look forward to

---

[18] Treaty of Washington, 1871, Article VI; the British government conditioned its acceptance of an arbitration on the basis of these 'rules' on their being, in future, 'binding internationally between the two countries' (the Foreign Secretary Lord Granville to the British High Commissioners, 17 March 1871 – FO 414/31, Confidential Print, 'Correspondence respecting the appointment of a Joint High Commission for the settlement of differences between Great Britain and the United States…' [hereafter High Commission Correspondence] p. 86)
[19] Newton, *Lord Lyons* esp. pp. 53-7; *Annual Register*, 1861 pp. 291-5 (de Thouvenel to Mercier, 3 Dec. 1861)

the disappearance of all dread of future wars between these great powers'.[20] The War of 1812 had seen a race to build first-class battleships on the Great Lakes. With peace, the United States sold or laid up all its armed Lakes vessels not required for revenue enforcement. Though Britain partially followed suit, it contemplated further building. The United States, financially much the weaker power, then proposed drastic naval limitation on the Lakes. Rather to its surprise, Britain agreed. The Rush-Bagot treaty of 1817 accordingly restricted each country to four warships of less than 100 tons; and though, over the years, both countries would exceed these limits, there was never again an overt building race.[21] There was no such agreement on land armies, but financial constraints and worldwide commitments kept British forces in North America low: regular troops peaked at 12,452 in 1842, while in 1861 they stood at a more usual 2,252 (though rising next year to 12,949 in response to the *Trent* affair). In 1840 the number of US regulars deployed on the northern border reached about 3,000, but generally it was much lower.[22]

These were not the postures of countries preparing for imminent conflict, but they were far from a guarantee of peace. Planning for the Lakes did not cease. America's potential there much exceeded Canada's; as a counter, Britain sought ways to rush ships in from the Atlantic. By 1834 £1,069,000 had been spent on strategic canals[23] and the locks above Montreal in an uphill struggle to provide access for modern warships. Moreover, as one historian remarks, 'every period of strained relations

---

[20] James Eayrs, 'Arms Control on the Great Lakes', *Disarmament and Arms Control* 2 (1964) p. 390
[21] C.P. Stacey, 'The Myth of the Unguarded Frontier, 1815-1871', *American Historical Review* 56:1 (1950) pp. 9-10, 12-14
[22] Bourne, *Britain and the Balance of Power* pp. 79, 88; J. Mackay Hitsman, *Safeguarding Canada 1763-1871* (Toronto, 1968) pp. 139, 144, 232; Francis Paul Prucha, 'Distribution of Regular Army Troops before the Civil War', *Military Affairs* 16:4 (1952) pp. 141-3
[23] Bourne, *Britain and the Balance of Power* esp. p. 41, and Map 1. Of this, £822,000 went on the Rideau Canal, the origin of what later became Canada's capital Ottawa. In winter it now furnishes the world's longest skating rink

produced its own expedients to circumvent' the Rush-Bagot treaty, mostly through preparations for 'break-out'. The strains were, perhaps, greatest in the 1840s: but when, in late 1864, the US added one armed vessel to guard against Confederate filibusters and gave notice that it might do more, there were British fears that it might spend the winter in building warships that, when transported to the Lakes in sections, would next spring secure it overwhelming naval supremacy.[24]

Both countries, too, spent substantially on fortifications. Americans worried over their long coast's exposure to British sea power, and sometimes also over incursions across the northern border. This occasioned substantial building, albeit by fits and starts. In 1816 the US moved to close the Lake Champlain invasion route by building at Rouse's Point – $113,000 had been spent by 1818, when astronomers discovered that it was on the *Canadian* side of the border.[25] More generally, expenditure dragged as the countries moved away from war, resumed with periods of tension – the US spent $612,300 on northern forts between 1839 and 1851, and appropriated $900,000 for them in 1862.[26] But the chief American efforts went on coastal defences: by 1867, 42 major works had been largely completed, of which the most famous, Fort Sumter, did indeed ward off an attack from the sea, though by the US not the Royal Navy.[27] Britain also spent considerably. For though the US army was small, it was (as the Mexicans discovered) geared to rapid expansion and backed by large state militias. So Britain needed fortifications to hold key positions pending reinforcement. Planning was inhibited by doubts as to whether Canada could be defended under any

---

[24] Stacey, 'The Myth of the Unguarded Frontier', p. 17; Bourne, *Britain and the Balance of Power* pp. 125-9

[25] £57,700 was spent between 1819 and 1825 on the countervailing Canadian fort just north of the border – Stacey, 'The Myth of the Unguarded Frontier' pp. 5, 8. Work on Rouse's Point resumed in a big way soon after the site had been confirmed to the US by the 1842 treaty

[26] Stacey, 'Myth' pp. 16-17

[27] *Seacoast Defense in the United States* and *Fort Sumter* (Wikipedia, accessed 10/12/14)

conditions, and by irritation over Provincial reluctance to spend money on the militias. But 1828-48 saw £462,100 spent on the key positions of Kingston (Ontario), Quebec, and Halifax.[28] And in early 1865 there were real fears that once its Civil War had ended, the United States would turn north: in February Queen Victoria talked over 'the danger, which seems to be approaching, of our having a war with ... [America], as soon as she makes [internal] peace; of the impossibility of our being able to hold Canada, but we must struggle for it. Far the best would be to let it go as an independent kingdom under an English Prince!'. The cabinet, more robustly, felt that 'the best security against [such] a conflict ... will be found in an adequate defensive force', and proposed renewed work on Canadian fortifications. Lord Palmerston told the Queen he believed such an American attack 'less likely than many suppose', but also that 'Canada can be defended, and must be defended'.[29] £497,800 followed on North American fortifications between 1865 and 1872; and in 1870 it was finally arranged that the new Dominion of Canada should raise an imperially guaranteed £1.1m. loan for the defences of Hamilton, Toronto, Kingston, Montreal, and St. John.[30]

To arms control and fortifications one can perhaps add mutual extended deterrence. Canada was vulnerable to US attack. Quite how vulnerable is unclear. The theme of the many British reports on the subject before the Civil War is that though Canada's defence really needed an (unattainable) superiority on the Lakes, it was achievable provided the recommended fortifications were in place and the province had upgraded its militia – conditions that

---

[28] Some £100,900 had already been spent on the Quebec citadel since 1820 – Stacey, 'Myth' pp. 4, 15

[29] Victoria's Journal account of conversation with the Secretary of State for India, 12 Feb. 1865, Lord Palmerston to the Queen, 20 Jan. and 13 March (*Letters of Queen Victoria ... between the Years 1862 and 1868*, i pp. 248-9, 262-3)

[30] Hitsman, *Safeguarding Canada* pp. 163, 218-19, 223-4, 231, and photographs between pp. 114 and 115. By way of comparison, Palmerston's great 1860s programme to end UK vulnerability to a lightning French attack cost £10m.

were never fully met.[31] On the other side, the American army respected the quality of the British regular troops there; and with his experience of the failed 1812-14 invasions, General Scott wrote in 1840 that, without the immediate expenditure of $15m. (of which there was no prospect),

> 'we may have a three years' war – the first year one of unmitigated disaster ... – captured cities; devastated frontiers; armies of militia & regular recruits, every where drubbed and driven like sheep; national credit (in loans) sunk from a premium, to, perhaps, 65 per centum, & the pride & spirit of all broken & destroyed. Whereas, *with* preparation, we can establish ourselves in Montreal, Fredericton & Halifax in *two* years...'[32]

So though the US was, by the 1830s, fairly sure that if war came it would conquer British North America, the anticipated costs, even on land, would be high. After the Civil War had demonstrated the United States' massive strength, things were different: Grant thought that General Sherman would deserve to be sacked if he could not seize Canada in thirty days;[33] and among the reasons for the final withdrawal of British troops from Quebec in November 1871 was the calculation that, if war came, imperial prestige would suffer more from their forced surrender than from that of their Canadian replacements.

But if the British empire was thus exposed on land, the United States was vulnerable by sea. At any time in the nineteenth century the Royal Navy could have swept up American commercial shipping on the high seas. In 1845 even the prospect of future war drove insurance premiums on US vessels to such 'impracticable' levels that 'British vessels are monopolizing the freights', and it led

---

[31] The repetitive cycle of planning for Canadian defence is well set out in Bourne, *Britain and the Balance of Power*
[32] To Col. William Jenkins Worth, 1 April 1840 (Winfield Scott Papers, W.L. Clements Library, Ann Arbor, Michigan)
[33] Nevins, *Hamilton Fish* p. 217

Whig New York merchants to look for deliverance to the Southern Democrat John Calhoun.[34] To some extent, too, the Royal Navy held the American coastal cities hostage: Boston in 1839 lacked any operational forts, and Governor Everett warned that the town was literally without a gun; next year US military engineers observed that the 1835 fire in 'a very small part' of New York had done $17m. damage, and asked what would be the loss 'from the fires that a victorious enemy could kindle'.[35] Attacks on American towns from the sea in 1814 had in fact met with only mixed success, and attempts to repeat them might well have run into trouble. But 'worst case' thinking often led Americans to exaggerate the advantages Britain would derive from the advent of steam power and the ease with which it could throw troops across the Atlantic. The British had, too, sailed freely up southern estuaries in 1813-14, bringing commerce to a halt and recruiting runaway slaves as 'Colonial Marines'. If war came, they meant to do so again, and there were Southern fears that this might now touch off a slave revolt. Such thoughts, though more salient during and shortly after crises, were always present to some degree. It would have been unwise to invoke them explicitly, so British signalling was more sophisticated: 'I mean to make a parade of it', wrote the First Lord of the Admiralty in 1855, 'to show the world, and the people of the United States principally, that [despite Crimean War commitments] we have a spare force after all.'[36] Similar motives

---

[34] Louis McLane to Secretary of State Buchanan, 18 Sept. 1845 (ed. William R. Manning, *Diplomatic Correspondence of the United States. Canadian Relations 1784-1860* ii (Washington, 1942) p. 980) and to President Polk, 1 Dec. (ed. Wayne Cutler and James L. Rogers, *Correspondence of James K. Polk* x *1845* (Knoxville, Tennessee, 2004) p. 393); Isaac Holmes to Calhoun, 18 Nov. 1845 (ed. Clyde N. Wilson, *The Papers of John C. Calhoun* xxii (Columbia: University of South Carolina Press, 1995) p. 298)

[35] Paul A. Varg, *Edward Everett. The Intellectual in the Turmoil of Politics* (London, 1992) p. 88; Bourne, *Britain and the Balance of Power* pp. 49-51, 95n.

[36] Sir Charles Wood to Admiral Fanshawe, 26 Oct. 1855 (Bourne, *Britain and the Balance of Power* p. 187). Andrew Lambert also sees signalling in the despatch to the North American station, in times of tension, of warships and officers associated with the victories of 1812-15 (*The Challenge: America, Britain and the War of 1812* (paperback edn.) pp. 453, 455-6)

presumably underlay the 1869 choice of the battleship *Monarch*, rather than (as originally intended) the frigate *Inconstant*, to carry George Peabody's corpse from London to burial in Massachusetts. Thereafter the *Monarch* went on to Annapolis, to the satisfaction of the British minister in Washington, Edward Thornton, who wrote that 'it is not amiss that the principal people, including the President ... should see what sort of vessels England can turn out in case of need.'[37]

Both countries, then, realised that they had good military reasons for avoiding war. In 1839 Maine found President Martin van Buren

> '*exceedingly averse to war*, the cabinet knows that we are unprepared, and nothing but necessity will bring the general government to our side. There seems to be a prevailing opinion that Maine ... is going faster than public opinion will sustain. Of this opinion ... are Mr. Clay, Mr. Webster and Mr. Davis. Mr. Calhoun thinks we cannot have war without previous preparation...'[38]

That said, military reasons could be disregarded: 'nine tenths of the democracy of numbers', the *New York Gazette* believed, 'would go for a general war'; and even Governor Everett, who both wanted peace *per se* and was well aware of Boston's vulnerability, concluded his pacific letter to the President with the assurance that 'if war must come, every man & every dollar in Massachusetts as far as my control or influence goes will be embarked at the call of the general Government'.[39]

---

[37] Thornton told the Foreign Secretary Lord Clarendon Britain's clear naval supremacy guaranteed that there would be no war – (private), 20 April 1869, 9 Feb. 1870 (Clarendon Papers, Bodleian Library, M.S. Clar. dep. C. 480, 481)

[38] Senator Reuel Williams to Governor Fairfield, 23 Feb. 1839 (Geraldine Tidd Scott, *Ties of Common Blood: a history of Maine's Northeast Boundary Dispute with Great Britain, 1783-1842* (Bowie, Maryland, 1992) p. 163)

[39] David Lowenthal, 'The Maine Press and the Aroostook War', *Canadian Historical Review* 32 (1951) pp. 324-5; Edward Everett to President Van Buren, 12 March 1839 (Van Buren Papers, LoC, Chadwyk-Healey microfilm Reel 32)

Another explanation often invoked for the maintenance of peace relations theorists is 'interdependence'. But conflicts can occur despite prior 'interdependence'. Most civil wars do so, and 1775 was a case in point. After the Revolutionary War, trade, financial, and cultural links were restored; the United States was the junior partner, but Britain needed American markets and supplies, especially after Napoleon had constricted European ones. Presidents Jefferson and Madison, indeed, sought to use this need to compel Britain to change the way it employed sea-power. They failed, since their embargoes proved unenforceable, both in peace and after the declaration of war – Wellington's Peninsula army fed on American grain. Nor did 'interdependence' stop the United States embarking in 1812 on what was clearly a war of choice, and continuing to fight despite great economic difficulties.[40] Thereafter the United States' vulnerability to British pressure was reduced by its westward growth away from its original Atlantic fringe, coupled with the development of its own manufacturing capacity and internal waterways. In the other direction, though, there were American claims, after the acquisition of Texas, that 'the monopoly of the cotton plant ... places all other nations at our feet. An embargo of a single year would produce in Europe a greater amount of suffering than a fifty years war. I doubt whether Great Britain could avoid convulsions.' But such rodomontade was never taken at face value on the other side of the Atlantic. And while there were British concerns over Lancashire's likely response to a collapse in cotton supply, these were, as the South would learn, not enough to determine policy: neither the United nor the Confederate States ever held 'England by a cotton string'.[41]

---

[40] US federal finances were squeezed as military expenditures ballooned while the chief revenue source, tariffs, shrunk; and Britain's wartime blockade cut into the coastal shipping required to move for bulk commodities internally – Peter Andreas, *Smuggler Nation. How illicit trade made America* (New York, 2013) pp. 74-80, 83-8; Lambert, *The Challenge* pp. 58-9, 104-5, 131, 228, 232, 274

[41] Ex-President Tyler to Robert Tyler, 17 April 1850 (Lyon G. Tyler, *The Letters and Times of the Tylers* ii (Richmond, VA., 1885) p. 483); Henry Wise to Secretary of State Buchanan, 24 Dec. 1845 (Thomas R. Hietala, *Manifest Design. American Exceptionalism and Empire* (Ithaca, N.Y., 2003 edn.) p. 74)

That said, 'interdependence' did, after 1815, help incline people towards peace. Economic and financial links were again quickly re-established, though their importance was very much a sectional matter. Daniel Webster was closely associated with the merchants and bankers of Boston, and was retained as legal counsel to the British bank, Barings – the most important external source of American credit. As Secretary of State, Webster conducted crucial negotiations (enlivened by culinary competition) in 1842 with the special British envoy Lord Ashburton, the senior partner in Barings. At their outset he was told by another Barings partner, the London-based Bostonian Joshua Bates, that in the event of success Barings would lend America $12m. But should Ashburton fail, it would be *'impossible* for anyone in the United States to negotiate a loan abroad' – a serious matter, since the country was still reeling from the crash of 1837.[42] Such considerations were not alluded to in the negotiators' correspondence, but they must have helped; and after Ashburton's treaty had been ratified, Faneuil Hall, Boston gave him a triumphant send-off. The Barings-Boston connection also operated in London: in 1845 Bates worked with US minister Everett (another Boston Whig) [and the Foreign Secretary Lord Aberdeen] to promote an Oregon compromise by planting articles in the British press; and after the furore occasioned by President Polk's Inaugural, Bates was used to pass a reassuring and potentially important message to Washington.[43] But financial influence could go only so far. Secretary of State Buchanan contrasted the

---

[42] Bates to Webster, 15 April 1842 (Jay Sexton, *Debtor Diplomacy: Finance and American Relations in the Civil War Era, 1837-1873* (Oxford, 2005) pp. 35-6)

[43] Frederick Merk, *The Oregon Question. Essays in Anglo-American Diplomacy and Politics* (Cambridge, Mass., 1967) pp. 287-95; Bates to the Boston merchant Sturgis, 1 May 1845 (Parliamentary Papers 1873 lxxiv pp. 753-4 [*North-West American Water Boundary. Memorial on the Canal de Haro as the Boundary Line of the United States of America... presented by the American Plenipotentiary George Bancroft, p. 25*]. Sturgis passed this to War Secretary Bancroft on 25 May – David M. Pletcher, *The Diplomacy of Annexation. Texas, Oregon, and the Mexican War* (Columbia, Missouri, 1975 printing) p. 247; Charles Grier Sellers, *James K. Polk: Continentalist, 1843-1846* (Princeton, NJ, 1966) pp. 247-8)

'Commercial interest which ... has a direct interest in the preservation of peace, and especially with Great Britain' with the 'strong and irresistible public opinion throughout the vast interior of our Country which controls the action of the Government [and] is but little if at all affected by the considerations which influence the mercantile Community.'[44] In August 1845 President Polk effectively broke off negotiations over Oregon; and he was not impressed when Baring's Boston agent Thomas Wren Ward told him in October that 'there was danger of war' if he claimed all of Oregon, and that this was inhibiting business ventures.[45] The dispute's eventual resolution was therefore due rather to other factors. Later, though, the resumption of Anglo-American negotiations over Fisheries and Reciprocity in 1852 (after both countries had sent warships to the Gulf of St. Lawrence) has been seen as made 'under the powerful influence of the Barings'.[46]

The impact of financial constraint was also in evidence after the American Civil War. When the Senate rejected the Johnson-Clarendon treaty in 1869, American stocks dropped by 10% on the London exchange, and Barings warned its agent that if the US wanted to improve the standing of its bonds in Europe, it should not anger Britain. Next spring President Grant exclaimed in cabinet, albeit only when irritated over Canadian fishery restrictions, that 'were it not for our debt, he wishes Congress would declare war' and take Canada. Grant's administration wanted to cut the interest paid on American overseas borrowing for the Civil War, and based hopes of re-election in 1872 'in great measure' on thus reducing 'the national burdens'. It had hoped to borrow also in other European centres besides London, but the Franco-Prussian war had crowded out this possibility. As the Canadian-British banker Sir John Rose

---

[44] To McLane, 26 Feb. 1846 (ed. John Bassett Moore, *The Works of James Buchanan* vi (New York, 1960 edn.) pp. 385-6)

[45] Polk's account of the interview sounds affronted – ed. Milo Milton Quaife, *The Diary of James K. Polk during his Presidency, 1845 to 1849* (Chicago, 1910), entries cited by their dates, here 27 Oct. 1845

[46] Adam Shorrt in *The Cambridge History of the British Empire* vol. 6 (Cambridge, 1930) p. 389; no evidence is cited to support this claim, but it is plausible

put it in November 1870, it was 'a pet object with Grant to reduce their rate of interest' from 6% to 4½%, and 'he is aware this cannot be done without a fair settlement of old scores with England.' Rose would stress this in December-January 1870-1 to a receptive Treasury Secretary Boutwell, and thus to the US cabinet.[47] But Britain, too, needed a settlement, though not for financial reasons. So Rose was sent on an 'unofficial' mission to Washington in January 1871, to work out a way of bringing most outstanding issues before a 'Joint High Commission' and so end a difficult period of estrangement. That said, *many* other factors were involved on both sides, and though America was financially the weaker party, it managed to drive distinctly the harder bargain.[48]

Other analytical approaches lean more towards the *primat der innenpolitik*, the dictates of domestic politics[49] and the

---

[47] Sexton, *Debtor Diplomacy* pp. 210-11; Sir John Rose as reported by Granville to Gladstone, 22 Nov. 1870 (*Gladstone-Granville Correspondence* no. 373), and Rose's 26 Nov. Memorandum (FO 414/31, High Commission Correspondence pp. 7-8); Hamilton Fish, Diary (John Bassett Moore's transcription, LoC, Hamilton Fish papers, Microfilm, shelf no. 17,634, Reel 4), esp. 22 March and 9 Dec. 1870, 24 Jan. 1871; Nevins, *Hamilton Fish* esp. pp. 431, 433. Rose's devotion both to peace and to British interests is not in doubt, but he hoped also to secure for his firm the management of the US refunding in London

[48] Both America's financial and Britain's international vulnerability were again in evidence in 1895-6. President Cleveland's unexpectedly tough Message on the Venezuela-British Guiana border on 17 December 1895 was followed on the 20th by Wall Street panic and a withdrawal of British capital that calmed exuberant American talk of war. Then on 3 January the Kaiser's telegram congratulating Transvaal's President Kruger on defeating the Jameson Raid emphasised Britain's general diplomatic isolation; and on the 11th the British cabinet overruled the Prime Minister (who saw the US as having no standing in the Venezuelan dispute) and opted to negotiate mutually acceptable terms of arbitration

[49] Ernest May feels that the positions of US policy-makers in 1823 can 'be best explained' not on the basis of their 'previous opinions ... or from knowledge of the external world' but 'as functions of their domestic ambitions' and 'political interests'. By contrast, the Tsar had few domestic constraints. 'The chief limitations upon his choices of policy were those imposed by his conscience ... and ... his calculations concerning the probable behavior of other governments' – Ernest R. May, *The Making of the Monroe Doctrine* (Cambridge, Mass., 1975) esp. pp. 255-9. And May would have had even stronger grounds for his opinion had he been examining not a simple Presidential pronouncement but a question needing Congressional assent and collaboration

subjective construction of interests and identities. In Britain, the Prime Minister, Lord North, took the votes against continuing the American war after Yorktown as 'the genuine sense of the House of Commons, and, I really think, of the Nation at large', and resigned. There followed a contest between Shelburne and Fox, with Shelburne pushing Fox aside to take personal control of the 1782 peace negotiations, Fox and North then ousting him next year to condemn the result and exclude the United States from the continued West Indian trade Shelburne had clearly intended.

Thereafter, though, British politics seldom turned on American issues. Far more important, between the 1790s and 1814, was the question of how, and whether, to conduct the wars with France, which was initially linked, at a more popular level, to the contest between ideas of radical reform and a more widely held 'Church and King' loyalism. America was usually peripheral; and though in 1814 Britain's American war aims were strongly influenced by lobbying and propaganda, actual policy was made by ministers, largely during the parliamentary recess. So the most that can be said is that *one* reason for Britain's making peace without achieving these recently adopted goals was the belief that parliament would be reluctant to continue wartime taxes to fight a further campaign. The next major intrusion of American questions into high politics did not come until 1842 when Palmerston (who had, when Foreign Secretary, been fairly conciliatory towards the United States) denounced the Webster-Ashburton treaty. He was not, he made clear, seeking to overturn the treaty – ratification was a matter of 'royal', in effect now governmental, prerogative. But he was mobilising press and extra-parliamentary support to build his personal position at a time when Lord Melbourne was withdrawing from the Liberal leadership. There proved to be important consequences in December 1845. For Palmerston's language had been such as to cause Lord Grey to veto his reappointment as Foreign Secretary lest he bring war over Oregon; and this in turn led Lord John Russell to decline to form a government and Peel to resume office to 'repeal' the Corn Laws, splitting his party in the process. Over Oregon, the Liberal leadership now firmly backed Peel's government, Russell rejecting Everett's plea that he call for a reversal of policy (as he had recently done over the Corn Laws), Palmerston huffing and puffing to encourage the US to settle before he was again back in office; and the eventual settlement, the closing act of Peel's government, was universally applauded in parliament.

The normal British nineteenth century pattern was for foreign policy to be left largely to the government of the day, albeit influenced by both parliamentary feeling and public opinion (which ministers themselves often shared). Only occasionally – over the Crimean War, the *Arrow* affair and the 1857 election, Palmerston's 1858 bill to stop political refugees plotting to murder their foreign opponents, and the 1878 'Bulgarian atrocities', none of them American issues – did overseas questions determine or seriously upset British governments. Nor were these governments as concerned with the colonies, India apart, as one might expect. It was quite largely to get him out of the way that Lord Durham was sent to Canada after the 1837 risings. And later, though both Liberal and Conservative governments in London supported Confederation, it was eclipsed in their minds by domestic electoral reform.

In North America, things were different. Amongst the First Nations, questions of borders with the area of European settlement, of the formation of coalitions to define and maintain them, and of alignment with the French, British or Americans could well be existential; and they sparked divisions both between tribes and individual leaders, notably (in the 1790s) that over whether to accept the Muskingum line or to hold out for that of the Ohio.

In 1760 American colonists, while certainly conscious of their local interests and identities, had seen themselves as loyal and enthusiastic subjects of the British Crown. Come the Revolution, a majority of activists, though retaining (in non-political matters) a largely British culture and tastes, recast themselves as citizens of both their own State and the 'United States'. The less politically involved gradually followed suit; a 'Loyalist' minority had to leave; and in a remarkably short time, the Revolution created a new and distinct national identity.

In peace time the 'United States' did not prove easy to operate, and much effort was devoted in the later 1780s to formulating a new Constitution and getting this adopted. The coalition that did so then split in the 1790s over whether to join France or remain neutral. The Federalists went for Jay's treaty securing British evacuation of the northern forts, and with it what eventually became a British-leaning neutrality. In the 1800s they were displaced by the 'Republican-Democrats', whose Presidents Jefferson and Madison took the US away from any British inclination and ultimately into the War of 1812. This proved divisive, for New England was brought to question a belligerence driven by states further south. But once peace had returned, no more came of this; and though popular identification with the United States would indeed later be challenged to the point of secession, this challenge came from the South, *not* from the sections bordering British North America.

The Treaty ending the War of 1812 set in motion the detailed determination of the US northern border east of the Lake of the Woods. The most contentious stretch proved to be that between the head of the St. Croix and the St. Lawrence. On both sides much of the difficulty was local. Lord Castlereagh had thought it 'a mere operation of Survey'; but to keep the border from crossing the river St. John and cutting their strategic overland route to Quebec, the New Brunswick men most directly involved managed to remove the Canadian surveyor Joseph Bouchette and tie the British side into claiming well south of the line Bouchette seemed to be envisaging. The question eventually went to arbitration and should have been settled by the Award of the Dutch King. President Jackson wanted to secure US acceptance, but in 1832 the Senate turned against him, and the Award was among the administration's measures that it then struck down. Though the state of Maine had never liked the Award, party loyalty brought the leaders of the Democratic party there to undertake to accept it if ratified by the Senate. The Senate's refusal to ratify discredited them and enabled the partisans of rejection to take control of the Maine party in 1833. Thereafter the issue remained a political football within Maine for a decade, and, with each party 'afraid that the other will get some advantage', compromise proved impossible. Eventually the combination of fatigue, F.O.J. Smith's clandestinely funded press and lobbying campaign, and skilled pressure by

Secretary of State Webster brought a bipartisan Maine delegation to Washington in 1842 to join in Anglo-American negotiations and reluctantly give the state's indispensable consent to their outcome.

The north-eastern boundary question was soon succeeded by the Oregon one. This too was strongly influenced by party politics, but more at the national (or sectional) than the state level. Believing that time was on the American side, the Tyler administration had been ready to let the issue run on. It was brought to the boil by the Democratic nominating convention of 1844. The front-runner, ex-President Van Buren, was cool on the then most salient issue, that of acquiring Texas, and was also outmanoeuvred over the convention's voting rules. The upshot was the adoption of James K. Polk on a platform of taking both Texas and all Oregon. Texas came quickly, and Polk moved on to seeking rapid resolution of the Oregon question. Probably he meant to move towards the 49ᵗʰ parallel 'to the sea' border that was ultimately adopted. But his initial proposal was very different. And when the British minister Richard Pakenham instead asked for one that would narrow not widen the gap between the two countries, Polk took this as releasing him from any obligation to stick with the limited requests of his predecessors, broke off negotiations, and demanded all Oregon. Opinion differs as to whether this was just a ploy to scare Britain into proposing the 49ᵗʰ parallel 'to the sea', or whether Polk really had adopted a '54° 40' or fight' posture. At the time most people thought the latter, and American feeling surged in its favour. To prevent war, Calhoun disregarded advice that he would thereby only destroy his own presidential hopes, and courageously returned to the Senate (a good deed by a man now seen as mostly on the dark side). By mobilising his Southern connections, Calhoun assembled enough swing voters to join the Whig opposition in taking control of the Senate and effectively inviting Aberdeen to propose the compromise 49ᵗʰ parallel 'to the sea' border. Working in the same direction was the administration's alarm at unexpectedly vigorous British naval preparations. This seems to have transferred the initiative within the US cabinet to Secretary of State Buchanan, whose wish to resume negotiations Polk had earlier repeatedly over-ruled. The eventual outcome was acceptance *in toto* of Aberdeen's take-it-or-leave-it proposal offering the 49th parallel 'to the sea' but insisting on a continued right of the Hudson's Bay Company to navigate the Columbia – something Polk always said he would never concede. Party and intra-Party politics were not, of course, the only factors – by the time Britain's final offer arrived, the US was already at war with Mexico. But politics was an indispensable component.[50]

The nineteenth century would see the advent of a Canadian state that, despite many commonalities, was determined to remain distinct from its southern neighbour, a process framed by both demography and politics. In and after the 1790s many Americans had moved into Upper Canada; indeed one observer believed that they and their children numbered half its population in 1814, and their allegiance to Britain was by no means certain. The next four decades saw mounting immigration from the United Kingdom, and at Confederation in 1867 about 60% of Canadians were of British origin.[51] In most provinces, identification with Britain was correspondingly strengthened. But in the largest, Lower Canada (Quebec), backlash against growing anglicisation led in the 1830s to a 'Patriote' movement that, under Louis-Joseph Papineau, took control of the elective house of the legislature to make steadily expanding demands. When the London parliament rejected its '92 Resolutions', the movement passed beyond constitutional declarations and petitions. In a land hit by bad

---

[50] As it was again after the Civil War, when treaties to address the *Alabama* affair and the Gulf Islands dispute were wrecked in the Senate by the wave of opposition to President Johnson, while the 1871 move back to negotiated settlements was enormously facilitated by the removal from the chair of the Senate Foreign Relations Committee of Charles Sumner (who had fallen out with President Grant over annexing San Domingo)

[51] Elizabeth Jane Errington, 'British Migration and British America, 1783-1867' *in* Phillip Buckner ed., *Canada and the British Empire* (Oxford, paperback edn. 2010) pp. 141, 144, 146; M. Smith, *A Geographical View of the British Possessions in North America...* (Baltimore, 1814) p. 288 – quoted in E.A. Cruikshank, 'A Study of Disaffection in Upper Canada 1812-15', Royal Society of Canada, *Transactions*, series 3 vol. 6 (1912), Section 2 p. 18

harvests, mass meetings and calls to boycott British products melded with rural discontent to create a pre-revolutionary situation, with clandestine preparations for insurrection. Actual risings followed when the authorities attempted arrests; but in November-December 1837 they were quickly put down, with Papineau and other leaders fleeing across the border. Upper Canada, too, had seen competition – legal, journalistic, and electoral – between a Conservative and Anglican establishment and advocates of 'Reform'. But while sympathising with the Patriotes, almost all 'Reformers' stayed well clear of rebellion – the exception being William Lyon Mackenzie, who was inspired by events in Lower Canada to try to seize Toronto. On meeting resistance, Mackenzie fled precipitately to the United States, where he enlisted the aid of American filibusters in an attempt to create a Canadian republic. Patriote leaders, notably Robert Nelson and more reluctantly Papineau, did likewise, Nelson leading two shambolic cross-border incursions in 1838.

The absence, in exile or in jail, of many Patriote leaders and the discrediting of rebellion left the way clear for Louis-Hippolyte LaFontaine. He had disengaged from the Patriotes as they moved towards insurrection, and he was in 1839 approached by Upper Canadian Reformers with the suggestion that they work together. Opportunity came when, to avoid restoring a Lower Canadian elective chamber, the British placed both Canadas under a single legislature, hoping that this would eventually lead to the swamping and anglicisation of Quebec. Upper Canadian Reformers had persuaded LaFontaine that together they might command a majority; and he took the important decision to promote Quebec's *survivance* by working *within* the new system alongside the chief Reform leader Robert Baldwin. Together the two polled so well in 1841 that next year Sir Charles Bagot could only manage the legislature by taking them into government. They had, in eighteenth century British parlance, forced themselves on the Crown. The next Governor broke with them when he felt they trenched on his prerogatives, and then defeated them electorally. But in opposition LaFontaine worked to develop his machine's electoral grip on Lower Canada. In 1848 the LaFontaine-Baldwin coalition triumphed, and the new Governor, Lord Elgin, invited them not merely to take offices (as in 1842) but themselves to form a government – one 'responsible' (as in Britain) to the legislature.

Baldwin had always believed, and had in 1838 so told Governor-General Durham, that 'Responsible Government' would strengthen the British connection. And so it proved. But it first occasioned a surprising movement in 1849 for annexation to the United States among Montreal Conservatives, who felt abandoned, politically by Governor Elgin, economically by the U.K.'s ending of tariff advantages. Their movement never reached far beyond Montreal, and subsided rapidly. But fears that it might revive led Lord Elgin, with diplomatic backing from London, into difficult but in 1854 successful negotiations for a trade treaty with the United States. This 'Reciprocity' was widely credited with the subsequent period of prosperity, and after the United States ended the treaty in 1866 Canada long sought to revive it.

However the flag did not follow trade, as many Americans had expected. Rather the three main British American provinces 'confederated' in 1867 to form the Dominion of Canada. There had been vague talk for some time. But the process that actually led to Confederation was touched off by electoral and political deadlock within the then province of Canada. The LaFontaine-Baldwin alliance had been on the political left. But by the early 1850s 'Clear Grit' radicals in Upper Canada were seeking to go further, while LaFontaine had recently moved his supporters towards an accommodation with the Church. They became the *bleus*, opposed within Lower Canada by the anti-clerical *rouges*; and they did not take to attacks on 'priestcraft and state churchism' from George Brown, the Toronto *Globe*'s Free Kirk owner, who became in the early 1850s the leading Liberal politician in Upper Canada. 1854 saw coalition government between the *bleus* and a Conservative party that had moved back towards the centre; and from 1856-7 this coalition, now directed by the liberal Conservative John A. Macdonald and the *bleu* Étienne Cartier (in 1837 a rebel), faced off against the Liberals (who had absorbed the Grits) and the *rouges*. The two sides were so evenly balanced that by the spring of 1864 there had been six governments in six years. To overcome this stasis, Brown moved for a constitutional committee, securing most of the Upper Canada votes, Conservative as well as Reform. Brown steered the committee towards a federal solution. Macdonald disliked this, but Cartier voted for it, presumably calculating that it would at least enable the *bleus* to remain *'maîtres chez nous'* in Quebec.

There soon followed a coalition negotiated between Macdonald, Cartier, and Brown to bring about a federal solution, whether simply within the province of Canada or one comprehending also the other British provinces. Fortuitously, the three Maritime provinces had arranged to meet in Charlottetown, supposedly to consider their own union but probably more in hopes of making progress on the 'Intercolonial Railway'. They were persuaded to let a large Canadian delegation join them and explain its ideas for a broad grouping. In a convivial atmosphere, these were well received, and it was agreed to try to work out satisfactory terms at another conference in Quebec. Those adopted there chiefly reflected the wishes of the Canadian government, partly because of Macdonald's drafting and man-management skills. But the Maritimes, with Québécois assistance, insisted that the new state should be, not a 'legislative union' on the United Kingdom model, but a 'Confederation' based on those existing provinces that joined it, plus Upper and Lower Canada (now renamed Ontario and Quebec). It should also undertake to build the Intercolonial Railway (which has been described as 'the *sine qua non* of' the Maritimes' 'entrance into Confederation').[52]

Many of Confederation's causes were thus internal to British North America: vague aspirations towards unity that antedated the American Civil War; the felt need to remodel the governance of Canada; concern in Nova Scotia and New Brunswick to secure the Intercolonial Railway. But Confederation also appeared the safest way of remaining 'British', and of escaping from the

---

[52] Peter B. Waite, 'A Chapter in the History of the Intercolonial Railway, 1864', *Canadian Historical Review* 32:4 (1951) p. 356. Another attraction of the Railway was that it would give Canada a winter access to the sea independent of the United States

pressures and reviving annexationist aspirations of a United States now liberated from a South reluctant to incorporate further 'free' states. Not everybody favoured exchanging a comfortable local autonomy within the British empire for what would inevitably be a Canadian-dominated 'Confederation': Prince Edward Island stayed out until 1873, Newfoundland until 1949. More seriously, in both New Brunswick and Nova Scotia one election went heavily against Confederation; but with the aid of pressure from London and astute politics, New Brunswick was brought round to joining, and Nova Scotia prevented from leaving, Canada.

Over subsequent decades the Dominion built up a Canadian identification based not on independence (which Macdonald saw as 'tantamount to annexation' to the US) but on an expanding position within the British Empire. Gladstone's first government would have liked to be rid of it. In 1869, amid ministerial gloom inspired by the US Senate's rejection of the Reverdy Johnson-Clarendon treaty,[53] the Colonial Secretary Lord Granville quietly invited Governor General Sir John Young to suggest 'measures which without implying on the part of H.M.G. any wish to change abruptly our relations, would gradually prepare both countries for a friendly relaxation of them.' Young did make a 'trial balloon' speech inviting Canadians to consider whether to retain the existing connection with Britain 'or in due time of the maturity of the Dominion to change it'. But his eventual reply to Granville was 'that the unanimous opinion of the Dominion is against separation, at all events for the present.'[54] The Foreign Secretary's view was that though he wished Britain's North American

---

[53] 'All agree that we could not defend Canada, and that our aim must be for independence' – ed. Angus Hawkins and John Powell, 'The Journal of John Wodehouse, First Earl of Kimberley for 1862-1902', *Royal Historical Society, Camden Fifth Series* 9 (1997), 8 May 1869 (p. 234); for the relationship between Kimberley's various 'Journal' drafts see ibid. pp. 7-13

[54] Granville to Sir John Young, 14 June and to Earl Russell, 28 Aug., 1869, Young to Granville, 11 Nov., summarised in Granville to Gladstone, 25 Jan. 1870 – D.M.L. Farr, *The Colonial Office and Canada 1867-87* (Toronto, 1955) pp. 282-4; ed. Agatha Ramm, 'The Political Correspondence of Mr. Gladstone and Lord Granville 1868-1876', *Camden Third Series* 81 (1952) no. 195.

possessions 'would propose to be independent, and to annex themselves', 'We can't throw them off.'[55]

The Grant administration was (despite clear evidence to the contrary) convinced that British North Americans wanted to join the United States, and Secretary Fish repeatedly pressed Britain either to boot Canada out into independence or, better still, to put annexation to a plebiscite (above pp. 621-3, 625). Thornton (the British minister in Washington) always replied that while London was not unwilling, it could not move without a request from the Dominion parliament, of which there was absolutely no prospect. By late 1870 this message had started to get through, opening the way next year to the Joint High Commission on Anglo-American issues. Several of these, like the fisheries, were Canadian, and the Commission's British side included Canada's Prime Minister, Sir John Macdonald. His position there was admittedly difficult. But the US recognised the Dominion's control of its canals and fisheries, and reluctantly accepted that some of the treaty's Articles could only be brought into effect through legislation by 'the Parliament of Canada'; and the 1871 Treaty of Washington that effected this became something of a landmark in US-Canadian relations.[56]

George Brown had initially been crucial to Confederation, but, following a cabinet defeat in December 1865, he resigned from the government to return to journalism, telegraphing his wife, 'I am a free man once more'. Macdonald and Cartier were left to control and bed down the new system. Both were determined to expand the Dominion westward; for if Canada was 'to remain a Country separate from the United States', it was essential that the latter 'should not get behind us by right or force and intercept

---

[55] Lord Clarendon to Lord Lyons (now Ambassador to France), 1 June 1870 (Farr, *Colonial Office and Canada* p. 313n.). Granville, too, hoped that eventually 'and in the most friendly spirit the Dominion should find itself strong enough to proclaim her [sic] independence'

[56] It is a measure of Canada's rising status that the issues before the next Joint High Commission, that of 1898-9, were US-Canadian, and that its 'British' side, while chaired by the former Chancellor Lord Herschell, consisted otherwise of the Canadian Prime Minister, three more Canadians, and the Premier of Newfoundland

the route to the Pacific'.[57] They were successful, securing Manitoba and the rest of Rupert's Land in 1870, British Columbia in 1871. Both men felt a western railway would be needed to bind in and develop these new acquisitions, with Cartier making over-enthusiastic promises of its speedy construction to ensure British Columbia's adhesion. The 'Pacific Railway Scandal' broke Macdonald's government in 1873, but he returned to office in 1878 on a 'National Policy' of tariff protection against American imports. From 1880 Macdonald was able to push forward the building of the Canadian Pacific Railway, insisting that, whatever the costs of driving it through the barren Canadian Shield, it should run entirely in Canadian territory. In the process, Conservative and Canadian Pacific interests became so melded that Macdonald would be told the 'day the CPR busts, the Conservative party busts the day after'. Aided by its services during Riel's 1885 rebellion in Saskatchewan, he managed to see the Railway through to trans-continental operation in 1886. By now he was getting old. But in 1891 (though the campaign killed him) Macdonald secured a final electoral triumph, countering the Liberal policy of 'unrestricted reciprocity' with the claim that it was bound to lead to annexation to the US (and was meant to do so by at least some Liberal – and all American – politicians). He offered instead, 'The Old Flag, the Old Policy, the Old Leader'. Admittedly the Liberals gained office five years later. But by then their leader, Sir Wilfrid Laurier, had shelved 'reciprocity'. Indeed, under pressure both from within his cabinet and from the Opposition, he was, during the 1898-1903 US-British-Canadian negotiations, markedly less convinced of American goodwill than were his U.K. counterparts – his Privy Council observing in 1903 that 'the most popular policy in the Republic is the extension of its territory', with its 'public men and the press' seeing absorption 'as the natural destiny of Canada'.[58] Only towards the end of the

---

[57] Macdonald to Edward Watkin, 27 March 1865 (Library and Archives Canada, on-line doc. MIKAN no. 566855)

[58] Memorandum enclosed in Governor-General Minto to Colonial Secretary Alfred Lyttelton, 3 Dec. 1903 (CO 42/893 fos. 316-18)

decade did Canada's stance soften; and then Laurier went too far the other way, negotiating a Reciprocity Treaty that the electorate repudiated in 1911.

In recounting the unfolding of events, we have inevitably highlighted the actions of specific individuals. Historical accounts always risk overstressing these. They record that X reviewed the situation and then did Y and Z. But A and B, had they been in X's place, might well have done the same. Still, it is hard not to see, for instance, the end of the Cold War as deeply shaped by both Gorbachev's qualities and his limitations. In everyday life, too, it is clear that, while some things can definitely not be done, others can be done either well or badly. And it is only sensible to look at past events in the same way. In 1842 there was a strong case for settling the 'north-east' boundary dispute. But this had long been true without any agreement being reached. Daniel Webster secured one, in part by clandestine and highly individual means. Equally there were questions (including Oregon) that, despite great goodwill, he and Ashburton could not then resolve. Competence, too, could take many forms. As British minister in Washington, Henry Fox handled the 1839 'Aroostook War' crisis well. But he became increasingly eccentric, kept unsuitable hours, and, though he accepted invitations, he did not give them. Hence Webster's advice that he be replaced with 'Some person of frank & social manners – whose house should be *known* to have an inside to it – & who should hold social & hospitable intercourse with members of Congress'. The advice was taken, and another British diplomat later observed that Pakenham, 'with infinitely less ability, was a far better negotiator. Mr. Fox went near to embroil the two countries ... by the keenness of his correspondence. Mr. Pakenham kept the peace and settled the Oregon question, by the cleverness of his cook.'[59]

---

[59] Webster to Everett (for tactful communication to Aberdeen), 25 Aug. 1842 (Kenneth Shewmaker (ed.), *The Papers of Daniel Webster: Diplomatic Papers, 1841-1843* (Hanover, N.H., 1983) p. 698); Thomas Grattan, *Civilized America* i (London, 1859 edn.) p. 176. One of Pakenham's 1843 dinners (for five Democratic Senators and others) featured nine courses: soup, sweetbread with

Individuals, of course, differ not only in sociability but over policy; and the potential importance of their decisions is well illustrated by events in and around British Columbia in 1858-60. When Indians started killing miners during the 1858 Fraser River gold rush, the larger current of opinion, led by H.M. Snyder of the 'Pike Guards', favoured intimidating them but then striking a deal that left the miners free to get back to their work. The alternative approach, that of Captain Graham of the 'Whatcom Company', was to achieve security by exterminating the Indians. On the other side, one Chief 'advised the people to drive out the whites', ending his speeches with a war dance. But David Spintlum (CexpentlEm) 'talked continually for peace, and showed strongly its advantages', eventually securing majority support and concluding peace 'treaties' with Snyder's miners (above pp. 800-1). A clash was thus averted that would have sparked an 'Indian war', with both sides drawing in supporters from across the American border at a time when British power on the ground was almost non-existent. Next year the 'Pig War' crisis was set off by General Harney's despatch of troops (without authority from Washington) to occupy San Juan island and exclude all British jurisdiction. The presence of several warships gave Governor Douglas a clear local superiority, and he later wrote that 'he would have taken immediate steps to drive' the American troops from San Juan 'had it not been for the opposition of the Civil and Military Authorities of this Colony'.[60] An initially tense stand-off ensued, with British warships shadowing but not interfering with American forces. It was sorted out, largely through the visit from Washington of General Winfield Scott, who rebuked Harney, praised British restraint, and remarked 'that we had never been so near war in all

---

tomato sauce, 'chicken curiously cooked', '*je ne sais_quoi*', ducks, boiled ham, lobster pie, mutton, ice cream, cakes, grapes, and so on (Senator Fairfield's account, cited in William Nisbet Chambers, *Old Bullion Benton. Senator from the New West* (Boston, 1956) pp. 287-8)

[60] Governor Douglas to Lord Lyons, 8 Aug. 1859 (Hunter Miller, *San Juan Archipelago: Study of the Joint Occupation of San Juan Archipelago* (Bellows Falls, Vermont, 1943) p. 85)

our previous disputes'.[61] Douglas' vigour and readiness to act on his own initiative, invaluable during the 1858 Gold Rush, might have been disastrous next year had he not been restrained by those around him.

There is then no single thread that controls each development in our story, and 'to some degree, all of the above' is a better explanation. We are told, too, that the flapping of a butterfly's wings in Brazil just *might* set off reactions leading to a tornado in Texas. Unpredictable lines of causation probably exist also in the political world. And even apart from these, we should note that accidents – what Harold Macmillan termed 'events, dear boy, events' – could strongly shape the way trouble arose; the *Trent* affair is an obvious example. Equally, adventitious events could help *resolve* difficulties. An obvious instance is the famous discovery of the two maps supporting Britain's border claim that Webster secretly used in 1842 to bring the State of Maine to accept, and the Senate to ratify, a border deal. His task would have been harder without them - much harder had the British map supporting Maine's claim been discovered that year, rather than in 1843 after the deal.

It may nevertheless be helpful to ask how far the border line that eventually emerged might plausibly have been different. This border arose initially from the 'War of the Conquest' which led France to leave the North American mainland, and from the 'Revolutionary War' through which Thirteen Colonies secured independence as the 'United States of America'. There followed the 'War of 1812' in which the US failed to take Canada, the British to create an 'independent' Indian barrier state and make other changes to the line of border fixed in 1783. Had these wars turned out otherwise, things would have been very different, as indeed they would, had later crises brought another war.

---

[61] Captain Hunt to Mrs. McBlair, Nov. 1859 – Keith A. Murray, 'Pig War Letters. A romantic lieutenant's account of the San Juan crisis', *Columbia. The Magazine of Northwest History* I (1987) p. 18

Treaties can, too, be revised through pressures short of war. Border treaties with First Nations were repeatedly so modified through some combination of intimidation, land purchase, and the offer to Chiefs of pensions and other favours. And even treaties between 'civilised' states were often prone to 'revision', as were those between the United States and Spain/Mexico up to the 1853 Gadsden Purchase. The 1783 Anglo-American peace treaty may at first also have been in this category: Britain did not surrender the 'northern forts' (as the treaty required) until 1796, and after St. Clair's 1791 defeat its ministers hoped to get the US to accept an Indian barrier state plus minor boundary concessions to improve British defences. Later it was from the United States that pressure for boundary changes came. In 1869-70 it repeatedly suggested that British compensation for the *Alabama* damages should take the form of turning over Canada (or at least forcing it into a transitional independence) and/or of ceding the land between Canada and the Pacific. But though Gladstone's government would gladly have disengaged from Canada, it would do so only on the request of the Dominion's parliament (which was never likely to be forthcoming). More generally, despite occasional remarks that there might be conveniences in an American takeover, government policy had always been to keep the lands beyond the Lakes in British hands. In 1858 the response to the Fraser River gold rush had been creation of the new colony of British Columbia; and in 1869 Governor Musgrave was sent to secure its accession to Confederation as the only viable way to keep it from slipping into the United States. Further east, the Colonial Secretary would in the early 1860s have liked a string of new Crown colonies to develop and safeguard Rupert's Land. Policy then switched to facilitating its purchase by Canada from the HBC, and in 1870 the British government contributed troops to complete the process. Britain, then, was not going to retract from the boundary lines already set. And the United States was still less likely to do so, as can be seen from its determined retention of the tiny enclaves of Point Roberts, Washington, and Northwest Angle, Minnesota.

There were, too, attempts to revise the established border from below. The first related to Vermont. This had proclaimed itself an independent republic in 1777. In 1780-1 its leaders, the Allen family and Governor Chittenden, negotiated with Quebec's Governor, General Haldimand, to make Vermont a buffer state under British protection. These talks dropped after Cornwallis' surrender at Yorktown, and the Paris peacemakers agreed a border that placed Vermont within the United States. Nevertheless, Vermont's leaders told Haldimand that it 'must either be annexed to Canada or become Mistress of it', since Canada was 'the only channel by which' their 'Produce ... can be conveyed to market', and in coming years members of the Allen family would try both courses. In 1788 the former 'loyalist' Levi Allen was sent to London 'to Assure the British Court that Vermont was truly from local situation as well as inclination firmly attached to them', and to secure the building of a canal to facilitate access to Montreal. Allen made little progress until taken up by the prospective Lt. Governor of Upper Canada, John Graves Simcoe, who saw Vermont as 'another Switzerland between Canada and the United States' and believed its alliance to be a prerequisite for Canada's security. In 1791 Allen was on his way home to promote such ideas when he was startled to learn that Vermont had instead joined the United States. Still, his brother Ira continued to hope for the ship canal: and, with a parade of secrecy, assurances were conveyed to the British government that the 'Verdmonters did wish to become a neutral Power like a Swiss Canton', their 'first view' being 'to secure an Alliance with Great Britain on Terms' including construction of the canal.[62] By 1796 Ira Allen was in London to promote it. But meeting no success, he switched course and told France he could set up a secret network of revolutionaries

---

[62] University of Vermont Libraries, Special Collections, 'Vermont Statehood: A Dissenting Opinion from the Allen Family' (accessed 1/11/19); Henry Motz to Evan Nepean 29 July, and Sydney to governor General Lord Dorchester 5 Sept., 1788 (CO 42/63 fo. 134, and CO 42/61 fo. 4); Simcoe to Nepean (clearly inspired by a letter from Levi Allen), 3 Dec. 1789, and to Henry Dundas, 26 Aug. 1791 (ed. E.A. Cruikshank, *The Correspondence of John Graves Simcoe*, vol. 1 *1789-93* (Toronto, 1926) pp. 7-9, 52-3); unsigned note of 18 March 1894 (CO 5/8 fos. 76-7, with map, MPG 1/252)

in Canada. An invasion from Vermont (aided by a French expeditionary force) would then set off a general rebellion. There would follow a republic of 'United Columbia' that would trade freely with Vermont and funnel strategic goods to France. The French government was persuaded to give Allen 15,000 muskets to start the process, but in November 1796 a British warship intercepted them.[63]

The 'War of 1812' revived the idea of effecting major changes through the combination of external force and internal assistance: General Hull's manifesto promised to annex Canada with the aid of Americans already settled there, while Brock and Tecumseh captured Detroit and briefly established what was meant to be the British protected Indian Territory of Michigan. But with peace in 1815, the border went quiet until disturbed in late 1837 by rebellions in both Upper and Lower Canada. While these were quickly put down, some of the leaders fled to the United States and recruited support there through propaganda, pay, and promises of land and booty. Sympathy from local officials often helped them appropriate weapons from militia armouries, and over the next year they staged a number of mini-invasions. These were always quickly repulsed by enthusiastic local forces backed by British regulars. But until 1842 the border continued to be disturbed by arson, raids, and rumours of raids.

For the Frères Chasseurs, Hunters' Lodges, and other secret societies advocating the 'liberation' of the Canadas had spread widely. Their membership fluctuated both seasonally and over time, estimates ranging from 20,000 to 160,000.[64] And while the 1838 invasions showed 'liberation' of Canada to be out of the question, there was always the chance of an incident touching off an American-British war that might lead to its conquest.

---

[63] J. Kevin Graffagnino, '"The Country My Soul Delighted in": The Onion River Land Company and the Vermont Frontier', *New England Quarterly* 65:1 (1992) 24-60, and '"Twenty Thousand Muskets": Ira Allen and the Olive Branch Affair, 1796-1800', *William and Mary Quarterly* 48:3 (1991) 409-31

[64] Robert E. May, *Manifest Destiny's Underworld: Filibustering in Antebellum America* (Chapel Hill, North Carolina, 2002) p. 302n.

The federal government and the regular US army, backed by 'respectable' opinion away from the border, were at pains to prevent any such catastrophe.[65] But one nearly developed with the November 1840 arrest of Alexander McLeod, the product partly of mistaken identity, but chiefly of resentment against his actions as a Canadian sheriff. The denial of bail under pressure from a local mob, and his trial for his life (charged with participation in the burning of the *Caroline* and murder of Amos Durfee) did indeed lead Britain to threaten war were he executed (above pp. 318, 320-1). McLeod should never have been charged, and he was eventually acquitted and rushed back to Canada.

The Frères Chasseurs and Hunters' Lodges had been, or at least aspired to be, filibusters. Filibustering continued in a big way. But following the 1842 Webster-Ashburton treaty, it did not again affect the British North American border until after the Civil War. Its revival then was due to Irish-American politics. Some 'Fenians' hoped to achieve Irish independence by seizing enough of Canada to establish a 'government' there that would attract US recognition, license privateers, and with this leverage induce Britain to quit Ireland. Resources came from post-dated 'Irish Republic' bonds – in 1869 one faction raised $101,000. With this, arms were readily bought, though it proved harder to deliver them to prospective invasion forces without attracting attention from the now more numerous US troops along the border. The Fenians could also recruit from former Civil War soldiers,[66] and their 1867 convention paraded 6000 armed and uniformed men through Philadelphia. With these advantages, they should have

---

[65] Albert B. Corey, *The Crisis of 1830-1842 in Canadian-American Relations* (New Haven, 1941) chaps. 5, 6; ed. C.P. Stacey, 'A Private Report of General Winfield Scott on the Border Situation in 1839', *Canadian Historical Review* 21:4 (1940) 407-14; Samuel Wilson, 'United States Army Officers Fight the 'Patriot War': Responses to Filibustering on the Canadian Border, 1837-1839', *Journal of the Early Republic* 18 (Fall 1998) 485-519

[66] cf. the supposed Fenian marching song, 'Many battles we have won, along with the boys in blue, And we'll go and capture Canada, for we've nothing else to do' – Robert L. Dallison, *Turning Back the Fenians. New Brunswick's last Colonial Campaign* (Fredericton, N.B., 2006) p. 73

been stronger than the Hunters' Lodges. But they were no more successful.

Their first operation hoped to seize Campobello, with a thousand Fenians foregathering on the Maine shore in April 1866. The venue was geographically ill chosen, since the British could easily bring up far larger forces. In any case, the largest arms shipload was impounded by the US military. Later that year some 5000 men are supposed to have made their way to the Buffalo area, but only a little over 800 crossed over under 'Colonel' John O'Neill. They routed some Canadian militia at the Battle of Ridgeway and took Fort Erie. But when a clearly superior force approached, they withdrew across the border, and were intercepted *en route* by the U.S.S. *Michigan*. This Niagara invasion had been meant as a feint to divert British troops away from the drive against Quebec's Eastern Townships. Here 'Brigadier' Spears had been promised 12,000 men with adequate supplies. He never had more than a thousand; and when they crossed into Canada, they merely foraged and looted, then 'retreated without even a token resistance' on the approach of British forces. At a time when Confederation was being brought into being with some difficulty, the invasions had not made British North America love either the Fenians or the United States that seemed so tolerant of them. The Ridgeway battle did, however, make O'Neill's reputation in Fenian circles, and he rose to 'General'. One of the associates he carried up with him, 'Henri Le Caron', fed information to the Canadian intelligence chief Gilbert McMicken. The next invasion (of Quebec in 1870) was fired on the moment it crossed the border and hurried back, while a second incursion, recognising the enormous imbalance of forces, was no more persistent. And when O'Neill took 40-50 men west in 1871 to rouse the Manitoba Métis and establish a 'Republic of Rupert's Land', McMicken travelled on the same train and enlisted American assistance. Most of the Fenians were arrested by US cavalry on the border at Pembina.[67]

---

[67] Hereward Senior, *The Last Invasion of Canada. The Fenian Raids 1866-1870* (Canadian War Museum Historical Publications, 1991); O'Neill, John, Beach,

Filibusters, then, were never going to overthrow the established British provinces in the East. Further west there were no filibusters. But the fear that there might be contributed to one major border change, *Russia's* decision to sell Alaska to the United States. Russia's leaders took hemispheric ideas very seriously, believing that the US would inevitably take over all North America, as they themselves hoped to dominate the Far East: 'following the natural order of things', Grand Duke Constantine maintained, the United States 'must strive to possess all of North America', and 'sooner or later ... they will seize our colonies', a view fed by the wild reports of the minister in Washington Eduard De Stoeckl. Initially the talk was of the impossibility of preventing a direct seizure by the United States (actually, Britain would have found the operation easier). But in the crucial period of 1866-7 the fear was less of direct US action than of the 'American buccaneers who have become bolder in raiding our shores after' the recall of 'our naval squadron'. Adventurers, Stoeckl explained, 'have more than once played the role of pioneers. It is they who, little by little, invaded Texas which later became a State of the Union. New Mexico and other parts of the South were acquired in the same way'. And he added a melodramatic account of the way in which the 1858 Fraser River gold miners had declared 'that they recognised no authority except that of the United States and formed a provisional government', concluding that had the gold not been quickly worked out, 'British Columbia would now be a territory of the United States'. Perhaps Stoeckl was hamming it up to defend his treaty, but even in private he wrote that it 'was a matter of either selling' the colonies 'or seeing them taken from us'.[68]

Thomas Billis (aka. Henri Le Carron), and McMicken, Gilbert, *Dictionary of Canadian Biography*

[68] Constantine to Prince Gorchakov, 22 March/3 April 1857, and to the Tsar 7/17 Dec. (Nikolay Bolkhovitinov, 'The Crimean War and the Emergence of Proposals for the Sale of Russian America, 1853-1861', *Pacific Historical Review* 59:1 (1990) pp. 29-30, 38); Stoeckl to Prince Gorchakov, 12/24 July

Russia's sale of Alaska constituted a major geopolitical change, but one of ownership not of borders, which continued to be governed by the treaties of 1824-5. And there have, indeed, only ever been two changes in established borders: the 1850 cession of Horseshoe Reef in Lake Erie to the United States to facilitate the construction of a lighthouse, and that to Canada in 1925 of 2½ acres of isolated water in the Lake of the Woods' Northwest Angle channel.[69] We must therefore look to the decisions on successive stretches of the border to see how easily these could have been different.

Minor matters might well have been decided otherwise. Canadians were pleasantly surprised to receive (from the Treaty of Ghent's Sixth Article Commission) St. Lawrence islands important for the defence of the Kingston naval base, but shocked when the Alaska Tribunal awarded the Portland Canal islets of Sitklan and Kannaghunet to the United States. Sloppy British drafting of the 1846 treaty left it unclear whether the boundary between Vancouver Island and the mainland should run through the Haro Canal or the Rosario Straits, a question finally resolved in favour of the former by German arbitration. Several other such cases could be noted. Sometimes, too, actors and negotiators canvassed lines other than those ultimately adopted. And had the US Senate not unexpectedly rejected the Dutch arbitration award of 1831, the miniscule 'Indian Stream' community at the head of the Connecticut would have become Canadian while New York's northern border would (with one strategic exception) have followed the real 45th parallel not the line surveyed in the 1760s and 1770s.

But more important turning points can also be highlighted, notably during the 1782 peace negotiations. The hardest to evaluate is the British decision to seek (the French Foreign Minister

---

1867, and to Baron Westman, July 1867 (Hunter Miller, 'Russian Opinion on the Sale of Alaska', *American Historical Review* 48:3 (1943) pp. 529-31

[69] US Lighthouses, 'Horseshoe Reef Lighthouse', https://www.uslighthouses. com/horseshoe-reef-lighthouse (accessed 9/1/19); International Boundary Commission, *Joint Report on the Survey and Demarcation of the Boundary between the United States and Canada...* (Washington, 1937) pp. 33, 137-9

Vergennes later said, to buy) a pre-emptive separate peace with the United States. Alternatively, Britain might have indicated a conditional readiness to evacuate New York but have stood on the approximate line of military control on the United States' fringes. Such a stance would have placed the American Peace Commissioners under far greater pressure, especially as it would (once Lord Shelburne had established a surprising degree of cooperation with Vergennes) probably have been assisted by a France that sympathised with the British wish to provide for the Loyalist refugees, rejected American claims beyond the Appalachians, and wanted a territorial balance in North America that would make the US continue to look to French protection. Elsewhere, Shelburne and Vergennes did, in the general peace negotiations, work together in a remarkably amicable 'adversary partnership' to persuade Spain to return West Florida as part of a compensation package for the projected British surrender of Gibraltar. But this fell through, and instead Britain ceded East as well as West Florida to Spain. Had Britain retained them both, the history of borders in eastern North America would probably have been very different.

Early in the peace talks, Benjamin Franklin had sought to replace Quebec's 1774 western borders by the restrictive ones originally appointed in 1763. With hindsight, these borders would have precluded the subsequent emergence of any significant Canadian state. In late August the British cabinet still seemed ready to accept them. But instead of settling on this basis, John Jay insisted on first extracting a recognition of American independence that could not be disowned if they failed. And by the time draft treaty terms had emerged, the British cabinet had decided that it must have more. The American Commissioners fell back on a westwards continuation of the 1763 border along the 45th parallel. This would have assigned Lakes Ontario and Erie to the United States, Lake Superior and the upper parts of Lakes Huron and Michigan to Britain, thus drastically cutting the Lakes' utility as a transport corridor. Probably, too, subsequent Canadian development would have remained limited, lacking the greater part of what became settled Ontario. However, struck by the advantages of an easily recognizable boundary, the American Commissioners gave London the choice between the 45th parallel and a border through the middle of the Lakes. It opted for the latter.

Such a border would naturally have ended at the head of Lake Superior, quite close to the Mississippi. But what was in fact agreed (whether by reason of faulty maps or, as has recently been argued, of American sleight of hand) was a more northerly line running up 'the water communication' from Lake Superior to the northwestern point of the Lake of the Woods, and thence 'on a Due West course to the river Mississippi'. As the British government could have ascertained by consulting London merchants, the Lake of the Woods is not on the same watershed as the Great Lakes. Even at the time, it was thought to be north, rather than 'Due West', of the Mississippi; and Britain's Fox-North government was remiss in not pressing for this to be corrected in the final 1783 Treaty.

The 1783 treaty had promised Britain free navigation of the Mississippi, but its 'Due West' boundary line from the Lake of the Woods would never reach that river. Montreal merchants lobbied for a correction. Lord Grenville tried for this in his 1794 negotiations with Jay, advancing two possible routes, but Jay insisted that their adoption would derail the entire treaty. Later, President Jefferson sought to conclude the matter by replacing the 'Due West' line with one running directly from the Lake of the Woods to the Mississippi's source. The 1803 King-Hawkesbury treaty provided for this, and had it been concluded earlier the terminus of the agreed border would no longer have been at the Lake of the Woods but further south. By then, though, the United States had just bought Louisiana. And to scotch any possibility of the border later being run west from its new terminus, Jefferson reverted to the Lake of the Woods and claimed a boundary extending west from there along the 49th parallel. This was an entirely new claim, and Britain was initially displeased. But to conciliate the US it would have accepted a 49th parallel border in 1807, and in 1818 it did so (as far as the Rockies), dropping its right of Mississippi navigation.

West of the Rockies the landmarks were different. Following the 1790 Nootka Bay crisis, Spain was forced to admit a general right to trade and establish posts beyond the most northerly Spanish settlement, San Francisco.[70] Spain was also to restore the British-owned buildings at Nootka seized in 1789, and Captain Vancouver was charged with accepting them. On his way up the coast, he missed the mouth of the Columbia, and it was first discovered and named by the private American trader Captain Robert Gray. Vancouver then had the lower Columbia surveyed, publishing the results in his 1798 Atlas. This Atlas established the Columbia, in public consciousness, as 'the line of communication from the Pacific Ocean, pointed out by nature as it is the only navigable river in the whole ... of that coast', and it attracted would-be empire builders. First among these was the Russian American Company, which would seek (albeit with very limited resources) to fill the vacuum resulting from the abandonment of Nootka. It established a small post in what is now northern California, and only shipwreck stopped it planting one at the mouth of the Columbia in 1808.

John Jacob Astor's American Fur Company did establish 'Astoria' there in 1811. The North-West Company had pressed the British Government to prevent this, saying it would probably 'involve the ultimate right of possession of the whole Northwest coast of America'. But while peace lasted, the government would not move. During the War of 1812, the North-West Company managed to buy Astoria, but a British warship nevertheless took formal possession, which enabled the US to secure its token return after the war. And though there would for decades be no American presence on the ground, the United States added discovery (by Gray, followed by Lewis and Clark) and first settlement to its list of claims to the Columbia basin.

In 1818 American negotiators secured British acceptance of a 49th parallel border as far as the Rockies. They also proposed its further extension to the Pacific, but their British counterparts wanted to run it down the Columbia to safeguard their right to

---

[70] Thereafter, Spain tried briefly to make the Juan De Fuca Strait the line between its possessions and the area where the general right to trade applied, offering Captain Vancouver in return the entire post at Nootka. Nothing came of this, but had he accepted, a border appreciably south of the present one might have come about

use that river; so the 'Oregon' issue was put on ice. In 1826 Britain offered the US in addition an enclave on the Olympic peninsula, and in 1842-3 Daniel Webster thought of so adapting this as to give Britain its border along the Columbia. In return, Britain would compel Mexico to cede San Francisco to the United States. But nothing came of this; and in 1846 (after a major crisis) Britain and the United States compromised on a border that would follow the 49th parallel only to the Gulf of Georgia and then turn south, leaving Britain all Vancouver Island.

Meanwhile, the basic course of what would become the Canada-Alaska border had already been laid down by the 1824 US-Russian and the 1825 Anglo-Russian treaties. In 1821 the RAC's territory had been extended south to 51°, but in 1824 Russia readily pulled back to islands terminating at 54° 40°. It did, though, in its negotiations with Britain insist on retaining on the mainland a protective lisière, whose precise borders were not easily defined in the then state of geographical knowledge. For its extension north to the Arctic Ocean, all three of the lines of 139°, of 140°, and of 141° West longitude were considered. That finally chosen, 141°, placed the 1890s Klondike gold strike just in Canada. Access usually ran via the head of the Lynn Canal, where the United States enjoyed both actual possession and a solid legal case under the 1825 treaty. But that treaty had not made it clear how far inland the American lisière should extend, and Canada went far to settle the question where it most mattered by pre-emptively stationing its Mounted Police on the summits of the mountains overlooking Skagway and Dyea.

* * *

Broadly there are two alternative approaches to the negotiation of borders between equals. In 1823 Russia proposed to set aside questions of 'strict right' in favour of 'an amicable arrangement [over Alaska] founded on ... mutual expediency'.[71] Both the

---

[71] Count Lieven to George Canning, 19 Jan. 1823, and Pierre de Poletica's report of his discussions with Sir Charles Bagot, 3 Nov. 1823 (*Proceedings of the Alaska*

British and the Americans sometimes adopted this approach. Indeed in the long sequence of boundary disputes there were only two points on which Britain absolutely insisted: retention of its strategic route up the St. John to Quebec; and that of the right to 'navigate' the Columbia that seemed essential for the HBC's continued operations west of the Rockies. Otherwise, Britain was the readier of the two powers to make goodwill concessions (like the 1818 abandonment of the link to the Mississippi prescribed in the 1783 treaty), and to suggest either compromises or arbitration. The United States was generally more drawn to the strict constructionist approach encapsulated in Secretary of State Cass's formula that if San Juan 'belongs to Great Britain she is entitled to hold it, whether it is valuable or not; and if it belongs to the United States the United States' Government is entitled to its possession, even though it should be conceded to be of superior value to Great Britain'.[72] This difference presumably reflected both the greater distance of British ministers from what they mostly saw as secondary issues of detail and their lesser exposure to political pressures on foreign policy. One must take President John Quincy Adams' protests with salt – his successor Andrew Jackson managed to be both more accommodating and more constructive; but no British Prime Minister could have written, 'One inch of ground yielded on the North-West coast, one step backward from the claim to the navigation of the St. Lawrence, one hair's-breadth of compromise on the article of impressment, would be certain to meet the reprobation of the Senate'.[73] Canadians, however, did not share the imperial government's relative detachment from these border issues, and they came to

---

Boundary Tribunal ... with respect to the boundary between the Territory of Alaska and the British Possessions in North America (Washington, 1904), ii pp. 116, 118, 140)

[72] Lord Lyons to Lord John Russell, 20 Dec. 1859 (reporting a conversation with Cass), and Russell's 9 March 1860 response (*San Juan Boundary. Abstract of Correspondence ... 1842 to 1869* pp. 227-8, 234-5)

[73] Adams to Gallatin, 20 March 1827 (ed. Henry Adams, *The Writings of Albert Gallatin* ii (Philadelphia, 1879) p. 368)

view British negotiators, notably Lord Ashburton and Chief Justice Alverstone, as appeasing the US at Canada's expense. By the end of the nineteenth century, the Dominion was of sufficient stature to take a harder line, not independently but by influencing the foreign policy of the Empire, though it did not obviously benefit thereby.

One result of the importance of law and the general predominance of strict treaty construction was emphasis on precedent. A border dividing North America from coast to coast was an entirely new phenomenon, but in defining its various segments people almost always managed to link them to earlier developments. When Nova Scotia had to be given a new western border in 1763, this was done by reverting to King James' obsolete 1621 grant.[74] Quebec also needed a new southern border, and the 1763 Royal Proclamation specified one that, crossing the St. Lawrence and Lake Champlain 'in 45 degrees of North Latitude, passes along the High Lands which divide the Rivers that empty themselves into the ... St. Lawrence from those which fall into the Sea'. This language passed (subject to the potentially importance replacement of the word 'Sea' by 'Ocean') into the 1783 Peace Treaty, and the process of interpreting it stretched until 1842. Beyond the St. Lawrence, the 1763 Proclamation had run Quebec's border west and north to Lake Nipissim; and when Congress came to consider the boundaries it hoped to get from the Revolutionary War, it sought to revert from the 1774 Quebec Act to the 1763 Proclamation, or, failing this, to extend to the Mississippi the Proclamation's 45th parallel line from the Connecticut to the St. Lawrence. Admittedly American negotiators were so struck by the attractions of a 'certainly distinguishable' natural water boundary that they also offered, and Britain accepted, a new line through the Great Lakes to the Lake of the Woods. But to take the

---

[74] Though the direction in which the border line should run above the St. Croix was altered from 'towards the north' ('versus septentrionem') to the much firmer 'due north', which, since it was incorporated into the 1783 treaty, would hamper attempts to find a mutually acceptable solution after the Senate's rejection of the Dutch arbitration award

border as far as Britain could legally concede, the peace then specified a line 'Due West' onwards from there to the Mississippi.

Before the War of 1812 these broad-brush definitions only really created problems in three areas. The most basic was the identification of the departure point for the border's entire circuit, the 'St. Croix' river. This was made in 1797-8 by archaeological excavation that revealed the river island where Pierre de Monts had wintered in 1604-5. The next question was the ownership of the islands in Passamaquoddy Bay. Legally this turned on whether they were 'or heretofore have been within the limits' of Nova Scotia, and copious evidence was collected on this, though in the end political considerations and those of convenience took precedence. The third was the replacement of the 1783 treaty's 'Due West' line by one that really would link the Lake of the Woods to the Mississippi. This should have been effected by the 1803 King-Hawkesbury treaty. But its apparent implications for the border west of that river prevented ratification. For buried in the thinking of the time was the presumption, harking back to casual grants in seventeenth century charters, that a boundary line once settled should be continued indefinitely west. To foreclose the possibility of any such curtailment of his new acquisition of Louisiana, President Jefferson came up with an entirely new claim. He might have anchored it on the 1783 treaty words, 'Due West' from the Lake of the Woods, but instead invoked an older authority, the (mistaken) belief that the 49th parallel had been chosen by Commissioners under the 1713 Treaty of Utrecht as the border between French lands and those of the British Hudson's Bay Company. This belief, unchallenged until 1840 and still a matter for debate at the time of the 1846 Oregon treaty, melded with the feeling that border lines *ought* to run indefinitely westwards to create a feeling that the United States was entitled to the 49th parallel as far as the Pacific. That cut across the HBC's claim to the Red River basin under its charter from Charles II. But the British government took little notice: in 1807 it would have accepted a 49th parallel border as far as the Rockies, and in 1818 it did so.

East of the Lake of the Woods border questions were governed by the 1783 treaty, so national interests had to be cast into contentions as to its proper interpretation. With no such over-arching treaty beyond the Rockies, other arguments were needed; but many related to the past. Discovery of a river's mouth was often held (albeit not in respect of the St. Lawrence) to convey title to the whole river basin; and the first to enter and name the Columbia was the American trader Captain Gray. Lewis and Clark then reached the river and wintered at its mouth in 1805-6. In 1811 Fort Astoria was established on the southern side of that mouth. And by the 1819 Adams Onis treaty, the United States assumed also the claims of Spain, which enabled it to claim not just the Columbia basin but the whole of Oregon up to the Russian border. The British too invoked discovery, notionally extending back to Drake, more realistically to Captains Cook and Vancouver, and to Lieutenant Broughton's 1792 mapping of the lower Columbia and formal claim of the territory for the Crown. The American Fur Company had admittedly been the first to establish a fort, Astoria, at the Columbia's mouth. But this, the British held, had been within the context of the Nootka Convention (whose continued currency in international law the Americans denied). So they saw their formal restoration of Astoria to the US in 1817 as merely that of property captured during the war, without prejudice to the sovereignty they derived from the explorations of Alexander Mackenzie and Simon Fraser and from the trading posts the North West Company had established on the upper Columbia.

These historically based claims raise counterfactual questions. What if Vancouver and not Gray had been the first to enter the Columbia? What if, when the Northwest Company already held Astoria by purchase, H.M.S. *Raccoon* had not in 1813 staged a military 'capture', thus rendering the post liable to restoration at the end of the war? The United States would probably still have invoked territorial propinquity and have demanded the westwards continuation of its 49th parallel border. But Britain, with what it might well have seen as a cast iron case, could have found it harder to make the concessions it did. What, too, if there had been no sand bar at the mouth of the Columbia? It came to be so generally accepted that the US required a proper Pacific port that in 1827 Britain offered one on the Olympia peninsula. Had there been no sand bar, this would have been unnecessary, and Britain's preferred solution, partition of Oregon along the Columbia giving both countries access to its mouth, would have been more persuasive.

The eventual outcome in 1846 turned on the 49th parallel border President Jefferson had conjured up. President Polk seemed to demand all Oregon up to '54° 40″. But a Senate majority fell back on the 49th parallel that had been central to the demands of Polk's predecessors. American commitment to this line, at least on the mainland, was absolute: even the 'more moderate' Senators, Pakenham warned, would insist on 'the Parallel of 49 ... as the basis of any arrangement.'[75] The requisite compromise was accordingly made on this basis. Thereafter the boundary was again defined by treaty. So the Gulf Islands dispute was, like earlier ones on the other side of the continent, conducted on the basis of rival treaty interpretations, and finally settled by German arbitration. And when the United States bought Alaska, its boundaries had already been defined by the 1824 and 1825 treaties with Russia. Canada's desire for sovereignty over a port giving access to its Yukon gold fields had, therefore, to take the form of a rather strained interpretation of these treaties. Canning and Nesselrode had left constraining footprints in the sands of time.

* * * * *

To settle the line of the North American border, it was often necessary to look back. But the whole point of doing so was to build for the future. Castlereagh had in 1818 hoped for quick agreement on the course of the border between the Columbia's mouth and the Lake of the Woods, since it was always easier 'to come to an arrangement ... where the territory ... is little known ... than where' people had established settlements 'which cannot

---

[75] Pakenham to Aberdeen, 28 April 1846, referring also to his earlier letter of 29 March (FO 115/92 fos. 72, 111-13)

be abandoned without loss'.[76] Castlereagh was clearly thinking of Europeans. For First Nations were already in place throughout the continent, and they were often adversely affected by the drawing of new boundary lines. In the area below the Great Lakes, Indians would, from Pontiac to Tecumseh, seek to divert or halt settler expansion, after 1782 often with attempted guidance, restraint, or supplies from British officials looking thereby to safeguard the Canadian border, and, during the two Anglo-American wars, also with active mutual military support. After 1815, First Nations resistance continued, but now with little impact on the border since British involvement was discontinued. Further west, the 49th parallel border was notionally drawn across the Great Plains in 1818. This might have been disruptive, for, as one Police Commissioner observed, the Indians on both sides of the 'International Boundary are one people, severed politically by an invisible line'.[77] Actually, both Indians and Métis buffalo hunters and carters long continued to move across it at will. But when the buffaloes failed at the end of the 1870s, the border became much harder: American authorities started first to restrict access, then to deport Canadian Indians, and the Canadian police later cut food doles on the border and shepherded Indians to newly appointed reserves well away to the north.

A more modern instance of borders creating rather than resolving problems is Akwesasne. Indians gathered in the eighteenth century at St. Regis and have remained there ever since. St. Regis happened to be where the 45th parallel, appointed by the 1763 Proclamation as the border between New York and Quebec, meets the St. Lawrence. In 1783 in theory, and in 1796 (with Britain's departure from the northern forts) in practice, this line became the international boundary. And matters were further complicated when Ghent Treaty Commissioners apportioned the

---

[76] Castlereagh's two official letters to Sir Charles Bagot, 4 Feb. 1818 (FO 5/129 fos. 17-24 and 26-9), and his private letter of the same date (Bagot Papers, National Archives of Canada, MG24 A13 Vol. 12 pp. 10-14)
[77] Paul F. Sharp, *Whoop-up Country. The Canadian-American West, 1865-1885* (Minneapolis, 1955) p. 133

adjacent islands in the St. Lawrence. The result is a Canadian Mohawk Reserve north of the international border that is itself split between the provinces of Ontario and Quebec, with, south of the border in New York, the St. Regis Mohawk Reservation. For good measure, one can only go from the Quebec to the Ontario sections by crossing the international boundary and passing through the New York section. Such a set-up necessarily gives scope for problems with the customs authorities. Moreover Mohawks maintain that the 1794 Jay treaty entitles them, as Indians, to trade across borders without paying duty – a view the Canada Border Services Agency does not share. Friction over Mohawk claims to unalienated sovereignty over Akwesasne is not new – in 1899 Jake Ince was shot by Canadian police while protesting against the planned imposition there of federal laws. But the issue really came to the fore with the First Nations' reassertion of rights in the later twentieth century. In 1968 traffic on the new Seaway International Bridge was blocked by Mohawks seeking to force recognition of their Jay treaty claims. In the 1980s an industry grew up smuggling cigarettes over the Canadian border for sale in the Kahnawake Mohawk reserve near Montreal, occasioning a police raid in 1988 that confiscated $200,000 worth of cigarettes and led to a brief Mohawk seizure of Canadian customs posts in retaliation. This smuggling was large enough to lead Canada to cut its cigarette taxes in the mid-1990s. There are many indications both that the trade nevertheless continued and that its practitioners also turned to other items – in 1996 a boat carrying illegal immigrants to the US capsized. Meanwhile a mixture of factional fighting and conflicts over both smuggling and the St. Regis reservation casinos led in 1990 to police interventions and the evacuation of 400 people to safety in Canada. Later, things calmed down, and indigenous governmental institutions developed. But frictions, protests, and disturbances have continued, most notably in the summer of 2009 when encampments against the arming of Canadian customs officers led these to pull out of the Reserve; instead, in June and July, Canadian authorities blocked access to the Seaway International Bridge from the north, and their American counterparts that from the south, thus effectively besieging the Akwesasne inhabitants.[78]

In Madawaska, too, the process of agreeing the border cut across a pre-existing community. Here Acadians had settled on both sides of the Saint John River, largely protected from Maine's attempts to control what it took to be its rightful territory. After the 'Aroostook War', some recent migrants from Quebec were drawn to Maine's emissaries. But the longer settled Acadians, who had taken the best lands on arriving and were now emerging as an elite, frequently asserted their determination to remain British subjects – Father Langevin (of the pre-eminent religious centre of St. Basile) even wrote that 'we would prefer war to ceding a single inch of our land of Madawaska to the Americans'.[79] In 1842 Lord Ashburton respected this loyalty, and did his best to keep southern Madawaska. But he had eventually to accept a border down the middle of the St. John. Though Maine's representatives had insisted on this, there were qualms as to the state's new citizens. Edward Kavanagh was told that, separated from other Maine settlements by 30-60 miles of unbroken forest, 'Their business intercourse has been wholly with New Brunswick and Canada – they have lived under British laws and are too ignorant to be at present capable of self-government.' In 1843 the projected withdrawal of US federal troops from Fort Kent occasioned alarm; and next year the state legislature stressed to Washington the French population's inexperience of American laws and the presence of 'powerful and armed bands of foreign marauders

---

[78] Websites of the Mohawk Council of Akwesasne and of the St. Regis Mohawk Tribe, and Wikipedia's Akwesasne article, accessed 4/11/2019. Google searches throw up plentiful press notices and comment, much of it hotly contested, including Chris Wood, 'Gunfire and Gambling', *Maclean's Magazine*, 7 May 1990 p. 22, Tim Shufelt, 'Akwesasne primer: A history of confrontation', *Ottawa Citizen*, 13 July 2009, and Tom Blackwell, 'Contraband capital: the Akwesasne Mohawk Reserve is a smuggling conduit, police say', *National Post*, 22 Sept. 2010

[79] W.S. MacNutt mentions many other protestations, 'invariably over the signatures of their priests' (*New Brunswick, a history: 1783-1867* (Toronto, 1963) p. 311); Thomas Albert, *Histoire du Madawaska* (Quebec, 1920) p. 221

encamped upon a weak and defenceless border'.[80] It was not a happy beginning. But Maine went to some trouble to survey Acadian holdings and grant land titles (which the border dispute had estopped their previous New Brunswick rulers from doing). Maine also encouraged schools, not yet on a large scale but sufficiently to attract children from the New Brunswick side of the border. And it provided its half of Madawaska with representation in the state legislature, whereas in New Brunswick Madawaska constituted only part of Carleton County.[81] All this no doubt helped to keep things quiet, and, as Maine's survey commission hoped, to transfer to the United States past traditions of loyalty to the British Crown.

Divergencies would develop between the two halves, most obviously in the movement for separate ecclesiastical institutions that led in 1870 to the transfer of Maine's Madawaska to the diocese of Portland.[82] But links across the St. John remained very close: the New Brunswick JP Joseph Cyr was the brother of Maine state Representative Firmin Cyr, while Representative François Thibodeau was the son, and Representative Paul Cyr the son-in-law, of New Brunswick JP Firmin Thibodeau.[83] At a lower level, a Maine official could write in the 1890s that as far as 'feelings, language and intercourse were concerned', the Madawaskans had until recently been 'as distinct from the other portions of Maine as though they were indeed a separate nation', with 'nearly all the necessaries of life' they could not themselves produce coming to them from Canada. A 1902 observer added that 'Racially and territorially' they were 'today more Canadian than American'.

---

[80] Charles W. Collins, *The Acadians of Madawaska Maine* (Boston, 1902) p. 51; Sheila McDonald, 'The War after the War: Fort Kent blockhouse, 1839-1842', *Maine Historical Society Quarterly* 29:3 & 4 (1990) pp. 193-4

[81] M. Ruth Nicholson, 'Relations of New Brunswick with the State of Maine and the United States, 1837-1849', M.A. thesis, University of New Brunswick, Aug. 1952 (microfiche, Rochester, NY, 1956, pp. 69-72). Maine's survey and land grants were completed by 1844, their New Brunswick counterparts not till 1847

[82] Albert, *Histoire du Madawaska* pp. 229, 247-8

[83] Béatrice Craig, 'Immigrants in a Frontier Community: Madawaska 1785-1850', *Histoire Sociale – Social History* 19 no. 38 (Nov. 1986) p. 294n.

So it is not surprising that at the great 1908 Acadian convention at St. Basile there were speakers from both sides of the St. John.[84] Later, enthusiasm for the preservation of minority cultures led to the establishment in 1938 of a notional cross-border 'République du Madawaska' with its own flag (now among those flown in front of Edmundston, N.B.'s City Hall), to which have been added a President (the Mayor of Edmundston), a Museum, and an annual 'Foire Brayonne' whose name reflects consciousness that the local French is neither Acadian nor Québécois. So, as Gary Campbell observes, despite Madawaska's cleavage by the Webster-Ashburton treaty 'the border was more a formality than a barrier', *'until the events of September 11, 2001'*.[85]

The other obvious border anomalies are Minnesota's North West Angle enclave on the Lake of the Woods, and Washington's Point Roberts which is surrounded by greater Vancouver. The British thought both would give trouble, and sometimes sought to negotiate them away: in 1824 Canning had suggested that rather than running up to the North-West Angle of the Lake of the Woods and then descending to 49°, the border should turn west as soon as it reached the 49th parallel, thus eliminating an anomalous US enclave on the Lake's western shore.[86] But the North West Angle did not develop, as feared, into a haunt of smugglers and criminals. With no more than 120 residents in 2010, it is lightly settled and hits the news only as a matter of curiosity.[87] Point Roberts is more significant. The British fear was that it would

---

[84] Quotations from State Superintendent Stetson in 'Our Schools in Northeastern Maine', *Maine Farmer* 67:2 (10 Nov. 1898); Collins, *The Acadians of Madawaska Maine* pp. 52, 58; Albert, *Histoire du Madawaska* p. 296
[85] Jacques Paul Couturier, 'La République du Madawaska et l'Acadie: la Construction identitaire d'une région néo-brunswickoise au XXᵉ siécle', *Revue d'histoire de l'Amérique française* 56:2 (2002) pp. 153-84; Wikipedia, 'Republic of Madawaska' (accessed 10/12/2019); W.E (Gary) Campbell, *The Aroostook War of 1839* (Fredericton, N.B., 2013 p. 127 – my italics)
[86] FO 414/2, Confidential Print, 'Negotiations between the Plenipotentiaries of Great Britain and the United States ... 1824' pp. 55-6
[87] In 1998, to the annoyance of the Chairman of the local Indian Reservation, a Minnesota Congressman introduced a bill providing for a referendum on joining Canada, though this was really a move to prompt action on a fishing dispute;

enable the US to interdict maritime access to Fort Langley and the Fraser River,[88] and during the 1857 negotiations (above, p. 570) Captain Prevost was told to seek Point Roberts' cession, offering 'a slight alteration of the Line of Boundary on the Mainland' by way of compensation, but to no avail. Similarly, Governor-General Grey would in 1907 have liked Laurier to seek its cession as a partial equivalent for abandoning Canada's right to pelagic sealing.[89] In 1858-9 a few people settled on the Point in hopes of avoiding the British taxes on participants in the Fraser gold rush, while in the 1860s it was the resort of smugglers. More conventional settlement began in 1873, and in the early twentieth century Point Roberts had both salmon canneries and farms. By 1949, with the canneries gone and the farms in trouble, there was talk of joining Canada. But Point Roberts developed later both as a holiday community and as the venue for Canadian purchases of cheaper American goods and gasoline, though these would be somewhat inhibited by the delays stemming from tighter US border controls after 9/11.[90]

Point Roberts' early history shows that there might be difficulties even when, as Castlereagh had wished, the border was defined before the real advent of settlement. Such difficulties can also be encountered along the 45th parallel. The border here was surveyed in the 1770s when it still ran through wilderness. In 1847 boundary monuments were erected, but next year one at Beebe Plain, Vermont, was removed to a more convenient position.

---

and in December-January 2018-19 2000 people signed a petition seeking transfer to Canada

[88] There was a US military reserve there from 1859 to 1892, but it was never used and may have been meant chiefly to discourage unsuitable settlement

[89] Grey understood, though, that William Templeman, a cabinet minister from B.C., did 'not attach much importance to this cession, and that Sir Wilfrid did not press it' (Grey to Sir Richard Cartwright, 11 April 1907 – Libraries and Archives, Canada, Albert Henry George Grey, 4th Earl Grey fonds: héritage, Film 1358, image 778)

[90] Phil Dougherty, *Point Roberts – Thumbnail History* (posted 15 Sept. 2009, HistoryLink.orgEssay9158), and Wikipedia, *Point Roberts, Washington* – both accessed 12/12/19

This may simply have been because it constituted 'a serious obstacle to the free passage of vehicles'; but Colonel Graham suspected an intention 'to cause' the border 'to pass through the middle of a store constructed across the line, making it easy thus to evade the authority of the Custom House officers [and Magistrates] of both Governments.'[91] By then building had, in several places, reached the border from both sides, with people moving readily across it.

We have seen that in the 1830s people from Canada proper, Indian Stream, and New Hampshire all foregathered at the Canaan, Vermont, store and tavern (above, pp. 231-2); and in 1820 Taillon's International Hotel (or Half-way House) was built literally on the line between Dundee, Quebec, and Fort Covington, N.Y. Though Customs officers sometimes caused difficulties, there 'were once hundreds of [such] buildings', inns, stores, houses, and factories, 'many' serving 'liquor during Prohibition'. Six small airstrips now straddle the border, some used in 1939-41 to deliver aircraft to Britain without quite breaking US neutrality laws: the planes were flown legally to the American end, 'autonomously' migrated overnight to the Canadian, and were then flown off by the Royal Canadian Air Force. The airstrips are still there, but by 2014 fewer than 40 of the buildings on or spanning the border line remain. For since the 1960s the International Boundary Commission 'has been authorized to regulate all construction ... within the 20-foot boundary zone', and it now 'refuses most applications for ... permits, even for repairs, for buildings inside' this zone.[92]

---

[91] 'Joint Report of Lieut. Colonels Graham and Ord upon the Replacement of the Boundary post at Beebe Plain, and the securing of certain other boundary monuments', 19 Sept. 1849, and Graham's 18 Aug. letter to Secretary of State Clayton (U.S. National Archives, Record Group 76, Entry P1 170, 128). The Report provides copious measurements, so that 'the true position of this monument may ... be readily found should it again be interfered with'

[92] The Centfor Land Use Interpretation, *United Divide: a Linear Portrait of the USA/Canada Border* (2015, reproducing a 2014 exhibition), chaps. 1, 5; 'Cross-border airports' in Wikipedia' *Canada-United States border* (though not all those

This process began well before 9/11, but the twenty-first century has seen such a tightening that the 'undefended border' now seems to western Europeans (if *not* to Mexicans) a hard one. Beebe Plain (split between Stanstead, Quebec and Derby Line, Vermont) was once

> 'viewed [locally] as one town … Now, the two [parts] are divided by an increasingly firm, and nearly invisible, line, prompting residents to stick primarily to their own side … everything began to change … after the terrorist attacks of Sept. 11, 2001. Surveillance has substantially increased…'

Some special Parks apart, the border should now be crossed only at official Ports of Entry, often, in less built-up areas, many miles apart. And the open space between them is 'usually' 'monitored by powerful cameras, on poles, along with movement sensors that alert the Border Patrol. Once triggered, the cameras begin recording, and can be zoomed in on suspects to see if anyone crosses the line…'.[93] Things used to be very different.

What has not changed is the border's location, which remains where surveyors marked it to give effect to the decisions of statesmen, Commissioners, and diplomats. They did so with considerable care; their work was usually cross-checked by opposite numbers from the other country; and picturesque traditions (as that Canada's possession of Campobello results from the unsteadiness of Webster's hand when drawing the boundary after a good dinner or that surveyors had 'too much to drink and decided to place the border right through the [Beebe] village') are, alas, myths. Still mistakes were made: during the 1872-6 survey there were 'wanderings of up to a quarter of a mile

---

there listed had been built by 1941); Adam Twidell, 'Shared Airports between the US and Canada' (posted online 17/8/2015 – accessed 10/12/2019
[93] Alexandre Silberman, 'On border road, a barrier marks a changing way of life', *VTDigger*, 27 Aug. 2018 (accessed 16/12/19); Center for Land Use Interpretation, *United Divide*, chap. 1 (with special reference to the Maine-New Brunswick border); 'Beebe Plain', Wikipedia (accessed 23/10/21)

from the true 49th' parallel. There is, though, little disposition to sort out either 'historical surveying errors' or the 'nonsensical enclaves' resulting from running the border along abstract geographical parallels. In the words of a 1990s US Deputy Boundary Commissioner, 'there is no interest ... in revising treaties that have served both countries quite well.'[94]

---

[94] *United Divide*, chap. 5; Hopper, 'Free the Northwest Angle, *National Post*, 3 Jan. 2019

Bibliography

(starred items relate exclusively to works cited in Volume 2)

Manuscript Collections

Those chiefly used are:

The National Archives, Kew, England – documents cited by their file references alone are from these Archives.

Despatches to and from the colonies of Vancouver Island and British Columbia and related documents (chiefly from the National Archives, Kew) are transcribed, digitally reproduced, and edited in *The Colonial Despatches of Vancouver Island and British Columbia 1846-1871* (ed. James Hendrickson and the Colonial Despatches project, University of Victoria, online (https://bcgenesis.uvic.ca)

The British Library, Additional Manuscripts – cited as Add. MS. followed by their identifying number

The National Archives, Washington, D.C.

The Library of Congress – cited as LoC

Besides its own MSS. holdings, the Library of Congress provides convenient access to the writings of many early US politicians through its 'Founders Online' series

Library and Archives Canada, Ottawa – sometimes cited as LAC

University of Oxford: Bodleian Library

All Souls College Library, Papers of Sir Charles Vaughan – many have been reproduced in the Archives Online, 'International Relations between Britain and America, 1796-1848' collection, from which most but not all of the book's citations are taken

References to other archives are given in the appropriate footnotes

Prints and Publications of Official Documents

i)   *Confidential Prints*: As the nineteenth century wore on, the British Foreign and Colonial Offices increasingly produced, for their own and/or Cabinet use, 'Confidential Prints', collections chiefly, but not exclusively, of British and other official documents relevant to specific topics. They are listed in the National Archives FO 881/ and CO 881/ series. (Of these Foreign Office prints, Adam Matthew Digital has digitised only their FO 414/ subsection, so references will as far as possible be given to this.) The *Confidential Prints* most used here are:

'Correspondence relative to the occupation of ... San Juan by United States' Troops, Part 1, 1 August to 31 October 1859', 'Part 2, October 1859 to July 1860' (FO 881/817, FO 414/16)

'Correspondence relative to the recent disturbances in the Red River Settlement'* [20 Aug. 1869-9 June 1870], and 'Memorandum relating to the Disturbances in the Red River Settlement. (Continued ...)', dated 13 April 1870* (CO 880/4/26, CO 880/4/25)

'Correspondence respecting the Canadian Pacific Railway Act so far as regards British Columbia ...'*(CO 880/7/5)

'Correspondence respecting the Rising in the North-West Territory'* (CO 880/9/18)

'Correspondence respecting the... Joint Commission for the Settlement of Questions pending between the United States and Canada, Part 1'* (FO 881/7135); 'Part X. Further Correspondence respecting the Boundary between the British Possessions in North America and the Territory of Alaska. February to September 1898'* (FO 414/158); 'Boundary between the British Possessions ... and ... Alaska. Further Correspondence XI, February to December 1899'* (FO 414/161)

Kenneth Bourne and D. Cameron Watt have edited *British Documents on Foreign Affairs: Reports and Papers from the Foreign Office Confidential Print*, Part 1 Series C North America 1837-1914. The volumes here cited are: 2 *Oregon and Texas, 1842-1848*, 10 *Expansion and Rapprochement 1889-1898**, 11 *Expansion and Rapprochement, 1899-1905** (University Publications of America, 1986, 1987).

ii) *Parliamentary Papers*: From the outset, the United States was commendably transparent in its publication of official documents, and these are often here cited in footnotes. But the British 'Parliamentary Papers' are better indexed, if generally less comprehensive; and in the 1830s Lord Palmerston deliberately sought to outdo the US in the quantity of documents (American as well as British) he published on the north-eastern boundary dispute. Much use is accordingly made of:

Parliamentary Papers 1837-8 xxxix, 'Correspondence relating to the Boundary between the British Possessions in North America, and the United States of America, under the Treaty of 1783' [Paper no. 118]; 'Proceedings and Correspondence relating to the Pretensions of the States of Maine, Massachusetts, and New Hampshire, and to the Question of Jurisdiction within the disputed Territory [Paper no. 146]

1868-9 xliii, 'Correspondence relating to the Surrender of Rupert's Land by Hudson's Bay Company and Admission into the Dominion of Canada'*

[The volumes of the Parliamentary Papers are paginated by hand, and I have followed the conventional form of citing by Parliamentary Session, volume number, and page within that volume – not by title and paper/command number (as preferred by ProQuest, when digitising them) and the printed *internal* pagination of each paper.]

iii) Canada followed the example of the Parliamentary Papers. Publications here used include:

'Return ... of ... Correspondence ... on the ... claims of certain Inhabitants of the Indian Stream Settlement ... for compensation for injuries received ... on the occasion of the arrest in 1835, of two individuals, under a Warrant from Alexander Rea, Esquire ...', 7 April 1853, *Appendix to the*

Eleventh Volume of the Journals of the Legislative Assembly of the Province of Canada, 19 Aug. 1852-14 June 1853, [Vol. 11 no. 8] Appendix B.B.B.B.

'Correspondence and Papers connected with the Recent Occurrences in the North-West Territories' (Canada, Sessional Papers, 1870 vol. v no. 12)*

'Report of the [Parliamentary] Select Committee on the Causes of the Difficulties in the North-West Territory in 1869-70' (Ottawa, 1874)*

iv) Many documents are also published in the material submitted to the King of the Netherlands for arbitration of the north-eastern boundary dispute, and to the Tribunal arbitrating the Alaska Boundary in 1903:

Statement, and *Definitive Statement, on the part of the United States, of the Case Referred ... between the said States and Great Britain, to ... the King of the Netherlands, for his decision thereon* (Washington, 1829); *First,* and *Second, Statement on the part of Great Britain ... [with] Reference to Arbitration of the Disputed Points of Boundary under the Fifth Article of the Treaty of Ghent* (London, 1829)

Alaska Boundary Tribunal [A.B.T], *Appendix to the Case of the United States* (Washington, 1903), also *Appendix to the Case of the British Government*

Published Primary Sources

Collections

Giunta, Mary A., ed., *The Emerging Nation. A Documentary History of the Foreign Relations of the United States under the Articles of Confederation, 1780-1789* (Washington, 3 vols. 1994-6)

Manning, William R., ed., *Diplomatic Correspondence of the United States. Canadian Relations 1784-1860* (Washington, 4 vols. 1940-5)

Individual Works

A Narrative of the Negotiations occasioned by the Dispute between England and Spain, In the Year 1790 (London, 1791)

Adams, Charles Francis, ed., *Memoirs of John Quincy Adams comprising portions of his Diary from 1795 to 1848* iii, v, vi, vii (Philadelphia, 1874-5)

Adams, Henry, ed., *The Writings of Albert Gallatin* ii (Philadelphia, 1879)

Barnes, James J. and Patience P., ed., *Private and Confidential. Letters from British Ministers in Washington to the Foreign Secretaries in London* (Selinsgrove, Pennsylvania, 1993)

Bowfield, Hartwell, ed., *The James Wickes Taylor Correspondence 1859-1870* (Vol. III, Manitoba Record Society Publications, 1968)*

Cruikshank, E.A., ed., *The Correspondence of John Graves Simcoe, with Allied Documents* (Toronto, 5 vols. 1923-31)

Cutler, Wayne, and Rogers, James L., eds., *Correspondence of James K. Polk* x *July-Dec. 1845*, xi *1846* (Knoxville, Tennessee, 2004, 2009)

Dmytryshin, Basil, Crownhart-Vaughan, E.A.P., Vaughan, Thomas, eds., *The Russian-American Colonies, 1798-1867* iii *A Documentary Record* (Portland, Oregon, 1987)

Doughty, Sir Arthur, ed., *The Elgin-Grey Papers 1846-1852* (Ottawa, 1937)*

Fortescue, Sir John, ed., *The Correspondence of King George the Third from 1760 to December 1783*, v *1780-April 1782*, vi *May 1782-December 1783*, (London, 1928, 1929)

Hopkins, James F., and Hargreaves, Mary W.M., eds., *The Papers of Henry Clay* v, vi (Lexington, Kentucky, 1973)

McElroy, Robert, and Briggs, Thomas, eds., *The Unfortified Boundary: a Diary of the first survey of the Canadian Boundary*

Line from St. Regis to the Lake of the Woods by Major Delafield American Agent (New York, privately printed, 1943)

Stevens, Paul, and Staywell, John T., eds., *Lord Minto's Canadian Papers* i *1898-1904* (Toronto, Champlain Society, 1981)*

Morton, W.L., ed., *Alexander Begg's Red River Journal and other papers relative to the Red River resistance of 1869-70* (Toronto, Champlain Society, 1956)*

'Papers relating to Nootka Sound and to Captain Vancouver's Expedition', *Report of the [British Columbia] Provincial Archives... for the Year ended December ... 1913)*

Pope, Sir Joseph, ed., *Correspondence of Sir John Macdonald* (Garden City, N.Y., 1921)

Quaife, Milo M., ed., *The Diary of James K. Polk during his Presidency, 1845-1849* (Chicago, 1910)

Richardson, James D., ed., *A Compilation of the Messages and Papers of the Presidents* (New York, 1897- 20 vols., but continuously paginated)

Rives, George Lockhart, ed., *Selections from the Correspondence of Thomas Barclay, formerly Consul-General in New York* (New York, 1894)

Shewmaker, Kenneth E., ed., *The Papers of Daniel Webster, Diplomatic Papers, Volume 1 1841-1843* (Hanover, N.H., 1983)

Schmidt, Louis, 'Les Memoires de Louis Schmidt, 8 Juin 1911' (typescript copy, Morton MSS Collection, University of Saskatchewan, *

Smith, William Henry, ed., *The St. Clair Papers. The Life and Public Services of Arthur St. Clair* ii (Cincinnati, 1882)

Stanley, George F.G., ed., *The Collected Writings of Louis Riel. Les Ecrits Complets de Louis Riel*, 5 vols. (Edmonton, 1985)*

Stanmore, Baron Arthur Gordon, ed., *Selections from the Correspondence of the Earl of Aberdeen* vols. 7 1845, 7a *From ... December 1845, to the French Revolution of 1848* [privately printed, 1885 – British Library., B.P. 12 (7 and 7a)]

Vane, Charles William [Stewart], Marquess of Londonderry, ed., *Correspondence, Despatches and other Papers of Viscount Castlereagh*, x, xii (London, 1852-3)

Wellington, Arthur Richard Wellesley, Duke of, ed., *Supplementary Despatches, Correspondence and Memoranda of Arthur Duke of Wellington, edited by his Son* ... ix (London, 1862)

Washington State National Guard, *Collection of Official Documents on the San Juan Imbroglio, 1859-1872* (Tacoma, typescript, 1964)

Wood, William, ed., *Select British Documents of the War of 1812* (Toronto, 4 vols. 1920-8)

Books and Articles

Moore, John Bassett, *History and Digest of the International Arbitrations to which the United States has been a Party* i (Washington, 1898) – description of successive arbitration Commissions and their outcomes, with documents and reproductions of relevant historic maps (chap. 1 'The St. Croix River: Commission under ... the Jay Treaty', chaps 2-6 Commissions under the Treaty of Ghent, chap. 17 'Fur Seal Arbitration'); Moore expanded this in his unfinished *International Adjudications Ancient and Modern. Modern Series* vols. 1-2 'St. Croix River Arbitration' (New York, 1929-30), 6 'Arbitration of the Title to Islands in Passamaquoddy Bay and the Bay of Fundy' (1933)

Hunter Miller, David, *Treaties and Other International Acts of the United States of America* (Washington, 1929-) esp. vol. 3 (1819-35), 4 (1836-46), 5 (1846-52) – printing the text of successive treaties, followed by often lengthy discussion of their negotiation, and incorporating in vols. 3 and 4 'Observations on Mitchell's Map' and on 'The Maps Known in 1842' based on the unpublished work of Col. Lawrence Martin *Dictionary of Canadian Biography* – longer biographies than those in its British or American counterparts, often very good, and including some of people who (like James Wickes Taylor and Jerry Potts), though deeply involved in events in Canada, were never British subjects

Classen, H. George, *Thrust and Counterthrust: The Genesis of the Canada-United States Boundary* (Toronto/Chicago, 1965)

Carroll, Francis M., *A Good and Wise Measure: The Search for the Canadian-American Boundary, 1783-1842* (Toronto U.P., 2001), chiefly a study of the 'Commissions under the Treaty of Ghent, 1816-27', their aftermath, and the resolution through the 1842 Webster-Ashburton treaty

Galbraith, John S., *The Hudson's Bay Company as an Imperial Factor, 1821-1869* (Berkeley, 1957, reprinted New York, 1977)

Ahrens, M.O., 'The Impact of Captain Jonathan Carver's Maps and Journal on the 1782-1783 British-American Peace Agreement', *Imago Mundi* 69:2 (2017)

Allen, Robert S., *His Majesty's Indian Allies. British Indian Policy in the Defence of Canada, 1774-1815* (Toronto, 1992); 'The British Indian Department and the Frontier in North America, 1755-1830', *Canadian Historic Sites: Occasional Papers in Archaeology and History* 14 (1975)

Andrews, Clarence L., 'Russian Plans for American Dominion', *Washington Historical Quarterly* 18:2 (1927)

Antal, Sandy, 'Michigan Ceded: Why and Wherefore?', *Michigan Historical Review* 38:1 (2012)

Atcheson, Nathaniel, *A Compressed View of the Points to be discussed in treating with the United States of America with an Appendix* (London, March 1814)

Barnes, James J., *Authors, Publishers and Politicians. The Quest for an Anglo-American Copyright Agreement 1815-1854* (London, 1974)*

Barratt, Glyn, *Russia in Pacific Waters 1715-1825* (Vancouver, 1981)

Bartlett, Fred Elmer, *William Mactavish: the last governor of Assiniboia* (University of Manitoba, M.A. thesis, 1964)*

Blakey-Smith, Dorothy, ed., *Reminiscences of Doctor John Sebastian Helmcken* (Vancouver, 1975)*

Blue, Verne, 'The Oregon Question [in Congress] – 1818-1828', *Oregon Historical Quarterly* 23:3 (1922)

Bolkhovitinov, Nikolai N., and Dmytroshin, Basil, 'Russia and the Non-Colonization Principle: New Archival Evidence', *Oregon Historical Quarterly* 72:2 (1971)

Bolkhovitinov, Nikolay, 'The Crimean War and the Emergence of Proposals for the Sale of Russian America, 1853-1861', *Pacific Historical Review* 59 (1990)*

'How it was decided to sell Alaska', *International Affairs* (Moscow) 8/1988*

Russian-American Relations and the Sale of Alaska, 1834-1867 (Kingston, Ont., 1996 – ed. and tr. Richard Pierce)*

Bourne, Kenneth, *Britain and the Balance of Power in North America 1815-1908* (London, 1967)

Brown, Joseph Henry, *Brown's Political History of Oregon. Provisional Government* (Portland, Oregon, 1892, Ann Arbor, MI, 1989)

Brown, Roger Hamilton, *The Struggle for the Indian Stream Territory* (Cleveland, Ohio, 1955)

Buckner, Phillip, ed., *Canada and the British Empire* (Oxford, paperback, 2010)

Burrage, Henry S., *Maine in the Northeastern Boundary Controversy* (Portland, Maine, 1919)

Burt, A.L., *The United States Great Britain and British North America from the Revolution to ... Peace after the War of 1812* (New Haven, Conn., 1940)

Campbell, Charles S., 'The Anglo-American Crisis in the Bering Sea, 1890-1891', *Mississippi Valley Historical Review* 48:3 (1961)*; 'The Bering Sea Settlements of 1892', *Pacific Historical Review* 32:4 (1963)*; *Anglo-American Understanding, 1898-1903* (Baltimore, 1957)*

Campbell, W.E. (Gary), *The Road to Canada. The Grand Communications Route from Saint John to Quebec* (Fredericton, N.B., 2005)

Christensen, Deanna, *Ahtahkakoop. The Epic Account of a Plains Cree Head Chief, His People, and their Struggle for Survival, 1816-1896* (Shell Lake, Saskatchewan, 2000)*

Coleman, E.C., *The Pig War. The Most Perfect War in History* (Stroud, Glos., 2009)

Combs, Jerald A., *The Jay Treaty. Political Battleground of the Founding Fathers* (Berkeley, 1970)

Cook, Adrian, *The Alabama Claims, American Politics and Anglo-American Relations, 1865-1872* (Ithaca, N.Y., 1975)

Cook, Warren L., *Flood Tide of Empire. Spain and the Pacific Northwest, 1543-1819* (New Haven, Conn., 1973)

Cozzens, Peter, *The Warrior and the Prophet. The Shawnee Brothers who defied a Nation* (London, 2020)

Davidson, Donald C., 'Relations of the Hudson's Bay Company with the Russian American Company on the Northwest Coast, 1829-1867', *British Columbia Historical Quarterly* 5:1 (1941)

Doan, Daniel, *Indian Stream Republic. Settling a New England Frontier, 1785-1842* (Hanover, N.H., 1997)

Dunbabin, J.P.D., 'The 1831 Dutch Arbitration of the Canadian American Boundary Dispute: Another View', *New England Quarterly* 75:4 (2002); 'Haro or Rosario? Maps, Navigation, and the Anglo-American Water Boundary Dispute, 1846-72', *BC Studies* 186 (2015)

Dykstra, David, *The Shifting Balance of Power. American-British Diplomacy in North America, 1842-1848* (Lanham, Maryland, 1999)

Eayrs, James, 'Arms Control on the Great Lakes', *Disarmament and Arms Control* 2 (1964)*

Edelson, S. Max, *The New Map of Empire. How Britain imagined America before Independence* (Cambridge, Mass., 2017)

Edney, Matthew H., *The Mitchell Map, 1755-1782: An Irony of Empire* (Osher Map Library, Maine, 1997)

Erasmus, Peter, *Buffalo Days and Nights. As Told to Henry Thompson* (Calgary, 1999 edn.)*

Fitzmaurice, Lord Edmond, *Life of William, Earl of Shelburne, afterwards First Marquess of Lansdowne iii 1776-1805* (London, 1876)

Flanagan, Thomas, *Louis 'David' Riel: 'Prophet of the New World'* (Toronto, 1979)*; *Riel and the Rebellion. 1885 Reconsidered* (2nd edn., Toronto, 2000)*

Foster, John W., *Diplomatic Memoirs* ii (Boston, 1909)*

Gaffney, Thomas L. Gaffney, *Maine's Mr. Smith: a study of the career of Francis O. J. Smith, Politician and Entrepreneur* (Ph.D. thesis, 1979 – UMI Dissertation Services, Ann Arbor, Michigan, 1999)

Ganong, William F., *A Monograph on the Evolution of the Boundaries of the Province of New Brunswick* (Transactions of the Royal Society of Canada, 1901 section II)

Garraty, John A., 'Henry Cabot Lodge and the Alaska Boundary Tribunal', *New England Quarterly* 24:4 (1951)*

Gay, James Thomas, *American Fur Seal Diplomacy. The Alaskan Fur Seal Controversy* (New York, 1987)*

Gluek, Alvin C., *Minnesota and the manifest destiny of the Canadian north-west: a Study in Canadian-American Relations* (Toronto, 1965)*; 'The Riel Rebellion and Canadian-American Relations', *Canadian Historical Review* 36:3 (1955)*; 'Canada's Splendid Bargain: the North Pacific Fur Seal Convention of 1911', *Canadian Historical Review* 63:2 (1982)*

Golder, Frank A., 'The Purchase of Alaska', *American Historical Review* 25:3 (1920)*

Grinev, Andrei V., 'Why Russia Sold Alaska: the view from Russia', *Alaska History* 19:1&2 (2004)*

Hall, D.J., *Clifford Sifton* i *The Young Napoleon, 1861-1900* (Vancouver, 1981)*

Harper, William A., 'The Alaska Boundary Question: the Seattle Commercial Interest and the Joint High Commission of 1898-99', *Journal of the West* 10 (1971)*

Donald J. Hauka, *McGowan's War* (Vancouver, 2003)*

Heglund, David G., and Onea, Tudor, 'Victory without Triumph: Theodore Roosevelt, Honour, and the Alaska Panhandle Boundary Dispute', *Diplomacy & Statecraft* 19:1 (2008)*

Henderson, George Fletcher, *Alexander Mackenzie and the Canadian Pacific Railway 1871-1878* (Queen's University, Kingston, Ont., MA thesis, 1964)*

Hietala, Thomas R., *Manifest Design. American Exceptionalism and Empire* (Ithaca, N.Y., 2003 edn.)

Paul S. Holbo, *Tarnished Expansion. The Alaska Scandal, the Press, and Congress, 1867-1871* (Knoxville, Tennessee, 1983)*

Hoffman, Ronald, and Albert, Peter J., eds., *Peace and the Peacemakers: the treaty of 1783* (Charlottesville, VA, 1986), esp. Jonathan Dull, 'Vergennes, Rayneval and the Diplomacy of Trust', and Charles R. Ritcheson, 'Britain's Peacemakers, 1782-1783 ...'

Horrall, S.W., 'Sir John A. Macdonald and the Mounted Police Force for the Northwest Territories', *Canadian Historical Review* 53:2 (1972)*

Horsman, Reginald, 'British Indian Policy in the Northwest 1807-1812', *Mississippi Valley Historical Review* 45:1 (1958); 'The British Indian Department and the Abortive Treaty of Lower Sandusky, 1793', *Ohio Historical Quarterly* 70 (1961); 'American Indian Policy in the Old Northwest, 1783-1812', *William and Mary Quarterly* 3rd series 18 (1961); 'On to Canada: Manifest Destiny and United States Strategy in the War of 1812', *Michigan Historical Review* 13:2 (1987); 'The War of 1812 Revisited', *Diplomatic History* 15:1 (1991)

Hunter Miller, David, *San Juan Archipelago: Study of the Joint Occupation of San Juan Archipelago* (Bellows Falls, Vermont, 1943)

Irwin, Leonard B., *Pacific Railways and Nationalism in the Canadian-American Northwest, 1845-1873* (New York, 1968 reprint)*

Jackson, C. Ian, 'The Stikine Territory lease and its Relevance to the Alaska Purchase', *Pacific Historical Review* 36:3 (1967)*

Jones, Wilbur Devereux, *Lord Aberdeen and the Americas* (Athens, GA., 1958)

Judson, Katharine B., 'The British Side of the Restoration of Fort Astoria', and 'The British Side of the Restoration … Continued', *Quarterly of the Oregon Historical Society* 20:3, 4 (1919)

King, Robert J., 'George Vancouver and the contemplated settlement at Nootka Sound', *The Great Circle. Journal of Australian Association of Maritime History* 32:1 (2010)

Lamb, W. Kaye, *History of the Canadian Pacific Railway* (New York, 1977)*

Lambert, Andrew, *The Challenge. Britain against America in the Naval War of 1812* (paperback, 2013)

Lass, William E., *Minnesota's Boundary with Canada. Its Evolution since 1783* (St. Paul, Minnesota, 1980)

Lenentine Melvin, Charlotte, *Madawaska – A Chapter in Maine-New Brunswick Relations* (Madawaska, Maine, 1975)

Longley, R.S., 'Cartier and MacDougall, Canadian Emissaries to London, 1868-9', *Canadian Historical Review* 26:1 (1945)*

Lowenthal, David, 'The Maine Press and the Aroostook War', *Canadian Historical Review* 32 (1951)

McCabe, James O., *The San Juan Water Boundary Question* (Toronto, 1964)

McDonald, Sheila, 'The War after the War: Fort Kent blockhouse, 1839-1842', *Maine State Historical Quarterly* 29 (1990)

Mailhot, Philippe R., *Ritchot's Resistance: Abbé Noel Joseph Ritchot and the Creation and Transformation of Manitoba* (University of Manitoba, D. Phil. Thesis, 1986)*

Manning, William R., 'The Nootka Sound Controversy', *Annual Report of the American Historical Association, 1904*

Marshall, Daniel P., *Claiming the Land: British Columbia and the Making of a New El Dorado* (Vancouver, 2018)*

Masters, Donald C., *The Reciprocity Treaty of 1854* (London, 1936)*

McLean, W.J., 'Tragic Events at Frog Lake and Fort Pitt During the North West Rebellion', *Manitoba Pageant* 17:2 and 18: 1-3 (1972 and 1973)*

Martin, Ged, 'How much did Canada "pay" First Nations for the Prairies?', & 'The Department of Indian Affairs in the Dominion of Canada budget', 1882, *Martinalia* (2020, online)*

Merk, Frederick, *The Oregon Question. Essays in Anglo-American Diplomacy and Politics* (Cambridge, Mass., 1967 edn.)

Merk, Frederick with Lois Bannister Merk, *Fruits of Propaganda in the Tyler Administration* (Cambridge, Mass., 1971); *Manifest Destiny and Mission in American History* (New York, 1967)

Messamore, Barbara J., *Canada's Governors General, 1847-1878: Biography and Constitutional Evolution* (Toronto, 2006)

Miles, Edwin, '"Fifty-four Forty or Fight" – an American political legend', *Mississippi Valley Historical Review* 44:2 (1957)

Middleton, Richard, *Pontiac's War. Its Causes, Course and Consequences* (New York, 2007)

Miller, David Hunter, *The Alaska Treaty* (Kingston, Ont., 1981)*

Miller, J.R., *Skyscrapers hide the heavens: a history of Indian-White relations in Canada* (Toronto, 2000 edn.)*

Mitchell, Elaine Allan, 'Edward Watkin and the Buying-out of the Hudson's Bay Company', *Canadian Historical Review* 34:3 (1953)*

Morris, Alexander, *The Treaties of Canada with the Indians of Manitoba and the North-West Territories* (Toronto, 1880)*

Munro, John A., ed., *The Alaska Boundary Dispute* (Toronto, 1970)*

Murray, Keith, *The Pig War* (Tacoma, WA, 1968)

Nevins, Allan, *Hamilton Fish. The Inner History of the Grant Administration* (New York, 1957 edn.)

Okun, S.B., *The Russian American Company* (tr. Carl Ginsburg, Cambridge, Mass., 1951)

Ormsby, Margaret, *British Columbia: a history* (Toronto, 1958)*

Penlington, Norman, *The Alaska Boundary Dispute: a Critical Reappraisal* (Toronto, 1972)*; *Canada and Imperialism 1896-1899* (Toronto, 1971 reprint)*

Penfold, P. A., ed., *Maps and Plans in the Public Record Office* ii *America and the West Indies* (London, 1974)

Perkins, Bradford, *Castlereagh and Adams. England and the United States 1812-1823* (Berkeley, 1964)

Pletcher, David M., *The Diplomacy of Annexation. Texas, Oregon, and the Mexican War* (Columbia, Missouri, 1975 printing)

Pope, Sir Joseph, *Memoirs of the Right Honourable Sir John Alexander Macdonald* ii (London, 1894)*; *Correspondence of Sir John Macdonald* (Garden City, N.Y., 1921)

Ritcheson, C.R., 'The Earl of Shelburne and Peace with America, 1782-3: Vision and Reality', *International History Review* 5:3 (1983); *Aftermath of Revolution. British Policy toward the United States 1783-1795* (Dallas, Texas, 1969)

Ronda, James P., *Astoria & Empire* (Lincoln, Neb., 1990)

Sellers, Charles Grier, *James K. Polk: Continentalist, 1843-1846* (Princeton, NJ, 1966)

Sharp, Paul F., *Whoop-up Country. The Canadian-American West, 1865-1885* (Minneapolis, 1955)*

Shelton, W. George, ed., *British Columbia and Confederation* (Victoria, 1967)*

Shi, David, 'Seward's attempt to annex British Columbia, 1865-1869', *Pacific Historical Review* 47:2 (1978)

Showerman, Grant, *The Indian Stream Republic and Luther Parker* (Concord, N.H., 1915)

Skelton, O.D., *Life and Letters of Sir Wilfrid Laurier* ii (London, 1922)*

Smith, Goldwin, *The Treaty of Washington 1871. A Study in Imperial History* (Ithaca, N.Y., 1941)

Spate, O.H.K., *The Pacific since Magellan* iii *Paradise Found and Lost* (London, 1988)

Stacey, C.P., 'The Myth of the Unguarded Frontier 1815-1871', *American Historical Review* 56:1 (1950)

Stanley, George F., *Louis Riel* (Toronto, 1963)*

Stockley, Andrew, *Britain and France at the Birth of America. The European Powers at the Peace Negotiations of 1782-1783* (Exeter, 2001)

Sugden, John, *Tecumseh's Last Stand* (Norman, Oklahoma, 1985)

Sword, Wiley, *President Washington's Indian War. The Struggle for the Old Northwest, 1790-1795* (Norman, Oklahoma, paperback edn. 1993)

Tallman, R.D. and J.I., 'The Diplomatic Search for the St. Croix River, 1796-1798', *Acadiensis* 1:2 (1972)

Tansill, Charles C., *Canadian-American Relations, 1875-1911* (New Haven, Conn., 1943)*

Taylor, John Leonard, 'Two Views on the Meaning of Treaties Six and Seven' [in Price, Richard, ed., *The Spirit of the Alberta Indian Treaties* (Calgary, 1999)]*

Thayer, William Roscoe, *The Life and Letters of John Hay* ii (Boston, 1915)*

Thompson, Erwin, *Historic Resource Study: San Juan Island National Historic Park* (United States National Park Service, 1972)

Tidd Scott, Geraldine, *Ties of Common Blood: a history of Maine's Northeast Boundary Dispute with Great Britain, 1783-1842* (Bowie, Maryland, 1992)

Tobias, John L., 'Canada's Subjugation of the Plains Cree, 1879-1885', *Canadian Historical Review* 64:4 (1983)*

Tovell, Freeman M., 'The Other Side of the Coin: the Viceroy, Bodega y Quadra, Vancouver, and the Nootka Crisis', *BC Studies* 93 (Spring 1992)

Vouri, Mike, *The Pig War. Standoff at Griffin Bay* (Seattle, 2013 edn.)

Waite, Peter B., *The Life and Times of Confederation, 1864-1867* (Toronto, 1962, 2nd edn. 2019)*

Warner, Donald, *The idea of continental union: agitation for the annexation of Canada to the United States, 1849-1893* (Lexington, Kentucky, 1960)*

Watkin, Sir Edward, *Canada and the States. Recollections 1851 to 1886* (London, 1887)*

Watt, Alastair, 'The Case of Alexander McLeod', *Canadian Historical Review* 12:2 (1931)

Weinberg, Albert K., *Manifest Destiny. A Study of Nationalist Expansionism in American History* (Baltimore, 1935)

Wharton, David, *The Alaska Gold Rush* (Bloomington, Indiana, 1972)*

White, Henry, *Sixty Years of American Diplomacy* (New York, 1930)*

White, James, 'Henry Cabot Lodge and the Alaska Boundary Award', *Canadian Historical Review* 6:4 (1925)*

White, Richard, *The Middle Ground. Indians, Empires, and Republics in the Great Lakes Region, 1650-1815* (Cambridge, England, 1991)

Willig, Timothy D., *Restoring the Chain of Friendship: British Policy and the Indians of the Great Lakes, 1783-1815* (Lincoln, Neb., 2008)

Willson, Beccles, *The Life of Lord Strathcona and Mount Royal* i (Boston, 1915 edn.)*

Index
(omitting titles/knighthoods acquired after last mention in book)

withdrew 1826 offer of
continued British use of the
Columbia, 505-6; Pakenham
asked for better offer, Polk broke
off negotiations, 506-7, 510-3;
rival explanations of Polk's
actions, 508-9, 531
Polk's well received all-Oregon
Message to Congress (Dec.
1845), 515-6; following 'grave
[cabinet] discussion of the
contingency of war', Polk agreed
to submit a British proposal for
some variant of a 49th parallel
border to Senate for advice, but
would give London no
encouragement to make one,
517-8, 521
Calhoun returns to the Senate to
avoid war, mobilises his Southern
friends, and on Oregon forms
controlling coalition with the
Whigs, 517-19, 524-5
US distaste for arbitration,
501-2; Polk's invariable blunt
(rather than 'friendly')
rejection leads Aberdeen to
withdraw his opposition to
'offensive' naval preparations,
520-2. McLane's report shocks
US cabinet, & Buchanan now
authorised to say Polk would
submit, and Senate probably
accept, a British proposal for 49th
parallel border 'to the sea', with
HBC allowed *temporary* use of
the Columbia, 523-4; Polk lets
this become increasingly known,
528-9
Senate attaches to Notice
terminating the freezing of
Oregon sovereignty the hope that
it would lead to 'speedy and
amicable settlement', 529-30;
war with Mexico adds to
pressure on the US, 554,
556

*British handling of the question
(1843-6):*
Everett brought Aberdeen to favour
a 49th parallel border to the sea,
leaving Britain all Vancouver
Island (1843), 478-9; Aberdeen
unsuccessfully sought such a US
offer that could then be put to
cabinet, while Peel favoured
arbitration (1844), 532-4
Polk's Inaugural prompted Liberal
opposition to further British
concessions, 495; government
investigation of the military
position in Oregon, 534, but Peel
& Aberdeen accepted HBC
memorandum envisaging
dropping the Columbia River
border, 535; Aberdeen's back-
channel intimation to US of his
readiness for a 49th parallel
border 'to the sea', & aid to
Everett's propaganda for this
(1845), 535-7; Aberdeen's
formulation of an acceptable
settlement not challenged by
Peel, 539-40
British rearmament, primarily
against France (1845) but partly
usable also against US, 496-8
December 1845 Corn Law political
crisis enabled Russell to drop
opposition to further concessions
& left Aberdeen free to seek
settlement, 541-2, 545; fears of
war resulting from Polk's
Message & his brusque rejection
of arbitration, 542, 542-8; with
these fading, Aberdeen used the
Senate's attachment to Note
terminating sovereignty freeze to
make final offer, 548-52
US accepts this linked proposal of a
49th parallel border 'to the sea'
and of the continued HBC right
to navigate the Columbia Polk
had always said he would never